The SCOTTISH GOVERNMENT YEARBOOK 1989

edited by
ALICE BROWN & DAVID McCRONE

First published 1989

Published by

Unit for the Study of Government in Scotland
Department of Politics
University of Edinburgh
31 Buccleuch Place

ISBN O 9509 626 7 8

Printed by
Drummond Street Reprographics Unit
University of Edinburgh

CONTEMPORARY Wales

AN ANNUAL REVIEW OF ECONOMIC AND SOCIAL RESEARCH

EDITORS:

Graham Day, University of Wales, Aberystwyth and Gareth Rees, University of Wales College of Cardiff.

An authoritative analysis of economic and social development in Wales, drawing upon the most up-to-date research. It will be of interest not only to academic researchers, but also professionals in local and central government, the private sector and the labour and trade union movement, as well as a general wider readership. *Contemporary Wales* fills a major gap in providing a forum for debate and an essential information resource for all those who are concerned about Wales' current problems and prospects for future progress.

Volume 1 December 1987, Volume 2 Summer 1988 and thereafter published annually in the Summer. Single issue £7.50 (£6.50 to regular subscribers)

UNIVERSITY OF WALES PRESS, FREEPOST, CARDIFF, CF1 1YZ
☎ (0222) 231919

ERRATUM

TABLE OF CONTENTS

TABLE OF CONTENTS

The Yearbook is edited on behalf of the Unit for the Study of Government in Scotland at The University of Edinburgh. Additional copies of the Yearbook, backcopies of the twelve previous volumes and further information about The Unit's activities can be obtained from Mrs. Helen Ramm at 31 Buccleuch Place, Edinburgh EH8 9JT, Scotland.

EDITOR'S INTRODUCTION

Alice Brown

In nineteen eighty-eight we witnessed further new developments in the governance of Scotland. The implementation of the Local Government Act 1988, the completion of registration for the community charge (poll tax), major education reforms, the development of the inner city programme, the introduction of new housing legislation, and the establishment of Enterprise Scotland are some examples of policies which have been enforced from Whitehall. These changes have progressed against the wishes and without the support of the majority of the Scottish people.

Following the outcome of the 1987 general election, Mrs Thatcher's stated view was that the apparent divergence between central government policy and Scottish public opinion could be overcome by improving communication of her government's objectives to the Scottish electorate. As one method of 'getting the message across', Mrs Thatcher herself visited Scotland on no less than six occasions in 1988. Her speech to the Scottish Conservative Party Conference in Perth where she claimed that the Scots had invented Thatcherism, her 'Sermon on the Mound' address to the General Assembly of the Church of Scotland, and the high profile given to Scotland at the party's annual conference in Brighton, gained much media coverage. However, as the District Elections of 1988 and Opinion Polls in Scotland show, either the message has still not been conveyed to the Scottish people, or there are other more complex factors involved than the government is prepared to acknowledge.

One area where the government has claimed success is in relation to the so-called economic miracle in Scotland. In an interview given to Scotland's new Sunday newspaper 'Scotland on Sunday' Mrs Thatcher pronounced that Scotland was flourishing. While it can be acknowledged that in certain sectors of the Scottish economy there have been signs of economic revival, it would be premature to say the least to state that Scotland is experiencing an economic miracle. The Scottish experience has been more in the nature of economic recovery than an economic boom. Related to the general economic picture in Scotland, the government has also taken the credit for the decrease in the official level of unemployment and the increase in the rate of growth in the economy over the last year. Leaving aside the rather obvious contradiction that the government previously claimed that it could not influence the level of employment/ unemployment and the disputes about the changes in the measurement of unemployment statistics issued by the Department of Employment, the government seems prepared to ignore other economic indicators such as the deterioration of the Balance of Payments, the rise in inflation, and the resultant increases in interest rates. These latter trends are likely to have a detrimental effect on the British and Scottish economy and to impact adversely on the level of unemployment.

Unemployment continues to be a major concern for Scottish people. A MORI poll conducted just before the Govan by-election in November noted that jobs were the most important issue for all those interviewed in the survey. The official seasonally adjusted rate of unemployment in Scotland in September 1988 was 11.4% compared with a rate of 7.8% for Britain. The average figure given for the whole of Scotland, of course, disguises very much higher levels of unemployment in some regions,cities and towns in Scotland and the uneven distribution of unemployment within and between the different locations. Therefore, the government's claim to have cured the problem of unemployment must ring rather hollow for people in areas where one in five of the adult population are unemployed.

Recent developments and proposed changes in Scotland are also causing concern. For example the redundancies resulting from the sale of the Royal Ordnance Factory at Bishopton; the continuing decline of the Scottish Coal industry; fears about the effects of the privatisation of the steel and electricity industries; and the impact on Scottish firms of the single European market. Another worrying feature is the proposed takeover of Scottish and Newcastle Breweries, Scotland's largest manufacturing industry, by Elders IXL an Australian owned company. The political row which developed over this takeover bid was fuelled by the part played by the Royal Bank of Scotland in providing finance for the takeover and the involvement of the former Conservative MP, Sir Alex Fletcher, in setting up meetings between Elders' executives and Malcolm Rifkind, the Secretary of State. The Bank's involvement is all the more ironic when one considers its own escape from takeover by foreign buyers not so many years ago. Also Fletcher's role in advising Elders led to calls for his resignation from the board of the Scottish Development Agency. At the time of writing (November 1988) the outcome of this takeover bid is undecided.

A significant change in the Thatcher government's approach to training poplicy took a particular form in Scotland, upsetting textbook models of policymaking. I am referring, of course, to what is known as the Hughes Plan or the Hughes Initiative. The context of the change in policy was the dispute over the implementation of the government's latest training scheme – Employment Training or 'ET'. Even before the decision taken at the TUC Congress in 1988 to withdraw support for ET, and the government's subsequent decision to abolish the Training Commission (previously the Manpower Services Commission), Bill Hughes, Chairman of the Confederation of British Industry Scotland, hit the front page of the

Scottish newspapers in June with his new plan. His proposals involved the amalgamation of the work of the Training Commission in Scotland with the Scottish Development Agency (and possibly the Highlands and Islands Development Board) and the creation of up to 60 employer-led enterprise agencies to deliver training and job creation policies at the local level. Mrs Thatcher personally put her seal of approval on the initiative – to be known as Enterprise Scotland – and a White Paper (with green edges) is proposed for the end of 1988. The plans have not obtained the approval of all Scottish employers or members of the CBI, and concern has been expressed by the SDA about their future role. Malcolm Rifkind has largely ignored the first and assured the latter that they will not suffer as a result of this new initiative. In spite of opposition in Scotland, it is likely that the government will move to implement the proposals in the 1989/90 session of Parliament.

The Community Charge (Poll Tax) also continues to be a major source of controversy in Scotland. Splits between the opposition parties in Scotland and splits within the parties themselves have prevented a united opposition to the government. In spite of attempts to oppose registering for the poll tax or delaying registration, the government was able to claim that over 90% of the forms were completed in Scotland. However, as the Opinion Poll data indicates (see Reference Section) there is clear opposition to the imposition of this tax in Scotland, although the large percentage of the electorate who disapprove of the tax is not directly translated into the numbers who will refuse to pay.

1989 will be the anniversary of the 1979 referendum on the Scottish Assembly. Ten years later the demand for some form of devolved government is growing in Scotland, with many of those who voted 'No' in 1979, now prepared to change their minds as a result of the experience of almost ten years of Conservative government. Frustration in Scotland over the imposition of unpopular policies from south of the border is mounting, and the 50 Scottish Labour MPs not surprisingly came in for heavy criticism from the SNP for alleged lack of effective resistance to Thatcherism. The Campaign for a Scottish Assembly's document 'A Claim of Right for Scotland' and its central proposal to establish a Constitutional Convention to prepare proposals for Scotland's future form of government, to include an elected Assembly has attracted much attention and support in Scotland. Jim Sillars' victory at the Govan by-election for the SNP (reducing the so-called 'feeble 50' to the 'frightened 49') will give added confidence to anti-Thatcher sentiments and the Assembly movement in Scotland. As one commentator stated, Scottish politics will never be the same again.

1989 then promises to be a testing time for the government as it continues to operate without a mandate in Scotland. In addition to the issues raised above, there is likely to be continued unrest, for example within the education sector with the creation of School Boards and 'opting out' of local authority control; and within local government as the government pursues its attack on local government finance and power.

This year's Scottish Government Yearbook continues to address key issues and debates within Scotland, some of which have already been referred to above. In addition to our regular features on the year at Westminster and election coverage, we are including articles on the coal and steel industries; housing and inner city policy; rural deprivation; and industrial relations. We also cover an assessment of TVEI in Scotland; the Arts Council; and the Media. Our two special sections highlight Social Work in Scotland with articles on the social work profession, social care policy and child abuse; and Women in Scotland with articles on the impact of Thatcherism, Women's Committees, Women in Trade Unions and Black Women in Scotland. The 1989 edition will also include a book review in addition to our regular Reference Section.

Our thanks to our regular contributors for their indispensable service; to all our authors who, despite the prevailing market culture, contribute their articles without any financial incentive; and to our advertisers, both old and new, for their support. My personal thanks to Dave McCrone, who is retiring as Editor of the Yearbook this year. I am indebted to him for passing on the skills of the trade to me and for his invaluable contribution to the Yearbook over the years. Last, but by no means least, to Helen Ramm, my thanks and gratitude for her advice and support, and for 'keeping me right' in my new role as Editor.

THE YEAR AT WESTMINSTER

Peter Hannam

It was the year in which Malcolm Rifkind led a fierce fight-back by the Scottish Conservative Party and Labour discovered that numerical superiority in the Commons by itself counted for little.

Anyone who had expected the Scottish Secretary to slope away to lick the wounds inflicted by the electorate in the 1987 general election had another think coming. His was to become an uncompromising counter-attack on several fronts, given added force by a higher profile north of the Border for the Prime Minister herself.

For Scottish Labour leaders, fresh from achieving a 50-seat target which had been derided by their opponents beforehand, it quickly became apparent that a position of responsibility with no power to implement election promises was fraught with danger.

With, in addition, the Scottish Nationalist Party constantly snapping at Labour's heels and rubbishing what it called the "Feeble Fifty's" inability to deliver, especially on devolution, the Shadow Scottish Secretary, Donald Dewar, and his colleagues were often forced on the defensive when they expected to be winning the argument.

The party's problems were compounded by the provocative antics of the vociferous Anglo-Scots (Scottish MPs from English constituencies) and their friends on the Tory benches who regularly sought a confrontation and complained about what they regarded (though even Rifkind himself dissented) as the public spending "feather-bedding" of Scotland.

Labour's attack tended, as a result of a combination of factors, to fragment, with deep divisions in the ranks about tactics inside and outside the Commons and a series of clashes at Westminster.

Meanwhile, Liberal/Social Democrat MPs pursued a two-pronged strategy of condemning the Government while rubbing salt in Labour wounds, but their effectiveness was blunted by internal strife over the creation of a new party.

The disastrous election performance of the Scottish Conservative Party provided the back-drop for the political year. With only ten MPs, morale slumped while the elected representatives were stretched. Rifkind provoked Opposition scorn when forced to take an Anglo-Scot, David MacLean, the young MP for Penrith and the Borders, as his Parliamentary Scottish Whip.

The problems of having just five backbenchers were highlighted at regular intervals, most notably in the manning of Parliamentary committees, sparking a series of rows over the drafting-in of MPs from English constituencies with Scottish links – and reaching their pitch in the epic of the Scottish Affairs Select Committee which never in fact materialised.

Rifkind's strategy and Labour's heart-ache

The Scottish Secretary had few options as the scale of Tory defeat became clear. The strategy which he brought quickly into effect involved capturing the initiative from Labour, carrying the Parliamentary fight to Labour and re-organising his own party in Scotland

Rifkind argued that the Conservatives' failure arose from their inability to get across the message that the Thatcher years had been good for the Scottish people who had not appreciated how well-off they had become thanks to the turn-round in the Scottish economy since 1979. Economic success was to be a constant theme of the new appeal.

It followed that there was to be no let-up in the pursuit of Thatcherite policies – which prompted accusations that Rifkind had sold out his earlier more liberal inclinations for personal gain – and that greater efforts must be made to persuade voters that they had never had it so good.

To that end, Rifkind enticed one of Whitehall's top communicators to the party's headquarters in Chester Street, Edinburgh. Alex Pagett – though, to his boss's dismay, he was to remain in post for only a year before moving to the industrial sector – was to play a key role in giving the message a real cutting edge and sharpening the Tory counter-offensive.

Pagett was to build up a press office and vastly expand contacts with the media (and not just the Scottish media) to make sure that journalists were kept fully informed about the Rifkind Revolution.

Meanwhile, the new chief executive, John MacKay, who had lost his Argyll and Bute seat the previous summer, began work, with the help of Central Office in London, trying to rebuild the party. It was tough going and there remains a handful of derelict constituency parties.

On the plus side, a group of Scottish businessmen was formed to bring in untold riches with which to finance the resurgence. Substantial new technology was imported. New and bigger offices were sought out.

At Westminster, the objective was laid down of out-manoeuvring Labour. Rifkind, one of the most intelligent and articulate members of the Cabinet, led from the front. He and his colleagues rightly pin-pointed the inexperience of Labour's new MPs and the disadvantages of the system to any Opposition as being to their own advantage.

Labour's contingent was undoubtedly more talented and enthusiastic than before the election with rising stars evident in the likes of Alistair Darling (Edinburgh Central), Sam Galbraith (Strathkelvin and Bearsden) and Henry McLeish (Fife Central). The Labour group's early tactics were, however, less than subtle and not very successful. They were to be reviewed by the turn of the year.

Two illustrations highlighted Labour's autumnal difficulties of presenting an effective and credible attack. One was the tabling of 2,000 Commons questions en bloc. The second involved a Commons filibuster of the Second Reading of the uncontentious Scottish Development Agency Bill which resulted in the embarrassing loss of a debate on the Scottish economy.

As Ministers gloated, an editorial in *The Scotsman* on October 23 mused: "By sheer force of numbers, Scottish Labour MPs can take the lead in filibustering and question-setting exercises but these are most unlikely to make the slightest difference to Scotland's political situation......The Government can take comfort from the Scottish Labour Party's display of frustration and limitation."

In November, Labour took another knock. The day after Dewar had addressed the full Parliamentary Labour Party on his intended tactics and won support for a clear run against Rifkind, four items of Scottish business were scuppered by English opponents in the party of the private Felixstowe Docks Bill. The Tories celebrated another example of Labour's suicidal tendency while Dewar uncomfortably tried to put a brave face on the setback.

Devolution

Labour leaders moved speedily to restore their attack on the Government by publishing their proposals for Scottish devolution. They produced a Scotland Bill for an elected Scottish Assembly with tax-raising powers and responsibility for domestic policy – the election manifesto commitment.

Devolution enjoyed broader support in the party than in the 1970s. But the Bill exemplified the impotence of the Scottish Labour Party for it could not be implemented. The attack fell away. The Bill ran into a traditional procedural block on its Second Reading. It ran out of steam. Opponents of devolution pointed to the low priority given to the proposals by voters in comparison with other matters.

The SNP, with their call for independence, and the Social and Liberal Democrats also raised the banner but devolution was not the political litmus that it once was.

Poll tax

It would be wrong, however, to create the impression that everything went badly for the Scottish Labour Party. Like the party nationally, it scored highly on social issues and industrial matters (as when Ravenscraig burst back onto the political map in the summer).

The community charge retained a high profile throughout the year, as England and Wales got to grips with the Local Government Finance Bill which introduced the "poll tax" enacted for Scotland the previous session. The Bill was used to bring forward a multitude of Scottish amendments in addition to several new Orders relating mainly to details of registration and exemptions. It also offered Labour a chance to go on the offensive.

The political campaign against the "poll tax" continued apace. Dick Douglas resigned as chairman of the Scottish Labour group to concentrate his fire on the charge. Brian Wilson, the new MP for Cunninghame North, chaired the STOPIT campaign. A growing number of MPs, including spokesmen such as Robin Cook, the Shadow Health Secretary, declared they would not pay it.

The SNP laid down a strong challenge to Labour by asserting support for a campaign of non-payment, but the Official Opposition stuck to tactics of disruption falling short of illegality. In the summer, the executive of the Scottish Labour Party endorsed that view.

The bickering between the Opposition forces again brought relief to the Scottish Office.

Meanwhile, individual Scottish politicians continued to enjoy a high profile and personal success. Rifkind and, in a different way, the Defence Secretary, George Younger, shone from the Treasury Bench. John Smith, the Shadow Chancellor much discussed as a successor to Neil Kinnock, and Gordon Brown, who devoted his usual skill and enthusiasm to the task of Shadow Chief Secretary to the Treasury, emerged as an influential economic duo.

Robin Cook out-performed the Health and Social Security Ministers.

Bruce Millan became one of Britain's new European Commissioners, forcing a by-election in Govan, the first in Scotland for some six years.

The fortunes of the Liberals and Social Democrats revolved around two Scots: David Steel, who had forced the pace on a merger in the immediate aftermath of election disappointment, and Robert Maclennan, who was thrust into the spotlight to lead the SDP when Dr David Owen walked off into the political wilderness.

Maclennan showed his lawyer's touch in the preparation of the new party's constitution. Steel was courted as its leader but after twelve dramatic, draining years as Liberal leader decided to return to the backbenches. But the two of them were responsible for the biggest political mistake of the year – the so-called "dead parrot" policy prospectus which they approved for the new party at Christmas.

Its over-hasty declaration of a myriad of controversial policies shocked the parties, particularly the Liberals, and an outright rebellion by Liberal MPs killed it. Credibility shattered, the parties produced a second draft based on known policies agreed at the last election.

Majorities in both parties eventually gave the merger the green light and Paddy Ashdown emerged as the new Social and Liberal Democrats' first leader – but the process had consumed a whole year.

Mrs Thatcher discovers Scotland

That Mrs Thatcher should pay more attention to Scotland and Scottish affairs was one of the central findings of the Tory Party's inquest into its electoral disaster north of the Border. Not least in the constituencies there was a feeling that she had neglected Scotland and ought to become involved, and be seen to be involved, much more in Scottish matters. It was a conclusion with which the Prime Minister agreed.

In the early months of her third term, a succession of Ministers visited Scotland only to provoke an outcry, and not just from their political adversaries, for being insensitive and uncaring in their attitude towards the Scots. The phrase which encapsulated their approach was about Scotland being a "dependency culture."

Take for example a passage from a speech in Glasgow by the Chancellor, Nigel Lawson, in November: "Despite the undoubted success so far, there is still a barrier along Scotland's road to prosperity. That barrier is the pervasive presence of a hostile attitude to enterprise and wealth-creation, to the enterprise culture on which economic success in a free society depends."

But the blunt and unsympathetic tones were to disappear altogether under the new regime once it became evident that, as the former Tory Minister, Alick Buchanan-Smith, so persuasively declared, they did more harm than good to party fortunes.

As telling the Scots to stop moaning vanished, so Mrs Thatcher's Scottish profile grew.

In May, in her own inimitable fashion, Mrs Thatcher rallied the Scottish Tory faithful at their annual Perth conference with a speech peppered with Scottish references and designed to underline her complete commitment to turning Scotland blue again. The following day, she exhibited previously unknown enthusiasm for soccer by attending, despite the obvious dangers, the Scottish Cup Final at Hampden Park.

There was more important work to do, too. The Prime Minister chose an invitation to speak to the General Assembly of the Church of Scotland to bid for the moral high ground of politics and associate the Conservative Party with the guardianship of morality. To note that it was a controversial declaration of personal faith would be a risky understatement; the row rumbled on for weeks.

Pity Mr Speaker

On the evening of April 18th, Labour MPs left the Commons in a state of special excitement and satisfaction following the embarrassing cut in the Government's national 101 majority to only 25 on the so-called Mates amendment to the "poll tax" legislation aimed at linking the charge to ability to pay. Their joy was to be short-lived.

The morning news headlines were to be dominated by the Hon Member for Leith, the unpredictable Ron Brown.

In what was surely the most extraordinary affair of the year at Westminster, Brown had stolen the limelight from the Government's difficulties by a late-night protest in which he picked up, dropped and damaged the Mace, symbol of the Speaker's authority.

And it got worse. Interfering with the Mace is a serious offence but not without precedent: Michael Heseltine had done something similar in 1977. He had been forced humbly to apologise next day. Brown was expected to do so. His Chief Whip, Derek Foster, went to great lengths to prepare the ground and a personal statement, to be read out by Brown, was agreed in the customary way with the Speaker.

He compounded his offence however by refusing to apologise without reservation, despite no fewer than nine attempts by the Speaker, Bernard

Weatherill, to let him. The anger of Labour MPs knew no bounds.

Conservative MPs held up the affair as proof of Labour's unruliness and even unfitness as Official Opposition. They wanted to suspend Brown for 60 days but eventually he was ejected for 20 days. Brown subsequently lost the party Whip and was reported to his constituency party amid dark rumours of an attempt to de-select him.

His was the most bizarre Commons outburst but by no means the only one in a year when some Opposition MPs appeared to have decided that there was no alternative to protest to try and make their voices heard.

The SNP MP, Alex Salmond, sought his moment of glory towards the end of Chancellor Lawson's Budget speech. No-one could remember that ever having happened before, but he also was thrown out of the House on refusing to end his interruption and sit down. Tam Dalyell (Linlithgow) was twice suspended for continuing his personal guerrilla campaign against Mrs Thatcher.

Protest was not confined to the Chamber. Labour's Dennis Canavan provoked the anger of his colleagues in January for disrupting two separate committees in fury at English Tory MPs taking part in the discussion of Scottish business. Labour reported him to the Speaker.

Paisley Grammar School

Correspondence between the Private Secretaries of the Prime Minister and Malcolm Rifkind was leaked to the Glasgow Herald in April, which caused the most serious clash of the session between the Government and Opposition parties. At the centre of the row was Paisley Grammar School.

The Scottish Office had already aroused political and educational opposition with its proposals in the School Boards Bill for a major extension of parent power. But now it emerged that the legislation was to be used as a stalking horse for the much more radical plan to allow individual schools to opt out of the state system. The letters revealed that the favoured option was for the former Scottish Education Minister, Allen Stewart, to introduce an amendment aimed at enabling schools to do just that. The amendment would be dropped after a declaration of similar intent by Rifkind.

To cut a long story short, the School Boards Bill proceded on the basis that the more controversial extensions of parent power were dropped. Rifkind took powers to intervene in school closure plans such as those of Strathclyde Council and save schools like Paisley. And legislation to implement the opt-out proposals is due in the 1988-89 session.

The two main pieces of legislation introduced by the Scottish Office in the session were the Housing (Scotland) Bill, to extend tenants' rights, and the School Boards Bill.

Both saw protests over the inclusion of Tory MPs from English seats to make up Government numbers: oddly enough, both Tories involved, James Arbuthnot and Ian Bruce, claimed strong Scottish pedigrees. But the arguments were a throw-back to the election result and the drastic cut in backbench Scottish numbers. There were simply not enough backbenchers to go round – as with the Select Committee, on which two of the five Scottish Tories refused to serve from the start.

In the unpromising realms of Private Members' Bills, two Scots scored notable successes.

Bill Walker, Conservative MP for Tayside North who had won pride of place in the annual Private Members' Bills ballot, saw his Scotch Whisky Bill make rapid progress to the Statute Book with cross-party backing. The measure was designed to protect real Scotch from poor imitations, much as the French protect their champagne.

Archy Kirkwood, Liberal MP for Roxburgh and Berwickshire who also unsuccessfully sought the leadership of the Scottish SLDs in a straight fight with Malcolm Bruce, steered a second Private Members' Bill to law in as many years to set something of a record. Again it was in the area of freedom of information. His Access to Medical Reports Bill enabled patients to see and challenge general practioners' reports about them commissioned by employers and insurance companies.

The way ahead

Scottish affairs occupied a large measure of MPs' time in this extended Parliamentary session: the future of Dounreay; tax hand-outs to the rich to develop private forestry, much of it in Scotland; inner city regeneration which brought Mrs Thatcher on an early visit to Glasgow; salmon netting; the Piper Alpha disaster which claimed 167 lives; orders for Yarrows from the Ministry of Defence; the future of Scottish Universities, particularly Aberdeen in its financial crisis; prison riots; nurses pay; and alleged Militant infiltration of at least one Glasgow Labour constituency party.

Of all these things and of all the mix of personalities was the colourful kaleidescope of Scottish politics made up.

But this has only been the start.

Scotland has now emerged as the most fascinating area of British politics. While Mrs Thatcher's own cultural revolution has swept across

England and Wales with the result that the Labour Party struggles even to hold onto its traditional heart-lands, Scotland has remained out of her reach.

Labour, which exceeded 50% in a couple of mid-session Scottish public opinion polls, remains the most powerful political force in Scotland and entrenched its local government superiority in the May elections.

But Rifkind has begun to change the political balance. This is not to suggest that he has solved all the Scottish Conservative Party's problems; but things are on the move and not all going Labour's way. In what is chiefly still a two-party contest, the protagonists have locked antlers.

There is no hint of any relaxation in Rifkind's battle-plans. The 1988-89 session will feature highly-contentious, radical legislation in the form of electricity privatisation, schools opt-out and the sell-off of the Scottish Bus Group. The three prongs of the Scottish Secretary's offensive to reverse the long-term decline of his party and pose a real electoral threat to Labour will certainly be pursued with determination.

The battle-lines have now been drawn. To date, more questions than answers exist as to future fortunes and a lesser degree of certainty than for some years clouds the field. It is impossible to adopt other than an Asquithian caution in looking to the future.

Much is at stake. For Mrs Thatcher, the prize of winning over the Scots would crown her political achievements just as failure would be an historical irritant. For Labour, Scotland could act as a spring-board for national revival and proof that there is life after Thatcher.

The fight for political supremacy is likely to be long and bloody.

Peter Hannam was Chief Political Correspondent of *The Scotsman* until becoming Features Editor of the Norwich-based Eastern Daily Press in August.

THE SCOTTISH DISTRICT ELECTIONS OF 1988

John Bochel and David Denver

The Scottish District Elections held on 5th May 1988 were the first electoral test for the parties in Scotland since the 1987 general election. In that election voting behaviour in Scotland deviated even more sharply from that in the rest of the country than hitherto. Whilst the Conservatives more or less held their own and Labour failed to make headway elsewhere, in Scotland Conservative support slumped to only 24 percent of the vote and they won only ten of the seventy-two seats – their worst performance ever. From an already strong positioin Labour advanced to 42.4 percent of the vote and won fifty seats; the SNP made a modest recovery (14 percent of the vote and three seats), and the Alliance slipped back to 19.2 percent of the vote while increasing its tally of seats to nine.

After their 1987 debacle the Conservatives sought to go on the offensive in Scotland. A review of party organisation was undertaken and radical changes were implemented. Scottish ministers and Mrs Thatcher herself began to preach aggressively the relevance of Thatcherism for Scotland. Few, if any policy changes seemed to be contemplated. The party remained firmly anti-devolutionist and the obviously unpopular poll-tax or community charge was to go ahead first in Scotland. The latter became the central issue in the 1988 local election campaign. One year was too short a time to see any significant results from the reform of party organisation or attempts to change political attitudes in Scotland. So the local elections became, to a large extent, a chance for Scots to pronounce a verdict on the proposed tax.

For the former Alliance parties the elections were also an important test. The formation of the Social and Liberal Democrats from the former Liberal party and a section of the SDP was a long and rather messy business, and inevitably support in the opinion polls for the new party fell compared with that for the former Alliance. Time was short for the new party to expect to make headway in the local elections. For the SLD, then, a holding operation must have been the most optimistic aspiration.

Having made some progress in the 1987 general election, the SNP was subsequently encouraged by good figures in Scottish opinion polls and some successes in local by-elections. It was vigorously opposed to the poll-tax and, unlike Labour, it was relatively united in its policy of non-payment as a means of resistance. The SNP had grounds for expecting to consolidate and advance upon its 1987 performance.

As ever, the Labour party could only hope to maintain its position in these elections. Since the reorganisation of Scottish local government in 1974, Labour had established a position of overwhelming predominance in the Regions and Districts. After the 1984 district elections Labour-controlled authorities contained three-quarters of the Scottish electorate, and in the 1987 general election it won almost 70 per cent of the constituencies. Clearly something extra-ordinary needs to happen to threaten Labour domination of Scottish politics.

Local elections are not, however, simply gigantic opinion polls recording voters' current preferences amongst the parties, although this is a legitimate view of them. These elections do decide who runs local affairs and, in these days of seemingly perpetual conflict between central and local government, and despite the limits placed on the discretion of local authorities, that is important. Local elections are also of intrinsic interest to those concerned with the developing patterns of party competition, electoral participation and trends in party support in Scotland. It is these themes that we wish to pursue in what follows.

Forms of Local Politics

We have in the past distinguished Scottish districts by the level of party competition in them. We identified three categories viz. (a) Partisan districts, in which party competition is the norm and councils are run on party lines, (b) Non-partisan districts, in which Independents predominate and (c) Mixed or Intermediate districts which fall between the first two categories. Table 1 presents our categorisastion of the fifty-three districts for the five sets of elections since 1974.

TABLE 1
Forms of Local Politics in Scottish Districts 1974-88

	1974	1977	1980	1984	1988
Partisan Districts	27	26	32	34	34
Mixed Districts	9	14	7	6	9
Non-Partisan Districts	17	13	14	13	10

Reorganisation resulted in much greater party interest and involvement in local elections than before and the level of partisanship has grown steadily since 1974. The number of purely non-partisan districts has fallen to only ten, and these are very small (in terms of population) and on the geographical periphery.

Candidates

Table 2 presents the number of candidates put forward by the different parties and groups at each set of district elections. 1988 showed the continuation of an upward trend which produced over 3,000 for the first time. The increase is entirely attributable to the growing involvement of the parties and indicates that, in this respect at least, local democracy is in good health.

TABLE 2
Number of Candidates 1974-1988

	1974	1977	1980	1984	1988
Conservatives	539	543	547	571	626
Labour	753	719	765	830	870
Lib/Alliance/SLD	148	136	153	417	333
SNP	269	465	439	493	769
Independent	644	521	426	402	373
Others	207	187	122	122	159
Total	2560	2571	2452	2835	3130

One of the weaknessess of Conservative organisation at local level in Scotland was the relatively low number of candidates they put forward at district and regional elections. This had a knock-on effect at Parliamentary elections because the local electoral machines were at best rusty and sometimes non-existent. Efforts were obviously made to remedy this and as a consequence they fielded a record number of candidates in 1988. The hope was not only to revive local organisation, but also to have as many candidates as possible to spread the Conservative message. Although Labour could hardly expect to improve upon the number of district councils it controlled, encouraged by some good results in unlikely places at the general election, it sought to improve its performance in some hitherto hostile territory. As a consequence it also fielded a record number of candidates. The SNP clearly perceived that its fortunes were on an upturn, morale had improved and so it was easier to attract candidates. These factors led to a spectacular increase in the number of candidates (+276) and for the first the SNP had more than the Conservatives. The break-up of the Alliance and the recent fraught birth of the SLD resulted in the new party putting forward fewer candidates (333) than the combined Alliance total in 1984 (417). It was still a creditable effort when we note that about half of the decline reflects our decision to treat the SDP (Continuing) candidates in 1988 as 'others'.

Overall, big increases in the number of candidates were recorded in Grampian (+85) and in Fife (+57) where all four major parties advanced upon their 1984 figures. Strathclyde had more candidates too (+67) largely because of a major increase in SNP intervention (+90). The total number of candidates rose in every region except Tayside which was the only one where the number of Conservative aspirants fell.

The Conservatives seem to have a major problem in attracting candidates in Central region where the SLD is also very weak as it is in Tayside and Strathclyde.

The decline in the number of Independent candidates continues unabated, as it has since 1974. Table 3 shows that they now constitute a tiny minority in partisan districts. In non-partisan districts Independent candidates were formerly in a near-monopolistic position, but in the last two sets of elections the major parties have made quite large incursions. In mixed districts the intervention of parties in 1988 was very substantial and Independents declined to less than half of all candidates. It seems likely that in these districts there will be a slow but steady move towards partisan local politics.

TABLE 3
Independents as a proportion of All Candidates 1974-1988

	1974	1977	1980	1984	1988
Partisan Districts (34)	10.7	7.1	5.1	3.3	3.0
Mixed Districts (9)	73.7	72.7	64.8	62.1	44.3
Non-Partisan Districts (10)	92.0	92.1	97.0	86.5	72.0
All Districts	25.2	20.3	17.4	14.2	11.9

Uncontested Elections and Party Competition

Uncontested returns have long been unheard of in parliamentary elections, and indeed, with the exception of Ulster, it is normal for the major parties to nominate candidates in all constituencies. But uncontested elections still persist at local level. Two major factors may account for this. Firstly there is the sheer number of wards – well over a thousand in Scottish districts – for which candidates must be found. Finding a candidate and mounting a campaign presupposes, or should, a ward party organisation and some resources of manpower and finance. It is very doubtful whether any of our parties has a viable organisation in every ward in Scotland, and so gaps arise in party slates. Secondly, the rewards of local government are few and the costs, in time, career prospects and disruption to family life are not inconsiderable. Of course many people do wish to serve as local councillors, and some even claim to enjoy campaigning in elections. But very often calls upon party loyalty and the promised support of the party machine are required to persuade party members to stand as candidates. There are, however, no such pressures for Independents and self-motivation is becoming increasingly rare. Parties do, however, have incentives to contest seats even where they have no prospects of winning. Headquarters are likely to argue that the electoral machine requires exercise, that party supporters should have a candidate to vote for, that the maximisation of the vote on a national scale is now important as a measure of party strength and so on. If electoral competition is good, then partisan politics contributes to a healthy political system.

Table 4 demonstrates that electoral competition is thriving. Overall the proportion of wards contested in 1988 was the largest since reorganisation but competition is uneven. Partisan districts have had a large and growing proportion of contests, but after an initial increase in competition in 1974 non-partisan districts have never had more than forty percent of wards contested; mixed districts have had an inconsistent level of competition, but 1988 saw a sharp increase to almost three-quarters of the wards contested.

TABLE 4
Percentage of Wards Contested 1974-1988

	1974 %	1977 %	1980 %	1984 %	1988 %
All Districts	79.5	77.9	74.0	78.3	86.1
Partisan	86.3	88.0	88.3	91.3	95.9
Mixed	64.3	51.9	43.6	52.2	73.3
Non-Partisan	53.8	36.6	20.7	27.5	40.0

The form that these contests have taken is shown in Table 5. The most significant long-term change has been the steady increase in major party contests and this accelerated sharply in 1988. Almost three-quarters of all district wards had contested elections involving two or more of the major parties compared with just over half in 1974. Wards in which the major parties were entirely absent declined to twelve percent of the total. In 1988 too, there was a marked decline in the number of wards in which a major party candidate was returned unopposed.

TABLE 5
Patterns of Competition in District Wards 1974-88

	1974 %	1977 %	1980 %	1984 %	1988 %
Ind/Others only	22	22	21	17	12
Major Party v Ind/Others	13	11	9	9	9
Major Party Contested	56	59	61	65	74
Major Party Uncontested	9	8	9	9	5

Another aspect of competition patterns is shown in Table 6. More than ninety percent of all the wards in partisan districts had major party contests. The spread of party activity is illustrated by the fact that even in non-partisan districts thirty percent of wards had at least one major party candidate.

TABLE 6
Patterns of Competition in Partisan, Mixed and Non-Partisan Districts 1988

	All Districts %	Partisan %	Mixed %	Non-Partisan %
Ind/Others only	12	*	27	70
Major Party v Ind/Others	9	4	33	14
Major Party Contested	74	92	31	9
Major Party Uncontested	5	4	9	7

* = less than 1%

The changing nature of party contests is illustrated in Table 7. Two-way contests, which were far and away the most common in 1974, have declined pretty steadily and significantly. In particular, straight fights between Labour and the Conservatives, which were again the most common, are now relatively rare. The increase in Conservative v. Labour v. SNP contests is a direct function of the larger number of SNP candidates. This also explains why, despite the fall in the number of SLD candidates, the proportion of four-way contests reached a high point of twenty-three per cent of contests in 1988.

TABLE 7
Selected Types of Party Contests in District Wards 1974-1988

	1974	1977	1980	1984	1988
Two-way Contests	%	%	%	%	%
Con. v Lab.	39	24	26	12	6
Lab. v SNP	20	22	23	16	23
Others	9	10	9	12	8
All Two-way	68	56	58	40	37
Three-way Contests	%	%	%	%	%
Con. v Lab. v SNP	17	30	26	17	26
Con. v Lab. v Lib/All/SLD	13	5	8	15	5
Others	1	2	2	7	5
All Three-way	31	37	36	39	36
Four-way Contests	%	%	%	%	%
Con. v Lab. v Lib/All/SLD v SNP	3	6	6	21	23

In 1988 the steady, and now very significant, trend towards a complex and competitive four party system continued in relation to candidacies. The nomination of candidates is but one aspect of elections however: harvesting of votes and their conversion into seats is quite another as we demonstrate below.

Trends in Party Support

Table 8 shows the distribution of votes at all district elections between 1974 and 1988. These are 'raw' figures which do not take account of the number of candidates put forward by the different parties or groups.

TABLE 8
Party Share of Votes in Scottish Districts 1974-1988

	1974 %	1977 %	1980 %	1984 %	1988 %
Conservative	26.8	27.2	24.1	21.4	19.4
Labour	38.4	31.6	45.4	45.7	42.6
Lib/All/SDL	5.0	4.0	6.2	12.8	8.4
SNP	12.4	24.2	15.5	11.7	21.3
Independent	14.1	9.8	6.7	6.8	6.4
Others	3.4	3.3	2.2	1.6	2.0

On these data the Conservatives dropped to their lowest level of support ever in district elections and the same can be said of their results in 1980 and 1984. On this occasion too, the Conservatives were pushed into third place by the SNP which improved its share of the vote by almost ten percentage points compared with 1984. The SLD emerged in a position half-way between the Alliance performance in 1984 and the Liberals' in 1980. Although there was a small decline in Labour's share of the vote its dominance was hardly dented. In three successive sets of district elections it has had around twice the number of votes obtained by the next placed party.

An analysis of the distribution of party support in the three categories of districts (Table 9) reveals, not surprisingly, that the results in partisan districts closely reflect the overall figures, with a nine point rise in SNP support, a five point fall for the SLD and small decreases for Labour and the Conservatives. There is distinctly more variation in mixed and non-partisan districts, but in both the Independents suffered sharp declines and the SNP made its largest gains, benefitting as it did from its increased number of candidates in these districts.

As we have cautioned before, the varying patterns of candidatures and the number of uncontested divisions can significantly affect the levels of party support. More precise and probably more reliable estimates of the

TABLE 9
Party Share of Votes in Three Categories of Scottish Districts 1984-1988

	Partisan Districts			Mixed Districts			Non-Partisan Districts		
	1984	1988	change	1984	1988	change	1984	1988	change
Conservative	22.2	20.7	−1.5	11.6	8.6	−3.0	–	4.1	+4.1
Labour	48.0	46.1	−1.9	9.3	9.9	+0.6	9.3	7.5	−1.8
Lib/All/SLD	13.2	8.2	−5.0	8.8	12.6	+3.8	0.9	2.5	+1.6
SNP	12.0	21.2	+9.2	8.2	25.1	+16.9	2.6	15.1	+12.5
Independent	3.0	2.2	−0.8	60.9	42.7	−18.2	87.2	68.9	−18.3
Others	1.7	1.6	−0.1	1.1	1.2	+0.1	–	1.9	+1.9

ebb and flow of support can be obtained by examining those wards in which the pattern of candidatures was identical in two successive elections.

In Table 10 we report the results in three types of contest, those in which the four main parties all nominated candidates, contests in which there were Conservative, Labour and SNP candidates and those in which there were straight fights between Labour and the SNP. The results in the four-way contests confirm that there was a genuine increase in support for the SNP. The overall figures are not simply an artifact of increased SNP candidacies. By the same token there was 'real' decline in SLD support. An

TABLE 10
Changes in Party Share of Votes in Selected Types of Contests 1984-1988

Four-way Contests (82)

	1984 %	1988 %	Change
Conservatives	29.1	27.6	−1.5
Labour	41.3	41.3	–
All/SLD	21.6	14.2	−7.3
SNP	8.0	16.8	+8.8

Two-way Contests (66)

	1984 %	1988 %	Change
Conservatives	24.4	19.7	−4.7
Labour	57.5	51.9	−5.6
SNP	18.1	28.5	+10.4

Two-way Contests (69)

	1984 %	1988 %	Change
Labour	64.0	59.7	−4.3
SNP	36.0	40.3	+4.3

analysis of the three way contests leads to the same conclusion, with the SNP advancing, apparently at the expense of Labour and the Conservatives. A study of two-way contests shows that Labour lost ground to the SNP. Together these data which, it should be remembered, control for the number of candidates, enable us to say with confidence that the 1988 district elections saw a marked revival in support for the SNP and a decline for the SLD. Conservative support fell a little from an already pitifully small base, and Labour at best stood still, but suffered a slight decline overall. The comfort for Labour was that the small loss it suffered was in relation to a record performance in 1984 and that its remarkable dominance of local government in Scotland was not in any immediate danger of erosion.

Council Seats Won

Labour's dominance in terms of votes has also brought a rich harvest of seats won. It advanced to (yet another) new record with almost twice as many seats as the next largest grouping, the Independents, and more than three times the number of the Conservatives. The Conservatives now hold fewer seats than at any time since reorganisation in 1974. The SNP, in line with the improvement in its share of the vote, nearly doubled its tally of seats, although this is still a long way from its 1977 performance. More surprisingly, despite a reduced share of the vote, the SLD came out of the election with an increased number of seats, but this was entirely due to their success in two small districts, Gordon (+8) and Annandale and Eskdale (+4). The decline in Independent representation continued and they now have one third fewer seats than they had fourteen years ago. (Table 11).

TABLE 11
District Council Seats Won 1974-1988

	1974	1977	1980	1984	1988
Conservatives	241	277	229	189	162
Labour	428	299	494	545	553
Lib/All/SLD	17	31	40	78	84
SNP	62	170	54	59	113
Independent	345	318	289	267	231
Others	17	22	18	11	11
Total	1110	1117	1124	1149*	1154**

* no nomination in three wards
** no nomination in three wards

The effects that changes in seats won between 1984 and 1988 had on party control in individual districts are shown in Table 12. Labour gained majority control in two districts (Clydesdale and Kyle and Carrick) but lost their majority in three others (Stirling, Dumbarton and Cumbernauld and Kilsyth). The Conservatives lost one of the four districts they controlled, (Kyle and Carrick) to Labour. The SLD added control of Gordon to North East Fife while the SNP gained Angus. Independents lost their majority in four districts (Moray, Kincardine and Deeside, Annandale and Eskdale and Inverness), but regained a majority in two others (Banff and Buchan and Roxburgh).

TABLE 12
Party Control in Districts 1984-1988

	1984	1988
Majority Control		
Labour	25	24
Conservative	4	3
All/SLD	1	2
SNP	1	1
Independent	16	14
No Overall Control	6	9
Total	53	53

Party cotrol of the 53 districts is now as follows:

Party Control of the 53 Scottish Districts 1988

Majority Labour Control (24)

Aberdeen	Midlothian	Strath	Renfrew
Dundee	East Lothian	Monklands	Inverclyde
Kirkcaldy	Clackmannan	Motherwell	Cunninghame
Dunfermline	Falkirk	Hamilton	Kilmarnock & Loudoun
West Lothian	Glasgow	East Kilbride	Kyle & Carrick
Edinburgh	Clydebank	Clydesdale	Cumnock & Doon Valley

Majority Conservative Control (3)

Berwickshire   Bearsden & Milngavie   Eastwood

Majority SLD Control (2)

North East Fife   Gordon

Majority SNP Control (1)

Angus

Majority Independent Control (14)

Caithness	Badenoch & Strathspey	Roxburgh
Sutherland	Ettrick & Lauderdale	Argyll & Bute
Ross & Cromarty	Banff & Buchan	Wigtown
Skye & Lochalsh	Tweeddale	Lochaber
Stewartry	Nairn	

No Overall Control (largest party in brackets) (9)

Inverness (Ind)	Perth & Kinross (Con)	Cumbernauld (Lab/SNP)
Moray (SNP/Ind)	Stirling (Con/Lab)	Nithsdale (Lab)
Kincardine/Deeside (Ind)	Dunbarton (Lab)	Annandale/Eskdale (SLD)

Conclusion

Local government throughout Britain is very much on the defensive just now. Councils see their powers diminishing, the range of services they administer contracting, their discretion over financial and other matters limited and, in Scotland at least, a question mark put over the entire structure.

In the circumstances it is surprising and encouraging to be able to observe that, in some important respects, the system of local government in Scotland is healthy and buoyant. A record number of candidates was willing to be nominated in 1988; the proportion of wards contested was at its highest since reorganisation in 1974 and so more electors than ever before had a choice of candidates; not only did more electors have a choice, their range of choice was also greater with major parties contesting almost three quarters of the seats. In addition, although we have not the space to go into detail, the number of women candidates and councillors continued to increase and turnout showed a modest but welcome rise. The inexorable advance of partisan politics is a more controversial 'gain', but its beneficial side effects are obvious. It has increased electoral competition in many areas and has, as a consequence, increased responsibility and accountability in a number of districts because, when electors have to give a verdict on a council's stewardship over the previous four years they can reward or punish the party that has administered the affairs of the district.

For good or ill local election results are scrutinised for what they might reveal about the electoral standing of the parties. The overall figures show that, despite the Conservative reorganisation of their machinery, their largest ever number of candidates and a formidable rhetorical counter-attack attempting to explain the advantages of Thatcherism for Scotland, their support continued to decline and they fell into third place in the popular vote. Labour, which has dominance in Parliamentary and local politics in Scotland did not lapse into complacency, it fought and won a record number of seats and its share of the vote remained at the high point attained in the 1987 general election. The SNP, which fielded its largest ever number of candidates, made more progress than any other of the main parties; its share of the vote (which put it ahead of the Conservatives), and the number of seats won was the highest since 1977, although these still fell some way short of the figures obtained then. It still controls only one District council, but of most potential significance perhaps, was the relatively good, but patchy performance of the SNP in Labour's heartland, the central belt. It has been there before, of course, and has not sustained its gains, and there is nothing about the current political climate which suggest that long-term change beneficial to the SNP is in prospect. Given the handicaps it faced the new SLD fought a commendable number of seats; its share of the vote (compared with the Alliance share in 1984) fell quite sharply, but it ended up with the largest number of seats won by the Liberals or the Alliance since reorganisation and added Gordon to North East Fife as districts that it controlled.

It is always difficult for an observer to determine with any confidence what the main issues are in any election or to divine what the electors are 'trying to say' when they vote. There is little agreement amongst the parties during a campaign about what they regard as the main issues, and their interpretations of the electors' verdict are perhaps even more varied. If, as we suggested earlier, these elections were some kind of judgement on the poll tax, then this innovation was overwhelmingly rejected. Equally, if they were an opportunity to show approval of Thatcherism as promoted by a newly aggressive Conservative party in Scotland, then the approval was clearly not given. The poll tax was indubitably an issue and an appropriate one, but local elections are, above all and properly, an opportunity for electors to pass judgement on the way in which their districts have been run over the previous four years. If this is indeed the case, then the results of the 1987 District elections can be read as a generous endorsement of the performance of the great majority of Labour councils. Labour's vote held, it won more seats than ever before and controls twenty-four of the thirty-four partisan districts in Scotland.

Probably no single interpretation of the results is correct, but it is probably not unfair to assess them as a muted, but pretty emphatic vote of confidence in our system of local government and in the people who run it.

John Bochel, University of Dundee.
David Denver, University of Lancaster.

Scottish Assembly • Take The High Road • Dreams And Recollections • Scotland Today • Taggart • Aly Bain And Friends • Enchanted Glass • Scottish Action • Reid About The USSR • Votes for Women • In Verse • Scottish Books • The Campbells • Festival '88 • Festival Cinema • Scottish Picture Show • Wheel of Fortune • McGinn • Night Talk • Scottish Questions • Split Second • Rescue • Get Fresh • MacDiarmid • Scottish Women • Englishing Of Scotland • Winners & Losers • Telethon • Out of the Elephant's Bed • Welcome to Gaeldom • Secret of Croftmore • Glen Michael's Cavalcade • The Macrame Man • Scotsport • Room For One More • Mayfest '88

SCOTTISH TELEVISION

SCOTLAND'S TELEVISION: HALFWAY HOME?

Ian Bell

THE PROSPECT of 1988's European Year of Film and Television had about as much impact on Scottish Television viewers as the average public information film. The underlying assumption of the year, that indigenous broadcasting is under threat from a flood of US product, is obvious (not to say ironic) enough to leave most of us cold.

In Scotland we have had little enough broadcasting of our own over the years. Traditionally Scottish Television, Grampian, BBC Scotland and Border have been the out-stations of English metropolitan producers and the country subsists on a diet of 'foreign' TV, from London or the US.

People who talk about the hegemony of US television tend to forget that the power of American producers has nothing to do with the size of their industry. Conversely, while Scotland supports TV stations it is regarded as being too small to sustain a TV service. We are, both literally and figuratively, a client state.

Put it this way; in the late 20th century television is perhaps the single most powerful medium for the shaping and projection of national culture and identity – if you are not on TV you do not exist. Yet in the year to March 1987, Scottish Television supplied (or was allowed to supply) only 2.5 percent of the 3,492 hours of networked programmes shown on ITV while Grampian supplied 0.7 percent. The figures for the BBC are little better. Scotland, with 10 percent of the UK population, earns only a 3.2 percent 'representation' at a time when our political distinctiveness has never been more marked.

Channel Four with special remit to serve minorities, fails the largest minority of all. They get £15 million of income from Scottish Television and Grampian and 10 percent of audience, but commissions to Scots about Scots amount to only 0.75 percent of production budget at a guess.

The Scottish broadcasting industry, meanwhile, is worth 2,000 jobs and our indigenous broadcasters carry a greater burden of responsibility in the areas of language, culture, religion, sport and education than their counterparts south of the Border. Scottish Television, for that matter, is the only major media outlet in the country which is Scottish-owned.

33

Twenty years ago Stuart Hood wrote an article entitled 'The Backwardness of Scottish Television' which depicted a broadcasting landscape scarred by a legacy of BBC cowardice in the face of authority at a time when the Canadian Lord Thomson was, not to put too fine a point on it, looting STV. Hood demanded more documentaries in the Grierson mould and more 'realistic' drama. He wrote: 'Both on a popular and on a higher creative level regional accents must be heard.' He concluded that 'a radicalisation of Scottish life in all areas' was the key to the development of Scottish Television.

It was not an encouraging picture. Yet twenty years on, if you should chance to talk to the people who run TV in London, you would be forgiven for thinking that little or nothing has changed. Michael Grade, the man who runs Channel Four, told this writer recently that Scottish independent producers 'moan' constantly about lack of access yet fail to generate sufficient programme ideas. Scottish commercial stations, which complain in similar terms, gather much advertising revenue from his channel, he suggested, and their grievances were not worth considering. More startlingly, he thought that SC4, the Welsh version of Four, was necessary and justifiable because of threats to that country's language and culture; similar considerations did not apply to Gaelic!

The real worry is that there is little or nothing that Scottish programme makers can do about such attitudes. Scottish Television recently won for itself a place on the ITV controllers' group representing the ten 'regional' companies in a network dominated by right of the Big Five who are fighting a rearguard action to defend their privileged position. Winning more access to the UK network can be very rewarding in terms of programme variety and production jobs. The extra access won in the last year allowed STV to double programme sales to £11 million. Its 'fair share' would be double that – enough to create hundreds of new jobs.

Politics aside, it is the demands of the networks which cripple Scottish broadcasting. With their own market too small to generate revenue for programme makers, the ITV companies must serve and protect Scotland while touting their wares to an English audience.

Nevertheless, Scottish broadcasting has changed immeasurably since Stuart Hood composed his critique. The very existence of independent producers is beginning, slowly, to establish a continuity of production and skills – a nascent industry, in other words. Both the BBC and Scottish have demonstrated, if only from time to time, that they can make programmes of quality which both reflect their origins and satisfy the networks, whether they be Tutti Fruitti or Taggart. Cable, meanwhile, is slowly extending its tentacles in Aberdeen, Glasgow and Edinburgh.

It is not going too far to suggest that even in their news reporting the

Scottish stations are beginning to achieve a style and an attitude which reflects the country's political condition and marks them out from their complacent and slavish English counterparts. It is no accident that the troubled Secret Society series, which so provoked Downing Street, was made in Glasgow.

Downing Street has a knack of hitting back, however. It seems more than likely that the hard-won gains of Scottish broadcasting over the past twenty years will be forfeited if plans for 'deregulation' and satellite broadcasting are carried out in their present form. Both Scottish and Grampian will, for example, have to fight hard just to survive if the Independent Broadcasting Authority is abolished and franchises are auctioned to the highest, multi-national bidder. Satellite, by definition, is no respecter of national boundaries or identities. The BBC, meanwhile, is running backwards in the face of a hostile government.

Unless and until Scottish broadcasting is regarded as a national asset such processes can only accelerate. The European Year of Film and Television has been an attempt to foster national identities within the continent while calling for more co-productions and EEC legislation to protect indigenous broadcasting. Scotland, forever on the periphery, needs that initiative more than most – and never more so than now. Just when we were half-way home and dry, the tide is rising again.

Ian Bell, Glasgow Herald.

THE CRISIS IN THE SCOTTISH COAL INDUSTRY

Suzanne Najam

Introduction

Nineteen eighty eight saw the unprecedented spectacle of two major nationalised power industries engaged in a legal battle in the Scottish courts to resolve issues with far-reaching ramifications for the Scottish economy. On 1st March 1988, after months of fruitless negotiations, British Coal (BC) sought an interim interdict against the South of Scotland Electricity Board (SSEB) in order to prevent the electricity board from accepting tenders from foreign suppliers of coal, (from which the latter argued it could buy more cheaply than from BC), by claiming that there were pre-existing contracts to supply Longannet and Cockenzie power stations with coal from Scottish pits into the 1990s. This interim interdict was granted to the coal industry, but was later set aside in an attempt to conciliate the SSEB and provide the grounds upon which to negotiate for a long-term contract to provide Scottish deep-mined coal to the power stations.

However, despite a three month negotiating period during which no imported coal would be burnt at the two power stations mentioned, the SSEB continued to buy coal from foreign sources. The main supplier, for these contracts, Shell, is said to have made a loss in its eagerness to secure the market. When the two sides met on the 30th June 1988 in order to seek ways to extend the ceasefire, it was these stocks of imported coal, amounting to 1 million tonnes, which were to prove the stumbling block to finding a settlement. For although prices and tonnages were agreed for a further nine months, the SSEB still insisted that it wished to burn the foreign coal at power stations other than the inefficient Kincardine station, which was not covered by the interim interdict, and which is estimated as having one-tenth of the combined power of Longannet and Cockenzie; BC, on the other hand, sought to ensure that some 750,000 tonnes would be burnt solely at Kincardine station.

On the surface, much of the controversy can be apportioned to an intransigent SSEB, eager to improve its financial and organisational position in the years prior to privatisation. The SSEB balance sheet looked particularly poor after an over-investment in unnecessary capacity, notably Torness, had put its total debts for 1987/88 at £1.82 billion. Financial advisors to the SSEB, and the Scottish Office, had informed the utility that its profit margin must be improved in the run-up to privatisation to increase its attractiveness. The new strategy of cutting costs must certainly be seen in this light. Yet there are also more practical problems for BC. With Torness coming on stream, previous investment in Hunterston 'B', and with Inverkip able to burn more oil since 1986, the SSEB's demand for Scottish coal has fallen. This is evidenced in its reduced need for coal from Monktonhall, which BC duly closed. It is for these reasons that the SSEB has sought only a one or two year contract, and to overturn the longer-term commitment to take Scottish coals for Longannet and Cockenzie. BC, in turn, has argued that not only has it invested £60 million in the new Castlebridge extension to Longannet, but that it needs a long-term contract until the end of the 1990s in order to plan its deep mine policy, necessary due to the massive input of planning and investment involved, and to ensure the redevelopment of the Frances Colliery in Fife.

Yet in many ways BC has wilfully, if unwittingly, placed itself in the unenviable position wherein it must resort to court action to keep the contract of its most significant customer as a result of the policies it has followed since the late 1970s. It is the purpose of this article, therefore, to trace, albeit briefly, the major ways in which, in this 'battle of the giants', BC has, by its own policies, exacerbated the weak position in which it now finds itself.

Governmental Policies and their Consequences for the Coal Industry

The 1980s have witnessed an international expansion in coal production, which can be seen as having developed from a growing concern from the early 1970s about oil reserves and supplies, and worries about nuclear energy. This increased world production, with resultant drives by foreign coal suppliers to secure markets, has served to lower world prices below the costs of production. Yet the same period has seen a contraction in the Scottish mining industry, as with the British coalfield as a whole, which has acted to enhance the exposure of Scottish coals to foreign competition. This has been, in no small way, the consequence of governmental policies since 1979.

The undermining of the coal industry by the Tory government is the result of two central thrusts of its ideological position; the first political, the second economic. The first factor is intimately connected to the seeming defeat of Heath's government at the hands of the National Union of Mine-Workers (NUM) in 1972 and 1974. It was in the climate of this apparent crisis that a report was sent to Derek Ezra by Wilfred Miron, National Coal Board member with Regional Responsibilities, in December 1973. In this document Miron sets out changes which would counter the potential threat from the Miners' Union in the future. He produced a programme which would implement technological changes, especially automated processes; alter payment structures; redirect investment to 'moderate' areas; limit future manning; remove 'subversive political influences', and ensure that as many employed as possible were outwith the NUM. Managerial attitudes were to be reorientated in compliance with the new proposals. The requirements for such moves hinged on Miron's perception of the political militancy of the miners. A quotation from this document serves to indicate its tone:-

> "We must keep in mind that the strategy of the NUM's Executive will become increasingly politically oriented and that its Left-Wing (Communists, Marxistsand their ilk, however organisationally fragmented) will maintain a unified strategy towards the ideological end – the overthrow of the present 'system'.... These Left Wingers now in office, or to achieve office, are not going to be changed; they will not be diverted from their political dedication[1]."

The activities surrounding the report were to be kept quiet yet Saville argues that by 1979 "the Miron proposals were mostly in place, or in process, aided by new micro-processor technology[2]." Evidence for this claim, and the effects for Scotland, can be seen from later arguments. Of greater public knowledge is the set of plans known as the Ridley Report, which was the final report of the Ridley Committee, leaked to *The Economist* on the 27th May 1978. It laid out a strategy for challenge from what it called a 'vulnerable industry', such as coke, which operated with "the full force of communist disruptors." The report stated:-

> "The group believes that the most likely battleground will be the coal industry. They would like a Thatcher government to: (a) build up maximum coal stocks, particularly at the power stations; (b) make contigency plans for the import of coal; (c) encourage the recruitment of non-union lorry drivers by haulage companies to help move coal where necessary; (d) introduce dual coal/oil firing in all power stations as quickly as possible[3]."

These two reports serve to demonstrate the preparedness of hostile forces within the NCB and Tory party to augment policy decisions for overtly political ends but which, as will be seen later, would also have important ramifications for the economic state of BC in the 1980s. We can see in such documents a political desire to lessen dependence upon coal in order to undermine the miners' industrial power. It could be argued that it is as a result of this desire that Britain has been the only country with indigeneous fuel supplies to invest heavily in nuclear power; investing around £10 billion in nuclear generating stations. Yet such strategies have also been supplemented by Conservative economic policies which have sought, financially at least, to lessen the ties between government and the nationalised industries. The demand by government for BC to break even, now set for 1988/9, has also been crucially connected to BC's policies in the 1980s.

BC Super-Pit Strategy and the Scottish Coal Industry

The financial restrictions placed on BC means that its recent policies have focused on ways in which costs could be cut whilst maintaining maximum output. To these ends, emphasis has been placed increasingly upon a 'super-pit' strategy. This has involved substantial investment in both new pits, (the best known of which is Selby, which cost £1.5 billion), and in new roadways linking some existing pits to greatly improve the time miners can work at the face each shift. This has operated in conjunction with the new advanced automation processes known as MINOS, (Mines Operating System). This system acts to increase the productivity of capital, reduce manpower and give greater managerial control over work processes. All of this was foreshadowed in the Miron Report, and formed the basis of the investment policies pursued by the NCB during the Labour government of 1974-79. However, the MINOS systems are best operationalised in pits where uncertainty in mining conditions is reduced to a minimum. The super-pit strategy consequently has been concentrated in the central coalfield where the geological conditions are more suitable to systems engineering, and in all cases has sought to place emphasis on production, associated with drastic reductions in manpower, and for one main purchaser, the Central Electricity Generating Board (CEGB). It is thus a production-oriented strategy, rather than a market-led one.

BC's policies were to have crucial effects for the Scottish industry. The domination of the CEGB, and SSEB, over BC's concerns means that BC has chosen to undervalue other potential markets; in particular, domestic and coking coals, and anthracite. Thus it has rundown its specialised products in favour of coal for the power stations, served by English super-pits. National funding in the 1980s has been available only for pits serving the power station market, whilst other forms of expenditure have had to be met from local resources. BC policy has consequently become overly-reliant on the CEGB and SSEB, and those pits unable to participate in the major market were to be those that were closed. Between 1979 and the end of March 1988 the number of collieries in Britain dropped from 319 to 96. In Scotland the position has become virtually terminal as, within the same period, the fall has been from 16 to 4; Bilston Glen, Barony, and Solgirth and Castlebridge, both in the Longannet Complex. The numbers employed have fallen from 21,000 to a mere 3,000.

BC's policies have served to make Scotland peripheral to its concerns. Both political and economic factors are important to this trend. Within the arguments laid down by Miron in the early 1970s, Scotland was seen as a politically 'unmoderate' area, where the communist president Mick McGahey and the young 'Marxist' Eric Clarke, later to become General Secretary of the Scottish Area NUM, were singled out for especial mention. It was in such an area that Miron believed moves should be made to lessen the power of the miners. Yet the technological side of his strategy also effectively managed to exclude the Scottish coalfield from being a main part of the NCB's plans, for it was unable to participate within the super-pit strategy due to more complicated geological conditions. These conditions require conventional management techniques due to a wider variety of underground environments than are found in the central English coalfield. The coalfield was thus doubly disadvantaged. Scotland has consequently been caught within a downward spiral wherein lack of investment has led to worsening Machine Available Time, (MAT), stagnation, rundown and final closures.

In 1987/88 BC claimed that all of Scotland's deep mines were uneconomic. Yet this claim is open to some considerable debate, for it hinges upon the particular accounting system used by BC[4]. In order to understand the crisis facing the Scottish industry it is, therefore, worthwhile to examine both the means by which Scotland's pits have been declared unproductive, and closed, over the last 9 years, and the problems which have confronted the Scottish Area, (now no more), which have engendered such an argument.

Clearly, part of Scotland's peripheral status is related to its minor strategic importance to BC's major market, the CEGB, to which sales have declined over the last few years to insignificance; some 11,873 tonnes going incoast from Leith in 1987 compared to 400,000 tonnes in 1986. BC decides whether to take Scottish coals for the English power stations dependent upon English production with its current strategy being not to use Scottish coals if there is stockpiling in England. Thus, BC only turns to Scottish supplies if there are problems with English supplies; for example, industrial action or logistical problems. At national level, therefore, Scotland plays only a minor role in BC's overall plans.

As was noted earlier, national funding largely goes to those areas which supply the power stations, which thus means that any Scottish investment must come from local resources; the exception being Castlebridge. However, under BC accounting systems, such major local investment counts as a loss against the area concerned, with minor developments being charged against the specific pit. For example, this was the case with the redevelopment of Polmaise, the cost of which was carried by the Scottish Area, and counted as a deficit in the accounts. This somewhat peculiar accounting system, which writes off investment as loss, acts to portray an even gloomier picture for the Scottish industry in two major additional ways. Firstly, although Scotland does not participate in large-scale national projects, with most funding going to Central England, interest payments on these are carried nationally by the 10 areas. According to the Latest Outturn Prospects, for example, the interest burden for 1988/9 will be some £430 million, to which the Scottish pits will contribute. Scotland, therefore, pays but does not receive. Secondly, the cost of pit closures is spread across the operating units, thus successive closures put additional burdens upon remaining pits. Again, the Latest Outturn Prospects estimate that for 1988/9 net restructuring costs will amount to some £54 million, with this figure rising with further potential Scottish closures. Yet if such strategies serve to disadvantage peripheral areas such as Scotland and, as the Scottish Coalfield Project argues, exaggerate its losses, the actual means whereby economic viability is assessed also serves to jeopardise Scottish pits[5].

The major criteria whereby Scotland is judged as unecomic hinges upon the somewhat crude analysis of output per manshift, (OMS), costs per tonne, and profits and losses. Substantial criticisms of this method have been made by both the Monopolies and Mergers Commission and the Scottish Coalfield Project[6]. The SCP, for example, argues that this fails to take into account that OMS is dependent not purely upon physical labour but also factors such as capital investment in both face and travelling machinery, and higher labour costs caused by overtime payments. If one adds to this the problems potentially caused by adverse geological conditions one can see how such judgements may serve to disadvantage Scottish pits over time. Such a situation acts as a 'Catch 22'. Scottish pits have been assessed by OMS figures which serves to 'establish' their unproductive nature, and then such judgements are used to determine whether pits should receive investment. However, low productivity may be seen as resulting from under-investment in the first instance. The SCP argues that all Scottish pits closed in the 1980s have been subject to under-investment in the years prior to their closure, as, indeed, has the Scottish Area as a whole. For example, in 1987 investment in the Scottish Area was the second lowest of the 10 areas of the British coalfield, at a mere £13 million, out of a total figure of £615 million; the lowest amount of £3 million going to the small Kent coalfield, and the largest amount, £232 million going to North Yorkshire.[7]

The consequences of under-investment will be looked at in more detail in the next section, in which we shall examine the particular case of Seafield Colliery in Fife. For the moment what is of interest is the way in which this acts to undermine the Scottish coalfield. The crude guidelines used to establish a pit's worth, outlined above, have had two effects. Firstly, under-investment as a result of BC decisions vitally affects the amount of MAT that is possible at a productive unit. Lack of financial input into the infrastructure of a pit lowers productivity in three potential ways; either by increasing the amount of time men take to get to the face by lack of investment in man-riding facilities, the use of out-moded equipment at the face, which may consequently be subject to breakdowns stopping production, or by leading to technological shortcomings in machinery to take coal to the surface which creates a bottleneck of coal underground. Thus, even whilst Scottish pits may not be suitable to all the high-cost investments in automated processes, under-investment in traditional engineering equipment may crucially impede a pit's performance.

Secondly, managerial decisions on the basis of the assessment of short-term productivity figures set against, again, short-term assessments of market demand, the need to break even or whatever, may result in pit closures which waste millions of pounds in closures, and further disadvantage remaining units. This progressive series of events resulting in economic catastrophe may be seen in relation to the closures of Highhouse, Sorn, Polkemmet, Comrie and Seafield, all of which suffered from declining MAT in the periods before closure between 1979 and 1988.

Associated with under-investment and closures, however, have been additional problems which have had a severe impact on Scotland's pits; namely, the loss of manpower through redundancy as BC has sought to minimalise the costs of production, and demoralisation among the workforce resulting from occupational insecurity. Gaining momentum since the end of the miners' strike, the redundancy payments offered until March 1987 meant men could leave the industry with £1,000 for every year worked. A new scheme introduced later that year and lasting until March 1988 was for redundancy terms which gave men with at least two years service a £5,000 bonus payment if they quit the industry before the end of the financial year. The eagerness with which increasingly younger men have chosen to leave the pits has been indicative of both low morale and faith in the industry. As Scottish miners have come to believe in the imminent demise of their pits, the choice has been one of choosing between staying in employment which may shortly be ended or leaving early with what is seen as a large sum of money.

Yet with growing numbers leaving the pits, the situation within the remaining units has deteriorated. This 'culling' of the workforce has been largely unplanned, with litle thought to the types of worker leaving. Consequently, some pits have experienced a loss of skilled men who, if anything, have become doubly necessary in a time when under-investment has meant that the infrastructure of the pits has become increasingly outmoded and unfit for production. Poor man management has had three effects.

Firstly, by losing the older, more experienced men productivity may decline, for lost skills means pits may increasingly witness time lost through machine breakdowns due to the lack of craftsmen to solve difficulties, a shortage of workers with experience of face problems, or of the necessary men to ensure materials get quickly to the point of need. Secondly, reduced manpower means that the remaining miners have had to spend more time working overtime to make up for worker shortages, leading to overtiredness on a job where mental alertness, or lack of it, may save or lose lives. Related to this may be the problem of high absenteeism due to overwork, and the disruption of the work schedule as men choose to work on shifts that will pay overtime rather than normal rates. Thirdly, undermanning has led to BC introducing contractors into the Scottish pits.

The advantages of contractors in pits without a guaranteed future are clear, for short-term contracts are more flexible and inexpensive; and BC does not have to pay redundancy money if a pit closes. Yet contractors have exacerbated difficulties for industrial relations in the industry for the miners resent the presence of such workers, often more highly-paid for the same work in their collieries.

All the factors outlined above have served to enhance the last major problem for the Scottish industry; namely, the profound demoralisation of the Scottish miners since the miners' strike. All too clearly aware of the under-investment in their collieries, the closures taking place around them which further limit employment opportunities, and the problems inhibiting productivity, all Scottish miners interviewed since the strike have attested to the belief that the Scottish pits will soon no longer exist. Under such circumstances, with morale at rock bottom, the will to mine coal has been lost. Even the Scottish Area Director, George McAlpine, has expressed grave concern over this issue. He stated, in May 1988 in relation to the ongoing feud with the SSEB:-

> "Our current below-par performance is undoubtably related to the fact that we have been living on the edge of a precipice, not knowing whether we will have a market for the coal we produce[8]."

Yet this crisis of morale has been in existence, as stated earlier, from prior to the current crisis, and whilst exacerbated by the SSEB dispute, demoralisation has been caused by BC's lack of commitment to the Scottish pits over the last 9 years, and more recently, since the end of the strike. All the points raised generally above can be amply demonstrated in the case of Seafield Colliery in Fife, which was closed in March 1988 for being 'unproductive'. A brief examination of the salient points raised by this closure will thus illustrate the crisis in the Scottish industry.

Seafield Colliery: A Test Case

Sunk in 1954, Seafield was to be one of the modern, mechanised pits upon which the young nationalised industry was to place its hopes. Drawing upon the rich reserves lying under the Forth, specialising in high quality household coals, it lay within the Fife coalfield, which was designated as the growth area of the Scottish coalfield by the NCB[9]. To were drawn men from all over the coalfield as older pits were shut. By 1979 it had an average yearly workforce of 2173. However, by 1984 this had dropped to some 1855 men, with further reductions being made in the wake of the strike, with only around 1050 miners starting in 1985. Two new faces were being brought into operation at this time to replace the older faces ceasing production, L11 and D17. One of the new faces, the L15, was lost due to fire in January 1987, and consequently the remaining new face, the D19, was rushed into production. During the same period the workforce suffered further reductions from 820 to 680. By 1987, Seafield was thus dependent upon only one face for its survival, and working with a much reduced workforce.

To guarantee the pit's future, therefore, new investment was imperative. This issue had become vital by Spring 1987, for the D19 had a life expectancy of some 2 years, approximately the same period as that necessary to bring a new face into production. However, when Mr McAlpine stated on 6th May 1987 that £10 million was to be invested in a new face, the D52, this was made contingent upon maintaining a production target of some 4 tonnes OMS; a higher target than the average for the British coalfield at that time. The management then claimed that the pit failed consistently to meet this target and on the 25th November Mr McAlpine stated that the pit had 6 weeks to meet the 4 tonnes OMS or the pit would close. He estimated that the pit would lose some £11 million in 1987/88. The closure decision was announced on the 11th January 1988. It was a decision which would mean the irredeemable loss of reserves of some 100 million tonnes, and related jobs, to the Scottish economy.

The closure of Seafield was, on the surface, caused by failure to meet BC's criteria for productivity. But the issue is not as simple as it seems, for managerial decisions and targets had placed the pit in a position which made it virtually impossible to succeed. The productivity target was set against ideal criteria wherein constant coal shear could be maintained, yet there were several factors which prevented this being achieved.

Firstly, Seafield, by its nature, was subject to geological difficulties, such as steep seams and coals prone to spontaneous combustion, which created particular problems for working. Secondly, failure to invest in the infrastructure of the pit resulted in problems in maintaining production. Between April and May 1987 breakdowns on the 6 year old conveyor belt systems, not modernised due to lack of cash, lost the pit an average of 2 to 3 shifts a week as production halted[10]. In September, problems over excessive dust led to a strike, and in the same month when the shearer broke down, managerial insensitivity in dealing with the issue led to a further strike. Thirdly, MAT was lessened due to under-investment in man-riding systems conveying men to and from their work. The face at Seafield was some 6 kilometres from the pit bottom and took over one hour to reach. Travel was by a combination of man-riding 'boggies' and a belt, with the last kilometre or so by foot, in wet conditions and excessively humid heat. The SCP estimated that some 3 hours 19 minutes were spent daily in travelling, thus reducing MAT to 4 hours 17 minutes[11]. Union officials constantly raised the isue of manriding facilities at Joint Consultative Committees, yet Mr McAlpine argued it was hard to get investment given Seafield's productivity statistics[12].

Problems with under-investment were compounded by redundancies at the pit, for many workers leaving the industry were from the skilled grades increasingly needed to maintain equipment. In March 1985 there had been 245 skilled workers at Seafield. By the end of 1986 111 had left, with a further 82 leaving after the loss of the L15. By the end of 1987 only 92 skilled men were left at the pit[13]. These losses presented two problems. Firstly, essential maintenance was neglected due to a shortage of the necessary men, and, secondly, workers had to put in increasing amounts of overtime, leading to overtiredness. The SCP notes that despite a great reduction in the workforce between 1985 and 1987, overtime hours worked remain roughly at the same level, indicating a greater burden on remaining men[14].

After the fire, by April 1987, some 80 Cementation contractors were brought into the pit. This move worsened the situation in two ways. The contractors were being paid at higher rates than the BC workforce. This became known to the men as the contractors' paylines were sent to their homes rather than given to them at the pit, and led to a great deal of resentment. Further, these higher wages were counted as part of Seafield's costs. When taken in addition to the redundancy payments made at the beginning of the year, this enhanced the pit's weak financial position.

In this atmosphere the morale of the men plummetted. Initially enspirited by news of the investment production figures rose from the end of May 1987, yet from July output dropped again as the men began to realise that the £10 million would not come[15]. Yet demoralisation was not the result purely of the events of 1987. When fieldwork commenced in the aftermath of the strike there was already a clear crisis of confidence among the Seafield men. As early as late 1985 men were predicting that the pit would be shut in the immediate future. They saw this as a fact; merely the date was uncertain. The rundown of the Scottish Area, managerial attitudes and lack of investment were already discernible signs to the men that their pit would be lost. Understanding the criteria by which their pit was judged, they foresaw that crisis would come. The last shift was on the 18th March 1988.

This example shows us how BC's policies and decision-making have brought about a self-fulfilling prophecy of crisis to Scottish pits. Yet they also carry ramifications for Scottish markets in coal. It is to the main trends in this area that we now briefly turn.

Coal Markets in Scotland

By 1987/88, closures in Scotland have reduced the deep-mine capacity to some 2.6 million tonnes per annum, a reduction of .8 million tonnes from 1986/87 caused by the closures of Seafield and Monktonhall. A further 2.4 million tonnes came from BC opencast, and c.5 million tonnes from private opencast during this earlier year. Of this 4.8 million tonnes went to the SSEB, BC's largest Scottish customer[16]. This concentration on the 'easy' market of the power stations has encouraged certain key trends in Scottish domestic markets, engendering a situation wherein Scotland, as with England, has become overly dependent upon the power station market to the detriment of other potential markets.

Marketing priorities have increasingly turned from specialist products, a policy which has led to closures of household coal pits such as Seafield and Comrie, and coking coal pits such as Cardowan and Polkemmet. The closure of these latter, for example, means that in 1986/87 Ravenscraig imported 2.6 million tonnes of coking coal at over £80 million due to the lack of available sources in Scotland. Today, domestic coal demand also is met by coals from outwith Scotland.

The closures of the Frances (1985), Killoch (1986) and Seafield (1988) mean that only Bilston Glen still produces household coals. Demand is therefore increasingly met by English coals, (for example, from Kellingley and Broadsworth), Welsh anthracite and manufactured fuels. Yet even here BC is not satisfying its market. Merchants and agents complain of bad quality, often caused by bad preparation, high prices and broken agreements for tonnages and sizes. Merchants are increasingly turning to alternative fuel supplies, whether imports or private opencast.

Much of this trend results from the miners' strike when, because of fuel shortages, other sources had to be found. In the aftermath of the strike the above problems with BC meant that many chose to stay with their new suppliers. Merchants prefer the cheaper prices, often savings in excess of £10 per tonne for foreign and opencast coals, the willingness of suppliers to fulfil contracts, and the greater choice in coals. Many argue that foreign and opencast coals are of superior quality, they have more come-back on opencast suppliers, and can readily change a foreign source.

Private opencast has been the main gainer from BC's problems. Scotland is the major opencast producer in Britain, and merchants find that they have greater access to such coals than with BC, which supplies from the south. But foreign coals are becoming increasingly available with overseas suppliers eager to break into Scottish markets. This trend goes unchecked largely due to BC's apparent lack of interest in the domestic coal market. Merchants complain, for example, that BC prefers to supply the SSEB as quality and preparation are unimportant to the power station market. Further, they claim, certainly with evidence in the case of Seafield, for example, that good household coals, which their customers seek, are being crushed to supply the power stations.

More importantly, BC is not fighting to retrieve lost Scottish markets which, indeed, seem as peripheral to its concerns as Scottish production. One large merchant, for example, argued that prior to the strike his company had bought £250,000 of BC's coals yearly, but that in 1987 they had bought only £10,000. Yet BC had made no attempt to contact the dealer to enquire whether there was a problem. Solid Fuel Advisory Service employees confirm such statements, by arguing that BC's concerns are dominated by the English market, and that marketing strategies are not sensitive to Scottish needs. Further they complain that too many resources are being wasted on unproductive schemes and given to private commercial agencies.

BC, therefore, appears to have abdicated from the declining Scottish market. With coal consumption coming under strong attack from gas and electricity, BC is failing to attempt to secure existing markets. At the present time Scottish household coals come largely from private opencast licensees, who pay BC a levy of £14 per tonne, and this is the only Scottish growth area, with some 23.3 million tonnes of opencast reserves with planning approval for either BC or private development. Failure to invest in the Scottish industry thus means not only declining jobs, whether directly in the pits or in associated industries, but also has weakened the domestic economy through the growth of imports. This failure may well become increasingly important to the Scottish economy in the future.

Conclusion

BC has, increasingly oriented its production to the English coalfield and, by failure to invest, critically undermined the Scottish industry. Yet its policies are extremely shortsighted for several reasons.

The over-dependence on the SSEB may well prove crucial in the next few years. The SSEB has commissioned 1,400MW of new nuclear capacity in 1988/89, and with the Torness AGR coming on stream SSEB demand is anticipated to fall from 4.8 million tonnes to 2.5 million[17]. Already in 1986/87, some 40% of this was met by opencast supplies, and by the 1990s the entire amount could be met from this source. Further, the government has stipulated that 25% of privatised electricity must be bought from nuclear energy at whatever the cost. The SSEB market, therefore, could well be lost.

This shortsightedness also manifests itself in relation to the international scenario. Although gas production is increasing, oil reserves are expected to be scarce by the mid-21st century. The future of the nuclear energy industry is still uncertain. The USA, for example, has not built any nuclear reactors for some 10 years, and has been expanding coal-fired capacity. In terms of BC's competitiveness on the world market, the current low prices are not expected to continue. There have already been world price increases from autumn 1987 as foreign pits selling at below production cost prices have closed. The SCP estimates that by the mid-1990s the world price will be higher than that of Scottish coals. Closures brought about by short-term policy decisions could thus prove more costly to the economy than already realised, for the end of the industry would mean the reliance on foreign supplies. Domestic supplies could not be met by the limited opencast reserves, for these are too small fully to replace deep-mined coals.

The picture, however, is not necessarily as gloomy as it appears, for several options are open to the Scottish mining industry. For example, the SSEB currently has excess capacity, which provides the potential for sending coal-generated electricity down the wire to England. The 400KV line and two 275KV lines linked to the Stella sub-station in Newcastle offer the possibility of sending some 1,500 MW to England, and would help overcome the financial burden involved with current plans to build eight new stations in the south of England[18]. Scandinavian power stations, which have ceilings on sulphur content, (for example, Sweden has a limit of .8%), offer potential markets for Scotland's low sulphur coals, such as that which would come from a newly-developed Frances Colliery. Ireland also offers a nearby market for it possesses few fossil fuels. Scotland could thus have a profitable future in industrial coals.

With household coals BC has three main possible options. Firstly, it could increase profitability by operating its own shops, something like British Gas shops, selling appliances and fuels, thereby cutting out the middle men. Secondly, it could exploit its opencast reserves itself, for if private suppliers can make profits after paying BC a levy, then surely BC could also make a profitable business from opencast coals, whilst operating a responsible policy of exploiting these limited reserves. Thirdly, it must secure markets in the highlands before more isolated areas are opened up by gas supplies.

These examples highlight certain potentialities for BC, and indicate that the current crisis is reversible. They must, on no account, be seen as exhaustive, however, but serve merely to demonstrate potential strategies which would generate a viable Scottish mining industry. They seek to illustrate that what is necessary to re-establish a productive industry is not the mere presence of coal, for that is abundant, but the will, the political will, so to do.

Suzanne Najam, Department of Sociology, University of Edinburgh. Researcher for the Scottish Coalfield Project.

References

1. The Miron Report, (3/12/1973).

2. R Saville, 'The Coal Business', (1988) *Scottish Economic and Social History*, Vol.8, p.93.

3. from J Saville, (1985/96), 'An Open Conspiracy: Conservative Politics and the 1984-5 Miners' Strike', *The Socialist Register*, pp. 296-7.

4. D Cooper and T Hooper (eds) (1988), *Debating Coal Closures*, Cambridge: University Press. This contains a range of arguments made in 1984/5 about how accounting systems can disadvantage a colliery or coalfield by comparison with others.

5. There is a further problem with the accounts. BC have claimed recently that opencast coals are more profitable than deep-mined coals. Opencast certainly does have lower capital costs, and can come on stream more quickly than a deep mine. Current costs work out at c.£1.13p GJ, (a gigajoule is a measure of heat produced), which is the target cost per GJ for the deep mines, not yet achieved. BC claimed to the unions in 1987 that the 'income' from opencast was c.£1.73p GJ for Scotland in 1986/87 mainly from sales to the SSEB. Thus, there appeared to be a profit of 60p GJ. Yet this claim is based on an accounting procedure with shadow prices, not on market decisions. What it disguises is a decision by BC to allocate a higher figure per GJ to opencast than to deep mines. Thus, whereas opencast was given £1.73 p GJ when the average price from the SSEB was £1.69 GJ, Longannet only received an average of £1.64p GJ for the year, with prices falling to below £1.60p GJ by the end of the year. These accounting figures were then used in the summer of 1987 to further demoralise and cajole the Scottish unions and workforce, for they exacerbated the seemingly poor financial position of the deep mines.

6. Monopolies and Mergers Commission Report, (1984); G Kerevan and R Saville, (1984), *The Economic Case for Deep Mined Coal in Scotland*, Edinburgh; The Scottish Coalfield Project, (1988), 'Scottish Coalfields Study 1988: A Plan for Scotland's Energy Future'.

7. BC Annual Accounts, (1986/87).

8. *The Scotsman*, 10/5/88.

9. NCB, *Plan for Coal*, (1950).

10. SCP, 'Scottish Coalfields Study', Vol. 3, p.122.

11. *Ibid*, p.124.

12. Joint Consultative Committee Minutes, 6/5/87.

13. SCP, 'Scottish Coalfields Study', Vol.3, p.128.

14. Average weekly overtime figures stood at 674 hours for the week 21/6/85 and 661 hours for the week 21/11/87.

15. On 16th May 1987 Seafield was meeting 90% (12,600 tonnes) of its production target, by 18th July 1987 this had dropped to 58.2% (8,150 tonnes).

16. M Prior and G McCloskey, 'Coal on the Market: Can British Coal Survive Privatisation?', *FF International Coal Report*, (1988) p.100.

17. *Ibid*, p.100.

18. *Ibid*, p.100.

I wish gratefully to acknowledge the advice, support and permission to draw on the SCP team's collective efforts given by Richard Saville and George Kerevan.

THE SCOTTISH STEEL INDUSTRY

J Love and J Stevens

Introduction

Recent months have seen a reintensification of concern within Scotland over the future of steel-making at British Steel's Ravenscraig complex. This concern is intimately linked with the privatisation of British Steel (BS). For most of the 1980s BS has been charged with the responsibility of preparing the industry for privatisation and in December 1987 Kenneth Clarke, the Secretary of State at the Department of Trade and Industry, indicated that the company was to the fore of the Government's privatisation programme. Following the July 1988 announcement of a strong financial performance for the trading year 1987/88, flotation was scheduled for November 1988.

The principal purpose here is to set out the most likely consequences of this privatisation for Ravenscraig. When he announced in December 1987 the intention to privatise BS, Kenneth Clarke indicated that the company would be privatised as a single entity and made a number of references to the position of the Ravenscraig complex. Specifically he pointed out that, subject to market conditions: the hot strip mill at Ravenscraig would continue in operation at least until 1989; Ravenscraig's iron and steel-making facilities will continue to operate for at least seven years; and there will be a requirement over a similar period into the 1990s for the output of the Dalzell plate mill adjacent to the Ravenscraig complex. In July 1988 the present Chairman of BS, Mr Robert Scholey, suggested that there might be little case for the retention of the hot strip mill beyond 1989. Before turning directly to such matters, however, it is important to outline the various stages of the steel-making process and the role of Scottish output within BS's activities. This will allow an informed discussion of BS's current production configuration and facilitate an explanation of why the plant is seriously threatened by the Corporation's investment plans. The argument is that BS can reduce the number of sites at which it operates, maintain production and increase profitability. In our view, this will prove attractive to private shareholders who can increase returns through elimination of the marginal plant at Motherwell. We conclude that, given present strategies, Ravenscraig has no future within BS. We set out details of a new technique which potentially affords a future for the works. We do not share the emerging view that large plant closures can easily be accommodated. Without minimizing the difficulties, we support the view that investments in this technique should be pressed on both BS and its future owners. In our estimation this remains the best strategy for North Lanarkshire.

The Production Processes of the Steel Industry

Steelmaking is an energy-intensive process in which iron ore is refined in a series of furnaces in order to produce a molten liquid of precise chemical composition and physical properties. The hot metal is then cast into semi-finished shapes which are rolled into a variety of final products (eg rails, rods, bars, sheets and plates). The production process presents five main stages each of which exhibit scale economies which are not exhausted by the largest plants so far constructed.

The first stage, iron-making, involves the removal of oxygen and other impurities from iron ore. In all BS plants the inputs to the process are prepared or produced on site. Coke is baked from metallurgical coal in batteries of coke-ovens and iron ore of different grades are mixed to allow the use of cheaper, less pure ores. In addition, finer grades of ore are agglomerated in a process known as sintering. A burden or charge of coke, ore and sinter is placed in the blast furnace and hot air is blown through. This causes the coke to burn, melting the ore and removing the unwanted oxygen as carbon dioxide. The molten iron is tapped into vessels and other impurities are separated off as a slag. At this stage the metal is over 90 percent pure iron and the molten liquid is transferred to a steel furnace for further refinement.

Within BS, the steelmaking stage is almost exclusively undertaken in Basic Oxygen Furnaces (BOF). The charge consists of a mixture of scrap and molten iron with small amounts of lime added to facilitate the removal of impurities. Oxygen is blown through the charge and carbon is removed as carbon monoxide gas. The process is precisely controlled to yield steel of the desired composition. It is increasingly common to further refine steel in secondary steelmaking vessels to generate higher quality output with more exacting mechanical and physical properties.

These major stages exhibit economies of scale. Aylen[1] estimates that the minimum efficient scale (MES) of operation of a blast furnace is 4 million tonnes per annum whilst for a BOF plant two 340 tonne vessels provide the optimum low cost unit. Capacity which is smaller results in significant cost penalties per tonne of output. BS presently operates eleven blast-furnaces, three of which are MES plants whilst only three of its five steelmaking plants approach the optimal capacity. All of BS's Scottish plant is significantly smaller than the MES and is regarded as a relatively high cost operation.

The third stage in the production process is the casting of molten steel into semi-finished shapes suitable for rolling into finished product. The traditional method involves pouring liquid steel into moulds. The resulting ingot is allowed to cool, the mould removed and the ingot reheated and rolled in a primary mill into the desired type of "semi". This procedure has been progressively replaced by the more efficient continuous casting process which generates "semi's" directly from molten liquid. The "concast" route has three distinct benefits: it improves product yield by eliminating the scrap which results from cropping the ingot in the traditional route; it reduces energy consumption by eradicating the need to reheat inputs and power a primary mill; and the concast product is of significantly higher quality than ingot steel. By European and Japanese standards BS has been relatively slow to adopt concast, although its investment intentions in the immediate future will result in over 85 percent of its product deriving from the concast route.

The fourth stage in the process is hot rolling. Flat products such as plate and strip are rolled from semi-finished shapes called slabs whilst long products such as rails and sections are derived from blooms. A slab has a rectangular cross-section while a bloom has a square cross-section. In both cases the semi-finished feedstock is passed through a series of rollers until the desired shape is obtained. Long products are often sold to consumers with no further processing although flat products are finished in a variety of ways. Plates are often heat-treated to install the desired mechanical properties whilst hot strip can be both cold rolled to improve surface quality and coated with materials such as tin, zinc and plastic. Since the closure of the Gartcosh cold rolling mill, Scottish hot strip output requires to be transported to Wales where all of BS's finishing mills are located. Again, scale economies exist in rolling mills and Aylen[2] estimates that only BS's two Welsh strip mills approach the optimal scale. In addition, both of BS's remaining plate mills at Dalzell and Scunthorpe are small and under-powered and present cost penalties compared with larger units.

In Scotland Ravenscraig produces slabs and hot strip. Both of these are intermediate products which require further processing. Dalzell produces plates of high quality and tolerances, eg armour plates, submarine hulls, plates for construction of high pressure boilers and plates for offshore applications. At present, as may be seen from Table 1, 20 percent of Ravenscraig's output goes to Dalzell. Around 35 percent of Ravenscraig's

TABLE 1
Current Disposition of Ravenscraig's Output (000 tonnes)

Export Slabs	300
Dalzell	400
Shotton	700
Tinplate	400
HRC Exports	200
Total Ouput	2000

output goes to Shotton, its single most important consumer, for further processing. Remaining output is disposed as exports slabs (15 percent), tinplate (20 percent) and hot rolled coil exports (10 percent).

The Evolution of BS's Productive Capacity

Following nationalization in 1967, the Steel Corporation operated all the major production processes at twenty-one sites. In addition to those integrated plants, the Corporation engaged in steelmaking at sixteen other locations, twelve of which possessed rolling mills. Rolling and finishing were undertaken at a further dozen locations. Much of this capacity employed obsolete production methods and was extremely small scale relative to the optimal plant size for the respective technology.

Following the Benson Report, it was widely believed that, because of scale economies, the UK industry required to concentrate production at a small number of large scale plants. Indeed, nationalization was regarded in many quarters as a necessary step to attaining this objective because the segmented ownership and poor performance of the private sector acted as a constraint upon the adjustment process. The model for the industry was the large scale coastal sites in Japan. A corporate strategy was thrashed out by BS executives, steel consultants and civil servants which envisaged that the Corporation would have 36 million tonnes of liquid steelmaking capacity by the early 1980s concentrated at five or six major plants all at coastal locations. This plan was fully set out in the Ten Year Development Strategy published by Government in 1973.

In the first instance, major investments were to be undertaken at the two Welsh strip plants at Port Talbot and Llanwern in South Wales, and at the long product sites at Redcar and Scunthorpe. The programme anticipated major increases in capacity at these plants which would be utilized fully through closure and withdrawal from sub-optimal locations. In Scotland the situation was a little different. Ravenscraig was to be expanded marginally and completely modernized with improvements made at all stages of the production process. However, it remained a smaller plant than the English and Welsh operations because it was regarded as a staging post for a 6-7 million tonnes per annum plant at Hunterston based on the Direct Reduction-Electric Arc steelmaking route.

The first Opec oil shock depressed the world economy in the mid 1970s. Steelmakers were simultaneously faced with falling demand, rising input prices and higher cost of capital. The Corporation's costs in this period rose particularly sharply because they were prevented from closing many of their smaller plants for social reasons. Market conditions continued to deteriorate as much of the Corporation's modern capacity came on stream and world-wide capacity rose as a result of expansion plans in Less Developed Countries (LDC's) and other countries. In 1979, BS were forced to retrench further by closing relatively modern works as at Consett, Shotton and Corby. The strategy became one of loading up their five Heritage plants and thereby attempting to reduce average costs. In addition, they embarked on Project Slimline which involved major changes in working practices and renumeration. Surviving works were eventually to be demanned in order to increase labour productivity whilst a greater element of earnings was in the form of a lump sum bonus linked to performance.

As early as 1980, however, following the second Opec oil shock, the Corporation were considering still further rationalization. The 1980/81 Corporate plan, projected likely demand and concluded that on the basis of pessimistic scenarios, savings could be made only by further concentration of activity. It is interesting to note that, given the total upgrading of Ravenscraig which took place during the 1970s, the option of closing the complex was not at the centre of the Corporation's thinking. The most likely option for strip products appeared to be mothballing of Llanwern's steelmaking and Port Talbot's rolling mills. In the event these options were not pursued in Wales but the position of the Scottish industry altered dramatically during the 1980s.

The shift in attitude towards Ravenscraig emerged from two sets of considerations: first, against a background of considerable world-wide excess steel capacity, the Corporation foresaw substantial difficulties in securing good margin business in highly competitive non-EEC markets and was constrained within Europe by adverse currency levels and by the Davignon quota arrangements designed to restore balance between European output and demand; secondly, the Corporation's strategic thinking shifted towards identification of Ravenscraig as the marginal plant among the five remaining integrated steelworks. This latter consideration was based essentially on a comparison between the attributes of the Corporation's operations in Scotland and in South Wales.

Locational and site-specific factors played a central role in determining the Corporation's outlook. Located inland from the ore terminal at Hunterston, Ravenscraig clearly did not, unlike Port Talbot, fit the "ideal" model of a coastal plant. Port Talbot's larger plant also presented the potential for the realisation of scale economies. Llanwern had the advantage over Ravenscraig of a well laid out site. Perhaps the most widely-discussed rationale for regarding Ravenscraig as the marginal plant lay, however, in the observation that Ravenscraig was more remote than the Welsh plants from final consumers. The decline of metal-using industries in Scotland imposed a cost disadvantage relative to the plants in terms of the higher transport costs involved in marketing Ravenscraig's output.

Concern that the shift in attitude towards Ravenscraig would result in attempts by Sir Ian MacGregor to close the plant precipitated a campaign of resistance within Scotland. This campaign was based on social and regional considerations and on the argument advanced primarily by Strathclyde Regional Council, that the Corporation was incorrect in its assessment that likely steel demand was inefficient to sustain five integrated plants. These efforts had a particularly successful conclusion. In 1982, following strong Scottish Office pressure, the Department of Trade and Industry prevented BS from commencing upon closure moves.

Thereafter, perhaps partly for tactical (political) reasons and partly because of some increase in UK steel consumption during 1983-84, the Corporation shifted away from seeking a complete and abrupt closure of an integrated plant and towards the idea of a phased contraction. In 1984, the then Corporation Chairman, Sir Robert Haslam, discussed the closure of an integrated plant in frank terms by indicating to the Trade and Industry Select Committee that:

"Our view would be that any closure would be phased and hence an immediate closure would be unlikely"(Cmnd 344 p.57).

The subsequent closure of the Gartcosh cold-rolling mill in 1986 should be viewed as representing one of those phases. That closure was consistent with the Corporation's oft-repeated argument that the objectives of commercial viability and privatisation are inconsistent with a five-plant configuration. Announcement of the Gartcosh closure made the Corporation eligible for State aid as part of the Community's capacity reduction and restructuring provisions. Simultaneously, the Corporation purchased and closed the privately-owned company Alphasteel and set about refurbishing Alphasteel's continuous casting facilities for installation at Llanwern as part of a massive programme of upgrading the Welsh plants.

Two important elements emerged from the Gartcosh closure. First, with the explicit support of Government Ministers, social and regional considerations were firmly relegated to a minor role with the Corporation's thinking being driven primarily by the need to enhance commercial viability. Secondly, the locational savings derived from closing Gartcosh were minimal suggesting that the bulk of costs continued to rest with the main Ravenscraig complex.

British Steel: The Current Situation

British Steel faces a difficult environment because of adverse long run trends in world capacity. In particular, it is faced with excess capacity for key products in its home market in Europe. This has prompted BS Chairman, Sir Robert Scholey, to openly speculate as to whether the company will require only three integrated plants by the mid 1990s.

LDC's share of steel production continues to grow faster than real consumption. Much of this is state-owned and constitutes a key element in overall development strategies. There is continuing protection of major markets, notably the EEC and USA. The net effect of this has been to restrict access to profitable US and EEC business for many steelmakers. Production has been diverted to third markets causing prices to be weak. In addition, European producers have found their restricted access to US markets progressively less lucrative in recent years owing to the strength of European currencies against the dollar. This is partially offset by lower domestic prices for essential inputs such as coal, oil and ore which are denominated in dollars. Because Continental producers export greater proportions of production to North America than BS, their profitability has been restricted to a more significant extent. However, BS, which exports 40% percent of its finished product has great difficulty finding good margin business in non-EEC markets. Until the uncertainty surrounding the dollar is settled and until the US protective regime is dismantled, it is likely that the EEC will remain the only market where BS can consistently generate reasonable margins on its export volumes.

In the Community the apparatus constructed following the declaration of manifest crisis in 1980 has been dismantled for most major products. After failure to generate voluntary capacity reductions, the Commission liberalized the strip products market in July 1987. Thus, the situation in Europe is now one of a free market in which operating subsidies and investment aid are strictly prohibited. Since the mid-1970s, BS has progressively increased the share of its turnover derived from Community markets. In recent years, the weakness of the pound against the key currency, the Deutschmark (DM) has significantly enhanced the Corporation's profitability. Recent City estimates suggest that a 5 percent adverse movement of Sterling against the Mark will lead to a £120m reduction in BS profits.

In addition to this currency advantage, BS has emerged as the world's lowest cost steel producer. This is the direct result of rationalization of capacity, investment programmes and manpower policies of the early 1980s. At present BS is one of the Community's few profitable steel producers and one would be tempted to conclude that BS's European market share will inevitably increase further through the ability to undercut the prices of EEC rivals thus contributing to the enforced exit of loss-making firms. However, three constraints can be identified which will limit such advances. First, the distribution channels on the continent are dominated by the producers. In France and Germany, 56 percent and 75 percent of stockholding activity is controlled by steelmakers. This contrasts with the UK situation where the British Steel Service Centres account for less than 20 percent of the stockholding market. In recent years, BS has sought to remedy this position through acquisition of Continental stockists and re-rollers and would not be adverse to acquiring a European steelmaker to further enhance market access. Secondly, there is a considerable degree of state involvement in the affairs of Community steelmakers. In both France and Italy, the steel industry is state-owned whilst the Dutch hold a golden share in Hoogovens. In Germany, the financial institutions own and control both steelmakers and major steel consumers. These factors restrict the ability of BS to expand in Europe through acquisition. Thirdly, because of the size of modern steel plants, they are often dominant employers in local economies. Indeed, since 1986, the EEC has been engaged in supra national negotiations designed to effect capacity reductions. The failure to achieve these aims largely reflects the reluctance of Government to face the social and political consequences of steel closures.

The ability of BS to capitalize on its cost and currency advantages is, thus, limited and the elimination of unprofitable excess capacity is likely to be slow. As Aylen[3] has pointed out, the immediate tactics are likely to involve joint production arrangements rather than merger and acquisition. Whilst such actions will contribute towards eliminating excess supply, contraction has to be negotiated which implies a less favourable outcome for BS than that which would emerge if the market for corporate control was more competitive. Therefore, although BS can look forward to a successful future in Europe, uncertainty concerning excess capacity and currency levels allied to the bleak outlook in third markets prompts senior executives to question both whether present high production levels will endure and whether activity at all five integrated plants can be profitably sustained.

On top of this long run contractionary pressure there are more immediate reasons to suspect that BS will withdraw from one or more of its present locations. First, all major forecasting agencies are predicting downturns in steel production in the first part of the next decade. Indeed, BS's own stockbroker, Philips and Drew has recently estimated that world steel demand will decline by 5 percent in 1990 and will not again reach current levels until the middle of the decade. In this analysis, EEC demand fares slightly better and it should be appreciated that BS is relatively well placed to weather a downturn in the cycle. However, such considerations rightly provoke concern about the marginal plant at Motherwell reinforced by the conclusions of the review of the Scottish steel industry undertaken for Motherwell District Council by Arthur Young.[4] This study draws attention to the plant configuration within BS and re-emphasizes the fact that, at all integrated sites, the Corporation's has iron and steelmaking capacity in excess of its casting and rolling capacity.

The exact situation has been fully set out in the papers submitted to Arthur Young by Dunbar and Associates, the steel consultants led by Jimmy Dunbar, the former Works Director at Ravenscraig. This analysis demonstrates that both Port Talbot and Ravenscraig are constrained by concast bottlenecks and that both have iron and steelmaking capacity which cannot be fully utilized. At Redcar, there is insufficient iron making capacity to fully utilize the downstream production capacity. Both Llanwern and Scunthorpe could increase output by bringing onstream idle blast furnaces. However, Llanwern is constrained by having a large proportion of its throughput processed by the ingot casting route. This not only results in cost penalties but generates output which is increasingly difficult to market profitably because of quality considerations. At Scunthorpe, the considerable iron and steelmaking facilities cannot be fully utilized because of both insufficient rolling mill capacity, a concast bottleneck and a low level of demand for the product range.

It should be appreciated that these bottlenecks effectively arise owing to the haphazard retreat from the scale of operation envisaged by the 1973 Development Strategy. The constraints, if removed, would allow a higher scale of activity and consequent reduction of average costs. The Arthur Young report made particular reference to the situation existing in BS's Strip Product Division and the plate making configuration evident within General Steels. The study basically concludes that it would be possible to eliminate the requirement for Ravenscraig's output by removing constraints at the two Welsh plants. This would mean no net loss of production potential and would lead to an annual increase in profitability of £100m at current levels of activity.

As indicated earlier, BS require to rationalise their plate making activity. It is possible that such a development could take place in Scotland although it would be costly to undertake this expansion at Motherwell. Given the situation at Scunthorpe, Arthur Young and most other analysts argue that BS's most profitable course is to proceed with any proposed single plate mill development at this site. However, such conclusions should not prevent the Scottish Lobby from pressing BS on this matter. The timing of plate mill rationalization, like the timescale of retreat from Motherwell, is uncertain. Although the Arthur Young study provides a timetable, its critics should note that this is illustrative rather than definitive.

EEC stipulations dictate that investment expenditure must be financed from commercial borrowing or cash flow. Thus the timing of all such output enhancing and cost reducing expenditures depends on the level of profitability which governs both possibilities. This in turn is a function of the market conditions which BS will face over the coming period. Indeed Bell et al[5] have surveyed major Scottish plate consumers and conclude that the likely level of North Sea activity will contribute to a continued buoyant demand for Dalzell plate. Given that Dalzell presents locational advantages with respect to many of its customers, this suggests that its future is indeed secure until well into the next decade. However, this study affords no conclusions and thus no comfort for the HSM whose closure BS estimate would save £15m per annum in operating costs.

The only possible conclusion from this analysis is that Ravenscraig faces a serious threat to its survival. This emanates from the external environment and the internal configuration of capacity. Thus, although it is demonstrably profitable, given current conditions, to operate on the basis of five integrated plants, it is more profitable to reduce the number of sites. In addition, because of the capacity enhancing nature of certain investment expenditure, this will not necessarily lead to the adverse effects on trade alluded to in certain quarters.

The Effects of Privatisation

Privatisation can be viewed to consist of two elements, the transfer of ownership and the liberalization of product and capital markets for the business in question. As has been pointed out above, the latter is not within the UK Government's control given that BS's home market should be properly regarded as the EEC block. Thus privatisation of BS, whilst it may lead to a more credible platform from which to urge removal of the barriers to rationalization within the Community, is merely a transference of ownership from state to private individuals, employees and financial institutions. The Government has retained a golden share which previous experience suggests will be used sparingly, if at all.

Our view, expressed over the last two years in the *Fraser Institute Quarterly Commentary*, is that an early flotation would seriously undermine the security of the Ravenscraig plant. The optimal outcome for Scottish interests would have been for the present owners, the State, to instruct BS management to prepare for flotation on the basis that they are required to build up profitable activity to a level which secures the future of the Motherwell plant. The guarantees given by BS and Trade Ministers fall far short of this. Indeed, recent statements by Sir Robert Scholey give further credence to the Arthur Young analysis. It would not be unfair to suggest that the Arthur Young scenario is that favoured by senior BS executives and that early flotation will be viewed by them as legitimization of this strategy.

Indeed, the guarantees provided by BS and Government for the Motherwell Works should be assessed rather carefully. During the process of preparing for flotation, a company requires to provide much information in order to allow investors to gauge future direction and calculate a market price with which to compare with the offer for sale. The bulk of this information can be provided to analysts via company visits, published reports and accounts and special documentation. Steel is historically a cyclical industry and one important signal which requires to be made is how management will react to declining earnings during a downturn. In this respect the Motherwell guarantees demonstrate that a feasible retrenchment strategy is available to offer some support to bottom line profits if the trading environment does deteriorate as certain major forecasters expect. In this view, the guarantees are directed towards comforting financial institutions rather than Lanarkshire workers. This is because the guarantees signal the likely timescale required for locational contraction whilst minimising the disruption to steel consumers. The qualification that the guarantees are subject to market considerations provides considerable flexibility and in the final analysis give BS *carte blanche* to dispose of their Scottish operation as they see fit.

In numerous press interviews, Sir Robert Scholey has forcibly spelt out that he intends to be a profit maximizer as opposed to an output maximizer. He has publicly welcomed the privatisation as a measure which facilitates a thorough review of site policy because it frees management to make decisions on commercial grounds without the need to heed wider political pressure. He is signalling to potential shareholders that his leadership will be robust in defence of the interests of the new owners. The bullish stance over the future of the Ravenscraig strip mill is part of this process. Given the benefits of contraction identified by Arthur Young, Scholey is giving every indication that he will sacrifice his Scottish capacity, if and when it is in the best interests of his shareholders to do so.

Scottish Steel – The Way Ahead

There is every indication that phased withdrawal from Motherwell is the scenario most likely to unfold over the next five years. The timing of each phase will depend on the commercial judgement of BS. However, abstracting from the evolution of the trading environment, there is an internal dynamic within the Corporation which appears loaded against the Motherwell plant. The STUC[6] has recently identified and costed the investment expenditure essential to maintain the efficiency and competitiveness of the works. This involves £24m to stabilize the medium term coke supply, £18m for a modern reheating furnace and £20-£25 million for various process improvements at the strip mill. The latter expenditure would improve the quality and range of output as well as improving the efficiency of the production process. Given the recent decision to "debottleneck" Port Talbot, it is unlikely that any of these claims will be entertained when the Strip Product Group reviews its operations in 1989. As Love and Stevens[7] conclude, there is a strong chance that the strip mill will not survive this appraisal and there is a high probability that the plant will be closed as soon as substitute capacity is brought on line. This could be two to three years ahead.

If the strip mill closes within this timescale, Ravenscraig's immediate major role will be one of supplying high quality slab for internal purposes. In the short run there could be considerable volumes despatched to South Wales to facilitate the debottlenecking of the two plants with minimum disruption. As indicated earlier the demand from the Dalzell plate mill seems secure until the mid 1990s. However, as investment increases the capacity of all four integrated plants and some resolution of the plate sector is undertaken, these internal markets will decline sharply.

The annual capacity of Ravenscraig's two concast machines is approximately 2.2m tonnes. Assuming a continuing delivery of 500,000 tonnes of slabs to Dalzell, this implies that by the early 1990's, BS will require to market 1.7 million tonnes of slabs externally. In 1987 the UK steel industry exported 1.5 million tonnes of semis (ie ingots, blooms, billets and slab). At present Ravenscraig slab exports total 350m tonnes pa. It is true to say that there is an emerging market for high quality slab but in all non-EEC markets the average realized sterling value of semi-finished export is low. This is particularly true of North American markets where approximately one third of such exports are placed. Fortunately, the dollar, whilst volatile, has recently moved favourably against the pound, but future access to this market depends on decisions to be taken in 1989 when import volumes will be determined for EEC producers.

Ravenscraig's advantage in export markets derives from its adoption of concast and secondary steelmaking and present favourable currency levels. Because of scale and locational considerations, it is likely to be relatively high cost output. A supply of such products to both US and EEC markets would clearly facilitate modernization and rationalization at inefficient sites. The most secure arrangement would be similar to the medium term contracts proposed and occasionally secured with US producers. In the short-term such ventures may prove possible within Europe although the difficulties of finding partners free and willing to sacrifice capacity to absorb Ravenscraig's slab output should not be understated. Thus it is not at all clear that a viable medium term slabmaking role exists for the Scottish Plant.

In addition to the question marks over the commercial attractiveness of slab markets, the issue of coke supply needs to be addressed. It is not apparent that BS will find it attractive to commit funds to perpetuate a small scale facility producing a low value added product. In our view given that market considerations do not pre-empt matters, the slab making role will not endure past the point when significant investment expenditure becomes essential.

It is apparent that a new role requires to be found to justify Ravenscraig beyond the mid 1990's. During the debates and committee stage of the British Steel Bill, Dr Jeremy Bray repeatedly drew attention to the direction of developments in casting technology. A new generation of casting machines is becoming available which generates thin slabs which require less processing at the rolling stage. Indeed this "thin slab casting" process effectively dispenses with the need to operate wide-hot strip mills. This new technique is less capital intensive and promises significant savings in energy consumption per tonne of final product. Adoption significantly reduces the MES of an integrated strip mill and in the US is set to provoke competition between the large BOF plants and the Electric Arc minimills in strip product markets.

In addition, the development and adoption of direct smelting over the next 20 to 30 years threatens to eclipse the dominance of the BF-BOF steelmaking route. This process refines iron ore to steel quality in one furnace and promises considerable savings in both capital costs and energy consumption. BS is currently constructing a pilot plant in conjunction with Dutch steelmaker Hoogovens. If technically and commercially sound, this process threatens to provide lower entry costs and yield output competitive with that of large scale BF-BOF operations.

In Europe, such developments could significantly undermine Aylen's conclusions concerning the inevitability of growing concentration in European steel markets. In this view,

> "It is evident that two minimum efficient scale plants (rather than five) would be ideal for supplying all the UK's heavier products coupled with, perhaps, two mini-steelworks (there are two at present). Comparable restructuring could be anticipated in Western Europe, where an obvious solution is for heavy product manufacture to gravitate towards a few well chosen coastal sites, with finishing facilities – which exhibit fewer economies of scale – located closer to mid-European markets. This implies that large swathes of the French, Belgian, Luxemburg and West German steel industries would close, as coastal sites in Holland, the UK and perhaps France and Italy are rounded out to nearer optimum capacity."[8]

This view that a small number of very large plants will come to dominate European production ignores the possible impact of revolutionary process innovations. Another likely long run trend is the closure of BF-BOS plants in the face of competition from smaller, better located and more flexible producers operating efficient mini mills. However, over the coming period the slow trend identified by Aylen is likely to dominate. The larger and better situated steelplants will continue to be upgraded and enlarged. As outlines above, this process has already started in the UK.

Recent Annual Reports indicate that BS has undertaken considerable research into thin slab casting. Love and Stevens[9] have pointed out that BS feels under little pressure to adopt this technology quickly because it possesses two large scale modern stripmills in South Wales which it can upgrade and expand. In the doming period, thin slab casting will become mandatory for competitive stripmaking and there is considerable merit in Bray's view that BS should install this process at Motherwell in order to gain operational experience and to develop the scope of the process. The threat of thin slab casting is imminent. As Bray has argued,

> "Port Talbot and Llanwern may well be the last of the old style hot mills in Europe to be modernized. It would not be the first time that British Steel has been the last to invest in an obsolescent technology."[10]

BS does not intend to diversify into non steel activity as many American, Japanese and European producers have done. This suggests that leading roles in new process innovations are essential if the business is to flourish. With expertise in both thin slab casting and direct smelting, BS would reduce the risk of being left behind towards the end of the next decade and in the first part of the next century. Such advantage will not materialise without undertaking the development work now. If this is done, BS shareholders can look forward to a competitive business in a strong position to engage in multinational expansion both in Europe and further afield.

Thus, a sustained campaign amongst BS's institutional shareholders must be undertaken to stress the importance of dynamic efficiency to an undiversified steelmaker. The case for the adoption and development of thin slab casting at Motherwell could be a major plank in this effort. As Bray[11] concedes, this technology can only be introduced on that site if the strip mill were closed and dismantled. This will present a job loss of over 700 direct employees plus additional losses through knock on effects. This has the advantage of making the remaining 2,500 jobs marginally more secure and promises rehires as the new casters and mill come onstream. This is progressive argument to put to BS during the strip products review in 1989 and can be argued alongside retention and investment in the HSM.

The attractiveness of either option depends on the immediate and expected outlook for strip demand. However, installing a new caster will remove a bottleneck and could lead to lower average costs at the iron and steelmaking stages. The timing of adoption could be left until market conditions permit. Thin slab casting affords cost savings which would offset the cost penalties inherent in a Scottish inland location. In the mid 1990's, Ravenscraig could find itself in the same position as during the early 1980's when technical advantage sustained the works in the face of severe locational disadvantage. This scenario may be difficult to sell to BS because it would ultimately provide capacity over and above that generated by removing production constraints in South Wales.

However, BS is known to be actively seeking European partners through either acquisition or joint venture. Any deal could be made significantly more attractive if the promise of involvement in new processes is part of the package. Thus, the Bray strategy not only makes long run sense but could facilitate the company's short run expansionist policy. Such implications should also be drawn to the attention of City institutions who are collectively noted for short termism. The pitfalls in this approach should not be minimised. BS may be inclined to promote sceptism or could attempt to pre-empt the discussions by admitting the general merits of the case and by announcing installation of thin slab casting at another site.

New technology provides a measure of credibility to notions that Ravenscraig could survive outwith BS as part of an overseas concern or even as an independent entity. The major difficulty with such proposals is that they present BS with competition in its UK markets from a UK location. It is unlikely that BS will look upon any such prospect favourably, in any case, there is no short term liklihood that BS will wish to sell the plant because, at present, they foresee a need for it's slab output. However, if the capacity issue is resolved in the way outlined by Arthur Young, then there may come a time when the works is genuinely surplus to requirements. An agreement with Government compels BS to offer the facility for sale at this point. It is highly likely that any such offer would be given only at a time of difficulty in steel markets. In addition, BS seem set to operate Ravenscraig with minimal investment expenditure thus reducing the attractiveness of the plant to potential buyers. Thin slab casting would offer future owners a low cost route into strip markets from a relatively high cost location. However finishing mills would be required to further process the strip for final customers. An independent Scottish operator would either have to construct these at suitable sites or link up with continental facilities. The former presents substantial capital costs above the purchase price and any sums required to modernize the capacity. The latter raises the question of whether partners could be found willing to close domestic steelmaking capacity in order to absorb Scottish output. Such an arrangement is not impossible to contemplate but does involve considerable suspension of judgement.

Although thin slab casting offers some hope of a future for Ravenscraig outwith British Steel, there are risks that it will not be a commercially sound step for anyone at a time when BS were prepared to part with the capacity. It would be less risky for Scottish interests if BS were persuaded to undertake this investment. They would be better placed to market the product and have knowledge of both the works and the new casting process. It should be appreciated that such an option would merely prolong the life of the existing iron and steelmaking operation and thus extend the timescale available in which to plan and execute policies to minimize the social and economic effects of steel retreat from North Lanarkshire. However there is nothing to be lost in a strategy which seeks to buy time.

Conclusion

Two scenarios concerning the future industrial structure of the steel industry have been presented in this paper. The first, that of Aylen and BS itself, sees the emergence of a smaller number of large, well laid out and situated plants supplying a progressively declining demand for bulk steel products. The second, that of Love & Stevens and Bray, sees new technology affording the possibility of entry by smaller, competitive suppliers threatening the markets and scale economies required by the large BOS-BOF plants. It should be appreciated that it is difficult to advance Scotland as an optimal location in either case.

The existence of an option which affords BS the opportunity of increasing profitability and maintaining volume via locational withdrawal is one which will be exercised sooner or later.

Privatisation significantly increases the probability of early implementation. Indeed, there is strong evidence that this course is currently being pursued and that BS management will shortly commend further stages to the new owners. This involves depressed earnings in the short run because of exceptional items such as redundancy costs and site closure costs. The benefit is a future stream of higher profits and thus a stronger equity price. To smooth out the impact on profits a phased withdrawal from Motherwell is likely in the manner set out by Arthur Young. The bulk of the total costs will fall on the community whose institutions will require to commit substantial resources towards repairing the social and economic damage which will inevitably result.

Baur[12] has argued persuasively that Ravenscraig assumes a significance in Scottish public affairs not justified by its role and status in the Scottish economy. This is certainly correct. However there are three recent studies of the economic impact of closure. Arthur Young[13] and Bell et al[14] estimate that 11-12,000 jobs will ultimately be lost whilst Pieda[15] forecasts a loss of 9,550 jobs and a reduction in Scottish GDP of £100m pa. Part of the discrepancy in estimates is accounted for by the exclusion of Dalzell in the latter analysis. All three reports are unanimous that the vast bulk of the impact would fall on the Lanarkshire economy. Baur advances the view that the Scottish Office believe that an orderly provision of alternative employment can be organized following a gradual withdrawal from steelmaking activity. Indeed this stance has been taken by Ministers in the face of several recent closure announcements, notably that at the Royal Ordnance Factory (ROF) at Bishopton. There has also been much Ministerial reference to 'success' in other steel closure areas with the experience of the Garnock Valley to the fore in such accounts.

These arguments should be approached with extreme caution. The loss of large numbers of relatively well paid manual and semi-skilled jobs in the traditional industries in the 1970's and 1980's has left its toll in Central Scotland. In the Garnock Valley, a small business development programme was initiated in 1979 following the closure of the majority of

Glengarnock Steelworks. Significant environmental work and provision of advance factories were undertaken to facilitate the creation of small and medium size industrial concerns. It is true to say that a significant number of jobs have been assisted but many employ a predominantly female workforce and most are characterized by low skill profiles and poor wage rates. This experience is mirrored across the Central Belt where many of the old industrial communities afford the choice of either no work or work in marginal employment at low wages.

Although a proper evaluation of the labour market experience of Glengarnock's steelworkers has not been undertaken, it is true to say that few ended up in the new enterprises set up in the Garnock Valley. However their offspring have and can be viewed to be stuck in a low skill-low wage trap. The main community concerned, Kilbirnie, lost both coherence and morale and is only now slowly recovering. Significant deprivation exists which will get worse as the pension income of former industrial employees declines. Indeed, there are few of the new jobs with adequate pension schemes or prospects for advancement. The Garnock Valley lost an opportunity structure which held out some prospects for economic advancement from a low human capital base and this has not been replaced. This is the picture which exists across Central Scotland in the face of the decline of core industries.

The state of industrial policy in Scotland is such that, on the back of growing skill shortages, the Scottish CBI have negotiated a new approach directly with the Prine Minister. The experience of the past decade should persuade one that a small business policy will create a high proportion of marginal jobs at low wages. The bulk of the returns appear to accrue to the entrepreneurs, especially in Scotland where high unemployment constrains the ability of labour to pre-empt a larger share of any rents which result from the firms activity. A complementary training initiative is likely to confer benefits on the labourforce itself. It would go some way to providing an equitable solution for those disadvantaged because they happened to come onto the labour market in the early 1980's. Indeed the experience of recent school leavers is not markedly better. To day, the vast majority of Scots displaced from traditional industry and their children, who have been largely brought up to follow suit, have been unable to share in the benefits offered by the Enterprize Culture. It is to be hoped that the 'Hughes Plan' leads to opportunities for the unemployed in peripheral estates and depressed communities and those in marginal employment to acquire marketable skills on which to base careers and plan futures.

Whatever the outcome of these deliberations, if arguments based on new technology fail to impress British Steel, then urgent consideration must be given to major economic initiatives in North Lanarkshire. Indeed, it is arguable that greater resources should be concentrated in this area in any case because it is part of the economy with manifest difficulties.

Ancilliary measures such as the upgrading of the A74 and the provision of fast rail links between the North and the Channel Tunnel would clearly enhance the attractiveness of the area for industrial and commercial development. In addition, further civil service dispersal is being sought and Lanarkshire should be considered for such projects. The notion that new SDA initiatives in North Lanarkshire undermine and betray the steel industry is palpable nonsense. Following privatisation, decisions on steel are wholly independent of the economic and social conditions in the area. Lanarkshire has nothing to lose from demanding greater resources and those who criticize such measures are flying in the face 1of common sense. Any offers of major expenditure should be universally applauded rather than treated with suspicion.

However, such initiatives should not be represented in any attempt to understate the severe and painful adjustments which would result as a consequence of steel closure. New economic activity would result in a pattern of labour demand markedly different from that which prevails in the steel industry and those closely linked sectors which would contract in tandem. Thus, even if there were tangible evidence of major and properly resourced business development and training programmes in Scotland, it would be imprudent to give up 11,000 jobs in an already depressed economy without first exhausting every commercial possibility for their retention.

Jim Love, Department of Economics, University of Strathclyde.
Jim Stevens, Department of Economics, University of Strathclyde.

References

1. Aylen, Jonathon, "The Privatization of the British Steel Corporation", *Fiscal Studies*, Vol.9, No.3, August 1988.

2. *Ibid.*

3. *Ibid.*

4. Young, Arthur, "A Study of the Impact of Privatization of British Steel Corporation on the Future of Ravenscraig and Dalzell Steel Works", Motherwell District Council, February 1988.

5. Bell, D, Findlay, J, Oughton, C, "The Importance of the Steel Industry to the Scottish Economy", Scottish Steel Campaign Trust, March 1988.

6. STUC, "Privatization and the Scottish Steel Industry", STUC, September 1987.

7. Love, J and Stevens, J. "RSD: A Comment", *Fraser of Allander Institute Quarterly Economic Commentary*, Vol.13, No.4, June 1988.

8. Aylen, *op.cit.* p.15.

9. Love and Stevens, *op. cit.*

10. Bray, J. "The City should make sure British Steel's strengths are built on", *Financial Times*, 19th October 1988.

11. *Ibid.*

12. Baur, C. "Long Shadow Hangs Over Ravenscraig", *Scotland on Sunday*, 16th October 1988.

13. Young, *op. cit.*

14. Bell et al, *op. cit.*

15. PIEDA, "BSC Ravenscraig Works: Economic Impacts of Closure", Scottish Television Ltd, December 1987.

TRADE UNIONS IN SCOTLAND: FORWARD TO THE 1990s?[1]

John W Leopold

Introduction

The Thatcher years have witnessed an overall decline in both the absolute numbers of trade unionists in Britain and in the proportion of workers who are trade union members. TUC membership has fallen from just over 12 million in 1979 to 9.1 million in 1987, while in the same period STUC affiliated members have declined from 1.09 million to 910,942. Trade union density has fallen from its peak of 55% of employed workers to just over 40% today. But it should be remembered that this decline only takes trade union density back to the levels of the 1950s and 1960s, not to those of the 1930s. Recently published figures indicate that, after allowing for industrial structure and workplace size and ownership, Scotland is still, marginally, the most unionised part of Great Britain.[2] Much of the recent decline in membership can be atttributed to the massive loss of jobs among male manufacturing workers who traditionally were well organised.[3] The decline of coal, steel and shipbuilding serves to illustrate the point. But Unions will have to adjust to the changing structure of the economy with the growth of part-time employment, increased numbers of women workers and sectoral change in the economy.[4]

The purpose of this chapter is to provide an overview of the state of trade unions in Scotland; to examine the pressure for change and to assess the extent to which they are ready to meet the challenges of the 1990s. Many of the issues facing the trade union movement in Scotland are the same as those facing the movement in Great Britain as a whole such as the trend towards merger into large general unions. But we will try to highlight Scottish issues and concerns and to focus on some of the particularly Scottish aspects of trade unionism, such as the role of the Scottish Trades Union Congress.

Union Membership in Scotland

A picture of trade union membership in Scotland from 1978-1987 is presented in Table 1. With one or two exceptions, the figures reveal a story of decline in membership of unions organising workers in manufacturing industry. This has particularly affected the traditional industries of coal, rail and steel. There are now more university lecturers who are trade union members than either miners or steelworkers. The decline has also affected

Table 1
Membership of Principal Unions Affiliated to the STUC 1979-1987

Union	1978	1979	1980	1981	1982	1983	1984	1985	1986	1987	% change 1978-1987
Section 1 Fuel & Power											
EETPU	40,000	40,000	40,000	40,000	40,000	35,000	32,000	29,000	27,000	25,500	– 36
NUM	15,752	15,981	15,558	14,202	13,010	10,198	10,088	6,422	3,763	3,538	– 78
Section 2 Transports and Docks											
ASLEF	2,734	2,756	2,788	2,639	2,489	2,404	2,329	2,284	2,199	1,975	– 28
NUR	16,429	16,592	16,532	15,603	14,920	14,310	12,907	12,376	11,577	10,672	– 35
NUS	3,000	3,000	3,000	3,000	3,000	3,000	3,000	3,000	3,000	3,000	0
TGWU	134,000	134,000	134,000	134,000	134,000	130,000	134,000	133,000	130,000	128,000	
Dyers & Bleachers	7,815	9,940	8,406	6,338	5,000	4,000	–	–	–	–	
Agric. Workers	1,500	1,500	1,500	1,500	1,500	3,519	–	–	–	–	
Total	143,315	145,440	143,906	141,838	140,500	137,519	134,000	133,000	130,000	128,000	– 11
Section 3 Shipbuilding and Engineering											
AEU	120,463	119,788	111,663	110,781	100,001	97,872	95,000	95,000	85,500	80,000	– 34
ISTC	10,436	9,673	8,904	8,751	8,733	8,000	7,000	5,292	4,702	4,160	– 60
TASS	15,155	20,000	20,000	17,988	16,728	15,721	17,705	16,729	16,950	17,998	
TWU	4,330	4,333	2,386	2,189	1,801	1,362	1,239	1,113	1,048	–	
Pattern Makers	800	1,000	950	900	800	700	803	–	–	–	
Sheet Metal Workers	4,500	4,600	4,002	3,400	3,256	3,000	–	–	–	–	
Total	24,785	29,933	27,338	24,477	22,585	20,783	19,747	17,842	17,998	17,998	– 27

Union	1978	1979	1980	1981	1982	1983	1984	1985	1986	1987	% change 1978-1987
Section 4 Building											
UCATT	39,884	39,884	39,884	31,908	30,313	30,313	30,313	30,313	30,131	38,971	– 2
FTAT	4,642	4,642	4,642	4,365	2,638	2,638	3,755	3,386	3,281	3,300	– 29
Section 5 Printing & Paper											
NGA(82)	–		–	–	2,247	2,382	2,382	2,617	2,613	2,563	
NGA	2,047	2,047	2,085	2,032	–						
SLADE	1,173	1,324	1,025	904	–						
Total	3,220	3,371	3,110	2,936	2,247	2,382	2,382	2,617	2,613	2,563	– 20
SOGAT(82)	–				19,219	19,792	19,350	19,095	18,587	18,145	
SOGAT	23,912	24,296	22,467	20,155							
NATSOPA	2,010	1,010	2,010	2,010							
Total	25,922	26,306	24,477	22,165	19,219	19,792	19,350	19,095	18,587	18,145	– 30
Section 6 Clothing etc.											
Scottish Carpet Workers Union	4,504	3,961	2,978	1,874	1,100	1,073	1,058	970	880	804	– 82
NUHKW	4,885	4,885	4,358	4,367	3,897	4,045	4,080	3,774	4,020	3,620	– 26
NUTGW	15,000	18,153	14,000	12,132	9,876	9,884	10,075	10,075	10,020	10,112	– 33
Section 7 Food, Drink, Tobacco											
USDAW	61,258	61,374	57,604	55,672	51,757	49,862	47,591	48,032	47,729	47,131	– 23
Section 8 Non-Manual Workers											
BIFU	15,513	17,463	18,196	18,911	19,957	20,228	20,479	22,154	21,505	22,316	+ 44
BETA	–					2,657	2,657	3,202	2,732	2,003	
ABS	773	854	891	734	958	–					
NATTKE	1,530	1,530	1,500	1,612	1,530						
Total	2,303	2,384	2,391	2,346	2,488	2,657	2,657	3,202	2,732	2,003	– 13
ASTMS	34,906	37,566	36,566	36,566	30,000	30,000	30,000	25,000	25,000	26,035	– 25
APEX	11,000	10,982	9,008	7,775	6,715	5,809	5,264	5,248	5,658	5,053	– 54

Union	1978	1979	1980	1981	1982	1983	1984	1985	1986	1987	% change 1978-1987
Section 9 Civil and Public Servants											
CPSA	21,204	20,513	19,868	19,983	20,205	19,849	20,081	17,954	18,564	18,799	- 11
NUCPS	-	-	-	-	-	-	-	-	-	12,228	
SCPS	8,200	9,000	9,000	9,000	9,000	9,000	9,000	9,000	9,000	-	
CSU	4,454	4,318	4,610	3,954	3,606	3,257	3,549	3,383	3,228	-	
Total	12,654	13,318	13,610	12,954	12,606	12,257	12,549	12,383	12,228	12,228	- 3
UCW	15,183	16,092	17,448	16,037	15,926	15,667	15,652	15,404	15,234	15,180	0
FBU	3,500	3,500	3,500	4,165	4,165	4,165	4,165	4,722	4,722	5,136	+ 47
COHSE	22,295	22,669	23,322	25,131	26,486	25,147	24,360	24,622	25,198	25,849	+ 16
IRSF	2,500	2,500	2,500	2,500	3,500	4,000	5,905	5,773	5,885	5,673	+127
NCU	10,251	9,554	10,959	10,893	11,003	10,853	10,498	12,517	11,901	11,654	+ 14
SPOA	2,553	2,567	2,652	2,668	2,736	2,760	2,904	3,021	3,127	3,228	+ 26
Section 10 Local Government											
GMBATU	100,000	105,000	102,400	102,400	102,000	101,368	118,487	115,000	111,892	108,889	
Boiler-makers	25,935	26,076	25,317	24,859	24,442	20,121	-	-	-	-	
The Scottish Lace & Textile Workers Union	600	1,200	1,200	1,041	1,000	-	-	-	-	-	
Total	126,535	132,276	128,917	128,300	127,442	121,489	118,487	115,000	111,892	108,889	- 14
NALGO	67,111	70,955	75,658	78,476	78,436	78,647	78,642	78,592	78,736	79,689	+ 18
NUPE	60,700	64,000	71,500	74,049	75,212	73,575	72,510	71,443	71,688	70,794	+ 17
Section 11 Education											
EIS	46,985	48,479	47,489	46,515	45,786	45,665	45,559	43,282	42,915	43,519	
ALCIS	N/A	650	650	650	660	652	660	-	-	-	
Total	46,985	49,129	48,139	47,165	46,446	46,317	46,219	43,282	42,915	43,519	- 7
ALCES	1,193	990	970	960	884	750	755	735	700	663	- 44
SFHEA	1,750	1,750	1,733	1,733	1,581	1,612	1,660	1,820	1,823	1,821	+ 5
SSTA	N/A	8,642	8,706	7,796	7,510	7,132	7,069	7,496	7,208	7,320	- 15
AUT(S)	3,983	4,089	4,196	4,538	4,488	4,339	4,471	4,188	4,519	4,888	+23
Non STUC organisations											
RCN	11,137	15,712	17,845	18,763	22,090	23,453	24,605	25,545	26,591	27,200	+143

Source STUC Annual Reports 1979-1988.   RCN figures supplied by the RCN.

lighter industries, such as clothing and knitwear manufacture, but particularly carpet making, with a decline in membership of the Scottish Carpet Workers Union of over 80% in the last decade. If the exactitude of the EETPU figures is accepted, then they reveal a sharp decline despite their 'single union no strike' approach to recruitment and organisation. The private service sector of the economy shows a more mixed pattern. The shop workers union, USDAW, has lost about a quarter of its 1978 membership, but USDAW always was in the position of having to keep recruiting in order to stand still, given the nature of employment in the retail industry and its 1987 TUC figures show a small increase. In the banking and insurance industry, however, BIFU has grown by nearly half.

The public sector also presents a mixed picture.[5] This sector of the economy traditionally was very highly unionised at around 80%. This figure does not look like changing very much, but within the public sector there has been a sharp decline in absolute membership in the trading sector, e.g. British Coal and British Steel and a less marked decline in union's organising in central government departments, e.g. CPSA and NUCPS. However, the picture is not all decline. The absolute number of fire brigade staff, tax inspectors and prison officers has risen and so too has the membership of the appropriate unions.

In local government, NALGO in Scotland has continued to grow slowly during the 1980s, although its membership on a UK basis has declined from the peak of 1981. Some of this change is due to privatisation of parts of the public sector and most of the relevant unions have amended their rule books to allow them to follow their members into the private sector. NALGO has agreed recently to take manual workers into membership to allow it to offer single union deals in competition with other unions when services are privatised. NUPE, however, has declined from a Scottish peak membership in 1982. In education, ALCES has declined markedly from 1978 to 1988 when it decided to amalgamate with the EIS. On the other hand, both the SFHEA and AUT(S) have grown in recent years despite falls during the early 1980s when education cuts first began to bite. The educational sector is virtually the only part of the Scottish trade union movement to retain separate Scottish unions, although the decade has seen the merger of ALCIS and ALCES into the EIS which puts pressure on the continued viability of other education unions outwith the EIS's banner.

The 1980s have seen a number of mergers of trade unions. While the decade has seen the disappearance of independent Scottish unions such as the Scottish Lace and Textile Workers Union, the main thrust of merger has been a UK wide phenomenon to create a number of large powerful general unions. The former General and Municipal Workers Union has expanded its name and its membership coverage to become the General, Municipal, Boilermakers and Allied Trades Union. A number of small regional unions have joined this organisation and its next major merger partner is the white collar workers union APEX. Similarly the TGWU have taken in Agricultural Workers and Dyers and Bleachers as well as a number of smaller unions. MSF (Manufacturing Science Finance) has recently been created combining ASTMS and TASS as a major force in the sectors of the economy suggested by its title. The creation of the National Union of Civil and Public Servants from the former CSU and SCPS is a sign of pressure for change in the public sector. Mergers will continue to be a major feature of trade union organisation in the 1990s and, although, to date, there is little evidence of a Scottish dimension to these changes it has been suggested that if the next general election produces a Labour Scotland but a Tory UK, then there may be moves to establish a separate Scottish public sector union.

Despite the success of some TUC/STUC affiliated unions in increasing their membership in this decade, it should be noted that the organisation which grew most rapidly, both in the UK and in Scotland, was the non-TUC affiliated Royal College of Nursing. The RCN now has more members than the main TUC NHS based union, COHSE. While it was clear during both the NHS dispute and the teachers' pay campaign that there was movement of members between organisations which were perceived as being more or less militant, it would appear that the balance of movement has been in favour of the 'no-strike' RCN in the health service. In teaching the Professional Association of Teachers has also grown although the EIS remains the dominant union in this sector. The issue of membership movement between organisations during dispute situations needs to be investigated further.

Pressure for Change

Having given this overview of the changes in trade union membership in Scotland in the past decade, it is now necessary to examine some of the pressures for change operating on the Scottish trade union movement. Many of these are not specific to Scotland, but can affect Scotland in particular ways. The issues to be addressed include the levels of unemployment, the changing distribution of employment, workplace size, etc. An overview of sectoral employment change is provided in Table 2.

The main reason for the decline in trade union membership has been the disproportionate rate of closure and job-loss among large highly unionised manufacturing plants. This could be redressed by a recovery in manufacturing, but the dominant trend in employment is away from manufacturing to non-manufacturing industries and from full time to part-time employment.[6] Both of these areas, non-manufacturing and part-time employment, are traditionally less unionised and thus are unlikely to be fertile recruiting ground for unions to recover the loss of members in manufacturing employment. Moreover, within manufacturing there is a

TABLE 2
Employees in Employment in Scotland at June by industry, 1980-1986
thousands

		1980	1981	1982	1983	1984	1985	1986
	1980 SIC Total Employment	**2,082**	**2,002**	**1,950**	**1,899**	**1,901**	**1,904**	**1,888**
0	Agriculture, forestry and fishing[1]	45	45	39	37	35	34	31
1	Energy and water supply	74	73	72	68	65	60	53
2	Metal manufacturing and chemicals	77	67	63	55	53	52	48
3	Metal goods, engineering and vehicles	239	215	204	195	189	188	182
4	Other manufacturing	248	229	209	194	192	191	181
5	Construction	155	141	135	134	136	136	134
61-63)	Wholesale distribution, hotels and catering	201	193	200	188	193	195	199
66-67)								
64-65)	Retail distribution	194	191	184	183	186	185	186
7	Transport and communication	134	129	124	119	115	115	110
8	Banking, insurance and finance	126	129	135	140	141	146	155
91-92	Public administration and defence[2]	171	167	168	171	170	170	175
93-99	Education, health and other services[3]	419	422	417	416	425	432	435

(1) There is a discontinuity in the estimates for agriculture: prior to September 1981, non-principal tenant farmers are counted as employees in employment; from September 1981 they are counted as self-employed.
(2) Excludes member of H.M. Forces.
(3) Excludes private domestic services.

Source: Scottish Abstract of Statistics 1987.

shift towards employment in smaller plants, employment in geographical areas which are traditionally less well unionised, such as the South-East of England and in small towns throughout the UK. The decline in employment in parts of the public sector is also weakening a traditionally well organised sector of the economy and means that this sector far from being able to add to overall union membership, will now have to work hard to maintain its own relative position. This will be particularly so if the government succeeds in its attempts to contract out local authority and NHS services in Scotland to the extent that it has already done in England and Wales.

If we examine trends in private sector employment, we can detect a number of factors which militate against trade union organisation. Within the manufacturing sector changes are taking place in terms of plant size, occupational structure, ownership and industrial structure. There is a strong association between large (over 500 employees), plants and unionisation. The trend, however, has been towards smaller plants, with average manufacturing plant size declining by half between 1979 and 1983.[7] The decline in Scotland has been less dramatic, but nonetheless the trade union movement will have to address the problem of organising and servicing members in smaller units where there will be increased costs and, perhaps, more resistance to unionisation on the grounds that 'we don't need outsiders because we have good direct relationships with our employer.'

It is also the case that unionisation is lower among white collar workers and the trend is towards more technical and managerial staff being employed. The 1970s witnessed a growth in white collar trade unionism which was attributed to a combination of three factors – the degree of employment concentration, the willingness of employers to recognise unions, and the extent to which recognition was encouraged by the Government.[8] There are signs that all three of these conditions no longer apply and any continued change in the occupational structure in favour of white collar workers will potentially pose difficulties for trade unions.

It is argued that Scotland has become a branch factory economy, particularly of US multinationals.[9] Such companies are more likely to prefer a non-union environment and therefore there is a possibility that a continued dependence on inward investment may pose difficulties for unions in Scotland. On the other hand, manufacturers tend to adopt a pragmatic line towards industrial relations and many Scottish branch plants have a long history of unionisation. The main approach to union recognition being adopted by companies establishing on greenfield sites is to favour single union deals or no-union arrangements and this also placed the trade union movement in Scotland, and indeed in the UK, in a considerable dilemma. This will be returned to later.

While unions face these difficulties in recruiting and organising in private manufacturing, they face even more difficulties in the private services sector. This has along been an area of low union density. Although the 1984 WIRS survey did indicate a slight increase in membership in this sector, compared to 1980, the figures are still well below those in manufacturing.[10] Moreover, much of the growth in this sector has been of the employment of part-time women workers and the evidence again shows that part-timers and women, but especially part-time women workers are less likely to be union members. Although there has been employment growth in private services, the increase of 30,000 jobs between 1979-1986 by no means compensates for the loss of nearly 250,000 jobs in manufacturing and primary industries.[11]

Any substantial increase in union members in the future will have to come from this sector. But a number of features of private service employment militate against such growth. This sector has been dominated by small workplaces which have been making union organisation more difficult. However, if the trend is towards smaller establishment size in manufacturing, then the reverse is the case in services.[12] Supermarkets are easier to organise then corner stores; estate agent chains linked to banks than one town partnerships. On the other hand, especially in retailing and catering, the nature of the workforce is not conducive to union organisation. These industries are characterised by high labour turnover often of temporary, part time and young workers. Two thirds of all temporary workers are employed in these sectors.[13] These characteristics of the workforce make the problems of trade union recruitment all the greater, and associated with low recruitment are problems with recognition. In June 1988 Pontins became the latest company to withdraw union recognition on the basis that union membership had fallen to less than 1 per cent in a workforce of 5,000. Similarly the Stakis and Norfolk Capital hotel chains have withdrawn recognition.[14]

Unions and New Towns

A general feature of the economy from the 1960s has been the relocation of manufacturing employment away from inner city areas and contributions in favour of more rural locations based on green field sites.[15] A key element in such a move in Scotland has been the expansion of the five Scottish New Towns. The implications for this for trade unions has been researched and has become the subject of debate.[16]

The state of union organisation in the New Towns is of particular importance as their employment structure has been heavily weighted towards the manufacturing sector and therefore any absence of unions in New Towns must be of particular concern since it cannot be attributed primarily to problems with the service sector.

The basic finding from research conducted into the state of union organisation in the five New Towns is that less than a fifth of all plants recognize unions.[17] As can be seen in Table 3, the figure is much lower for Livingston, but higher for Cumbernauld if all premises are included not just those established post 1979. Or, from the viewpoint of individual workers, around 90% of firms in Cumbernauld and East Kilbride have no non-manual employees in a union and nearly two-thirds have no manual unionised employees. Moreover, where unions are recognised this, in most cases is, on the basis of single union recognition. Irvine is the partial exception to this.

TABLE 3
Extent of Unionisation in New Towns in Scotland

Town (Date of survey)	% of plants recognising a union for bargaining purposes		% of firms which recognised unions, which did so on a single union bases
	All plants	post 1979	
Cumbernauld (1987)	30.4	20.2	69
East Kilbride (1986)	19.0	n/a	78
Irvine (1985)	n/a	19.4	45
Glenrothes (1985)	n/a	19.6	76
Livingston (1986)	n/a	6.6	54

N/a = not available

Source: Cairns *et al*

Further analysis of the survey results indicate that non-unionism is associated with new plants and small plants (which usually, but not always, are the same thing). For example, 30% of all plants in Cumbernauld recognised unions, but only 20% of those established post 1979. Non-union plants in East Kilbride had grown from 65% to 85% of the sample between 1982 and 1986.[18] Similarly as can be seen from Table 4, a large proportion of firms in New Towns are small, and these firms are overwhelmingly non-union.

TABLE 4
Size of Plant and Union Recognition
In New Towns in Scotland

Town (Date of survey)	% of companies with less than 10 employees	% of companies with less than 10 employees not recognising unions
Cumbernauld (1987)	40	85
East Kilbride (1985)	70**	–
Irvine (1985)	63*	91
Glenrothes (1985)	72*	88
Livingston (1986)	65*	97

** 1-15 employees
* Post 1979 companies only

Source: Cairns *et al*

Non-unionisation is not simply a function of size. In East Kilbride the two largest employers are non-union, accounting for about a third of manufacturing employment. In Cumbernauld, the larger firms were much more likely to recognise unions, but there were very few with more than 200 employees.

The general conclusion of this research is that the five Scottish New Towns exhibit a similar pattern of non-unionism. This is not unique to Scotland. Beaumont and Townley found that a relatively high proportion of recently established plants in the three New Towns in the North West of England (Central Lancashire, Skelmersdale and Warrington Runcorn) were also non-union.[19] Milton Keynes is estimated to have only a 20% unionisation rate and was the subject of a special recruitment drive organised through the Trades Council.[20]

Non-unionism in Scottish New Towns cannot be blamed on US multinationals alone. Small indigenous firms, some of which do not have a long life span, are a key feature of new town employment. But while the unsuccessful may fade away, the successful ones will grow. If they start non-union, develop non-union, then they may well remain non-union. Taken together, we are talking about substantial numbers of people – an estimate of 10,500 in Irvine, Glenrothes and Livingston.

On the other hand, it could be argued that unions have always had difficulty in recruiting in small firms and that those that grow will eventually be organised when it becomes worthwhile, say once over 100 employees. This view may be overcomplacent now, especially as average plant size is declining and thus fewer plants may expand to this size.

A different interpretation of the state of unions in New Towns is to be found in the work of John MacInnes. MacInnes surveyed New Town manufacturing plants with more than 100 employees.[21] The results (from only 30 companies covering only a quarter of employees in manufacturing in the New Towns) showed that over 8 out of 10 plants, accounting for 87% of employment, recognised unions for collective bargaining. Manual union density was put at 95%, but only 50% for white collar workers. In line with this finding, 30% of the plants which recognised unions did so for manual workers only.

These figures would appear to suggest that unionism is well established in large plants in the New Towns and as these cover a high proportion of all workers, then fears of New Towns being at the vanguard of non-unionism are unfounded. However, two further findings reported in MacInnes work lend support to a more pessimistic viewpoint. First, manual recognition was usually agreed when plants were first opened and 85% had been opened since the 1970s or before, indeed 30% before the New Towns were designated. Thus these plants and manual trade unionism at least are long established. However, half the plants without recognition had been established since 1980 and the newer plants were smaller in size which is in line with national trends, but also in line with a concern about unions' ability to organise smaller plants.

MacInnes argues that the figures on new plants not recognising unions are 'too small to be able to say whether this represents any trend away from recognising unions in the 1980s'.[22] But the earlier findings clearly indicate that plants established post 1979 are much more likely to be non-union and employment patterns in the Scottish New Towns are characterised by a simultaneous high rate of job creation and of job loss. All this suggests that the position of non-unionism is an issue which trade unions ought to address.

There are virtually no trade union offices in the New Towns which could serve as a focus for recruitment drives (assuming there was agreement over which union should organise which workforce). The STUC have begun to tackle this issue by seeking agreements with the New Town Development Corporations to alert them to incoming investment so that the appropriate union can be advised of the recruitment opportunity.

Unions in Electronics

It is often alleged that the 'high-tec' industries, especially electronics are a feature of non-unionism.[23] This is partly associated with location in New Towns. There is some evidence in support of this contention. Cairns' New Town Survey found 70 companies in the electronics sector, all but two of which were non-union.[24] The East Kilbride study found all the firms in this sector to be non-union.[25] The reason for this may not, however, be due to location, but to more salient features such as plant size and date of opening which are explored in the next section.

MacInnes has disputed the conventional wisdom. In a recent report, MacInnes and Sproull have compared trade unionism in the electronics industry in 1987 with that in 1984. They found that 'union membership in the industry is quite robust and shows little sign of falling off. Overall, six out of ten employees in the industry work in unionised plants and more than four out of ten are union members.'[26]

They found 'no statistically significant evidence that non-unionism in the industry was associated with the nationality of ownership, new town location, style of workforce, sector of production or employment, performance of the plant.'[27] They did find, however, that larger plants were more likely to be unionised, but that plants established in the 1980s were less likely to recognise unions. Plants which had all their employees on staff conditions were less likely to recognise unions and there was some evidence that semi-conductor manufacture may be significantly associated with non-unionism, but their data did not allow this to be adequately tested statistically.

Additionally, they found a low incidence of single union deals which contradict any belief that those are the automatic pattern for future union organisation. Moreover as they point out only just over two in every hundred employees in Scotland work in the electronics industry; a proportion below the GB average. Thus they suggest that it would be wrong to assume that the future patterns of work and employment in Scotland will be mainly shaped by what happens in electronics.

One feature of their work which must however be a cause for concern for the trade union movement, is the finding that younger plants are more prevalent in this sector of manufacturing industry and that these are less likely to recognise unions. Coupled with the finding that some companies in this industry are developing non-union human resource management policies, this should again ring alarm bells about what might happen in the future. While the old established plants may remain stable in terms of employment and recognition, newly established plants (if they survive) may not be under any pressure to become unionised when they grow, especially if the 'single status' human resource management policies help create a climate where unions are unwelcome to management and perceived as unnecessary by employees. Indeed MacInnes and Sproull found that of the plants with recognised unions, 55% had been recognised at the time of establishment, and 13% had come after a period of operating of over six years and in 7% of cases over 11 years. This they argue 'suggests that there are some large plants which unions have successfully organised after some years of either indifference or resistance to their efforts',[28] but they go on to concede, virtually all of these cases date to the mid-1970s when trade unionism was more buoyant than it is today. Coupled with their finding that recognition is less likely in newly established plants, then it is clear that the successful pattern of establishing recognition at the time of opening has been broken and that therefore new ideas and new methods may be necessary to tackle this problem.

Gender and Trade Unionism in Scotland

One of the key Labour market changes we have detected is the continued increase in women workers, particularly of part-time women workers in the service industries. Indeed the rate of increase of the proportion of women workers has been greater in Scotland compared to the UK in the period 1980-85, so that women were 46.4% of the Scottish 1985 labour force compared to 44.3% in the UK as a whole.[29] This means that trade unions will have to recruit more women members if they are to maintain, far less increase, their membership. This in turn may influence the composition of union executives and delegations, and, it could be argued if it does not, male dominated unions may not be able to appeal to the vast army of potential women members. We now turn to an examination of the position and status of women with the trade union movement in Scotland.

In doing this we are fortunate that there have been two studies of women in unions in Scotland. One, conducted by Esther Breitenbach, reports the situation to 1979[30], while the Trade Union Research Unit (Scotland) has updated the figures to 1986.[31]

Breitenbach estimated that in 1979 just over 40% of women workers in Scotland were unionised (compared with just under 38% for GB) and that women formed 35.2% of STUC membership (compared with 28.4% of the TUC).[32] She attributed this to the greater preponderance of full time women workers in the Scottish labour force. She also discovered that the unions with a higher proportion of women members in Scotland compared to their GB average were GMWU, TGWU, COHSE and the NUHKW. In the first three cases, this could reflect greater organisation among the higher proportion of public sector workers in Scotland. The second survey was unable to estimate an accurate figure for 1986 due to a low response rate to its questionnaire but put the absolute bottom line of women members at 27.2%, and the 16 (out of 63) affiliates which gave accurate figures had 41.5% women members.[33]

Whatever the accurate figure is, it still remains the case in Scotland, as in GB as a whole, that women are under-represented in the hierarchies of trade unions. Breitenbach concluded that the numbers of women full-time officers (FTOs) in unions in Scotland was, with the exception of the Post Office Engineering Union 'in no case commensurate with the size of female membership'.[34] On examining women's participation in other levels of union hierarchies she found considerable variation in the level of their activity as measured by office holding from union to union, but felt that 'the most striking feature of women's level of activity is, in general, that it in no way reflects adequately the level of women's membership'.[35]

The report prepared from the STUC in 1986 attempted to use statistical analysis to argue that 'the proportion of women in official positions in Trade Unions is directly related to their proportion of membership in Trade Unions.'[36] They produced statistically significant evidence to support this view only in the case of women on leading committees in Scotland. This is done on a sample of only 9 unions and all the other regressions were not statistically significant. This seems rather weak evidence, indeed. In fact, Breitenbach had already dismissed the point the STUC researchers were trying to prove when she wrote 'clearly there is a connection between the size of women's membership and their occupation of such positions, at least in the sense that we would not expect women to occupy such positions in unions where they formed only a small minority.'[37]

The figures produced in the STUC report, however, continue to show that women do not hold leading positions in proportion to that which would be expected going simply by membership share. In the case of FTOs only BIFU (one woman rather than two) comes anywhere near a proportionate share. There is evidence of some change in that the TGWU, USDAW, and the EIS have all marginally increased their proportion of women FTOs, but within the EIS, for example, although two thirds of the membership is female, all of the senior officials are men. Similar figures are to be found for other positions such as branch secretary or chairperson. There is evidence of some change since 1979 in that the proportion of women members of the leading Scottish committee of APEX has shot up from 14% to 38%, and of NUPE branch secretaries from 4% to 18%. On the other hand, however, the proportion of women branch secretaries in APEX has declined from 54% to 37%. Where comparisons can be made between the two surveys, the movement is generally small, but in the right direction. We must conclude, therefore, that women are still under-represented in the hierarchies of trade unions and that this continues to be an issue which unions must address.

GMBATU, for example, discovered in 1987 that its female membership was declining less rapidly that its overall membership and consciously began to regear its activities and concerns towards women. It was recognised that this would pose problems for many male officials who were being asked to bargain on issues they have previously considered soft, or secondary. By the spring of 1988 this policy appeared to be paying off as GMBATU reported a membership increase for the first time since 1979. As John Edmonds put it, 'We are trying to become less macho, distant and remote'.[38]

The research evidence on the lack of woman's involvement in unions points to the attitudes of men and the continued expectations of women's domestic roles.[39] Many more male trade unionists will have to adopt John Edmond's maxim before women play a fully proportionate role in unions.

The Role of the STUC

It would not be possible to conclude an overview of trade unionism in Scotland without giving some consideration to the role of the STUC. The STUC has a long tradition of independence being formed in 1897 in response to the 1895 decision of the British TUC to exclude trades councils from direct affiliation.[40] Ninety years later there are hardly any separate Scottish trade unions left (SCEBTA, SCWU, SPOA, EIS, SSTA, SFHEA), but the trades councils are still as vociferous as ever, being the main source of left wing views put to Congress. They have also been at the forefront of the moves to create unemployed workers' centres.

While the STUC is an important forum for debate, it has been unable to influence the policies of a Conservative government led from London with little regard to the precarious parliamentary position of the Tory party in Scotland. The STUC to a large extent operates in a political vacuum without a Scottish Assembly to which it can address its policies and concerns to. Nowhere can this be seen more than with the fate of the document *Scotland: A Land Fit for People*.[41] This was presented to the 1987 Congress and represented the STUC's analysis of the state of the Scottish economy and its prescriptions for change. The document was well researched and a widespread circulation had taken place in the movement about its content. It was well received by the media, but two months later a Tory government was again returned to Westminster and so the prospects of implementing the policies were reduced to zero.

As the report stated, 'the establishment of a Scottish Assembly with side ranging economic powers, was 'central' to the creation of a climate and framework within which Scotland and its people can once again flourish'.[42] The impetus then shifted to the work of the Standing Commission on the Scottish Economy which drew together a range of expertise across the political spectrum to produce a report on the future of the Scottish economy.[43] However, the Conservative party did not play an active part in the proceedings and once again it is unlikely that the government will change its policies.

Clearly, the STUC will continue to champion the cause of industries under threat and initiate campaigns such as the Scottish Health Service Campaign to defend public services and the anti-poll tax campaign. But in the absence of a Scottish Assembly, coupled to the existence of a Tory government, it is unlikely that the STUC will be able to influence decisively key political and economic decisions which will confront Scotland in the next few years.

One area where the STUC is likely to be more involved is that of union recruitment. Campbell Christie expressed his concern at a FBU School at the end of 1987. Unions, he said, had been 'complacent about seeing recruitment as a key union activity and putting resources into the areas where recruitment takes place.'[44] The STUC is concerned about the state of unionisation in New Towns and as stated earlier is seeking agreements with the New Town Development Corporations on getting early warnings of new investment.[45] This would be with the aim of advising appropriate unions of recruitment opportunities. Here, however, lies a potential problem. While it is in the general interest of the trade union movement and the STUC to ensure as high a union density as possible, it may not be in the particular interest of an individual union to let a rival union organise a new plant, especially if it is on the basis of a single union deal.

This issue came to a head at the beginning of 1988 with the crisis over the proposed Ford plant at Dundee and the dispute between the AEU and TGWU over recognition. The STUC played a very conciliatory role throughout this affair and is attempting to establish an agreed mode of operation so that new plants will become union rather than non-union plants, even if, from time to time, some particular unions have to suffer disappointments. To this end, the STUC have established a sub-committee on Trade Union Recruitment and Organisation.

The STUC is seeking agreement with the SDA so that the STUC could advise the SDA on the appropriate union(s) to seek recognition. A 1988 Congress motion also committed the STUC to establishing an appropriate mechanism to deal with representation at new work places, with a view to avoiding disputes and being more effective in obtaining recognition.

This issue is related directly to the ability of the TUC to secure an agreement on handling prospective Single Union agreements. At the time of writing this seems likely, at least in the short term, but at the expense of the EETPU being expelled from the TUC. The STUC, unlike the TUC, has not got bogged down in the sole issue of single union deals to the detriment of other policies to aid recruitment and organisation. Nonetheless it is an urgent issue as our earlier overview of the changing state of the labour market and the pressures on trade union recruitment and organisation shows.

Summary and Conclusion

There are a number of key points which arise out of this overview of the position of trade unions in Scotland. Both the absolute numbers of people in trade unions and the density has been falling in Scotland as in Great Britain as a whole. But it should be noted that some unions have been expanding and the 1987 TUC figures reveal that 33 out of 83 affiliates increased their membership between 1986 and 1987.[46] Much of the decline is attributable to the loss of jobs in the traditionally heavily unionised manufacturing industries. But it is also due to changes in the composition of the workforce – more self-employed,more women, more part-timers, more people in the service industries, fewer in manufacturing and potentially fewer in the public sector. Any future recovery of trade union density cannot rely on the traditional areas of strength; such as manufacturing – because of jobs losses which are unlikely to be recovered – or the public sector – because of the existing high levels of penetration and because the absolute numbers of union members is likely to decline as the number of jobs in the public sector declines.

Unions in Scotland must therefore address certain key questions about recruitment and organisation. The issue must come to the fore. There are signs that this is happening – the establishment of the STUC sub committee on Recruitment and Organisation; the special campaigns by unions such as the TGWU and GMBATU addressed to women, part-timers and youth; the deal for financial services for union members concluded between

GMBATU and TSB (Scotland) and the possible outcome of the TUC Special Review Body. These moves are necessary to develop recruitment tactics relevant to the groups of workers who are under unionised at present – women, part-timers, youth, workers in the service industries and in small companies. Unions will also have to examine ways in which word processing technology can be used to service members directly from permanent offices so that members can receive most of the benefits of membership without there necessarily being employer recognition. The balance of evidence from research in the New Towns suggests that special measures need to be addressed there. Arriving fast is the single European Market and its potential impact on unions.

The STUC appears set to play a leading role in this. It is anxious to see present trends reversed and willing to play an overarching role in the interests of trade unionism rather than that of particular unions. It has the scope to develop such activities in a political climate which precludes the establishment of a Scottish Assembly on which much of its economic and social policies for Scotland is based. In passing such a policy it will, from time to time, come up against objections from particular unions, but the question has to be asked whether fiercely competitive unionism is appropriate in the present circumstances. If the alternative is no trade unionism, then unions will have to co-operate through the medium of the STUC in order to reverse the decline of the 1980s in the 1990s.

John W Leopold, Department of Business ans Management, University of Stirling

References

1. I am grateful for discussions with Larry Cairns, Jim Devine, Mike Jackson, John MacInnes and Kath Ryall. None of these is, of course, responsible for anything that follows.

2. N Millward and M Stevens 'Union density in the Regions' in *Employment Gazette*, May 1988, p 293.

3. N Millward and M Stevens, *Workplace Industrial Relations Survey*, Gower, Aldershot, 1986, p 52.

4. For an overview of this see J MacInnes, *Thatcherism at Work*, Open University Press, Milton Keynes, 1987 Ch 5.

5. For an overview of this sector, see J W Leopold 'Developments in the Public Sector' paper prepared for TUC Seminar, promoting Trade Unionism: The Challenges and Choices, University of Strathclyde, November 1987.

6. J MacInnes, *op cit*.

7. J MacInnes, *The Changing Economic and Industrial Environment, and its Implications for Trade Union Membership and Organisation in the 1980s and 1990s*. Paper prepared for the STUC, p 4.

8. See, for example, G S Bain, *The Growth of White Collar Trade Unionism*, Clarendon, Oxford.

9. J Firn 'External Control and Regional Policy' in G Brown (ed) *The Red Paper on Scotland*, EUSPB, Edinburgh, 1975.

10. N Millward and M Stevens *op cit*. pp 54-60.

11. P Smith and M Burns, 'The Scottish Economy Decline and Response', in D McCrone and A Brown (eds) *The Scottish Government Yearbook*, 1988, p 262.

12. J MacInnes, STUC paper *op cit*, p 6.

13. *Ibid*. p 7.

14. *Financial Times*, 11/6/88.

15. C Handy, *The Future of Work*, Basil Blackwell, Oxford 1984.

16. See P B Beaumont and L Cairns 'New Towns – A Centre of Non-Unionism?', in *Employee Relations* Vol 9, No 4; L Cairns, J W Leopold, M P Jackson and S Butts 'New Towns, No Unions!' Mimeographed University of Stirling 1987; J MacInnes, *Employee Relations in Large Manufacturing Plants in the Scottish New Towns*, Centre for Research Into Industrial Democracy and Participation, University of Glasgow, 1987; J MacInnes, *Economic Restructuring Relevant to Industrial Relations in Scotland*, Centre for Urban and Regional Research, University of Glasgow, 1987.

17. L Cairns, et al. *op cit*.

18. Strathclyde Business School. *East Kilbride a Labour Study*, East Kilbride Development Corporation 1986.

19. P B Beaumont and B Townley 'Greenfield Sites, New Plants and Work Practices' in V Hammond (ed) *Current Research in Management*, Francis Pinter, London 1985.

20. *Financial Times*, 9/5/87.

21. J MacInnes, *op cit*. C.R.I.D.P. Report.

22. *Ibid*. p 9.

23. P Bassett, *Strike Free*, Macmillan, London 1986, pp 28-81.

24. L Cairns, *New Towns Unionisation Survey – Glenrothes, Irvine and Livingston*, unpublished M Phil. University of Glasgow, 1984, p 24.

25. Strathclyde Business School, *op cit*. p 9.

26. A Sproull and J MacInnes, *Trade Union Recognition, Single Union Agreements and Employment Changes in the Electronics Industry in Scotland*, Department of Economics, Glasgow College 1988, p 41.

27. *Ibid*. p 41.

28. *Ibid*. p 22.

29. Cited in M Jackson, 'Strikes in Scotland', in the *Industrial Relations Journal*, Vol 19 No 2, Summer 1988, p 115.

30. E Breitenbach, *Women Workers in Scotland*, Pressgang, Glasgow 1982.

31. K Morrison 'Trade Union Women in Scotland' reported in STUC, *General Council Report*, STUC, Glasgow 1987, pp 23-26.

32. E Breitenbach, *op cit*. p 48.

33. STUC, *op cit* p 23.

34. E Breitenbach, *op cit*. p 50.

35. *Ibid*. p 51.

36. STUC, *op cit*. p 24.

37. E Breitenbach, *op cit*. p 50.

38. Quoted in *The Independent*, 14/3/88.

39. For discussions of this see, for example, A Pollert, *Girls, Wives and Factory Lives*, Macmillan, London 1981 and J Beale, *Getting it Together, Women as Trade Unionists*, Pluto, London, 1982.

40. For a history of the STUC, see A Tuckett, *The Scottish Trades Union*

Congress: The First 80 Years 1897-1977, Mainstream, Edinburgh 1986. Also, J Milne talks to J Leopold – 'Industrial Relations in Scotland' The Role and Work of the STUC' in *Employee Relations*, Vol 6, No 6, 1984.

41. STUC, *Scotland – A Land Fit for People*, STUC, Glasgow 1987.

42. *Ibid.* p 81.

43. The Standing Commission on the Scottish Economy, Interim Report, Glasgow 1988.

44. *Financial Times*, 11/11/87.

45. STUC, *General Council Report*, 1988, p 41.

46. *Financial Times*, 23/6/88.

Glossary

ABS	Association of Broadcasting Staffs
AEU	Amalgamated Engineering Union
ALCES	Association of Lecturers in Colleges of Education in Scotland
ALCIS	Association of Lecturers in Scottish Central Institutions
APEX	Association of Professional Executive Clerical and Computer Staff
ASLEF	Associated Society of Locomotive Engineers and Firemen
ASTMS	Association of Scientific and Managerial Staff
AUT(S)	Association of University Teachers (Scotland)
BETA	Broadcasting and Entertainment Trades Alliance
BIFU	Banking Insurance and Finance Union
COHSE	Confederation of Health Service Employees
CPSA	Civil and Public Services Association
CSU	Civil Service Union
EETPU	Electrical, Electronic, Telecommunications and Plumbing Union
EIS	Educational Institute of Scotland
FBU	Fire Brigade Union
FTAT	Furniture, Timber and Allied Trades Union
GMBATU	General Municipal Boilermakers and Allied Trades Union
IRSF	Inland Revenue Staff Federation
ISTC	Iron and Steel Trades Confederation
NALGO	National and Local Government Officers Association
NATTKE	National Association of Theatre Technicians and Kinomatic Employees
NATSOPA	National Association of Operative Printers, Graphical and

	Media Personnel
NCU	National Communication Union
NGA	National Graphical Association
NUCPS	National Union of Civil and Public Servants
NUHKW	National Union of Hosiery and Knitwear Workers
NUM	National Union of Mine-Workers
NUPE	National Union of Public Employees
NUR	National Union of Railwaymen
NUS	National Union of Seamen
NUTGW	National Union of Tailors and Garment Workers
RCN	Royal College of Nursing
SCEBTA	Scottish Colliery Enginemen, Boilermen and Tradesmen's Association
SCPS	Society of Civil and Public Servants
SCWU	Scottish Carpet Workers Union
SDA	Scottish Development Agency
SFHEA	Scottish Further and Higher Education Association
SLADE	Society of Lithographic Artists, Designers, Engravers and Process Workers
SOGAT	Society of Graphical and Allied Trades
SPOA	Scottish Prison Officers' Association
SSTA	Scotish Secondary Teachers' Association
STUC	Scottish Trades Union Congress
TASS	Technical and Administrative Staffs Section
TGWU	Transport and General Workers Union
TUC	Trades Union Congress
TWU	Tobacco Workers' Union
UCATT	Union of Construction and Allied Trades and Technicians
UCW	Union of Communication Workers
USDAW	Union of Shop Distributive and Allied Workers

THE SCOTTISH DIMENSION OF TVEI

Colin Bell, Cathy Howieson, Kenneth King, David Raffe

The Technical and Vocational Education Initiative (TVEI) was launched in November 1982 by the Government as a pilot scheme to stimulate the provision of technical and vocational education for 14-18 year-olds within the educational system. It is one of the major innovations in education in recent years and one that, as part of the Scottish evaluation of TVEI, we had the opportunity to observe at first hand. The findings of our evaluation are reported elsewhere[1]; this article focuses on two themes, one is the Scottish dimension of TVEI and the second the reality of an attempt to implement an initiative embodying many of the ideas and ambitions of the "new vocationalism". By this is normally meant making education less based on a highly theoretical and academic curriculum geared to high ability pupils which is irrelevant to the 'needs of industry' and demotivates the majority of educational consumers.

Much of the discussion and indeed opposition to TVEI has centred on TVEI as the flagship of "the new vocationalism". Our consideration of this aspect of TVEI does not debate the rights and wrongs of such an approach but discusses what happened in practice and the tensions, contradictions and unexpected outcomes thereby revealed. But first we look at a very neglected area: the development of TVEI in Scotland. In Scotland, TVEI has been confronted with a very different educational system and climate from England and Wales and this influenced both the initial response to TVEI and its subsequent implementation. It has meant that TVEI projects in Scotland have faced unique problems but at the same time have benefitted from the recent developments in Scottish education.

TVEI in Scotland

What does TVEI look like in Scotland? It was introduced in stages in Scotland starting with five projects in 1984, a year after the first starts in England and Wales. These were located in Borders, Dumfries and Galloway, Fife, Renfrew and Glasgow. A single project (in Lothian) began in 1985 and another (in Tayside) in 1986. By 1987 there were projects in all mainland regions in Scotland, and in all divisions of Strathclyde Region. Most pilot TVEI projects are based on a consortium of three, four, five or six schools and colleges, and on a cohort of 200-250 pupils in each of five consecutive year groups. Most pupils enter TVEI at around 14 years at the beginning of third year. They variously choose to be in, were chosen or picked at random for the first cohort, although the exact procedure varied between projects and between schools. The pilot TVEI projects have set out to "explore and test the ways of organising and managing the education of 14-18 year olds across the ability range" so that various educational aims, discussed below, can be met. They are self-consciously *pilot* projects from which educational authorities are meant to learn. The national extension of TVEI to all schools and all regions was announced in the summer of 1986 in the White Paper *Working Together – Education and Training* (Cmnd 9823). This was actually before the full teams of Scottish evaluators of the pilot projects had been assembled.

TVEI's ambition is to give 14-18 year old boys and girls of all abilities a more relevant and practical preparation for adult and working life. Within the broad criteria set for TVEI by the Manpower Services Commission, projects have taken different approaches. Some have a greater technological slant than others which perhaps pay more attention to personal and social development. It is also the case that whilst the stated aims of TVEI have remained the same, the emphases have changed and been reinterpreted over time. TVEI programmes consist of a *core* that is common to all TVEI pupils, plus *options*. Together core and options range from about 30 to 60 per cent of Scottish TVEI pupils' timetables but the modal figure is nearer 30 than 60. In Scotland the core usually includes information technology, personal and social development, careers education, work experience and a residential experience. Options include subjects chosen by students to meet their needs, such as business studies, computing, catering, textiles, control technology, pneumatics and caring. Many established curriculum areas have also been 'enhanced' through TVEI funding in the sense of adding to existing subjects by providing resources, introducing a more technological dimension into the curriculum or helping to change teaching methods. English, maths, music, art, geography, Latin and home economics are all examples of subjects that have been enhanced in this way. Both in these enhanced subjects and in the TVEI core and options (above) there has been an attempt to introduce technology across the curriculum. There have been equally important changes in the modes of teaching, emphasising a problem-solving approach, experiential learning and more negotiated, individualised study. TVEI aims to give students more control and responsibility for their own learning and thus to motivate youngsters "turned off" by traditional teaching methods. This has been one of the most popular aspects of TVEI.

This description of TVEI in Scotland hints at the "Scottish dimension", for example, the later introduction of TVEI, a year after England and Wales. In fact, although TVEI is one of the largest and most important cross-border initiatives ever seen in British education, its origins and centre of gravity are in the south. TVEI was devised to fit the English education system and framework, for example, patterns of certification, staying-on rates and participation in post compulsory education. The results of applying an English design in a Scottish context have become evident as TVEI has been implemented and we return to this later. First we consider the response in Scotland to TVEI and the particularly Scottish reasons for its late arrival on the Scottish educational scene.

The Scottish Response to TVEI

The announcement of TVEI was greeted with considerable hostility by many educationalists, politicians and others in Britain as a dangerous extension of MSC's responsibilities into the secondary education sector; as an attack on the comprehensive system; and as an effort to move towards a narrowly vocational education geared to the needs of employers who would be given a direct and damaging influence on the school curriculum. In Scotland opposition had an extra dimension on several counts. Firstly, TVEI was seen as a threat not only because of MSC involvement in schools but also because it represented the imposition of an English system in Scotland, a country with different traditions. Opposition on the grounds of this "colonising" aspect of TVEI was clearly expressed by the Educational Institute of Scotland (EIS) in 1985.

"The involvement of MSC in the education system represents a damaging intrusion from England and Wales into the established pattern of Scottish education ...the whole thrust is assimilative"[2]

A second distinctive feature of Scottish reaction to TVEI was the strength of opposition to it as undermining the comprehensive principle. Although similar fears were being voiced in England, there was a strong feeling in Scotland that England had never fully taken on the comprehensive ideal and that some there were not unhappy about the direction in which TVEI was moving the education system. This widespread opposition was well captured by the EIS when it stated that

"Scottish teachers and parents are more strongly supportive of the comprehensive system ... than would ever have been thought possible ... TVEI represents a further threat to the comprehensive system. It originates in England and Wales where there is a much stronger ongoing lobby for selective education."[2]

A third aspect of the Scottish reaction was simply that Scotland did not need TVEI. A common response was that Scotland had already addressed the issues of educational relevance for which TVEI was designed and had come up with its own solutions, better suited to Scotland, in the Standard Grade and Action Plan. Once again, the EIS summed up this feeling

"Little consideration has been given so far to the effect of MSC activities on the ethos of Scottish education. The debate about balance between vocational and general education has been suddenly overtaken by intervention on one side ... when Munn and Action Plan developments had come near to achieving some kind of consensus in the debate."[2]

This quote also illustrates the view that Scotland was not only ahead of England in tackling the question of educational relevance but had managed to do so in a way that preserved a balance between vocational and general education unlike TVEI. TVEI was seen as threatening the Scottish tradition of general education, a principle maintained and endorsed by the Munn Report and Action Plan.

Such views of TVEI as divisive, narrowly vocational, unsuited to and redundant in Scotland all contributed to the delay in introducing TVEI in Scotland. The auspices for TVEI seemed to be discouraging: its Scottish launch in 1984 coincided with the start of a prolonged and bitter industrial dispute in schools which involved a boycott of curriculum development work of the kind essential to TVEI.

Paradoxically, these very difficulties may have strengthened TVEI and encouraged its assimilation into mainstream educational developments. Within schools and education authorities, those most closely associated with and committed to TVEI had to spend much time defending it and emphasising its continuity with other education-led reforms. This process forced them to give serious consideration to the philosophy and practice of their projects. It seems that in Scotland, a consequence both of the educational doubts about TVEI and of the industrial action, has been that the philosophy of TVEI is more developed and more explicit as well as more consistent with current educational developments. It may also be better reflected in practice. These same difficulties may also have encouraged the MSC, anxious to see any positive movement in TVEI in Scotland, to be more flexible in interpreting the TVEI criteria.

TVEI was extended to Scotland only after acceptance of COSLA's demand that in Scotland TVEI would have to be compatible with Standard Grade and Action Plan developments. Such an acknowledgement of this Scottish dimension of TVEI is made clear, for example, in the White Paper *Working Together – Education and Training*. In announcing the extension of TVEI it states

"In Scotland, the arrangements will take into account the need to ensure full harmony with Standard Grade and Action Plan developments"[3]

and

"The Government is publishing a statement of curricula criteria based on the relevant passages of ... for Scotland the Munn Report and the 16 Action Plan."[3]

From the beginning TVEI in Scotland was a different animal from that in England and it bore the imprint of the Scottish educational tradition and of its recent developments. It is our impression that the principles of compatibility with Munn and Dunning and the Action Plan have generally been honoured and as a result TVEI has been more fully assimilated into the educational mainstream than seems to have been the case in England. (In making this comparison we are aware of the enormous diversity of TVEI projects in England; our point is not that TVEI in Scotland is different from all English projects, rather that it is more homogeneous, at least in this respect).

The extent of this assimilation is reflected in the option choices offered to pupils after second year where TVEI has been fitted into a structure based on Munn modes. It is also evident in the extent of "enhancement" where TVEI funding has been used to add to or enrich an existing subject in a school. It is significant to note that enhancement is a Scottish invention. There is no mention of it in early literature about TVEI, the idea arose within TVEI in Scotland and later spread to cover English projects. Consequently enhamcement has meant that from its inception in Scotland there has been a large measure of "extension" of TVEI to other pupils which has helped to counter some of the criticism of TVEI as a divisive initiative. In Scotland TVEI has been domesticated.

Certifying TVEI

The relative uniformity of Scottish education with the existence of a single examination board and single vocational education body has been another factor in determining the particular shape of TVEI in Scotland. Projects have been able to gain national certification for their activities through SCOTVEC modules and the Standard Grade. (From 1985 a special agreement allowed TVEI projects to offer SCOTVEC modules to 3rd and 4th year pupils). In England certification has been more of a problem: there have been difficulties in finding appropriate certification and with the slow response of the different examination boards to develop suitable provision or validate modules and courses developed by projects. The number and variety of examination boards and the diversity of the non-advanced further education sector in England has created a very different picture in relation to certification. In Scotland projects have been able to offer young people nationally recognised certification and, at the same time, the availability of this certification has reinforced the trend for TVEI in Scotland to resist separate development and to be more integrated into mainstream provision and certification.

Post 16 Problems

Although the particular nature of the Scottish education system has had a positive effect on TVEI, it has also created difficulties for projects in Scotland and we now turn to this aspect of the "Scottish dimension".

TVEI was conceived of and remains a four year programme for 14 to 18 year-olds. This ambition has presented certain problems in the Scottish context. Although TVEI was introduced with the expectation that it would improve staying-on rates, this has not transpired and both Scottish and English projects face a common problem of retaining their cohorts beyond the compulsory leaving age. (The lack of any real impact by TVEI on staying-on rates is not surprising given the strength of the traditional early leaving pattern in Britain compounded by the fact that the first TVEI cohort had more mid to low ability pupils). In response to the numbers leaving TVEI after two years, projects in Scotland recruited extra pupils (known as "infill") who had not previously taken TVEI to make good the lost numbers.

Once those leaving after two years had done so, English projects can assume that the majority of remaining or new "infill" pupils will stay for the next 2 years. This state of affairs is not shared by Scottish projects which face further difficulties because of the distinctive characteristics of post-compulsory education in Scotland. 48% of the first cohort left at the end of 4th year but in addition projects have to cope with that Scottish phenomenon, unknown in England, of the Christmas leaver: about 3 in 10 pupils are too young to leave at the end of 4th year and have to remain in school for the first term of 5th year. A significant number of pupils therefore leave at Christmas of 5th year. Consequently, TVEI projects in Scotland experience another exodus of pupils at this stage. For example, 31% of the first cohort were still in TVEI in October of 5th year (i.e. 1986) but this figure had dropped to 18% by the following spring. Most of this decline is accounted for by Christmas leavers. Having experienced the flight of the Christmas leavers, Scottish projects then face another migration at the end of 5th year since more Scottish pupils leave from 5th year than 6th year – only 1 in 5 Scottish pupils stays on for a 6th year. Thus TVEI projects in Scotland have to cope with not one but three significant transition points: at summer of 4th year, Christmas of 5th year and the summer of 5th year. In Scotland young people might experience TVEI as a 2, 2½, 3 or 4 year programme or if they join as "infill" at 16 might stay for 1 term, 1 year or 2 years. Confronted with this bewildering set of permutations of possible involvement in TVEI, projects have experienced management and resource problems at the post 16 stage. This situation also makes it very difficult for projects to provide a coherent, progressive and meaningful programme for pupils.

The nature of 5th year in Scottish schools adds another turn of the screw on TVEI projects in Scotland. The majority of those who remain for a full 5th year are those who have been relatively successful in their 4th year examinations and who are attempting Highers. The 5th year is very pressurised and the timetable crowded because of the nature of the Higher as essentially a 2 term course. There is little room for TVEI if pupils have a full timetable of Highers. We know that such pupils are frequently TVEI in name only since they have little time for any TVEI activities other than perhaps after SCE exams at the end of the year. In an effort to overcome the time pressures, one TVEI projects organises very popular "Twilight Classes" when pupils attend the TVEI centre after school. But in other cases there is a tacit acceptance that for academic pupils TVEI in 5th year will be a very limited experience. In contrast the Scottish 6th year, compared to its English equivalent, is a time when many pupils have a relatively light timetable and so it provides an opportunity either to concentrate on TVEI after little involvement in 5th year or to take TVEI for the first time.

As the first TVEI projects in Scotland have progressed they have been confronted with a set of managerial problems unenvisaged by MSC. These problems have arisen largely because TVEI, although a British wide innovation, in fact reflects the nature and structure of English education and does not fit readily into the different pattern and character of post-compulsory education in Scotland. While MSC have been willing, almost anxious, to acknowledge and accommodate the Scottish situation in terms of curriculum and certification, they have been less so in relation to the management of TVEI in 5th and 6th year. Perhaps this is not surprising: they have had to recognise that the early aims of TVEI as a 4 year programme could not be sustained, that it would be more of a 2 years plus 2 years programme and so have been understandably reluctant to see their ideas further disintegrate by sanctioning a variety of modes of participation post 16. But in Scotland there needs to be the opportunity to schedule TVEI more flexibly across 5th and 6th year to take account both of the numbers leaving TVEI at several points and the varying timetable loads over this period. Projects have had to argue strongly to be allowed to "infill" new pupils after Christmas of 5th year and especially after the summer of 5th year. Moreover when the numbers problem is resolved, it still leaves Scottish TVEI with the major task of constructing coherent programmes suitable for the different categories of youngsters leaving and joining TVEI over these 2 years.

THE NEW VOCATIONALISM IN ACTION?

The announcement of TVEI was greeted by a combination of disapproval and support both based on the same grounds: that TVEI was a radical attempt to put into practice many of the ideas advocated in the debate about the vocational relevance of education. We were particularly concerned with education/industry relationships in our evaluation of TVEI and were able to observe at first hand the reality of the best resourced and most sustained effort of recent years to make education more responsive to the needs of the economy and the wishes of industry and to achieve a greater involvement of employers in secondary education. We were told forcefully about the issues on both sides of the debate but were perhaps most struck by the fact that whatever the ideological positions adopted on this question and the intentions of practitioners, reality was more complex and full of unexpected and unintended outcomes. It is some of these complexities we discuss in the second part of this paper.

Vocational Relevance

Early statements about TVEI, for example by David Young the then chairman of MSC, demonstrate a belief that by following a programme of vocational education youngsters would be better recruits for employers, thus improving their own job prospects and, later as employees be more able to respond to changing skill requirements and economic circumstances. The criteria set by MSC for TVEI reflected this thinking. Projects were required to ensure that

> "They should provide four-year curricula, with progression from year to year, designed to prepare the student for particular aspects of employment and for adult life in a society liable to rapid change;"[4]

and

> "The vocational elements should be broadly related to potential employment opportunities within and outside the geographical area for the young people concerned; and there should be appropriate planned work experience as an integral part of the programmes."[4]

Each TVEI project was to be supported and guided locally by a mechanism that would include local industry and commerce; to give details of how co-operation with local industry, commerce and the public services would be achieved especially in terms of work experience provision; and to ensure "close collaboration between local education authorities and industry/commercial public services etc. so that the curriculum has industry's confidence".[5]

In the face of such requirements there was considerable fear of an industry "takeover" of education, that employers would have the major say in determining the curriculum which would be geared to their requirements. In our research (which included over 200 interviews in both industry and education) we found that this has not happened. On the one hand, although many employers we interviewed were critical of secondary education and wanted schools to be more responsive to industry, very few wanted to direct the curriculum closely. On the other hand, the reality of efforts by projects to involve employers highlights vividly the practical issues often overlooked in the frequently heated debates in this area. In practice, far from industry taking over education, projects have had problems making contact with employers, in getting their support, in sustaining initial interest over time and in transforming promised help into action because of employers' work pressures. Projects have also discovered the limitations of some employers' understanding of education and training and what they could be expected to contribute to courses and modules. The scenario we encountered was not the one that many had expected, hoped for or feared.

TVEI and the Youth Labour Market

If TVEI has not resulted in industry domination, has it had the desired effect of making youngsters better recruits and improving their job prospects? While it would be too much to expect TVEI to have made a marked impact after only 2 years we were interested to see whether there were any indications or trends, for example in the labour market destinations of TVEI leavers and in employers' recruitment practices. But reality belies the simplifications that underpin much of the rhetoric about education and vocational relevance. Aims to make the curriculum more relevant to the needs of industry assume that industry's requirements are known and agreed and that what happens in industry, for example in relation to recruitment and work practices, coincides with its statements. Apart from the lack of even medium-term manpower and skill forecasting in industry, there are other factors that complicate the question of vocational education, its value and its outcomes.

Although the employers we interviewed were all involved in TVEI and supported its aims, they did not appear to translate this approval into practice when they recruited young people. When asked how much account they would take of an applicant's TVEI experience and in particular any course that seemed to be related to their own industry, very few said that a youngster's TVEI experience would significantly influence their recruitment or selection decisions. This seemed to be due to several inter-related factors: the strength of support for and reliance on traditional academic certification both as an initial screening device and as a measure of competence; a greater value attached by employers to academic rather than vocational skills in potential employees; the poor image and low status of vocational education in Britain and its association with the "non-academic" or "less able". Of course, employers' practice reinforces the latter problem. As long as young people know that employers prefer academic certification, they, and especially more able pupils, will take their cue from this, whatever the merits of alternative, more vocationally oriented, courses. Industrialists might call for a more relevant and vocational education but so far they have not demonstrated that they value it.

Employers' disregard of the vocational education of the TVEI youngsters coming on to the labour market at 16 raises the question of whether such training is seen to be of much practical value. It seems that it is not, at least in any direct way. Employers explained to us that for the jobs and YTS schemes entered at 16, the skill levels required are usually fairly low so that previous experience and training in them through TVEI does not confer an advantage, the necessary skills can be picked up quickly once in the job. This attitude to TVEI is in keeping with the traditional disregard for broad-based vocational education of many British employers.

Another area where there seems to be a gap between the rhetoric of industry and the practice is in the area of enterprise. We hear a great deal these days from the government and from industry about the need for 'enterprise'. We are told that employees need to be flexible, creative, able to use their initiative and tackle any problem that comes up. Education is criticised for failing to produce such creatures. Yet the work practices of many employers do not match their statements. The extent of their demand for critical, enterprising employees is limited in many instances and is frequently related to the level of job. How much enterprise does an employer really want an operative to show? The lower the level of the job, the less employers need workers to be innovatory and enterprising. And even in higher level jobs, when employers talk about employees using their initiative, they frequently assume that the exercise of this initiative will be within fairly narrow parameters set by themselves. This provides another illustration that there is not a simple equation between what employers say they want and how education should respond. It also raises an issue about the likely impact on young people who have experienced a more enterprising education who then find themselves in jobs where they feel bored and their initiative stifled. This is a tension which is not being confronted in TVEI.

Value in the Labour Market

Turning to the other side of the question – the young people concerned – has TVEI improved their job prospects?

When we asked TVEI staff about the types of jobs and YTS schemes that TVEI pupils had found, none felt they could point to any appreciable TVEI influence. From our data on the labour-market destinations of the first cohort of TVEI pupils from the Scottish Young People's Survey[6] we can see little evidence of a direct TVEI effect on finding employment and training. More than half the TVEI cohort was on YTS, nearly three in ten were unemployed, and only one in five was in a full-time job outside YTS. Those proportions were much the same among the non-TVEI pupils.

Status of labour-market entrants in spring 1987 (percentages)

	TVEI schools			Rest of Scotland
	TVEI in S3/4	others	all	
Males and Females				
YTS	53	53	53	48
Full-time job	20	22	21	27
Unemployed	28	25	26	24
Total	101	100	100	99
Unweighted n	(394)	(901)	(1295)	(2690)
Males				
YTS	52	50	51	48
Full-time job	23	22	22	27
Unemployed	25	28	27	26
Total	100	100	100	101
Unweighted n	(232)	(480)	(712)	(1440)
Females				
YTS	54	58	57	50
Full-time job	15	22	20	28
Unemployed	32	20	24	23
Total	101	100	101	101
Unweighted n	(162)	(421)	(583)	(1250)

Source: 100% sample

The survey also collected data on young people's own perceptions of TVEI's value in the labour market. We asked former TVEI pupils who were in a job or on a YTS scheme, if TVEI had been useful to them in getting their job or scheme and in doing it. In answer to both questions, around a quarter felt that TVEI had been useful. We can contrast their response to these questions with their responses to the more general question of whether they thought TVEI in 3rd and 4th years had been worthwhile or not. More than four in five of these youngsters in jobs or on YTS rated it as very worthwhile or worthwhile in some ways. This suggests that TVEI was valued by its students for considerably wider reasons than its perceived relevance to their employment prospects. They expressed appreciation at being 'treated like adults' and at working in groups as well as getting out of school onto work experience and residentials.

It is evident from the implementation and development of TVEI that the debate about the vocational relevance of education, the correct role for education in the economy and for industry in education is a far more complex affair than some of the protagonists on both sides would maintain. Roger Dale identifies this as a central problem in efforts to promote closer links between education and industry. He points to

> "the *simplification* of both the educational attitudes, preferences and requirements of employers and of the available institutional provision and in the consequent *simplification* of the attempts to bring the two together"? (our emphases)[7]

The experience of TVEI reveals the inadequacy of any simplistic answer to the thorny question of the proper relationship between education and industry.

Colin Bell, Department of Sociology, University of Edinburgh
Cathy Howieson, Centre for Educational Sociology, University of Edinburgh
Kenneth King, Department of Education, University of Edinburgh
David Raffe, Centre for Educational Sociology, University of Edinburgh

References

1. Bell, Howieson, King, Raffe *Liaisons Dangereuses? Education Industry Relationships in the First Scottish TVEI Pilot Projects*, Edinburgh University, July 1988.

2. Educational Institute of Scotland *Technical and Vocational Education Initiative*, Minute No 574 (15) (iii), Annual General Meeting, June 1986.

3. HMSO *Working Together – Education and Training* (Cmnd. 9823) London, July 1986.

4. Manpower Services Commission *TVEI Operating Manual*, Annex 3, Sheffield, 1983.

5. Manpower Services Commission *TVEI Operating Manual*, Annex 2, Sheffield, 1983.

6. The Scottish Young People's Survey is a postal survey of a national sample of young people from across Scotland carried out by the Centre for Educational Sociology of Edinburgh University in conjunction with the Scottish Education Department.

7. Roger Dale *Education, Training and Employment: towards a new vocationalism*, Pergamon, Oxford, 1985.

MUNICIPAL HOUSING IN SCOTLAND: THE LONG GOODBYE?

Duncan Maclennan

INTRODUCTION

For more than 100 years municipal governments in Britain, and especially Scotland, have been regarded as the key public organizations implementing housing policies. At the end of the last century it was municipal action, to cope with the public health externalities of slum housing, which prompted central government policies. At that time with rudimentary systems of data recording and retrieval and high real communication costs it made good sense for municipalities to be, at the very least, the agents of central government. Also, central government then hoped that municipal housing would be subsidized from local rates rather than central taxes.

After 1919 and the introduction of subsidies for council housing, municipalities became key providers of social housing for low and middle income groups as well as acquiring powers to control and intervene in more general market provision. This expanded even faster after 1945 with welfare state policies. Nowhere, in Britain or Western Europe, has the association of housing policy and municipal provision been so extensive and so clearly defined as in Scotland (See Tables 1 and 2).

TABLE 1
The Construction of Housing in Postwar Scotland
(quinquennial periods)

Period	Total Output	Private Sector	Public Sector	Council Share of Public Sector
1946/50	89,200	6.0	94.0	83
1951/55	166,100	7.1	92.9	81
1956/60	132,100	2.5	97.5	83
1961/65	154,300	22.6	77.4	81
1966/70	205,000	19.8	80.2	80
1971/75	165,000	34.7	65.3	77
1976/80	133,800	50.6	49.4	60
1981/85	90,800	70.3	29.7	47

TABLE 2
Tenure Pattern, Scotland (percentage figures)

Year	Owner-Occupied	Local Authority Rented	Private, Rented & Other (inc. H.A.)
1966	29.1	47.3	23.6
1976	33.6	54.2	12.2
1986	41.8	49.6	8.5

Source: BSA Bulletin No. 50.

The proportion of Scottish homes rented from municipalities, New Towns and Scottish Special Housing Association (SSHA), has fallen from a peak of 56 percent in the 1970s to just under 50 percent at the end of 1986. Even now some 22 of the 56 district councils have more than half of their stock in municipal housing. It is not just large cities such as Glasgow, Dundee and Aberdeen (63, 57 and 48 percent respectively) which have large municipal sectors. The smaller districts, at the edge of metropolitan areas which had early industrial growth often now have very large public housing sectors. For instance Monklands and Motherwell with 81 percent and 79 council units, respectively, are extreme but not untypical.

The municipal sector is readily identifiable in any Scottish town or village from Aberdeen to Ardrishaig, not just because public and private sectors have been spatially separate in their development but because of the often distinctive styles and materials used in the council sector. In Glasgow, the largest municipal housing authority in Western Europe, some 75 percent of political wards have 50 percent municipal housing and indeed 50 percent of wards have more than 75 percent municipal units. The architecture, geography and visual environment of much of Scotland's cities and small towns is dominated by this municipal movement. And moving beyond the physical, the scale of council housing has permeated economic, social and political relationships in Scotland. These interactions were so strong and pervasive that criticism of social housing was seen as a wider attack on particular social and economic policy approaches. However these correlations of beliefs, objectives and means of policy no longer hold true, if they ever did. Fifty years of intensive housing policy leads us to the current context where there are now doubts that the state will provide more acceptable housing for low and middle income groups than will the market (appropriately assisted). And even if we are to have a social housing sector it is no longer obvious that its governance should be by municipalities. Recent and soon-to-be-announced legislative proposals seek to curtail the municipal role in Scottish housing provision, both by promoting increased private provision and stimulating the rate of non-municipal housing agencies.

This paper, after setting the context of recent developments in the role of municipalities in Scottish housing policy, Section II, considers a number of key issues related to the proposed shifts in policy. The possible reasons for municipal difficulty are considered in Section III and the case for curtailment probed. Section IV, recognizing that there exists a strong government preference for home ownership growth, considers the possible role of municipalities in a new rental sector for Scotland. Finally, in Section V, the likely influences of new legislation is discussed in relation to possible municipal roles.

DE-EMPHASISING THE MUNICIPAL ROLE

Reducing Roles to 1980

In my view, there has been no clear strategy for British, and therefore Scottish, housing policy since the early 1970s. By clear strategy I mean a set of policy actions in which clear objectives are pursued efficiently by appropriate agencies or individuals.

The municipal growth strategy of the period 1955-75 was, on its own terms, quite consistently developed. The key objective was to build shelter units for as many people as quickly as possible. Central government facilitated this process with specific grants. Pooled rents and costs distorted rent-quality relations but favoured increased output. Development issues forestalled the introduction of management systems and monitoring. Tenants views were not regarded as very important. Such procedures would not now all be regarded as desirable, but they were quite consistent with the objectives of the time. Those building the "welfare state" gave scant attention to how it was to be managed and maintained in the long run.

The Housing Finance Act of 1972 whilst never threatening the role of municipalities, was a coherent attempt to relate income subsidies to household needs, and dwelling rents to dwelling characteristics. Since then, until now, we have had no coherent strategy. Labour wandered along from 1974 to 1979 introducing ad hoc subsidy systems and commencing the housing spending cuts so forcefully implemented by its successors.

The 1977 Green Paper on housing in Scotland did recognize, perhaps a decade too late, that a new pluralistic structure was required for Scottish housing. It was the first Labour document to advocate measures to sell council houses and to assist first time home buyers. Thus it recognized, at least implicitly, that municipalities would decrease in relative importance as providers of housing. On the other hand it suggested new roles. Assisting in the private market, cooperation with associations in rehabilitation and special needs provisions were tasks which gave credence to a burgeoning strategic planning and coordination role for housing departments. Municipal housing planning and enabling roles, it was accepted, would offset any losses in municipal control or status implied by their reduced share of direct housing provision.

Finance and De-municipalization Since 1979

The first traces of the 1977 Green Paper were barely in place when the Conservative administration of 1979 was returned. Since 1979 there has been a sharp reduction in housing policy spending in Scotland, but until 1985 it is also arguable that there was no clear, constructive housing strategy.

From 1979 to the present, government has been committed to reducing the public sector borrowing requirement and government expenditure. In the period 1979 to 1984 there was a clear anti-housing expenditure stance in government policy which, as is indicated below, had a major effect on municipal housing. At the same time the key thrust in "housing policy" was tenure change, fuelled by transfer of council and SSHA dwellings to owner occupation. From April 1977 to June 1987 some 8.1 percent of Scottish municipal housing stock has been transferred in this way, often with the lowest sales in the authorities with the highest council shares and vice-versa. Clearly this transfer has reduced the municipal role, though notably New Towns and SSHA had disposed of 26.4 and 17.4 percent of their stock in the same period.

An analysis of current and capital expenditure on housing in Scotland does not sustain the continued cutting perspective of the popular press (See Tables 3 to 6). Analysis of real capital expenditure on social housing in Scotland indicates that overall expenditures fell from 1979/80 to 1985/86, with the exception of election years. As estimates for 1988-89 have also risen by 5 percent after the 1987-88 figure, there has, in fact, been a sustained real increase in social housing investment in Scotland since 1984/85, with the Conservative government of 1987/88 spending more than the Labour administration of 1977/78.

Rising social sector investment need not mean increased municipal investment. The figures in Table 3 make it apparent that in the period of housing investment cutback, the municipalities were particularly curtailed, and their share of spending fell from 78 percent in 1978/79 to 58 percent in 1982/83. It is important to stress that this trend has been reversed in recent years. Each year since 1984/85 municipalities have been given an increasing share of a growing programme.

These shifts do not represent a softening of the government's views on municipal competence. Rather it reflects a growing recognition, by central government, of the need to re-invest in and modernize social housing areas. Almost ninety percent of municipal housing investment is now devoted to modernization. To cope with this growing problem (the COSLA estimated

TABLE 3
Gross Public Sector Capital Spending on Housing in Scotland
1977/78 to 1987/88 (Real, 1987/88 prices)

Spending on Social Housing

	Total spending on Social Housing (real)			Share of Spend Percent		Indices of AM Council Spending on Housing	
Year	Amount	Real Expenditure Index	Councils New Towns	SSHA	HC	HRA	Non-HRA
1977/78	529	100	72	17	11	100	100
1978/79	573	108	78	11	11	99	81
1979/80	639(E)	121	73	13	14	90	68
1980/81	564	106	70	13	17	78	66
1981/82	496	94	65	12	23	75	85
1982/83	500	95	58	15	27	72	104
1983/84	612(E)	116	69	10	21	83	94
1984/85	482	91	61	15	24	63	158
1985/86	445	84	63	12	25	69	100
1986/87	502	95	63	11	24	80	93
1987/88[1]	585(E)	111	69	9	21	99	121

(E)   indicates Year of General Election   [1]   Estimates

TABLE 4
Investment by Social Housing Sectors in Scotland
1983-84 to 1987-88

	Distribution of Scottish Spending on Modernisation			Distribution of Scottish Spending on New Social Sector Construction		
	Percent spent by			Percent spent by		
Year	LAs & NTs	SSHA	HC	LAs & NTs	SSHA	HC
1983/84	66	13	21	59	7	35
1984/85	64	15	21	54	12	34
1985/86	69	11	20	55	10	35
1986/87	71	9	20	55	13	33
1987/88	75	7	18	58	13	20

Source: Public Expenditure to 1990: 91.
HMSO, Edinburgh, 1988.

TABLE 5
The Structure of Revenue Sources in the Scottish HRA

Year	Average Revenue	Proportional Source of Revenue		
		Rents and other payments	HSG	RFC
1977/78	415	52	36	12
1978/79	465	53	34	13
1979/80	579	47	39	14
1980/81	688	50	37	13
1981/82	729	59	25	16
1982/83	758	66	16	18
1983/84	764	71	11	18
1984/85	810	71	9	20
1985/86	826	77	9	14
1987/87[1]	861	83	7	10
1987/88[2]	892	88	6	6

[1] Estimated   [2] Projected
Source: COSLA

TABLE 6
The Growth of Rents and Incomes in Scotland and England
(1977 = 100)

Year	Real Scottish Rents	LA Rents Normal		Average Gross Weekly Earnings		Rent as percent of Average Earnings		RPI
		Scotland	E&W	Scotland	E&W	Scotland	E&W	
1977	100	100	100	100	100	6.1	8.3	100
1978	104	111	106	114	114	5.9	7.7	108
1979	104	122	116	129	133	5.7	7.3	126
1980	103	146	147	153	155	5.8	7.9	146
1981	119	191	205	173	172	6.7	9.9	163
1982	127	224	242	188	188	7.3	10.7	174
1983	130	245	252	203	206	7.3	10.2	183
1984	130	260	264	217	220	7.3	10.0	192
1985	137	287	280	235	238	7.4	9.8	202
1986	145	323	294	251	253	7.8	9.7	208

required modernization cost for the social sector in Scotland is in the range of £7-10 billion) government has increased municipal spending permissions.

This respite may be temporary. Until 1988 SSHA and the Housing Corporation have acquired municipal units for modernization on an ad hoc basis and only with municipal agreement. These agencies were therefore only able to invest limited amounts in previously municipal stock. Urban policy proposals for Scotland, which are in the infancy of their implementation, envisage much wider transfers of municipal stock to other agencies and the private sector. This issue is discussed further below, here we note that if 'Scottish Homes' is successful we cannot expect that real municipal housing budgets will continue to increase in scale.

Central government has also, in an important structural shift, de-municipalized revenue sources in the Housing Revenue Account (see Tables 5 and 6). Real rent increases for council stock are indicated in Table 6. With reduced Housing Support Grant from 1980 onwards, many councils matched subsidy cuts with a combination of rent increases and increased subventions from the Rate Fund. Since 1984/85 comments on Rate Fund spending have reduced the RFC from 20 to 6 percent of current expenditure.

The figures in Table 5 are often used, it should be emphasized *incorrectly*, to suggest that council housing subsidies have fallen sharply since 1980. This deduction is nonsense. Housing benefit now pays 60 to 75 percent of rent increases in Scottish local authorities and, indeed, subsidies arising from historic cost accounting procedures have grown in value over time. The fact that the rent to income ratio has only risen from 6.1 to 7.8 percent over the decade would tend to suggest that real net subsidies may not have altered significantly.

Housing Planning in Retreat

The beginnings of a more pluralistic social housing sector and the cutback environment did not greatly stimulate the planning/enabling role of all Scottish municipalities. Some authorities were hostile to associations, and the Housing Corporation was hardly systematic in the spatial development of its programme across Scottish authorities. Indeed by 1988 an Institute of Housing (IoH) report indicated that only half of Scottish authorities felt that they had developed a "working together" approach with other social housing investors. In most cases cooperation was relatively token in nature.

A review of Scottish Housing Plans by the Centre for Housing Research (CHR) in 1985 also indicated that most were short, bidding documents which provided no analysis and little hard information. Aside from a few notable authorities which prepared well argued plans, such as Glasgow or Gordon District, municipalities were stupid enough to give the government what they asked for.

As an outside, albeit interested, observer it has never failed to amaze me that Scottish housing authorities were never prepared to put a well researched, incontrovertible case for their programme to the Scottish Office. Instead political statement and a few crude figures have driven the reaction against government policies. If it were not for the fact that so many poor Scots live in bad council housing, it would be laughable that in 1985 Scottish local authorities began to argue for a Scottish House Condition Survey. Why, if municipalities have been large scale providers since 1890, don't authorities keep property records? Why do fewer than 20 percent regularly inspect their stock? Why do they not have property record files on repair and disrepair? If authorities were good, caring landlords why did they not already know the conditions their tenants resided in?

It is only in a particularly incompetent or self-deluding industry that 25 years of self-neglect can form the basis of an anti-government campaign. Of course we should have a Scottish Housing Survey, though not like EHCS, but it should not be imposed from the centre but aggregated up from below. Local authorities have to demonstrate an interest in and commitment to strategic and resource planning. The 1980's experience of housing planning in Scotland suggests that central government would be unwise to adopt the view that when municipal management is poor that local authorities should retreat to an enabling, strategic rate. These roles require vision, resources and a good understanding of management. Poor managers may be even worse strategists. We return to this point below.

The Evolving Context

Against this background of shrinking policies and perceptions the Scottish housing system has continued to evolve. On the positive side, over the last decade, more people now live in their preferred tenure, the level of dwelling amenity has improved and the vast bulk of Scots are satisfied with their generally improving homes.

The problem of the last decade has not been falling or slowly rising averages. Rather it has been increasing dispersion around the means. Clearly there is a problem of low income access to rental housing, the numbers of homeless have doubled, needs provision estimates for a range of client groups greatly outstrip present provision and housing and neighbourhood conditions have sharply deteriorated in, say, the bottom 20 percent of the council stock. In spite of still extensive housing subsidies (properly measured) and new targeting measures, it is still the poorest households who receive least effective support from the state. This outcome, in part, reflects the way in which municipalities allocate, price and manage the scarce housing resources provided to them. Recent developments in Community Charge legislation and social security reform which have potentially damaging impacts in poor, rundown estates do not absolve central government of all responsibility for the difficulties in these areas.

Reverting to housing issues, the next section summarizes the causes of the present disorder in many, but not all housing departments.

PROBLEM EVOLUTION IN COUNCIL HOUSING

The remaking of areas council housing has become is the key policy issue of Scottish housing since 1985, perhaps a decade late. The changing context has placed growing demands upon management services. As in England, council vacancy rates increased into the early 1980s but have more recently declined. Rates of rent arrears have doubled since 1980, with the Scottish pattern broadly similar to England outside of London. Repair requests, according to 1985 research evidence[1], had increased by an average of one third between 1980 and 1985. At the same time analysis of 1981 census data indicated that the most deprived small areas in Scotland were no longer in older, private neigbhbourhoods (as in 1971) but in council estates.

The critical issue for Scottish council housing is that rising service demands and deteriorating conditions are usually concentrated into neighbourhoods containing the poorest households. Such locations whilst being most evident in the large cities are by no means restricted to them. Paisley, Perth and Hawick, for example, have all experienced such difficulties.

As noted in the previous section, critics of government policy have argued that council house sales and reduced Housing Support Grant (HSG), with consequent rent rises largely created these difficulties. These arguments are open to doubt. From 1979 to 1986, the Scottish public sector sold around 100,000 units, less than 10 percent of the stock. As most purchasers were middle aged households, often in middle-to-better quality properties, it is unlikely that these houses would have been relet during the 1980s as these groups have particularly low mobility rates. Sales receipts have been available for reinvestment and by the mid 1990s, when the relet effects would have been occurring, shortages of council housing may well not exist. Of course in some smaller, usually rural areas, their negative relet effects are more obvious at an earlier stage. Sales of council houses have so far, had little influence, positive or negative, on the key problems of Scottish council housing.

The difficulties now faced in Scottish council housing, albeit that capital expenditure restrictions have limited the extent of their removal, arise from at least three long term processes. First, council housing has matured adversely. Not only has there been a failure of municipalities to maintain housing stock adequately, and this problem dates from the 1950s and not the 1980s, but relatively new, non-traditional stock has deteriorated at alarmingly early vintages. The physical environments of these areas have matured adversely in the last two decades and dissatisfaction with housing conditions is also highly correlated with neighbourhood dissatisfaction. As residents had little direct involvement in estate design and management, and, of course, have no equity share in dwellings, the external public spaces in public schemes have often fallen into a cycle of disuse and then misuse. Indeed surveys of tenants usually indicate that vandalism, petty crime and inept environmental improvements are the three main sources of irritation in their lives. These were management issues ignored for too long, and indeed the postwar public sector has, for four decades, seemed oblivious to the research observation that the demand for higher quality housing and environments increase with income.

The families who entered the public sector in the boom periods between 1955 and 1975 have also aged and a disproportionate share of those left behind are elderly and single person households. Council housing has become primarily a tenure for the elderly. In Glasgow, for instance, more than half of tenants are over the age of 60, though in general the elderly live in the better council areas. Because of the pricing system, more than a third of these households still live in the house to which they were first allocated when they entered the council sector. At present there is a gross inefficiency in the use of council dwellings with elderly households often living in larger, better quality council houses with younger, poorer families living in overcrowded conditions in the less populated areas.

Much of the public policy debate in housing has argued for better, appropriate housing for the elderly. Of course high standards for all the elderly are laudable. But these standards should not be achieved at the cost of families with children, especially the children of single parent families. We are in danger, perhaps for the first time in half a century, of offering a declining quality of life to children in housing schemes. Infant mortality is actually rising in some areas, Scottish fitness standards of children are low and falling, more smoke and use drugs than ten years ago and educational performance in the most deprived areas is abysmal and reportedly deteriorating. Low housing quality and no prospect of a job is the expectation not the exception for "Jock Thompson's Bairns" in the 1990s. The youngsters of Castlemilk have, now, more in common with those of Northeast Philadelphia, Les Minguettes etc. than with those of their parents only 20 years ago. And worst of all, the housing schemes are becoming self-absorbing systems. In Glasgow's big schemes, 80-90 percent of net new lets go to existing scheme residents forming new households. Such households are generally unwaged and unmarried. We need a housing policy for the young, just as much as the elderly.

The second related process is that these areas, whilst the absolute levels of real council incomes increased into the 1980s, became relatively poorer over time. Aside from the fact that elderly tenants had no stored-up housing asset with which to trade down and extract capital as they aged and retired, the working age population were particularly susceptible to the general increase in unemployment from the early 1970s onwards. Those who would argue that a "dependence culture" is a cause rather than a consequence of neighbourhood decline, would do well to note that the majority of non-elderly adults who are now benefit "dependent" in Glasgow were active in the labour force in the 1970s. Taking the unemployed and the elderly together only one council household in three in the city has an adult in employment. By implication, these social housing areas would still be problematic even if the overall unemployment rate in Scotland were returned to the low levels of the 1960s.

The third process operating is what is often referred to as residualisation and, in Scotland, it is the least important of the three. As areas decline in physical quality and as their residents become relatively poorer they become unattractive to households with any degree of choice. As a result, the poorest areas attract only young unemployed households, jobless single persons and single-parent families in particular. Longer-established council tenants are offered better council housing, or they can wait for the right offer, and younger households with incomes enter the owner-occupied sector. In the longer term, sales policies can aggravate this problem.

SHOULD COUNCILS REMAKE RENTAL HOUSING?

It is now obvious, including to the Scottish Office, that a major reinvestment programme is needed. What is less obvious is whether councils should be the main reinvestors or whether different forms of socially oriented housing landlords, such as associations, co-operatives and trusts should have this major responsibility. This judgement must be based upon an understanding of whether the management capacity or style of councils has improved over the last decade and whether they can operate effectively at the localized scale required for the revitalization of housing and communities.

Although there has been no systematic review of the effectiveness of housing management in Scotland (as there has been for England and Wales between 1985 and 1987) there are some signs that the structure and style of management in Scotland is now changing.

A recent review[2] suggested that around three-fifths of Scottish housing Departments have an integrated structure. Smaller, rural councils, as in England, often spread housing functions to different departments and may not have a "Director of Housing." The reorganization of local government, with housing as the predominant District level function, and the 1980s demise in the power of "planning" departments have often placed the Housing Department at the centre of Council activities.

If "integration" has proceeded apace with England, decentralization of housing management provision is less marked. Some 40 percent of Scottish councils, once again the smaller councils, operate from a single main office. Only a fifth could be said to be operating a decentralized form of management and even in these authorities the frontline management units may be large. For instance, Glasgow regards itself as decentralized, but the average office size is greater than the average size of council housing Departments in England! Small may be beautiful, but it is also a relative term. Allocation, repair provision and rent accounting are the commonly decentralized services.

Almost all decentralized authorities are also extensively computerized. In 1975/76 no Scottish authorities used computers for management purposes. The recent Scottish survey, by J S Aboud, indicated that by 1986 some 80 percent of authorities used computers for rent accounting and housing benefit administration, 45 percent of the organization of jobbing maintenance but only 20 percent for allocation tasks. This latter figure is surprisingly low. However, few Scottish Authorities had developed an integrated computing system capable of adequately serving local or decentralized offices.

Regarding the details of the provision of key services, again Scottish authorities were broadly similar to patterns in England. In the area of allocations policy, points schemes of various kinds were operated in three-fifths of authorities, in contrast to a much smaller proportion in 1976. A further third operated variants of date order schemes and less than 5 percent used policies with officer or councillor discretion as the key consideration. Over the last decade councillors have been removed from day to day involvement in housing allocation in Scotland. More recently, especially in Glasgow, there has been a growing debate as to whether control of allocations policy should be devolved to local area groups including tenants.

Regarding maintenance provision, Stanforth et al indicated that, in common with England, less than a quarter of councils have a clear planned maintenance strategy for their stock. A variety of approaches to response maintenance provision existed. More receipting, better training of staff, increased inspection levels and decentralization were all seen as key requirements for improving the service. Cost effective providers often had large scale usage of Direct Labour Offices (DLOs), as is the case in England, but a worrying place-to-place variation in service administration costs was noted.

Rent collection services in Scotland are more centralized than in England. Three quarters of councils rely on rent collection at offices and only 10 percent use door to door collection methods. Rent payment periods are broadly similar to England with a quarter collected monthly and 40 percent weekly.

There has been no attempt to assess the effectiveness of management of these policies in Scotland. But existing approaches are not entirely consistent with what is widely regarded as good practice. Glasgow is often described as a forward-thinking landlord but in that city three quarters of tenants are dissatisfied with the repairs service and more than half of tenants have expressed an interest in organizing their own repairs. Research has also claimed that the council's allocation policy exacerbates small area social composition problems. And centralized rent collection is generally associated with higher rates of rent arrears.

Compared with the efforts of the Audit Commission, and Department of the Environment (DoE) in England, the Scottish Office have done relatively little to review or reinvigorate housing management practice in Scotland. An exception to this general statement is in the area of tenant participation. The 1980 Tenants' Rights (Scotland) Act extended to tenants new rights concerning succession and consultation in relation to tenancy agreements. Scottish tenants did not gain, in contrast to England, the automatic right to consultation regarding a broad range of housing management matters. However, two other aspects of Scottish Office action did boost tenant involvement. First, in 1980 the Tenants' Participation Advisory Service (TPAS) was set up under the guidance of the Scottish Council for Social Services. TPAs and related measures appear to have had a considerable impact since 1980. In 1980 few authorities had a formal participation policy, there were no housing officers with specific participation responsibilities in the field and there were around 300 tenants' groups and only one Tenants' Federation, in Glasgow. By 1986, 22 of the 56 landlords had a formal tenant participation policy and only 4 had explicitly rejected this management style. The number of tenants' groups has grown to more than 1,000 and there are now 16 Tenants' Federations, generally in larger authorities.

The shift toward management styles and structures involving more and more tenant action, has also been reflected in Scottish Office advice encouraging the formation of tenant management and ownership co-ops. And, in Scotland, much of the current repute of the housing association movement has been earned through their participative approach.

In Scotland, in 1988, no one now doubts that remaking social housing areas and in the process involving tenants is the key priority of Scottish housing policy.

Desiderata in the New Order

There seems to be a number of key desiderata, on the part of central government, regarding the agents to undertake such change. First, does the organization provide levels and qualities of service which are consistent with customers preferences? Secondly, does the consumer have the facility to be consulted or involved in management as well as invest in management decisions? Thirdly, are the service bureaucrats locally accessible and involved? Fourthly, is the organization committed to keeping costs under control, consistent with good service delivery, and in order to do so, is it prepared to contract out services? Fifthly, is the organization amenable to facilitating the shift of units and households to owned tenures? Sixthly, is there a commitment to economize on public finance? Finally, will rents reflect dwelling quality, insofar as this is consistent with client group affordability?

Some councils, in at least some of their stock, may already be implementing such desiderata, but many will not be. Even more would resist such changes, and in these cases municipalities cannot probably expect direct government support. The real question is whether or not housing associations in Scotland can, with stock transferred to them, accept an expanded role.

Recent research in England suggests both large regional associations (of which there are no equivalents in Scotland, except perhaps SSHA) and small associations provide quality services, involve tenants and are locally accessible. And some have stimulated low cost home ownership and equity sharing schemes. However many small associations are high cost, many larger ones fail to capture economies of scale and the use of private finance is only now growing. As in England, the average association spends almost twice as much as councils on management. Associations are better service providers, but at a higher cost. The design of legislation to transfer management does, in theory, leave this choice open to tenants. Government has been correct not to back a single tenure or organizational form for remaking Scottish housing. There is little expectation that proposed changes will produce any long term result other than the de-municipilization of social housing. There is evidence from Canada, Sweden, France and the Netherlands to suggest that good social housing is a function of good design, realistic pricing, targetted subsidies and good management and not on specific municipal forms of provision. Our recent experience of municipal housing in some parts of Scotland is enough to suggest at least a partial de-municipilization of social housing.

MUNICIPALITIES AND THE HOUSING BILL

There is little doubt that the 1988 Housing Bill contains measures which could fundamentally change rental housing provision in Britain and in favourable ways. Whether or not it will do so depends upon the way in which Ministers select the specific measures and provisions, for instance the HAG rate, to achieve the broad objectives of the Bill. For unlike many legislative statements forming British housing policy, the 1988 Bill was long on important ideas and principles and very short on particular measures.

Equally, in relation to 'Scottish Homes', as the location, staffing, budget and style of this organization are yet to be determined, it would be unhelpful to speculate on the details of its future operation. However this section sets out key tasks which, as well as existing SSHA stock and association activity, will confront 'Scottish Homes' into the 1990s. The 1988 legislation discussed in this paper should be regarded as an experiment, with the terms and location of the trial as yet to be determined. In broad terms, the experiment is concerned to increase the scale of private investment in rental housing (private and social tenures alike) and to upgrade the housing and neighbourhood qualities of rental areas. Although the renewed interest in rental housing, which dominated discussion of the Bill, is to be welcomed, it is important to bear in mind that government still regards further expansion in home-ownership as its key housing objective, especially in Scotland.

New Private Renting?

The private housing sector is both now small (6 percent of households) and still declining in scale, even if the furnished letting sector in Scottish cities appears to have stabilized in scale in the 1980s. Critics with a free market orientation are right in identifying rent controls as a deterrent to new investment and, therefore, as contributing to the decline in scale and quality of the sector. However they would be wrong to suggest that controls were the sole or main source of decline since the 1960s and that their removal will provoke a sudden burgeoning of market rented housing. For most British households long-term housing solutions are provided by the owner occupied sector, reflecting taxation arrangements, financing systems etc., or the social rented sector, usually where income levels preclude access to owner occupation.[3] Government does not wish to prioritize renting tenures ahead of owner occupation (given its wider "property owning democracy" ethos) and it is not at all clear that, even if there were to be more generous Housing Benefit levels, private lets are a desirable solution for low-income "family" housing.

There is, however, a case for liberalizing private rental housing in order that it might play its "specialized" housing tenure role more effectively. The 1988 Act adopts this argument for deregulating rents on new lettings and moving away from the Fair Rent regime. New lets will have rents agreed between tenant and landlord and security of tenure will be either on a shorthold or assured tenancy basis. The key advantage of private rental housing is that it has low entry and transaction costs for residents. The tenure is potentially useful for those who know that they will shortly be moving again or those who are uncertain about future housing requirements. Mobile households of all ages, couples living together prior to selecting a longer term residence, temporarily relocated employees, etc. all constitute potential markets. Demand is further diversified by households with relatively limited short term access to capital, such as young singles setting up home for the first time or the recently separated or divorced.

Much of this demand is presently met by the furnished rental sector and although as many as two-thirds of such lets are already made outside the Rent Acts, there are obvious signs of shortage of such accommodation, particularly for good quality apartments. These patterns suggest, in the foreseeable future, that deregulation will neither greatly increase rental supply nor will there be a significant increase in rents vis-a-vis housing prices in general. The new landlords such as Quality Street and the Business Expansion schemes, initiated by solicitors in Glasgow, are likely to find a profitable but unlimited niche in providing central city, quality lets for young mobiles and singles.

Calls for a more generous tax regime for rental housing to extend the middle income rental market are unlikely to receive Treasury support. The eligibility of private rental schemes for Business Expansion Schemes, tax concessions announced in the 1988 Budget, are likely to mark the full extent of such concessions. A general tax break for landlords would largely mean competition with tax-subsidized owner occupiers. Wasted tax expenditures and higher land and housing prices, especially in the more pressured and popular area where such schemes appear to be most widely advocated, are the likely outcome. Such effects would be less pronounced if landlords received tax subsidies to upgrade existing properties or convert derelict or commercial properties into homes.

Looking further to the future, demographic patterns are not now greatly conducive to a marked increase in the stock demand for private rental housing. The unfurnished relict will literally die off. A more promising market for private landlords may be to induce the growing elderly population, and particularly the post 75s to release capital by selling to responsible landlords and leasing back. Such a market would be curtailed, of course, by any major growth in maturity lending. None of these changes in private rental provision seriously threatens the role of municipalities.

Transfers and Municipal Housing

Although a large scale expansion of private renting seems unlikely there is some prospect of expansion in direct private investment in stock transferring away from local authority ownership and thus facilitating de-municipalization. The legislative proposals of early 1988, whilst in no way discouraging individual right-to-buy sales, contained the radical proposal that council tenants should be allowed to select an alternative landlord. Stock transfer proposals came to be regarded in a number of different ways. Many critics saw the measure as being driven by central government's continuing pressure to curtail the role of local government. And many argued that 'privatization' was the key theme. There is no doubt that transfers could reduce municipal roles in the housing field and tilt the balance of ownership and provision tilt from public to private sectors.

There is another possible interpretation, namely, that the government attack is aimed at monopolies rather than council status per se. Council monopoly provision in the low income sector could produce low quality services. Naturally, some right wing commentators believe this to be true of all councils. Interestingly, major speeches by Mr Rifkind (Secretary of State for Scotland) have made it clear that efficient councils, meeting their tenants' aspirations, would be little influenced by transfer activity. Certainly, from the housing analysis standpoint it is difficult to see how competition or potential competition in social rental housing provision, if adequately supervised, could have an adverse effect on tenants. In due course it could also be argued that tenants should be able to transfer to councils and away from other social landlords if tenants prefer such solutions. The pick-a-landlord proposal is then, potentially, a rapid route to a more pluralistic social rental sector. There is no inevitable connection between good social housing and municipal ownership and provision. Nor indeed are social housing slums the preserve of municipalities, and government should note this for the future – changes in ownership will not solve all of the key issues in rundown estates.

If there is a case for the general principle of pick-a-landlord, it is still possible to be less than convinced that the proposed implementation strategy is adequate. In England, during 1988, more than 100 local authorities, many of them rural authorities or authorities with a council stock of less than 5,000 units, approached DoE, the IoH and potential alternative landlords to discuss the possibility of transferring stock. Voluntary municipal interest of this kind appears to have been on a much smaller scale in Scotland, with no more than four or five authorities making such plans.

As yet there have been few approaches originating from tenants groups in either Scotland or England. The Housing Corporation are to be charged with promoting and approving alternative landlords in England. 'Scottish Homes' and 'Homes for Wales', the new quangos constructed from existing organizations to promote new rental sector policies, will have these responsibilities in Scotland and Wales.

If pick-a-landlord is to operate pervasively in Scotland, 'Scottish Homes' will have to counter quickly the active and vigorous campaigns of opponents, who are out in the estates on a day-by-day basis, and which are sometimes fuelled by fear rather than fact. Recent research shows that less than 1 percent of council tenants know what a housing association is, that less than 10 percent of tenants will undertake participation to change their areas and that pick-a-landlord is perceived as 'a return to the private landlord'. Many older tenants in council housing suffered costly indignities at the hands of private landlords for decades. They will stick to the 'devil they know' unless the alternatives are promoted locally and clearly and continuously. How will 'Scottish Homes' do this? Will it create incentives for associations to promote transfers or create co-ops from municipal housing? If associations follow this route, will the smaller, high-cost associations adapt their management systems to cope with change, will they lose their caring reputation if they grow markedly in scale? Financial inhibitions to transfer are considered further below.

Transfer votes for a potentially transferring area, are to be organized independently but paid for by the new potential landlord. A majority of tenants have to vote against the transfer proposal for it to fall. That is abstensions/non-votes count as 'yes' votes. Government may have been better to stick to basic democratic principles on this issue and to have devised a more intensive promotion strategy.

Obviously tenants will not transfer solely on the issue of service quality of municipal/anti-municipal ideology. They will be concerned with tenants' rights, their security of tenure, rents and future rents, opportunities for involvement and prospects for modernization. The Government, after much internal discussion, came to the view that tenants in transfer schemes would not have a 'Social Housing Tenancy' but rather rely upon selecting the contractual terms of assured tenancies. This decision, may demonstrate a lack of understanding of how many tenants perceive such issues – if they have a complaint or grievance they will generally prefer to visit their councillor or area housing manager rather than have recourse to lawyers and contract enforcement. Such a view pays scant regard to the income and indeed educational levels which now prevail in many of our worst housing estates. In the absence of Social Housing tenancies, securing customer confidence may take a long time and much patience on either side.

The prices at which estates transfer will be critical in determining the attractiveness of transfer. Currently it is proposed that 'tenanted' values are set but clearly this is an area for much dispute where councils are hostile to transfers. Naturally, central government can encourage stock transfer through finance and subsidy systems. As long as central government controls overall housing capital spending, it may shift potential modernization resources from councils to other investors through 'Scottish Homes'. However, major changes in capital grants to housing associations (see below), could compromise the potential rate of transfers. In autumn 1988 the Government produced its consultation documents for housing revenue accounts and capital spending. These papers suggest quite major changes which could increase council rents and discourage rent pooling, all of which facilitate transfer policies.

There is now a potential for a major reorganization of social housing in Britain. Poor promotion and conflicting financial decisions could compromise such changes. And where changes do take place, care will have to be taken that competition continues and we do not see the formation of new, local and non-municipal monopolies. In general growing pluralism will not mean extensive privatization. Private landlords such as 'Quality Street', are not likely to have access to higher modernization subsidies than associations and co-operatives (in my view they should have equal subsidy rights if competition is to be tenure-neutral) and they do have a requirement to make a surplus. Unless private landlords are going to be more efficient than social landlords by a considerable margin they will not be able to compete extensively.

Housing Association Finance

Housing associations, in spite of their past and likely future dependence of public subventions, are now to form an "Independent Rented Sector" along with Private Rental Housing. This grouping makes no real sense, but let us leave aside the labels and examine the substance of the movement. There are more than 180 associations in Scotland, providing homes for more than 50,000 households. Aside from a few large national associations they have been accustomed to operating on a small, often local scale, building houses and rehabilitating homes with the support of communities and municipalities. Most have little experience, in recent years, of fast growth and of coping with local political hostility.

Housing associations, as a number of recent studies have shown, do not now constitute a "privileged" sector of social housing provision. Their resident populations are as poor as council tenants, unemployment rates are similar and age structures are not dissimilar. As associations mature, some of them are also showing some signs of inadequate maintenance, serious mismatches of stock size and household type and symptoms of wider neighbourhood deterioration. Set beside this, however, the majority of associations have achieved impressive levels of customer satisfaction. Rent levels approximate those of authorities, although capital grants (HAG) have commonly financed 80 percent (and more) of development work. As indicated above, associations, apart from lower cost regionals/ nationals, are good but expensive managers. It is not surprising that government has often chided councils to aspire to the service performance levels of associations (at least on most management indicators). But government advocacy of the virtues of associations has peaked, just as a new financial regime for associations is being devised. Government discussions of associations, throughout 1987 and 1988, stressed that neither capital grants (HAG) nor current subsidies (RDG) and external rent setting encouraged efficient resource use. In general the marginal additional costs of capital projects fell upon HAG expenditures rather than rents or association surpluses. External rent-setting and the clawback of surplus revenues (Grant Redemption Fund) meant that associations had minimal incentives to economize on current spending until allowance levels were reached.[4],[5]

If government were correct in the identification of these problems there are fewer grounds for being convinced by the proposed solutions, particularly in relation to capital grants. Private finance, whether raised by individual associations (expensively) or the Housing Finance Corporation (less expensively through economies of scale and expertise), can only be raised where investors are satisfied by investment returns and risk prospects. The value of existing housing as an asset base against which to secure further borrowing is a concept which has gained a fresh currency since 1987, and major finance institutions are showing a renewed interest in funding housing in the rental sector. Even if the security of the asset base reduces risk, rates of return still have to be earned. Early "mixed funding" schemes in England were financially viable through a number of ad hoc financial adjustments. Land and property was made available to associations at below market values, some subsidized new investment from existing surpluses and assured tenancies allowed rent levels above "Fair Rent" levels. Clearly such ad hoc arrangements could not underpin a major expansion in private financing.

To secure more widespread use of private finance, government has proposed that HAG levels be reduced and rents increased. Scottish housing associations are now expected to have an average HAG level of 75 percent, some 10 percent below those of 1987. Where schemes contain at least a 50 percent share of private money the government will class this proportion of investment as "private"; if the private share is less, the whole project will be regarded as public (as the public sector will be regarded as bearing the investment risk). Associations could choose to build upmarket schemes with low HAG rates, say in rehabilitation activity competing with grant aided private landlords (whose investment is all regarded as "private" even with 50 to 75 percent improvement grants)! These could then be "mixed" with schemes for more traditional client groups. Naturally if HAG is reduced rents will rise, even if major economies in management and maintenance could be secured, and the proposed HAG reductions are likely to increase rents by 50-100 percent on new projects.

At this juncture the exercise becomes frustrating for central government. A series of surveys, albeit that none of them recorded income levels in the exhaustive but expensive fashion of government surveys, has revealed that almost two-thirds of association tenants in Scotland and England alike receive Housing Benefit and for those in employment wages are sufficiently low that more than half of tenants in employment would have rent to income ratios in excess of 30 percent in the new financing regime. It might have, in retrospect, been easier to stretch association finance if a revised (correct) conception of "public" spending had been adopted by the Treasury and some of Hill's suggestions on index linked financing has been adopted. As a result of these proposed changes, government now faces some very difficult choices. If HAG rates are reduced with no change in Housing Benefit arrangements associations and their tenants will face considerable difficulties. And if these difficulties are severe, there is little prospect that associations can become the new landlords for disintegrating council empires. If that is the case the bold conception of the 1988 Bill will not give birth to a new order for social housing in Scotland.

CONCLUSION

During the next decade we are likely to see a marked reduction in the role of municipalities in the Scottish housing system. Home-ownership growth will continue, transferring households from municipal to private sectors. Investment in social rental housing will be aimed at upgrading the quality of the sectors rather than expanding its role. To the extent that modernization capital is channeled via non-municipal agencies and that council tenants pick alternative landlords, then the municipal role will diminish.

The pattern of response will differ from area to area but the management systems and financial structures of council housing will have to be altered markedly if councils are to compete. Local authorities will have to upgrade their performance as housing planners if they are to be regarded as the key strategic housing planners.

Professor Duncan Maclennan, Centre for Housing Research, Glasgow University.

References

1. Stanforth, J, MacLennan, D, and Malcolm, J. 1986, 'The Delivery of Repair Services in Public Sector Housing in Scotland'. *Central Research Unit Paper*, Scottish Office, Edinburgh.

2. Aboud, S J, 1988. 'An Integrated Computing System for Housing Management'. Ph.D. thesis, University of Glasgow.

3. Kemp, P. 1988, 'Privately Rented Housing'. *Report* to the Rowntree Trust.

4. Hills, J. 1987. 'When is a Grant Not a Grant?'. *LSE Suntory-Toyota, Discussion Paper Series*, No.18.

5. Kearns, A. 1988. 'Affordable Rents and Flexible HAG: New Finance for Housing Associations.' *Discussion Paper No.17*, Centre for Housing Research, University of Glasgow.

WHOSE RESPONSIBILITY?

ANALYSING CONTEMPORARY URBAN POLICY IN SCOTLAND

Robin Boyle

Introduction

In 1988, the future of urban Scotland, and the appropriate policy response, was once again a topic of considerable political interest. While Mrs Thatcher was on her travels north to analyse the failure of the Scottish Conservatives in the 1987 election, particularly in the urban constituencies, she came to learn and be impressed by the recent "success" of Scottish urban policy. Moreover, in the summer of 1988 she was intrigued by a plan suggested by Bill Hughes, Chairman of the CBI Scotland, to create "Enterprise Scotland" based on a merger between the Training Commission (TC) in Scotland with that of the Scottish Development Agency.(SDA)

Going back twelve months, following the June 1987 election victory, the Conservative Government announced renewed commitment to the "inner cities", linking urban Britain into a wider domestic policy programme based on the central tenets of: securing a strong private economy; shifting responsibility away from the state; creating a climate of opportunity; removing obstacles to development; promoting choice and investing in people. Mrs Thatcher's Foreward to the brochure "Action for Cities" launched in March 1988 clearly articulates the link between her ideology and urban policy:

"There is, of course, nothing new in urban change. Throughout our history towns and cities have risen and fallen only to rise again. Some have responded to new markets and technologies. Others have clung to old ways and allowed opportunities to pass them by. A number have suffered from civic hostility to enterprise. All too many have had their problems intensified by misguided post-war planning and development which had the best of intentions but the direst results for the people living there".

"Every area covered by the term (inner city) shares one common need: new hope for the future. The Government is resolved, in partnership with the people, to generate that hope and help create a new, lively environment in which to live, work and prosper."[1]

Closely following this (largely) English initiative, a "new" urban policy for Scotland was announced in March 1988, with programme details lavishly presented in the brochure *New Life for Scotland*.[2] Publication of this report presents an opportunity to examine critically recent government statements on and affecting urban policy in Scotland and perhaps isolate commonality of policy redirection. This paper examines the relevant policy statements from "New Life", and reviews the urban policy implications of: the 1987 consultative document "Scottish Homes"[3] and the subsequent White Paper[4] on changes to Scottish housing legislation; the "Enterprise" White Paper from the Department of Trade and Industry (DTI)[5] the National Audit Office's review of the Scottish Development Agency[6] and their own 1988 Annual Report.[7] Comment will also be made as to the relevance for urban policy of the so-called Hughes initiative to create Enterprise Scotland.

A theme common to these and other urban policy statements, and one very much in line with the overall direction of Conservative policy, is that of disengaging the State from certain urban problems and placing *responsibility* for improving urban Scotland on to a combination of the private sector, acceptable community groups, the family and ultimately the individual. Hence, the focus of this review is to assess the likely impact of the "new" urban policy, and to gauge the response such initiatives will have on the wider policy community throughout Scotland.

Policy Comparison

First, a few introductory comments that will serve to place developments in Scottish policy into a GB context. It is important to draw certain distinctions between Scotland and England in terms of the objectives, the delivery and the implementation of urban policy. In 1987 and certainly in the first half of 1988, English urban policy was directed from the DTI, with Lord Young and Kenneth Clarke (both originally working together in the Department of Employment) extending the activities of the *City Action Teams (CATs) and particularly the Task Forces* to spearhead developments in urban policy.[8] Neither of these mechanisms operate in Scotland. The original purpose of the CAT was an attempt to improve inter-departmental coordination between the Department of the Environment (DoE), DTI and Department of Employment (DE)/Manpower Services Commission (MSC) and, after changes in 1985, to increase the importance of employment and training through the Urban Programme, thereby enhancing the status of DE/MSC.

It is important to stress that the CATs were not designed as a conduit for substantial additional urban funding. Other than receiving funds for administrative and promotional activities, their initial role was to influence the pace and direction of existing resources. The original five CATs were, however, each allocated an additional £1 million just prior to the June 1987

General Election. These funds were to be used for projects falling between or outside the guidelines issued by the four main Departments. This level of funding was repeated in 1988, suggesting that the CAT's have the capacity to develop a modest executive function. Moreover, the allocation of a recurrent grant, the emergence of the CAT "Action Plans" and the recognition of inner city problems within the DTI, suggests that the CAT's have matured beyond mere promotion and now play a more proactive role in urban policy implementation.

The Task Force was the second Young/Clarke urban initiative while they were both at the Department of the Employment. Eight "pilot" areas were launched in February 1986, with a further eight announced in April 1987. This variant on the Task Force model was once again introduced with the objective of coordinating and channeling existing resources. The key difference was that the Task Forces would also have additional funds to target at particular communities – indeed to local people – within defined inner city areas. All Task Forces began with additional funding of £1 million per annum to be allocated in the form of grants or soft loans to appropriate projects in each area.

While the broad structure of the 16 Task Forces is similar, the implementation and management of each is different. All Task Forces are led by senior civil servants, mainly from the DTI, DE or MSC, seconded to the local area for the duration of the initiative. They "employ" a range of assistants, some funded from the seed capital, others, such as local business advisors, sponsored by local businesses or by branches of national companies. All operate from within the designated area: some from shop units on the High Street, others in small offices or converted industrial units.

In Scotland, the co-ordinating role of the CATs was taken by the SDA, particularly in their programme of Area Projects that had evolved from earlier Government initiatives to address severe economic problems in Glengarnock and Clydebank. The Department of Employment Task Forces has no Scottish equivalent but the Hughes model, launched to an unsuspecting public in August 1988, would appear to have the same enterprise-led focus. It is not altogether surprising, therefore, that the Hughes plan caught the attention of Mrs Thatcher and Lord Young.

Towns and cities in Scotland have also been spared the imposition of the Urban Development Corporation (UDC). Originally established in 1981 on Merseyside and in the London Docklands, this model of urban regeneration was extended in 1987 to cover another five main UDC's in the Black Country, Teeside, Trafford Park, Tyne and Wear and in Cardiff and then four "mini-UDC's", in Bristol, Leeds, Sheffield and Central Manchester. While originally given a wide remit that embraced the concept of "ensuring that housing and social facilities are available to encourage people to live and work in the area"[9], the direction of UDC activity and indeed the balance of expenditure reveals a marked shift in programme intention.

Indeed, this is a feature common to both Scotland and England. Looking at the latter, where the data are more readily available, it is clear from Government reports that urban policy is concerned, first and foremost, with support for the private sector and that spending through the Urban Programme is now part of a wider policy of supporting profitable urban enterprise, with government funds increasingly used to "lever" private investment. In 1979/80, the so-called "Urban Block" (including spending on the UDC's) was made up of £207m for "spending to assist private investment" and £109m allocated for "spending on social and community projects". Expenditure in the financial year 1988/89 is expected to reach £593m in support of the private sector, with £118m for social and community activities, in effect, a considerable cut for the latter activity over the past nine years.[10] Comparable data for Scotland are not available but the refocussing of policy – and the new lead being taken by the Scottish Office – suggests that a similar ratio of expenditure will be a key objective in the coming years.

A central feature of English urban policy, especially those parts driven from the DoE, has been a sustained assault on the powers and responsibilities of local government. Central government certainly no longer believes, as it once did in the 1977 White Paper on the Inner Cities, that "local authorities are the natural agencies to tackle inner area problems". Instead, the DTI/DoE have evolved an approach to urban policy based on the centralisation of certain functions (an example being the way in which local government has effectively been excluded from the operation of the new City Grant) and a proliferation of agencies, public and private, that fragments the implementation of policy, "further diluting the role of local government".[11] Moreover, the new housing legislation in England and Wales, introducing the Housing Action Trust to the lexicon of urban policy, serves to residualise accountable local government, turning housing responsibilities over to community organisations, or householders or indeed, private companies.

New Life for Scottish Urban Policy?

Originally trailed as a White Paper, *New Life for Urban Scotland* was issued in March 1988 as a hybrid "Blue Paper": a combination of colourful brochure and detailed issues analysis, objective formulation and "proposals for action". In comparison with the English Action for Cities, however, 'New Life' is indeed a robust document. Its strengths are that it draws together the different, often confusing, strands of urban policy; gives credit for specific urban achievements: "results are there for all to see and the economic potential of areas (in GEAR) once neglected is now being realised"; clearly identifies the key problems – unemployment, lack of investment, run-down housing; and, in marked contrast to what can be found in the English report, states that urban policy must address the problems of:

> "people suffering from multiple deprivation; a combination of the problems of poor environment, high dependence on state benefit and poor housing. Related problems are a lack of social and recreational facilities. These problems co-exist with high crime rates (including vandalism), poor health and low educational achievement" (para.12)

Similarly, the objectives laid out in the report focus on the priorities identified from the earlier analysis of urban problems. Social objectives are clearly ranked in first place, with the subsequent economic goals linked to "improving the abilities of residents in deprived areas to initiate small businesses and to compete for jobs" (para. 13 vii). Moreover, there is recognition that different towns and communities require different prescriptions; there are no cure-alls. But in looking to the "Way Ahead", New Life shows the influence of the dominant thrust of central policy with the principle of making the residents responsible for their communities. In Malcolm Rifkind's Foreword to the document he states that:

> "Future action should be based firmly on the principles of helping residents take more responsibility in various ways for their communities, of full involvement of the private sector, and of partnership between different public bodies and the private sector."

> "It is especially important that we renew the self-confidence and initiative of local people and help them to assume increased responsibility for their communities. That is why, for example, our housing policies aim to increase people's control over the houses they live in, and our education policies offer parents increased responsibility for their local schools. We must make it easier for people to exercise greater influence over their own lives and make it easier for them to use their fair share of the opportunities provided through economic recovery and growth."

And in line with that other component of government policy, 'New Life' sees a central role for the private sector:

> "The Government are committed to increasing further the involvement of the private sector in urban renewal, both their wider economic policies which increase business confidence, and through encouraging investment in deprived areas" (par.17);

> "The Government look to the private sector to continue to regenerate urban areas by pursuing opportunities for profitable

investment, and *hope* (emphasis added) it will examine carefully the scope for investment in areas currently neglected. For example, the peripheral estates enjoy very little private investment in any form. Where necessary the private sector must work in close partnership with the public sector. We *want* (emphasis added) to see the private sector involved from the outset in new urban regeneration initiatives".(para.19);

No evidence is presented to justify the "hope" that private investment will flow into the most problematic areas. Indeed, the Blue Paper conspicuously ignores academic and government studies that show how very difficult it is to attract large scale private investment into marginal locations.[12] There is a real danger that the success of "leveraging"[13] private capital into the city centre can be simply transferred to the peripheral estates. Indeed, 'New Life' does just that, where photographs of warehouse renovation in Glasgow's Merchant City are juxtaposed with public sector housing improvements in Barlanark. Ironically, the successes then cited in the report are almost exclusively determined, funded and implemented by the state: by Government itself, by its agencies such as the SDA and the Housing Corporation in Scotland (HCiS), and by other organisations in receipt of state subsidy, including the "remarkable" network of local enterprise trusts.

The report is at its weakest when prescribing on Scotland's urban problems. While "attaching great importance" to four initiatives in selected peripheral estates: Castlemilk (Glasgow), Ferguslie Park (Paisley), Wester Hailes (Edinburgh) and Whitfield (Dundee), it says almost nothing about what will be done, nor does it give any indication of additional funding. While briefly mentioning existing work in areas such as Barlanark (Glasgow) and Forgewood (Motherwell) it clearly fails to identify the lessons learned by the SDA and local authorities in a variety of very difficult urban locations – in Barrowfield, in Wester Hailes and in Drumchapel. Moreover, the authors of the Blue Paper have short memories. In selecting Ferguslie Park, they make no reference to the failure of the Community Development Project (1970-1975) centred on the same locality nor do they comment on the experience of the Comprehensive Community Programme introduced to Craigneuk (Motherwell) in 1976. Both initiatives were funded by central government and directly involved Scottish Office civil servants.

Predictably, political comment on the Blue Paper was divided, Scottish Labour MPs were less than impressed: "Too little, too late," (David Marshall, Glasgow Shettleston); "He's given us the HP sauce but where's the bloody meat" (Norman Buchan, Paisley South); "The statement does not face the problems of the mining communities which are suffering severe dereliction" (Dick Douglas, Dunfermline West); "a sad anti-climactic, gathering up of bric-a-brac from the past, packaged in a way that borders upon dishonesty" (Donald Dewar, Glasgow Garscadden). On the other hand, the Secretary of State called the programme "the most significant initiative ever taken to change the face of Scotland's giant estates" and commenting on the reaction of the Labour MP's, Nicholas Fairbairn (Perth and Kinross) speculated that "if Mr Rifkind were to announce Christmas the Opposition would treat it like the Crucifixion."

What Role for Scottish Homes?

The Government places considerable emphasis on the new housing agency, Scottish Homes, for the delivery of their urban initiatives. First announced in May 1987 in the Consultative Paper, the proposal to create a merger of the Housing Corporation in Scotland with the Scottish Special Housing Association was developed in the 1987 White Paper, *Housing: The Government's Proposals for Scotland*, then taken through Parliament as the Housing (Scotland) Bill for enactment in the summer of 1988.

Much has already been written about changes to Scottish housing legislation but for the purposes of this paper, three points are worthy of additional comment. First, the rhetoric of new housing policy is the same as in the Blue Paper. The White paper states that:

"The Government will continue to support the growth of home ownership to which it is clear the vast majority of people aspire. Home ownership gives people independence and control over their housing; it gives them a sense of greater personal *responsibility* (emphasis added); and it helps to spread the nation's wealth more widely" (para.1.7)

"The dominance of the public rented sector has become a negative factor in some parts of Scotland, effectively constraining choice and detracting from the achievements of the public sector." (para.1.11)

Yet, as in *New Life for Urban Scotland*, the details of achieving such a strategy are not discussed. The implications of shifting responsibility for housing are not assessed, and while rental deregulation and support for assured tenancies are promised, there is no indication, other than allowing market forces to operate, how the new legislation will assist those families currently living in the poorest living conditions, on both sides of the tenure divide.

Second, the White Paper indicates that Scottish Homes will "promote a co-ordinated approach to the complex problems of large peripheral housing estates" (para.2.5). Moreover, Scottish Homes will have certain powers to assist with the environmental aspects of urban renewal and will be able to provide "financial assistance to employment-related aspects of projects primarily related to housing" (para.2.11). A concern widely expressed, however, is that these and other powers will be used to lever private sector investment that may, once more, have little bearing on those families already living on the poverty line. A recent study of the possible impact of Scottish Homes in the Pollok Scheme in Glasgow suggests that less than 10% of existing households maintain an income capable of sustaining investment in even the most heavily subsidised owner-occupied property.[14]

Third, from comments made by Scottish Office Ministers, Scottish Homes may take a very active role in subsidising private sector housing, perhaps even taking some of these responsibilities away from the SDA, LEGUP[15] support for private housing development being a case in point. Again the evidence suggests that such subsidies are useful and can induce house builders into the peripheral estates, but often only for a short period. Instead, a classic cycle may be introduced: policy is developed on the basis of objective urban analysis that identifies the most distressed localities; programmes are then devised and implemented to induce private investment into the most marginal areas: evaluation criteria are developed in order to determine policy impact including measuring leverage ratios; policy analysis reveals the "best" leverage ratios are found in communities favoured by the private sector, and not surprisingly these may not be in the worst localities; and policy is then changed to support developments with the highest ratios of private to public investment. Consequently the areas in most need look the least attractive. Moreover, staff taken from the private sector to run Scottish Homes may indeed feel that such policy redirection is indeed correct.

Will There be an Entré for the SDA?

The evolving functions of Scottish Homes in the field of urban regeneration need, however, to be viewed in a wider policy context. The different "enterprise" initiatives: the White Paper, *DTI – the department for enterprise*, its Scottish Counterpart, the Hughes plan for Scotland, the organisational re-organisation of the SDA and the role envisaged for Enterprise Trusts in the Blue Paper, all suggest that central responsibility for urban policy is shifting, that the nature of programme implementation will be very different and that the distribution of urban resources will no longer follow familiar routes.

Looking at the SDA in more detail, the appointment of Iain Robertson in 1987 as the new Chief Executive resulted in a significant reorganisation of the Agency structure. Central functions were simplified with urban policy and programme support mainly channeled through two central directorates: Property Services and Urban Renewal and Industry and Enterprise Development. Seven Regional Directorates were then created, each responsible for: property development and management, business development, land engineering, investment and area projects. On paper, the new structure has considerable merit with a much closer and clearer link between specific companies/communities and the advisory/support/ investment functions of the Agency. While it is much too early to pass judgement on the effectiveness of the new structure, sources within the SDA suggest that the detailed knowledge of urban policy, especially complex urban development skills, has been dispersed to the regions and that the new Property Services and Urban Renewal directorate may, despite the confident listing of their functions in the Annual Report, be unable to capitalise on the knowledge of urban development carefully built-up over the past decade. Only time will tell. Yet, it may be significant that *New Life for Urban Scotland* was not issued from the SDA but was clearly the product of the Industry Department in the Scottish Office (IDS).

What is significant, however, is that the Blue Paper effectively marks a sea-change in Scottish Urban policy. For the best part of twelve years[16], the SDA has been at the very centre of urban policy, in terms of analysis and innovation, programme development and project funding. Indeed, with the benefit of hindsight, the series of Area Projects that covered much or urban Scotland had three valuable assets that no longer appear as important in current thinking: (1) a clear urban focus, (2) a measure of community commitment, and (3) involvement by the local authorities at member and officer level. Instead, 'New Life' focusses more narrowly on specific problems (mainly in public sector housing schemes), finds little space for local government and places considerable emphasis on the future role of some 40 local enterprise trusts (agencies):

> "The local enterprise agency movement in Scotland, led by the private sector through Scottish Business in the Community exemplifies the potential role of partnership in encouraging and assisting local communities to adopt an entrepreneurial approach to their problems. Such arrangements offer a cost-effective means to encourage local growth through self-employment, small business development and the creation of community enterprises. There is ample scope to develop such activities" (para.21)

And that is precisely what the Hughes initiative of combining the activities of the Training Commission in Scotland with that of the SDA, would seem to suggest. The SDA's new regional structure is not sufficiently localised for what Mr Bill Hughes sees as the future enterprise structure in Scotland. Instead, and building on the lead given by the DTI White Paper and the accompanying document from the IDS, Hughes "wants the whole package of support for enterprise – factory space, financial support, market intelligence, and the supply of trained workers – to be delivered through a network of local, one-door user-friendly agencies, where existing business talent makes the lead contribution."[17]

The Hughes plan also gives Government another opportunity to trim the sails of the SDA. Earlier, following publication of the National Audit Office (NAO) report on Agency involvement with the private sector, the influential Public Accounts Committee had been less than impressed by the answers to their questions given by SDA's senior management. At issue was the "but for" question: would a particular product or company or property development become commercially viable "but for" the investment, in grant, loan or equity, from the SDA? The funding arrangements and assistance to Laing Homes in connection with the Glasgow Garden Festival and SDA's financial commitment to the Scottish Exhibition and Conference Centre attracted the Committee's attention, generating an amount of critical press coverage. Notwithstanding the poor press, the NAO was generally satisfied that there had been no commercial impropriety, that the SDA operated basically sound appraisal procedures and that previous weaknesses in monitoring arrangements were being remedied.

But viewed from a different angle, the NAO report and the criticism from the Public Accounts Committee represent further pressure on the SDA to look to the private sector to take responsibility for a range of activities. Three points from the Report stand out. First, the NAO applaud the transfer of factory provision from the public to private sectors; second, following the 1986 Treasury/Industry Department for Scotland review of Agency activities, the Report repeats the conclusions that "the SDA could do more to encourage the private sector to provide (advisory) services" (par. 2.13); and third, "the Agency have stated however that they would not intervene in a way which would impair commercial decisions in order to secure wider development benefits" (par. 3.34). This suggests that private, commercial, interests come before the public good, representing a marked change from the original activities of the SDA, when it was expected to use its powers in such a way as to secure the maximum public benefit; and that market intervention should be part and parcel of its work.

Thus, what Hughes is suggesting and appears to be eagerly supported by Ministers, is a set of "enterprise" initiatives whose fall-out will affect urban policy. Control will be firmly held at the centre, the SDA's role will change, funding will be based on leverage principles with the private sector expected to pay for much more, and programme implementation will become the *responsibility* of local agencies mainly staffed from the private sector.

Conclusion

Recent reports and statements concerning Scottish urban policy – from the Blue Paper through to the possible impact of the Hughes initiative – make light of the difficulties of urban economic adaptation. Change is painful and costly. Individuals, families and local communities are often the most vulnerable and least capable institutions for withstanding the pressures of economic adaptation. Families in poverty and communities racked with deprivation of all forms are even more vulnerable to the impact of change. Moreover, shifting responsibility for improving community on to individuals and families can have unintended consequences, not least the problem of neighbourhood protectionism. There is already sufficient evidence from local education reform of the negative aspects of fierce community protectionism. Taking another example, increasing personal responsibility through home ownership may indeed improve parts of the housing stocks but at the expense of other, less fortunate, areas. Is there not some danger that terms such as "shifting responsibility" and "increasing personal choice" is a code for diverting or indeed reducing public support for problem areas?

Second, despite the rhetoric of the Blue Paper, there is little evidence from recent Government pronouncements that the new shape of urban policy has any real concern for *place*. Some fifteen years of political restructuring, supported by right-wing philosophical reasoning, has resulted in an effective assault on "place". When Mrs Thatcher declares there is no such thing as society, she offers even less prospect for urban society. Her vision for the future of the UK would, as in much of the US, be simply an endless collection of comfortable suburbs where personal redress to property law would replace any form of collective land use regulation. In the city centre, the market will determine the shape and pace of development, perhaps with the help of simplified planning zones and the like. It is no accident that the Adam Smith Institute, a major influence on spatial legislation over the duration of the Conservative governments, modelled its land use ideas on Houston, Texas. Unfortunately, the Adam Smith Institute have not looked at Houston for a number of years as it is this major US city that has suffered most from the decline of the petro-dollar. Subsequently there has been a withdrawal of investment capital from a number of downtown projects resulting in mobilisation to strengthen the powers of the city council, not least in terms of land use planning.

Not only does Government listen to the views of the right wing on urban policy, it is also attracted by the critique of urban administration, especially a set of arguments that conveniently undermine local politics. To dismiss "place" – towns, cities, maybe even the Regional Councils in Scotland – as a unit of government is to dismiss the basis for accountable governance at the local level. Not surprisingly, British local authorities, of all political hue, offer a measure of opposition to centralised policy. Such opposition, however, doesn't figure in the plans of the present Administration.

Strong, place-related urban policy therefore is as much about government as it is about improving economic, social and physical conditions. Mrs Thatcher knows that, and has set a course that will effectively dismantle meaningful urban government in England. Mr

Rifkind has not, as yet, gone quite so far, but his policies will eventually lead to the same result. And it comes as no surprise to learn that the Adam Smith Institute is already pressing for a root and branch review of Scottish local government. With the regions dismantled, with education fragmented to the School Boards and with housing powers passing to 'Scottish Homes', accountable local government in Scotland's towns and cities could become little more than a feature of the past. And who then will be responsible for urban Scotland?

Third, and at a more prosaic level, this interpretation of urban policy *ownership* has potential implications for Scotland. In the policy gap before Scottish Homes, in the midst of the SDA's corporate reorganisation, and with increasing central direction from New and Old St Andrew's House, urban policy is drifting perilously close to the English border. With the SDA under considerable pressure to disengage from active urban involvement, the IDS will assume control. But what experience do they have of working closely with local government and local communities? Experience from the recent past would suggest very little indeed. At best they exhibit a cool detachment, at worst down-right hostility, towards Scottish local government. Furthermore, the Hughes model, enhancing the role of Enterprise Trusts, therefore presents an ideal opportunity to combine this central control with the parallel objective of extending the role of replacing local public agencies with a private alternative.

This then appears to be the strategy. Both the enterprise culture and the future shape of urban Scotland will be created by a shift towards more personal and family and business *responsibility*. And this neatly squares the policy circle – less cost, weaker local government, more privatism – just like the South East. The Conservative answer to the Labour's domination of urban Scotland?

Robin Boyle, Centre for Planning, University of Strathclyde.

References

1. Cabinet Office (1988) *Action for Cities*.London.

2. Industry Department for Scotland (1988) *New Life for Urban Scotland*. Edinburgh, Scottish Office.

3. Scottish Development Department (1987) *Scottish Homes*. Edinburgh, SDD.

4. Scottish Development Department (1987) *White Paper – Housing: The Government's Proposals for Scotland*. CM 242. Edinburgh, HMSO.

5. Department of Trade and Industry (1988) *White Paper: DTI – the department for enterprise*. CM278. London, HMSO.

6. National Audit Office (1988) *Report by the Comptroller and Auditor General. Scottish Development Agency : Involvement with the Private Sector*. HC 478. London, HMSO.

7. Scottish Development Agency (1988) *Annual Report*. Glasgow, SDA.

8. Boyle, Robin (1988) City Action Teams and Task Forces. *LEDIS Overview Series*. Planning Exchange, Glasgow.

9. *Local Government, Planning and Land Act*, 1980.

10. Cabinet Office, 1988, *op cit*, pp 15.

11. Stewart, Murray (1987) "Ten years of inner cities policies". *Town Planning Review*, 58, 2, pp. 129-145.

12. for example see, Keating, Michael and Robin Boyle (1986) *Remaking Urban Scotland*: Strategies for Local Economic Development. Edinburgh, Edinburgh University Press; and Donnison, David and Alan Middleton (1987) (eds) *Regenerating the Inner City: Glasgow's Experience*. London, Routledge and Kegan Paul.

13. "Leverage" is the term applied to the ratio of public-private investment that occurs in particular areas or projects. Originally used in US urban policy, leverage ratios are now commonly applied to projects in the UK.

14. "Scottish Homes and Pollok" (1988). Unpublished report, *The Centre for Planning*. University of Strathclyde, Glasgow.

15. LEGUP: Local Economic Grants for Urban Projects, administered by the SDA.

16. see, Boyle, Robin (1988) "Private Sector Urban Regeneration: The Scottish Experience", in Michael Parkinson, Bernard Foley and Dennis Judd (eds) *Regenerating the Cities: The UK Crisis and the American Experience*. Manchester, Manchester University Press; pp. 74-92.

17. Young, Alf (1988) "Positive blueprint for Whitehall". *Glasgow Herald*, September 3, Glasgow.

THE POLITICS OF RURAL DEPRIVATION*

Arthur Midwinter, Colin Mair and John Moxen

Bacground

For about twenty years, successive British Governments have had policies for tackling deprivation. In government, the problem of deprivation has been regarded as an urban one, reflected in physical and environmental decay, unemployment, poverty, and overcrowded housing conditions. By contrast, images of rurality have consistently been highly romanticised versions of everything that rural life is not, and particularly so in the Scottish Highlands. According to Knox and Cottam, there is a fictional image of:

> "a spectacular heatherclad landscape dotted with picturesque cottages and inhabited by hardworking but unimaginative ginger-haired people who love accordian music, dressing up in kilts and sporrans, and live on whisky and porridge – has been particularly effective in obscuring some of the harder aspects of rural living conditions."[1]

There have been attempts recently to redress the balance[2], but nevertheless, these two sets of images, on urban and rural deprivation, are completely consonant with the present urban focus of deprivation policy. Deprivation is regarded as an urban *phenomenon*; a *multiple concept* combining several facets of disadvantage, including low income, unemployment, poor housing, lack of basic amenities and services, and a poor physical environment, whose interaction provides the problems of the disadvantaged; and *spatially concentrated*, and this areal focus led policy-makers to believe the problems were politically containable within identified geographic areas. Most of the policy initiatives, such as the Urban Programme, Educational Priority Areas, or Housing Action Areas, sought to practice *positive discrimination* through the preferential concentration of resources to areas or institutions in greatest need, and *community regeneration*, whereby patterns of economic and social decline would be reversed through community action and self-help.[3]

In England, rural responses to government policy began in response to Peter Shore's 1977 announcement that the causes of urban decline were structural, and required shifts in resources in mainstream programmes, such as the Rate Support Grant, as well as the special schemes of assistance.

Several reports recording the existence of rural deprivation were produced, and demands for additional funds for tackling rural deprivation were made. So far, these have been resisted. These argued that rural deprivation is less visible and less concentrated than urban deprivation and, moreover, has qualitatively different manifestations in social isolation and inaccessibility to public services on grounds of both location and low levels of provision.[4]

In Scotland, the lead in raising the initiative on rural deprivation was taken by the regional and district councils in Strathclyde. A Joint Working Party was formed in 1979, which reported in 1982. It concluded there were special problems in Strathclyde's remoter rural areas. This research showed that these remoter rural areas typically have a higher cost structure and lower income base than the Strathclyde average. These three factors combined – special problems, low indigenous income and high costs – put the remoter rural areas at a serious disadvantage compared with more favoured areas. It made recommendations for local policy changes to respond to these needs, and suggested the creation of an independent rural aid fund as a desirable and necessary complement to existing provision.[5]

The Joint Working Party Report was submitted to the Convention of Scottish Local Authorities (COSLA) who agreed to raise the matter with Government. In 1985, the Scottish Office and COSLA met to discuss the proposal by the local authorities for the creation of a Rural Aid Fund, with aims and format similar to Urban Aid.

The Scottish Office Minister, Mr Alan Stewart, responded by pointing to the recent evidence of the article in the June 1985 issue of the *Scottish Economic Bulletin*, which purported to show that in general rural areas were faring better than other parts of the country and the level of government assistance in the main sectors of economic activity was higher per head of population than elsewhere. He saw a need to define what problems the proposed fund should assist, given the assistance already available through the Scottish Development Agency and other services, to ask whether such purposes were not already served by local authorities existing powers, and which new resources outwith the Rate Support Grant were needed.

The Convention's response was to associate its proposals with a counter-deprivation strategy. It saw the fund as serving the remoter rural areas of rural Scotland as distinct from the generality of rural areas, some of which had problems of social deprivation which paralleled those of deprived urban areas and justified a similar response from Government. The main orientation of the fund would be of a social and community nature, and therefore be complementary to the work of the SDA. The Fund was needed as authorities lacked the resources to tackle the problem.

The Government was unconvinced by these points, and rejected the proposals formally in a letter of April 1986, arguing along the lines used by the Minister at the meeting. In doing so, it linked COSLA's request for a Rural Aid Fund with the Committee on Scottish Affairs' recommendation for a Rural Development Fund, and saw the general considerations set out in the Government's reply to the Committee as being equally relevant to the COSLA proposal. This must in itself be dubious, as one proposal was concerned with economic development, and the other with social and community development. But, in short, the Government's response was to say it was *already allocating a lot of resources to rural areas, and the case for increasing this was not justified.*

The response to the Committee simply set out the main government spending programmes. It noted that the SDA spends 25% of its main programme budgets in rural Scotland, which represents only 20% of the total population. The Government gives extensive financial support to rural areas in the area of *transport.*

In terms of the *health* service, the formula for resource allocation (SHARE) recognises the particular problems of sparsely populated areas by a weighting in the assessed demand for community health services, and through other specific schemes. For *local authority services*, the RSG provides a further means of support for rural areas, as the client group approach to grant distribution takes special account of the needs of authorities in sparsely populated areas, by ensuring that their extra costs of providing services are recognised more precisely and systematically. The combined effect of these measures, it was claimed, was that the Government was already providing a range of assistance to rural areas well in excess of the £25 million proposed budget for a Rural Development Fund and, therefore, such a fund would be unlikely to make any significant contribution to the needs of rural areas beyond the present extensive measures of support.

The local authority initiative in response to this rebuttal was taken by Dumfries and Galloway Regional Council, who commissioned consultants to provide a critique of the Government's position. This was completed in March 1987 by economist Tony Mackay. In reviewing the article in Scottish Economic Bulletin, which formed the essential basis of the Government's response, he concluded that it was "more an attempt to provide evidence to support the view of the Scottish Office that rural areas are treated favourably in central government spending programmes than an objective analysis of the data available. By a selective choice of statistics, it gives a misleading picture".[6]

Mackay's analysis concentrated on the economic statistics in the paper, and did not tackle the issues raised by the Government over the Scottish Health Service Resource Allocation Scheme or RSG. He argued that the concentration was on direct support of economic activities in rural

Scotland and Scotland as a whole, thereby excluding public expenditure where the economic impact is indirect, e.g. through infrastructure provision. In terms of agricultural assistance, Mackay argued that it was misleading to imply that agricultural expenditure is a form of rural subsidy, as it is intended to help consumers throughout the UK and the EEC. Moreover, the focus on support for the rural economy ignored special assistance to 'urban' economic activities and, as a result, the conclusion that rural Scotland received about 49% of relevant central government expenditure was erroneous. A more accurate figure would be 19%.

As important, for present purposes, the emphasis on economic development monies ignored a whole dimension of COSLA's proposal which related to social and community development, not economic development. A central concern in relation to rural areas is the low availability and accessibility of public services, and this in itself may compound the problem of rural economic development by making many rural areas unattractive prospects for business and industrial location. Within the Convention, the whole issue has been referred to its Economic Affairs Committee, and the emphasis has shifted somewhat to a rural "Development" Fund rather than a Rural Aid Fund. Our concern, however, is with rural deprivation. In this article, we seek firstly to evaluate the arguments made by government about rural needs and, secondly, to examine the evidence about the existence of rural deprivation in Scotland.

Deprivation and Resource Allocation

We should begin, therefore, with a definition. An official Scottish Office study suggests the following:

> "Deprivation is a concept frequently used in the discussion of social inequality. It has no precise meaning, but a household may be said to be deprived when its welfare falls below some generally agreed standards. The concept goes beyond the single notion of financial poverty, i.e. insufficient income in terms of some standard of need, to encompass other aspects of welfare observed from or influenced by the activities of the state, for example, the provision of health care, education, housing and recreational provision."[7]

In short, it is clear that it is 'resources' not simply financial income that should be related to needs and this includes central and local government service provision in support of "generally agreed standards". Although part of the aim of measuring deprivation is to target public services, access to public services themselves will also be central to measuring deprivation in the first place.[8]

In our view, this creates a major conceptual and measurement problem for public policy, as the most readily usable data, the Census, takes no account of the "access" issue, and we shall return to this later in the paper.

We noted that the Government's response to COSLA was simply to point to its general expenditure programmes which benefit rural areas. From a *rural deprivation* perspective, the key mechanisms are those in support of public services, and here the Government's response is quite disingeneous. For example, the benefits gained by rural areas through SHARE arise from the weighting they receive which reflects the widely recognised high unit costs of service provision in rural areas, rather than the existence of deprivation. In fact, the Government only recognises deprivation as a needs factor in two programmes, Urban Aid and the Rate Support Grant, and therefore the rigour of Government's argument that existing resource allocation systems already take account of rural needs stands or falls by these two programmes. Spending on other programmes per se is not evidence that rural deprivation, the focus of the COSLA initiative, is adequately covered in existing programmes when these have entirely different objectives. Moreover, existing resource allocation mechanisms also purport to take account of the needs of urban areas, but they still benefit from additional monies through the Urban Programme.

In the main, resources are allocated to tackle deprivation through two main spending programmes, the Rate Support Grant and the Urban Programme. Local authority revenue expenditure programmes amount to something over £3 billion in Scotland, but only a very small proportion of that is in recognition of problems of deprivation. Expenditure under the Urban Programme is about £30 million per annum. The Urban Programme seeks to channel funds to local authorities with problems of social deprivation. A recent review of the Urban Programme in Scotland stated the intention of "agreeing lists with authorities to focus the Programme's resources in the deprived *urban* areas of greatest need".[9]

This report notes that the statutory power for the Urban Programme requires the expenditure to be incurred in ....."any urban area of special need" but does not in itself define 'urban', and confirms the political decision to continue with the broad approach of defining areas with a population of over 10,000 as urban. In terms of multiple deprivation the resources will be concentrated in those areas in the worst 10% based on enumeration districts.

In short, as a second Scottish Office paper makes clear, urban aid is "seen as a main funding mechanism for inner city policy", with the emphasis on encouraging local authorities to adopt an area-based approach to problems of urban deprivation.[10]

The governmental review of the programme concluded that the Urban Programme has proved itself to be of value in mobilising resources to tackle the problems of areas of special need. Its priorities are:

- to continue to use an *area-based* approach focusing upon deprived areas and those at risk of deprivation.

- to emphasise the importance of *voluntary effort* by giving priority to projects undertaken by voluntary effort.

- to support projects involving the *mobilisation of private sector resources*.

- *no net increase in local authority staffing* should result.

We would draw attention to two dimensions of the Urban Programme that cast doubt on the efficiency and equity of concentrating additional resources on a narrow band of urban areas. First, although area deprivation is presented as *the* central criterion of the programme, it is at present a necessary but not sufficient condition for resource allocation. It acts as an initial filter in the sense that authorities can apply for funding only on behalf of certain areas. Thereafter whether a project put forward is funded or not depends entirely on the merits and relevance of project applications.

Central to this will be demonstrating client need (for innovatory social services, for playgroups and nurseries, play areas and schemes etc.), and the degree to which a proposed project meets other criteria suggested by government from time to time, e.g. co-ordinating voluntary, private and statutory provision. The decision to fund any particular project is therefore based on client need and related criteria, *not* area deprivation criteria. All the area criteria do are to ration the right *to apply for* resources; they are not used to ration the resources themselves.

The Urban Programme, therefore, combines area and client criteria within the one programme. The problem is that it does so in an illogical, inefficient and inequitable way. It is illogical because, in allocating resources to client based services, areas warranting additional resources should be defined in terms of concentration of client need for particular provision. In the Urban Programme, the right of concentrations of clients to have their needs met is determined by where they live. Location becomes the primary criterion, not concentration of need, yet within the targeted areas specific projects are then funded in terms of demonstrated client need.

Further there is now considerable evidence that deprivation is far more widespread than originally assumed, and this is certainly true of Scotland as a whole, with the major exception of Glasgow.[11] Where the majority of deprived people do *not* live in 'areas of deprivation', and substantial numbers of those living in such areas are not themselves deprived, the basis of the area approach is highly questionable. Equivalently sized client groups with equivalent needs, e.g. poor elderly people with high support needs, will have their access to additional service determined by where they live, not in terms of their living conditions and state of welfare. Equally, non-deprived families in deprived areas get the benefit of additional educational provision, while deprived families in non- deprived areas do not. Where the basis of service provision is client need, it is unfair to ration resources by locational criteria.

It is also inefficient as a mechanism for meeting need. Again, for client services, any resource mechanism based on the 10% worst areas, by given deprivation criteria, will target resources on a minority of deprived households. It is inefficient because areas viewed as deprived because of their elderly populations can apply for additional resources for child services, and vice versa. *The combinations of indicators used to identify areas stand in no direct relation to the projects actually funded.* Finally, it is inefficient because it assumes that putting additional resources into areas is an effective mechanism for getting services across to the most deprived households, whilst in practice, the better off in these areas may also benefit.

The second major point is that, though the deprivation element is emphasised, the programme has emphasised innovation and experimentation in service development, and the need to co-ordinate statutory and voluntary effort. It has also emphasised projects that diminish demands on mainstream budgets and are therefore cost beneficial. Indeed, Strathclyde Region, the major beneficiary of the programme makes service innovation and cost-benefit in relation to mainstream budget control criteria for evaluating funded projects.[12]

The Urban Programme may therefore be viewed as an action research and development fund that finances attempts at improving the cost effectiveness and target efficiency of local authority provision by permitting experiments in alternative types of service and patterns of service delivery. The evidence is that urban authorities have used the opportunity intelligently and well. Intermediate treatment (IT) in the social work area is now widely recognised to be a cost-effective alternative to previous institutional provision, and is now part of mainstream provision. In education, home-school link initiatives and pre-school education initiatives have become part of mainstream policy. In leisure and recreation, community development approaches that evolved within urban programme funding have become central to recreation policy. All these experiments were possible because authorities were not forced to carry the initial funding liability alone, and successful experiments can then be taken over into mainstream funding.

The research and development dimension of the Urban Programme would be of crucial importance to rural authorities. Given the initially lower service base available and given the serious problems of service delivery to a highly dispersed population, rural authorities have a particular need to experiment and innovate in both types of service and strategies for service delivery. Equally, given low resources overall, the availability of monies to stimulate and co-ordinate voluntary and informal provision with public provision would be of great importance. At present, rural authorities who perhaps most need it are denied the experimental capacity that the Urban Programme gives urban authorities. Indeed, innovation in service development and improved cost-effectiveness is, perhaps, the major success story of the Urban Programme, and it is a very questionable economy to withhold resources to facilitate this from rural authorities.

The second major resource allocation mechanism is the Rate Support Grant, which the government believes systematically takes account of the needs of rural areas.[13] It is certainly true that the Resources Element of the Rate Support Grant, which seeks to equalise the tax raising capacities of local authorities, provides considerable benefit to the majority of rural authorities who have a low rating resource base. However, the biggest portion of the grant is distributed through the Needs Element, based on a series of factors deemed to be indicative of an authority's need to spend, and it is in this portion that any allowance for rural deprivation would be made. In fact, as it operates, allowances for deprivation uniformly allocate money *to* urban areas, and *away from* rural areas.

Assessments of needs are based on the Client Group Method, which allocates a predetermined level of expenditure provision among local authorities, or estimates of their relative needs. A primary indicator is defined for each component of a service, which is seen as being the main determinant of demand and having the strongest influence on expenditure. Thereafter, secondary indicators redistribute allocations of resources where factors outwith the control of the authority also influence expenditure.

In our view, the basic principles of the Client Group Method are sound. There have been some problems of conceptualisation and measurement in practice, but client group treatments are subject to a continuing process of refinement and development, and this has also been the case with "deprivation".[14]

The use of multiple deprivation as a need indicator in the client group approach has been as a *secondary indicator*, though the variable itself has changed on several occasions. The Client Group Method was used first as the basis of current expenditure guidelines in 1982-3, and then for Rate Support Grant in 1984-5. When first used, however, there was only *one* secondary adjustment for multiple deprivation. This was in the social work casework and administration category, where a strong relationship was found between expenditure per client and multiple deprivation.

As a result, the government decided to make an *ad hoc* adjustment of £18m to direct resources to certain urban local authorities, because:

"The government consider it important that local authorities where the incidence of multiple deprivation is higher than average should receive more resources to cope with this problem."[15]

However, the Convention of Scottish Local Authorities argued against such ad hoc policy adjustments. As a result, the Multiple Deprivation Allowance was withdrawn in 1983-4, and reviews of the impact of both sparsity and multiple deprivation were included in the Work Programme of the Distribution Committee of the Working Party of Local Government Finance.

The impact of the introduction of the Client Group Method was a broader recognition of the incidence of deprivation and sparsity across authorities. By 1984-5, only three regional and two district services had adjustments for deprivation whilst seven regional and three district service treatments had adjustments for sparsity, and rural authorities gained resources as a result. This would appear to support the Scottish Office view that the method takes systematic account of rural expenditure needs, but that needs qualification.

It is certainly the case that client group assessments successfully identify high unit costs of provision *in some services*. Where service provision is heavily influenced by national standards, and broadly comparable throughout the country, the higher unit costs in rural areas will be revealed through regression analysis. There is, however, a second dimension to sparsity, which is central to evaluating whether the method takes account of the manifestations of rural deprivation, this reflecting the case for additional resources in a Rural Aid Fund. That is, where the costs of service provision are so high that only minimal provision is made, then the expenditure need for such provision *will not* be revealed by correlations with past expenditure. In short, the unmet need resulting from low levels of public service provision, which is central to any concept of rural deprivation, is ignored for the purposes of Rate Support Grant.

The Central Research Unit noted this problem in a report on sparsity to the Distribution Committee:

"Either the need for the service, as judged by the providing authority is low and the service is not provided at all in parts of the area, or is provided at a lower level, or that the costs of *providing a service* are so high that only a minimal service can be afforded."

Moreover, the paper shows that the method cannot take account of the latter factor:

> "In the light of discussions held recently with a number of authorities, it is evident that *local discretion* is a major factor in determining expenditure and therefore authorities having the same rating on the sparsity measure may expend a *significantly different* amount of money per unit of primary indicators on the same service.
>
> The Client Group Method attempts, through its use of secondary indicators, to distinguish between those demand factors which reflect actual need (usually a large number of clients together with those production factors which affect costs of provision locally) from these factors which reflect the demand for a higher quality of service.
>
> If needs factors are not *reflected in actual expenditure*, then the method *assumes that need is low* and therefore it *cannot* take into account situations where, even with *high need* and/or *high unit provision costs, expenditure is low*." (our emphasis)

This is precisely the situation pertaining in many remoter rural areas.

The result is, therefore, that the service availability dimension of rural deprivation *will not be* revealed by correlations with past expenditure, as low provision will result in low spending. Moreover, the only adjustments made for deprivation are based on the urban indicators developed in connection with the Urban Programme, and have the effect of directing resources away from rural areas, although conceptual improvements have been achieved in some services by shifting from area or household measures of multiple deprivation to more direct indicators of deprived groups.

In total, some £25m of expenditure need is redistributed for deprivation factors, and this is only 0.43% of total expenditure provision for regions, and 1.1% of district expenditure provision. However, this amount in total is almost as large as the entire Urban Programme, and the resources are concentrated in Strathclyde Region. At regional level, Strathclyde Region gained the resources at the expense of all other authorities, whilst at district level, ten districts in Strathclyde and Dundee gained from the adjustments.

There is little evidence that the problems of rural deprivation are accommodated within either the Urban Programme or the Rate Support Grant. Certainly, in the latter case, one of the important characteristics of rural areas, namely sparsity, is recognised as causing high unit costs. But the initial approach from COSLA to the Scottish Office was for a rural equivalent to Urban Aid. As we have seen, rural areas and the rural poor have no equivalent scheme, and in the Rate Support Grant, deprivation is still treated as mainly an urban phenomenon.

In fact, the Rate Support Grant takes *no account of the accessibility dimension* of rural deprivation at all. In areas of high discretion, where provision and spending are low, then need is also regarded as low. This is a serious defect of the client group methodology as it stands. Finally, rural expenditure needs have been under-assessed because of the inappropriate measures of urban deprivation which have been used.

CONCLUSION:

Rural Deprivation exists and warrants a Public Policy Response

The Government's response to local government's request to establish a Rural Aid Fund and that rural needs are adequately met from existing public expenditure is an inadequate one. We have shown that *no* allocation of resources to tackle the specific problems of rural deprivation exists, and that the effect of deprivation allowances in the RSG is to take resources *away* from rural authorities. Yet a large number of studies point to the existence of rural deprivation on a scale which warrants a public policy response. Miller's study, for example, shows that area measures of deprivation considerably under-estimate the extent of rural deprivation.[16]

Moreover, there is evidence that poverty and deprivation is concentrated amongst the same groups in rural areas as in urban areas; the elderly, the unemployed, and low income families. Rural areas have a "top heavy demography", a disproportionate proportion of elderly people in the population. As Knox notes "a disproportionate number of the poor are elderly and a disproportionate number of the elderly are poor". On his estimate, the incidence of multiply deprived pensioner households is higher in rural than in urban Scotland, and accounts for well over 50% of multiply deprived households in rural areas.[17]

The predominance of agriculture in the rural economy as a source of employment has in recent years been highly associated with low income occupations and unemployment. The Rural Indicators study, for example, suggest that the proportion of households in low socio-economic groups is higher in rural Scotland than in urban Scotland.[18] On Knox's data, family size does not significantly differentiate the urban and rural deprived, therefore the needs – financial resources balance is at least as bad proportionately in rural as in urban areas. However, it should be noted that whatever the proportions of population involved, the absolute number and concentrations are very much lower in rural areas. This should be balanced however by noting that low income rural households face higher costs of living, a point demonstrated by the Scottish Consumer Council's "Rural Price Survey".

The demographic and socio-economic composition of rural Scotland is therefore indicative of levels of deprivation equivalent to urban areas. This, however, has been argued on the basis of income considerations above. The third theme emergent from rural deprivation studies focuses on access to the other resources that support lifestyle and welfare, and the interaction of economic, demographic and public service factors in reinforcing patterns of deprivation. Studies have emphasised what are regarded as the two quite distinctive features of rural deprivation, namely low levels of public service provision, and poor accessibility to services, which underly the pattern of rural deprivation.

Constraints on public expenditure have over a number of years led to the contraction of rural services and the concentration of service provision in larger settlements. This adds to the problem of access, although only a minority of households do not have access to a car, and Moseley has argued that what matters is not households without the use of a car, but groups such as children, women, the elderly and the disabled, in short, the rural majority.[19] With the decline in rural public transport, and the contraction of services, the problem is real indeed.

Finally, we believe that the conceptual basis of deprivation policy, and the measurement problems which results from it, serve to compound the mistaken views of the incidence of rural deprivation. Deprivation is a more widespread phenomenon than originally envisaged and in part this original failure reflected the attempt to provide measures of multiple, concentrated deprivation. Edwards rightly notes that it is unacceptable to adopt a 'hotch potch' approach "in which any variable deemed by the researcher to be vaguely relevant has been thrown in to the statistical melting pot".[20] As Hatch and Sharrot argue, there is a need for more precise and relevant indicators with greater illustration of causality.[21]

In practice, area-based positive discrimination is difficult to implement through the mainstream programmes of local government. A Scottish Office study, which monitored the impact of the Urban Programme, showed that 40% of the projects served all the residents of a particular area.[22] Strathclyde Regional Council, which has one of the most extensive deprivation strategies in local government, found a very high use of nursery schools in Areas of Priority Treatment by children from outwith the area.[23]

That Region's review of its own social strategy shows that the sheer complexity of the process of designing Urban Programme projects diverts attention from the fundamental issue of directing mainline policies and budgets to the problems of the disadvantaged. After seven years of an area based strategy, this review still concluded that in future:

"...the Council will adopt a more rigorous and aggressive approach to the implementation of its policy of positively discriminating in favour of the most disadvantaged. It will be particularly important to ensure that this policy is applied to all appropriate mainline budgets of the Council.

Conventional budgeting and staff dispositions have largely been inherited and as recent information has shown there had been only a limited levelling up of services in the Areas of Priority Treatment. The annual budget review is concerned only with the marginal activities of the Council. There has been a reluctance to examine how services can be made more relevant to local needs and indeed how staff, our most valuable resource, should be deployed."[24]

The existing stance of government towards rural deprivation is therefore one of complacency. There is clear evidence that poverty and deprivation exists on a substantial scale in rural areas, and that the extent of rural deprivation has been consistently under-assessed by government. Secondly, the access dimension of rural deprivation is ignored for public resource allocation.

We do believe, however, that these issues could be tackled through a Rural Aid Fund which recognises the rural dimension of deprivation. As the Scottish Office's Urban Renewal Unit noted, deprivation:

"is not a single or simple concept – there are many different forms of deprivation which require to be measured in different ways, and proposed action must be based on detailed knowledge of particular circumstances."[25]

This means that, in the rural case, rather than defining areas of eligibility, the emphasis should be on concentrating benefits on deprived groups, within a policy framework which accommodates that diversity. This would require a concern for specific projects meeting the needs of specific deprived groups, within a coherent local deprivation strategy.

Each project would therefore:

1. Identify the deprived groups at which the project is targeted.

2. Identify the *relevant community* at which the project is targeted, in terms of settlement. This would discuss both the distance from 'service centres' and the adequacy of public transport availability. In our view, with limited resources, there is a case for limiting approval to settlements more than ten miles from service centres rather than the five miles suggested by the JWP.

3. *Specify the policy objectives* that the project is seeking to meet.

4. Illustrate that the proposal is both *innovatory* and *cost-effective* in relation to mainstream programmes.

5. Demonstrate that the project is part of a *coherent local strategy* for tackling deprivation, and not simply an ad hoc way of supplementing mainstream service provision.

There is a substantive case for the introduction of a Rural Aid Fund, as part of the national commitment to retain and invigorate rural communities. Our view is that the £3m proposed by the JWP is too modest, and does not reflect the incidence of rural deprivation, which at individual household level is about the national average, and the rural share of the total population, which in terms of the definition used in government, is about 30 per cent in settlements less than 10,000. If the Urban Programme is the comparable government programme, then an appropriate sum would be about £10m. To date, an understandable concentration on urban deprivation has led to the neglect of those socially deprived in rural areas. The creation of a Rural Aid Fund would be a recognition of that, and stimulate community-based renewal in the remote rural areas. Equality of access to public services may be difficult to achieve in practice, but that is no excuse for not trying. A Rural Aid Fund would be a valuable step in the right direction.

*The authors are grateful for the financial support of Angus, Annandale and Eskdale, Clydesdale, Ettrick and Lauderdale, Nithsdale, Sutherland and Wigtown District Councils, Highland Regional Council, Shetland Islands Council, and Community Work North, for their research programme into Rural Deprivation in Scotland.

Arthur Midwinter, (Department of Politics) and Colin Mair and John Moxen, Department of Administration, University of Strathclyde, Glasgow.

References

1. Knox P and Cottam M B (1981) "Rural Deprivation in Scotland: A Preliminary Assessment" in *Tijdschrift voor Econ in Soc. Geographie*, No 3.

2. See for example Walker a (ed) (1978) *Rural Poverty: Poverty, Deprivation and Planning in Rural Areas*, Poverty Pamphlet No 17 (Child Poverty Action Group) and Mosely M (1979) *Accessibility: The Rural Challenge* (Methuen, University Paperbacks).

3. For analysis of urban deprivation policy, see Higgins J, Deakin N,

Edwards J, and Wicks M (1983) *Government and Urban Poverty* (Basil Blackwell) and Lawless P (1981) *Britain's Inner Cities: The Problem and its Solution* (Harper and Row).

4. Association of County Councils (1979) 'Rural Deprivation', (Report).

5. JWP Report (1982) The Remote Rural Areas of Strathclyde: Strengthening the Response (Strathclyde Regional Council).

6. Report prepared for Dumfries and Galloway Regional Council.

7. Miller A (1980) A Study of Multiply-Deprived Households in Scotland (*Report*) (Central Research Unit, Scottish Office).

8. For a fuller discussion of these issues, see A Midwinter, C Mair and J Moxen (1988) Rural Deprivation in Scotland (Report) (Department of Administration, University of Strathclyde, Glasgow).

9. Scottish Development Department (1985), the Urban Programme 1986/87 (Circular to the Local Authorities).

10. Central Research Unit (1984) The Urban Programme in Scotland: Results of a Monitoring Exercise (Scottish Office).

11. Knox P L (1985) "Disadvantaged Households and Areas of Deprivation: Microdata from the 1981 Census of Scotland" *Environment and Planning* volume 17 pp 413-425.

12. Strathclyde Regional Council: Notes accompanying Urban and Project Evaluation Form.

13. Central Research Unit (1981) Client Group Studies of Expenditure Need (Report: Scottish Office).

14. For a critique of this view, see Mair C, Midwinter A and Ford C (1985) Assessing Local Expenditure Need: Problems of Theory and Measurement in the Scottish Client Group Approach, *Certified Bulletin No 15*.

15. Midwinter A, Mair C and Ford C "The Politics of Rate Support Grant Distribution" in D McCrone (Ed) *Scottish Government Yearbook 1986*.

16. Miller A *op cit*.

17. Knox P L (1985) *op cit*.

18. Central Research Unit (1978) Rural Indicators Study (Scottish Office).

19. Moseley, *op cit*.

20. Higgins J et al, *op cit*.

21. Hatch S and Sherrott R, "Positive Discrimination and the Distribution of Deprivations", *Policy and Politics*, Vol 1, No 3 1973.

22. Central Research Unit (1984) the Urban Programme in Scotland: Results of a Monitoring Exercise (Scottish Office).

23. Strathclyde Regional Council (1983) Social Strategy for the Eighties (Report).

24. Strathclyde Regional Council, *ibid*.

25. Urban Renewal Unit (1978) Area Based Policies Approach to Urban Deprivation (Reports) (Scottish Development Department).

THE SCOTTISH ARTS COUNCIL GROWS UP?
AN IDENTITY CRISIS

Sara Krusenstjerna

"The day is not far off when the Economic Problem will take a back seat where it belongs, and the arena of the heart and head will be occupied, or reoccupied, by our real problems – the problems of life and of human relations, of creation and behaviour and religion."[1]

It is perhaps ironic to begin a discussion of the Scottish Arts Council in its twentieth birthday year with such a quotation from the first Chairman of the Arts Council of Great Britain, parent organisation to the SAC. In fact, both bodies are currently under siege over economic and other issues, a controversy which is intensified by the fact that the entire concept of state patronage for the arts is seriously being called into question for the first time since its inception in 1945.

Any crisis, whatever its extent, is useful insofar as it exposes the essence of the parties involved. The Scottish Arts Council (SAC) in its present dilemma emerges as a spongelike, amorphous entity, adroit in the employment of survival tactics. This fact is central to the assertion that the SAC, with its inherent contradictions, typifies other bodies attempting to administer the state, and therefore warrants examination for insight into questions facing Scottish society as a whole. In effect, the problematic existence of the SAC may be viewed as a microcosm of Scotland itself.

Discussion of these ideas begins with the current operation and predicament of the SAC. Then follows an analysis of its evolution in light of the underlying themes of money, power and questions pertinent to the role of the SAC and the arts in Scottish society. This process will, it is hoped, substantiate the premise that the SAC can serve as a mirror for Scotland and thereby stimulate further discussion of issues relevant to the future of both.

Current Operation

At present, the SAC is the Scottish arm of the Arts Council of Great Britain (ACGB), a QUANGO established by the government and charged with the responsibility for state subsidy of the arts. The stated aims of the Arts Council are:

1) to develop and improve the knowledge, understanding and practice

of the arts

2) to increase the accessibility of the arts to the public throughout Great Britain

3) to advise and co-operate with government departments, local authorities and other bodies on any matters concerned directly or indirectly with these objects.[2]

The SAC negotiates with the ACGB each year for its apportionment of the ACGB parliamentary allocation. It then has complete autonomy in disbursement of these funds to grant-seeking artists and arts organisations in Scotland, although it has no administrative authority over them. The SAC is accountable financially to the government at the end of each fiscal year.

The council itself is comprised of 20 members, appointed by the ACGB, final approval resting with the Scottish Secretary of State. Nominations are open to the public, and once appointed, members may serve a maximum of two three-year terms. The Chairman and Vice-Chairman are members of the Arts Council of Great Britain, and with recommendations from the SAC Director and senior officers are influential in the selection of council members. An assessor from the Scottish Office Education Department attends all council meetings, although the SAC is directly answerable to the Minister of Arts and Libraries.

The SAC is advised by a Policy and Resources Committee (comprised of the SAC chair and committee chairs); by the various art-form committees responsible for the review of individual grant applications, and by specialist panels for the most time-consuming evaluations. Committee and panel members are appointed by the council. All members of the council, committees and panels serve on a volunteer basis.

The SAC also has a staff of 40 full-time and 6 part-time professionals which includes the Director, Deputy Director, and five departmental directors. The staff is responsible for the coordination and implementation of policy, serving as the administrative liaison point for the Council and its constituencies. In-depth review of grant proposals and on-site investigation is done by the staff in preparation for appropriate committees and panels.

Current Predicament

It is difficult at first glance to determine the actual scope of the current dilemma. The evidence of unrest consists of isolated protests against the Arts Council, and may not seem to warrant the crisis label. It is legitimate to ask: at what point do these individual sparks constitue a raging inferno?

There is a crisis, but clarification of one key point is essential in order to realise this. It is the very fact that these portents are isolated which explains the nature of the Arts Council's survival strategy. Such fires may be stamped out relatively easily, provided they do not become too numerous and out of control. This divide and rule tactic serves to eliminate the possibility of a coherent opposition (the raging inferno), and allows the Arts Council to exist not peacefully, but without threat of extinction. It must act to preserve itself, employing whatever defusing devices are necessary to maintain status quo.

In December 1986, the Scottish Arts Council announced its 1987-88 allocation: £14.12 million, a 4.4% increase over present year funding, representing 12% of the unearmarked ACGB grant, the SAC indicated that it had fared well in winning this 12% during a year when the total ACGB allocation had been increased by only 3.4% to £138.4 million. (Note that of the £138.4 million, £26.2 million were previously earmarked for the SAC.) Thus:

£138.4 million	(total ACGB)
− 26.2 million	(earmarked SAC)
£122.1 million	(un-earmarked ACGB)

Total 1987-88 SAC allocation is therefore:

£14.12 million	(12% of ACGB)
+26.20 million	(earmarked funds)
£40.32 million	

SAC Chairman, Professor Alan Peacock, did warn that "there may be a number of difficult and possibly unpleasant decisions to be taken"[3] regarding apportionment of these funds; but he upheld an essentially optimistic view of the arts future for Scotland.

By the end of January, distribution decisions were made, with 45% of allocated funds going to four major organisations: Scottish Opera (21.9%, up 2%), Scottish National Orchestra (9.8%, up 4.3%), Scottish Ballet (9.1%, up 5%), Scottish Chamber Orchestra (4.2%, up 5.7%). These groups face cost increases well upwards of 5% merely to maintain status quo.

The fires of protest began with a flurry of media activity subsequent to these announcements. Frank Dunlop, Edinburgh Festival Director, accused the SAC of a "complete lack of confidence in the Festival and horrifying disregard for its well-being."[4] *The Scotsman* Arts Editor, Allen Wright, proclaimed the "Scottish Opera Seeking Cash,"[5] referring to the SAC's "parsimony" and "punitive financial increase of only 2%."[6] An announcement that the Scottish Theatre Company is having to cancel its spring tour[7] resulted in SAC committee investigations and a subsequent article forecasting a "Bleak Future for Scots Drama."[8] Most recently, the attacks have extended into the political arena, with SALVO, the Scottish arts lobby, calling for "a review of the SAC structure, functions and accoauntability."[9]

Events climaxed on 11 May with an announcement of publication by the right-wing Adam Smith Institute of a report which "proposes ending of subsidies to arts." Taking the position that any cultural activity should be left to find its place in society by persuading the public of its worth, the report condemns "noncommercial elitism that takes pride in its unprofitability." It proposes rapid phasing out in as little as three or four years – because the arts lobby "is nothing if not articulate and organisations would seek charitable status to exempt them from VAT, and businesses would receive extra tax relief for cultural investment."[10]

In the face of this adversity, the SAC has maintained a dual line of defence: first, that it has done well in procuring this level of funding, and second, that it is not responsible for arts funding decisions made by the government. Says Alan Peacock, "If the inadequacy of this amount stirs the blood and calls for action, then let that action be directed toward Ministers of the Crown and eventually Parliament... The most SAC can do is to see that it is fairly treated by the ACGB, and that the resultant sums are sensibly used."[11]: a predictable diversion.

Clearly, the structure and operation of the SAC leave it vulnerable to the numerous and frequent criticisms levelled against it. Almost by definition, the integrity of its decision-making processes is suspect; personnel selection, grant allocation, policy determination are all subject to unsympathetic scrutiny.

Evolution

The evolution of the SAC (and necessarily, the ACGB) is characterised by three themes which underlie all relevant issues, very simply: money, power, policy. A brief history of both institutions will provide a basis for discussion of these themes. It is interesting to note that its development, like the SAC itself, is rather ambiguous, without major surprises or pivotal issues.

During the Second World War, the government established an organisation under the auspices of the Minister of Education, known as the Council for the Encouragement of Music and the Arts. CEMA was responsible for the wartime provision of music, art and drama to the British populace, largely through direct provision of its own productions, but including subsidy of existing enterprises as well. Following the war, on 12 June 1945, the Chancellor of the Exchequer announced the replacement of CEMA with a permanent organisation, the Arts Council of Great Britain, which would receive its grant-in-aid directly from the Treasury. A royal charter was granted on 9 August 1946 establishing the ACGB as an autonomous corporate entity with official status.

By 1 April 1947, the Scottish Committee of the ACGB was granted authority for independent administration of its funds. In general, a high degree of control over "associate" organisations and a large proportion of directly provided activities characterised this early period. The scope of activities widened steadily until the mid-1960's, with the trend away from directly provided activities. In February 1965, the government issued a white paper, for the first time seriously addressing the issue of state arts funding. Arts Council responsibility was re-shifted from the Treasury to the Department of Education and Science, with Under-Secretary Jenny Lee appointed to oversee the arts.

On 7 February 1967, a new charter redefined organisational objectives and established an independent Scottish Arts Council. Also during this year, Jenny Lee became Minister of State of the Department of Education and Science. By 1972, the SAC was producing its own annual reports and well-established in its "autonomy." Growth and general optimism continued through the 1970's despite inflation, and the expanding role of business in arts funding was signalled by the establishment of the Association for Business Sponsorship of the Arts (ABSA). With the imminent prospect of a devolved Scottish Assembly, the arts emerged as a more overtly political issue, evidenced in part by the appearance of the Scottish arts lobby, SALVO.

The 80's saw a change from rising to stable (and possibly declining) arts funding in real terms, a profound difference whose ramifications are even now not fully realised. A general pessimism beginning with the devolution failure in 1979 seems to have accompanied the Scottish (and British) arts to their present state of crisis.

Money

Money, not surprisingly, is by far the dominating theme throughout the development of this, and any, government funding agency. Without exception, the annual reports of the ACGB, and later, those of the SAC, plead for proper financial recognition of the arts by the state. Apparently at no time, even during the periods of rapid growth in the 60's and 70's has there been enough to meet the needs of the developing arts. It is possible that the Arts Council must resign itself to the fact that this is, was, and ever shall be its fate. It is also possible that the Arts Council has cried wolf on one too many occasions, thereby lessening its own effectiveness in soliciting government funds. In the mid 1950's, the ACGB proclaimed "the living arts in peril of extinction,"[12] and similar warnings by both the ACGB and SAC have recurred in subsequent decades.

For the sake of perspective, a few figures may prove useful:

Fiscal Year	Total Government Expenditure	ACGB Allocation	SAC Allocation
1945-46	£5,967 million	£175,000	*** [13]
1987-88	£173.7 billion	£138.4 million	£14.12 million [14]

*** no separate budget figures for the SAC

Interestingly, government expenditure for "Arts and Libraries" for 1987-88 is listed at £.8 billion with the Arts Council's £138.4 million representing only 17% of the total. It is difficult to imagine where these "arts" funds are going if not to the Arts Council, a body established to manage state arts subsidy. Arts practitioners are understandably disillusioned with such encouraging and untraceable figures.

In a similar vein, the Scottish arts "achieved" a 28-fold increase in real terms from their 1948 to their 1985 appropriation, from £429,860 to £12,024,000. (See table following.) Note that actual percentages of government spending are much less attractive and tend to be avoided by politicians.

Growth in Scottish Arts Appropriation from the ACGB as Compared with Inflationary Adjustment of Original Grant

	Actual	Adjusted Original [15]
March 1948	36,000	36,000
March 1955	75,750	49,585
March 1965	202,789	67,245
March 1975	2,421,700	145,936
March 1985	12,024,000	429,860

Money is the governing force behind the other two recurrent themes of power and policy. It is the endless quarrelling over a) whether there should be money, b) who should distribute it, and c) who should get it, which gives rise to the questions of power and policy. It may seem too obvious to state that were there enough money to go around, no one would bother much about the rest. Such is not the case, and thus we are confronted by power and policy issues which affect the decision-making processes mentioned previously.

Power

Power is a multidimensional theme: the relationship between the government and the ACGB, the ACGB and the SAC, and the SAC and its various constituencies, not to mention the internal power dynamic of these institutions. "The method in this country... is to recognise a chain of responsibility all along the line, from Parliament to the Little Nessing Music Club. Parliament votes a block of money to the Arts Council to distribute at its discretion, in turn the Arts Council does not interfere with policies of bodies it assists: respect for self-government in the arts."[16] This is an interesting, quasi-military structure which absolves those at each level, regardless of their degree of influence, of any responsibility for decisions made by those farther up the pyramid.

To illustrate: periodically, the Arts Council has called for funding of grants on a triennial basis, to assist recipients with long-term planning. In 1962, the ACGB enthusiastically announced that the Treasury finally agreed to advance fixing of grants: "the most important financial innovation of the fiscal year."[17] However in 1965, when inflation rendered an additional funding request necessary, the ACGB noted with regret that "it has always seemed obvious to the Arts Council that the rigid determination of grants three years ahead in our line of business must be based on guesswork."[18]

The successful operation of this system depends upon the complacency of those at each level. When there is resistance or pressure of any kind from below and a reverse flow occurs, normally the divide and rule principle serves to defuse the tension. It is the nature of such a hierarchy, divided and subdivided, which allows such conflict to be absorbed into the system. Petty squabbling becomes the norm, but poses no serious threat to the perpetuation of the whole.

Primarily important in this discussion of the power theme is the relationship between the ACGB and the SAC. While the official landmarks in the emergence of the present-day Scottish Arts Council have been duly noted, additional evidence is necessary to portray accurately the complex nature of this relationship.

In the earliest days of the Arts Council of Great Britain, no separate budget figures existed for Scotland, which was regarded as one of the 'regions'. With the establishment in 1947 of the Scottish Committee and its autonomy in fund disbursement, more information became available. Total complacency in the acceptance of its allocation, and a provincial approach to both its problems and its reporting characterised the Scottish Committee at this time. Complacency remained while professionalism replaced provincialism during the relatively modest growth and expansion of the 1950's.

The 60's brought a developing confidence, and by 1966, on the eve of its SAC metamorphosis, the Scottish Committee was able to say: "The State's entry into the field of artistic subsidy is only 27 years old and already willy-nilly the Arts Council is bearing the financial responsibility for life and death over most of the professional organisations in Scotland. It is a responsibility which has not been sought but which the pressure of rising costs and social change has imposed upon it."[19] And one year later, as the Scottish Arts Council, "Scotland has often looked backward to a dimly remembered golden age... The present report perhaps suggests that this is no longer necessary."[20]

Then followed a period of rapid expansion in Scottish arts funding to the present levels of 11-12%, and consequently, of Scottish artistic enterprise. A corresponding rise was evident in the SAC's self-confidence. Faced with the ACGB endorsed prospect of the establishment of a National Touring Board, the SAC responded: "In all these discussions the SAC has taken the view that the degree of autonomy which it has always enjoyed, and which it believes to have been valuable in the management of the arts in Scotland, would seem to be threatened by any proposal for a supranational Board to control touring on a United Kingdom basis. It feels that it must remain 'master in its own house...' "[21]

The eagerness and apprehension with which Scotland looked forward to the prospect of a devolved Scottish Assembly was certainly felt by the SAC. Involved discussions of the implications of devolution constitute the SAC reports during the mid-late 1970's. Apparently it felt the need to justify its own existence, advocating the "arms' length principle" which is the basis of the QUANGO concept. "The advantage of this arrangement is that it enables the Minister of the day responsible for the arts to consider public support of the arts on a long-term basis, and to represent these needs to Parliament on a longer perspective, leaving responsibility for individual day-to-day support decisions and priorities to the Arts Council."[22] It is amazing to note that subsequent reports make absolutely no reference to the failure of the devolution referendum.

The SAC and the ACGB are in many respects involved in a parent/child relationship. The SAC was created by the ACGB and granted a sufficient degree of independence to develop its own identity. It remains, however, answerable to and financially dependent upon the ACGB. It has, in addition, the adolescent luxury of being able to present itself to its peers in an alternately dependent or independent relationship with its parent. It can take refuge in ACGB authority when faced with peer pressure or criticism, or distance itself from the parent and claim credit for actions met with approval. Further, the parent can speak for the child, with or without the child's consent: states the ACGB in 1960, "... the Scottish Committee accepts two primary responsibilities, one of the Scottish National Orchestra and the other for the Edinburgh Festival."[23]

In this context, it is easy to understand how the ambiguous use of the term Arts Council has evolved. Both parent and child have the same surname; references to common philosophies and practices may be attributed to the family name, while specific attitudes and actions belong to the individuals. Problems of semantics arise when family members refer to themselves by their family name. In any given instance it is important to ask whether the SAC is speaking for itself (child), the ACGB as a separate organisation (parent), or the Arts Council collective: ACGB, SAC and Welsh Arts Council (family). Such confusion (planned inocuousness) can be used very conveniently as a cloaking device, another method of defusing potential conflict. We are justified in wondering: what is meant by "Arts Council?"

An attempt to determine who controls the money and the best way to get it inevitably leads those on the receiving end to attack the power distribution (or lack thereof). The fact that the entire structure is built on appointments, no matter how apolitical, merely adds fuel to the critical fire. Both the ACGB and the SAC have repeatedly found it necessary to defend themselves against accusations that they are "undemocratic" in structure and in operation. "The efficiency of the system depends on the predominantly sensible contribution of all concerned, rather than on any particular combination of checks and balances."[24] This seemingly naive, blind faith approach gives the Arts Council great flexibility in assuming and shedding responsibility as it "tries to escape formality in its dealings".[25] "It can initiate change as well as reflect it, it can lead as well as respond."[26]

It is not surprising then that appointments to both the Arts Council of Great Britain and the Scottish Arts Council are closely scrutinised. Arts practitioners refer to the "curious presence" of people on committees, while council members insist that there is an optimum ratio of stability and fresh blood maintained through membership rotation.

Generally speaking, a glance through these lists does reveal an extraordinary number of recurring names: staff members who were once council or committee members and vice versa, council members who retire to become committee members, council members who retire and reappear in later years. While it may be true that the Arts Council is relatively free from political bias and that Lord Goodman, while he was ACGB Chairman "never heard a political discussion at any Arts Council meeting"[27] (whether or not this is a desirable goal is another issue entirely), the assertion that this is a fairly insular system does seem justified.

It follows then that it is difficult to determine the exact nature of the internal power dynamic of the SAC (or the ACGB). Outsiders attribute ultimate authority to staff members, claiming that they have too much influence over the volunteer element. In general, council and committee members believe that they have sufficient freedom in their decision-making duties. Indications from the annual reports are that a gradual shifting of responsibility to staff did take place over the years, and was in fact intentional. In 1975, ACGB Chairman Lord Gibson was "no longer convinced of the effectiveness of volunteerism"[28] and wanted the staff to assume more evaluation responsibilities. Internal restructuring during the late 1970's shifted details of finance to senior officers, leaving committees freer to attend to policy.

Policy

Where the power and policy themes overlap is in the area of Arts Council control of British arts development. Needless to say, funded organisations believe that they are at the mercy of seemingly whimsical changes in policy; noncompliance means no money and therefore is not an option. It seems safe to assume, further, that those who are denied funds do not look kindly upon the Arts Council's censorious powers.

As for the council itself, from its earliest days it has expressed intentions not to interfere too much. "This is a very important experiment – State support for the Arts without State control. We prefer not to control, though sometimes we must; we want to support, encourage and advise."[29] This at a time when the council acted virtually as a manager for recipient organisations, entering into complicated and restrictive legal contracts with them.

By 1962: "Our responsibility for effective leadership at the grand strategy level thus has to be discharged piecemeal, at the tactical and operational level, entirely by seconding the activities of others."[30]

By 1971: "It is quite clear that a change is taking place which must involve the Council more in the affairs of its client companies. The Council has always held firmly to the view that it should not interfere in matters of artistic policy; but artistic policy and finance, and even survival, are becoming more and more closely linked and the Council is finding it more difficult to stand apart."[31]

The point is clear that for any funding agency to deny its influence over grant recipients and the consuming public is naive. Discretionary fund disbursement means having the power to dispense money at will. The manner in which the Arts Council money is spent inevitably has a direct bearing on practitioners and partakers alike, and in addition affects the cumulative artistic legacy of the society. Current council members hasten to point out the fact that the Arts Council hasn't the absolute live or die authority of a Minister of Arts. Arts initiatives are not determined by the Council; the Council merely decides whether and how much it will fund them. Further, it cannot determine the fate of under- or non-funded bodies; they are free at least in principle, to develop outside the auspices of the Arts Council.

The Arts Council policies which affect all of this may be viewed simplistically as a quality vs. quantity dilemma. When the Arts Council is emphasising quality it tends to channel its funds to a limited number of highly visible institutions; quantity means lesser amounts to a larger number of recipients. Not surprisingly, in the first instance the Arts Council is criticised for elitism, and in the second for trying to be all things to all people. The fact that it has swung back and forth inumerable times over the years leaves it vulnerable to attack for being indecisive: a no-win situation on all counts. It is quite telling that a 1985 self-conducted survey by arts administrators resulted in a vote of no confidence in the Arts Council. [32]

On behalf of "quality" in 1962: "The essence of the Arts Council policy nowadays is to sustain the best possible standard of performance at a limited number of institutions..." [33]

Four years later, in its own defence: "The Arts Council has been criticised in the past for apparent snobbism. Shortage of finance has limited support to the top end of culture. The best, the highest and the finest at least one must support, and it has been necessary to deny support to worthy, but less worthy causes." [34]

And again, in 1976: "There is a new creed emerging, to which we are totally opposed. This is the belief that because standards have been set by the traditional arts and because those arts are little enjoyed by the broad mass of people, the concept of quality is irrelevant.... Inevitably and rightly, most of our money has gone to the traditional arts." [35]

For an institution attempting to dispel the notion that it is elitist, the Arts Council has managed some awkward postures over the years. "The public, it seems, is not unwilling to pay a little more for the best. But second-best establishments cannot persuade their customers to pay more, especially as they have to compete with such other forms of entertainment as television and cinema" [36] – a rather back-handed method of championing the underdog. Indeed, the Arts Council has looked with great disfavour upon the television and film industries, while admitting that "despite the inanities which both these media abundantly disseminate, they have unquestionably enlarged the public appreciation of music and drama." [37] Without a doubt, "the distinction must be drawn between art and entertainment." [38]

The Arts Council's emphasis on quantity has taken various forms: first, in increased funding of smaller organisations; second, in the funding of new initiatives; and third in the funding of large institutions with the understanding that outreach programmes will be developed. Also, during times of 'quantity' emphasis, pressure is increased by the Arts Council on the local authorities to share responsibility of 'bringing art to the people.' Outreach falls basically into two categories – touring and audience development with young people being an especially favoured target: "if now battle is joined for the allegiance of young people between the attraction of facile, slack and ultimately debasing forms of sub-artistic, under-civilised entertainment, and the contrary attraction of disciplined appreciation and hard, rewarding work, then we need to know and to enlist all the allies we can get."[39] (Dare we mention the word elitism?)

The "potential conflict" of its twin obligations: 1) to improve standards of execution, and 2) to increase accessibility of the arts to the public[40] (essentially quality vs. quantity), was finally recognised by the Arts Council in 1964. It was afforded the luxury of continuing to shift its emphasis until the late 1970's when it found itself "faced with a difficult choice: whether to try to sustain all existing clients at existing levels of activity and thereby to say 'no' to all new initiatives and so stultify enterprise, or to finance a few new activities, knowing that this can be done only at the expense of some existing activity."[41] Indeed, and this was a forecasting of the pessimism of the 80's: "the implication is clear that no body has the automatic right to subsidy forever, no body can any longer expect always to expand. Any new proposal will need to withstand the closest scrutiny."[42]

Current council members, however, acknowledge the existence of "sacred cows" in the funding decisions, as well as the importance of supporting new initiatives. Thus it tends to be those "steadies" in the middle who are reduced or cut to accommodate the others.

What constitutes the immediate crisis, then, is the fact that there simply is not money enough to meet anyone's need. The Arts Council is well beyond the dilemma of deciding whether to emphasize quality over quantity or vice versa. All recipients are in danger, and the Arts Council can no longer rely on the effectiveness of the divide and conquer principle. Mobilisation of a coherent opposition is a very real prospect indeed. Furthermore, pressure from above is being forcefully exerted in the form of government policy toward the arts. The position that the arts should be supported in the marketplace spells ultimate death for the Council, to say nothing of the effect upon the arts organisations themselves. It appears that the system, not designed to withstand such internal pressures and counter-pressures, will have to change radically or self-destruct. The Arts Council, being caught in the middle, is not in an enviable position.

The Questions

What then, does all of this tell us about Scotland, if in fact the SAC does serve as a mirror for the Scottish experience? A satisfactory solution to any problem requires asking the "right" questions – questions which are unrestricted by parameters established by the status quo. Implicit in the very name of the organisation are three exploratory questions, a discussion of which will elucidate the Arts Council's present identity crisis as well as impart a possible means for resolution. Parallels to Scotland's own dilemma should become clear simultaneously. The questions prompted by the

"Scottish Arts Council" are, in reverse order:

1) Should arts subsidy exist?

2) What is art in the context of this organisation and its role?

3) Does Scottish culture exist?

Should Arts Subsidy Exist?

Where the SAC is concerned, the first question is the most basic. A negative response destroys the institution, while an affirmative response invites further interrogation. State subsidy of the arts began as an experiment, somehow never undergoing a conscious and thorough evaluative process; and it gradually became the more or less accepted status quo. The Arts Council itself articulated this non-committal attitude in 1949, "it is a mistake to think that the arts must necessarily be subsidised."[43] Viewed by some as an essential practice by a responsible and enlightened society, by others as frivolous spending by an imprudent government and by most as a sort of necessary evil ("We don't like it, but we don't know what else to do about it."), arts subsidy has survived and periodicaly flourished up to the present.

Scotland has been accused of having a "public client mentality" with the typical response to any societal problem being that someone should give money. This passionate passivity, at least in part, seems to be the philosophy behind arts subsidy as it has developed here. The fact that viable alternatives have not been explored judiciously, and that extreme dependence of the arts organisations on the council has been allowed to develop "willy nilly", provided a sound basis for the present state of crisis. Subsidy through a government agency may in the end by a desirable goal, but it must be determined as such by an enlightened consensus. Only then can the system function effectively and without paranoia. As previously explained, it is inherently impossible under the present structure for the SAC to undertake such a limitless and necessary self-review, for it must act always in its own preservationalist interests. Such action must therefore be initiated outwith the system.

What is Art?

Consistent avoidance of the second and controversial question on the part of the SAC has given rise to the general confusion and numerous criticisms regarding policy discussed earlier. In an attempt to placate the situation, the SAC has adopted a sort of add-on philosophy, accommodating demands and vested interests as the need (and pressure) arises. This reactionary approach to institutional growth and planning is very much in character with the SAC's survivalist strategy.

It is counter-productive for the SAC to deny that its conscious selection of fund recipients is a process which defines art – not certainly in an ultimate sense, but within this context. It must acknowledge and accept this not insignificant responsibility, before it is free to explore its role in the development of the arts in Scotland. It must determine which constituencies it is to serve and how best to serve them. It will then have established an identity for which it will have no need to apologise.

Does Scottish Culture Exist?

If viewed strictly in politico-economic terms the third question must be answered in the affirmative, for Scotland consistently receives a greater per capita allocation for arts funding than other areas of Great Britain. However, a non-numerical approach immediately confronts the inherent contradictions mentioned earlier.

First encountered is the British/Scottish dilemma. Can there be a distinctly Scottish culture when the primary source of funds for the vast majority of the arts organisations says, of itself, "The SAC is not a Council for Scottish Arts but an Arts Council for Scotland?"[44] Given the discussion thus far, the fact that the SAC fails to address its Scottish identity is perhaps not incredible, but certainly illuminating. As a British government agency in Scotland, the SAC becomes a confrontation point between these two societal divisions. Is it possible for one organisation to function simultaneously as the cultural epicentre of Scotland and as the ambassador to Scotland of the ACGB? Must it ignore one role in order to fulfill the other? Or make token gestures toward the fulfillment of one, while emphasizing the other? To date these seem to have been the SAC's chosen methods for coping with this dilemma.

If (when) the SAC denies its Scottishness, it can more easily fulfil its role as government messenger. This is a direct manifestation of the "branch plant" syndrome which has permeated the Scottish economic and political communities over the past several decades. In this role the SAC exists simply to funnel money, power, policy (themes earlier discussed), a one-way channel from the government to its Scottish constituency. As we have seen, a reverse flow in this system is problematic. It is when this occurs that the SAC is confronted by its Scottish responsibility and resorts to one or another of various placating gestures – e.g. special allocations to Gaelic initiatives, opposing stances to unpopular ACGB policies. These compromise moves on the part of the SAC neatly avoid a full-scale confrontation of the duality of its nature.

The British/Scottish dilemma of the SAC is but a smaller scale version of that which besets Scotland. Indeed, Scotland itself may in many respects be said to be a branch plant of Britain, administering on a more local level for a larger political, economic and cultural machine. Is it then possible for

Scotland to fulfil its role as a participant in the British state and yet protect its own interests at the same time? And more to the immediate point, what are the Scottish interests and do they warrant 'protection'? It is not within the scope of this discussion to explore the former question in detail, but the latter question effectively returns us to our original: Does Scottish culture exist? Here "culture" implies a broader context than that served by the Scottish Arts Council; however, the underlying issue is constant: establishment of Scotland's (cultural) identity through clarification, not necessarily elimination, of its contradictory roles.

It is also important, in probing the concept of Scottish culture on behalf of the SAC, to note the dominance of external influence in the Scottish arts. Significant numbers of administrators, creators and performers – influential and otherwise – are from England and other countries. Moreover, a great proportion of Scotland's artistic talent has migrated southward and abroad for many years. This replacement, albeit unintentional, of indigenous talent with the foreign element extends to virtually every realm – political, economic and cultural – of the Scottish experience. Thus, the SAC shares with Scotland in general the burden of, and consequently the need to address, this additional inherent contradiction. Is there a distinction between the Scottish and the foreign; can the two be reconciled?

An extreme and negative syndrome stemming from this particular internal conflict is the "Scottish Cringe", a general lack of confidence on the part of individuals, institutions and Scotland as a whole, based upon the notion that "if it's English – or foreign – it must be better". This crippling outlook automatically precludes the existence and value of a Scottish culture and is a vivid manifestation of the identity crisis (of the SAC and of Scotland) under discussion.

Also important in this exploration is the issue of media influence. Ironically, the media have had an inhibiting effect on Scottish culture, or at least on how Scottish culture is presented and perceived. Images of Tartanry and Kailyard have been swept up by the tourist industry, promoting the backward stereotypes of romanticism and provincialism. These narrow definitions of what constitutes Scottishness have become so entrenched both internally and externally as to hinder Scotland from recognising and promoting other forms of cultural activity. To uphold the standard media images as evidence of a Scottish culture is as extreme a perspective on the one hand as the Scottish Cringe is a denial on the other. The question of whether such a culture exists, and if so how best to nourish it, deserves more than a simply defined yes or no.

Perhaps a more enlightened perspective can be gleaned from the historians and writers. Tom Nairn affirms repeatedly that Scottish culture is not whole, a view echoed by Hugh McDiarmid in his references to the

Caledonian split personality.[45] This concept of internal conflict (the basis for any identity crisis) is further substantiated by T C Smount's reference to Scotland's "remarkably strong native culture."[46]

Smout does a thorough job of portraying the pre-1707 Scotland as a nation fraught with turmoil. Ethnic, economic, geographic, class and religious struggles prevented real internal unity for many centuries. Despite all of this, and even after the union of the Parliaments under the British Crown (1707), Scotland was able to preserve its own cultural identity, in part through the strength of some key institutions: legal, educational and religious. The continuation of this sense of separateness in Scotland gave birth to the now fully developed British/Scottish dilemma. Thus from the beginning, Scottish culture existed in a state of increasing and seemingly permanent internal conflict. The inevitable complexities imposed upon this general confusion by the industrial age have brought Scottish culture to its present debilitated state of affairs.

The third question then is the link between the Scottish Arts Council's identity crisis and that of Scotland. Constructively critical self-examination on the part of both, through questions unhindered by present convention, is the only process which will permit resolution. Quarrels over policy change and staff interference are not the problems of the SAC. These are merely symptoms which serve to divert attention from the real issues of long unanswered questions; they belie a system which expends energy on the irrelevant at the expense of the relevant solely in order to sustain itself. So too with Scotland. In diverting attention to treatment of symptoms (be they council housing or North Sea oil), Scotland has historically avoided confrontation with the underlying conflicts causing its political, economic and cultural problems. As a result, it now finds itself caving in beneath a centuries-old accumulation of unresolved internal and external pressures.

Is there a Scottish culture? Only by stepping entirely outside the bounds of convention and conceiving and accepting the possibility that it may cease to exist in its present form, will the Scottish Arts Council – and Scotland – find a solution to this problem.

The author spent 1986-7 in the Department of Sociology at Edinburgh University examining the arts in Scotland. The chapter takes no account of events subsequent to this date.

References

1. Arts Council of Great Britain, *Annual Report*, 1945-46.

2. Scottish Arts Council, *The Next Five Years*, June 1984.

3. A Wright, December 20, 1986.

4. A Wright, January 30, 1987.

5. A Wright, February 23, 1987.

6. C Wilson, April 23, 1987.

7. A Wright, February 13, 1987.

8. A Wright, April 27, 1987.

9. A Wright, April 6, 1987.

10. "Report Proposes Ending of Subsidies to Arts," May 11, 1987.

11. A Peacock, March 9, 1987.

12. Arts Council of Great Britain, *Annual Report*, 1958-59.

13. "National Income and Expenditure of the United Kingdom," April 1946.

14. *Government Expenditure Plans*, 1987-88.

15. Government Statistical Service, 1986.

16. Arts Council of Great Britain, *Annual Report*, 1952-53.

17. Arts Council of Great Britain, *Annual Report*, 1962-63.

18. Arts Council of Great Britain, *Annual Report*, 1965-66.

19. *Ibid.*

20. Arts Council of Great Britain, *Annual Report*, 1966-67.

21. Scottish Arts Council, *Annual Report*, 1969-70.

22. Scottish Arts Council, *Annual Report*, 1977-78.

23. Arts Council of Great Britain, *Annual Report*, 1959-60.

24. Arts Council of Great Britain, *Annual Report*, 1962-63.

25. Arts Council of Great Britain, *Annual Report*, 1948-49.

26. Scottish Arts Council, *Annual Report*, 1972-73.

27. Arts Council of Great Britain, *Annual Report*, 1978-79.

28. Arts Council of Great Britain, *Annual Report*, 1975-76.

29. Arts Council of Great Britian, *Annual Report*, 1948-49.

30. Arts Council of Great Britain, *Annual Report*, 1962-63.

31. Arts Council of Great Britain, *Annual Report*, 1970-71.

32. Arts Council of Great Britian, *Annual Report*, 1984-85.

33. Arts Council of Great Britain, *Annual Report*, 1961-62.

34. Arts Council of Breat Britain, *Annual Report*, 1965-66.

35. Arts Council of Great Britain, *Annual Report*, 1975-76.

36. Arts Council of Great Britain, *Annual Report*, 1952-53.

37. Arts Council of Great Britain, *Annual Report*, 1954-55.

38. *Ibid*.

39. Arts Council of Great Britain, *Annual Report*, 1965-66.

40. Arts Council of Great Britain, *Annual Report*, 1963-64.

41. Scottish Arts Council, *Annual Report*, 1976-77.

42. *Ibid*.

43. Arts Council of Great Britain, *Annual Report*, 1948-49.

44. Arts Council of Great Britain, *Annual Report*, 1971-72.

45. T Nairn, 1977.

46. T C Smout, *Review*, 1980.

LOTHIAN REGIONAL COUNCIL
WOMEN'S COMMITTEE

*The Women's Committee aims
to promote the welfare and
interests of women in Lothian.*

*The Committee have highlighted issues that affect women
employed by the Council eg. Maternity Rights Cervical Screening,
inequalities in the Local Government Superannuation Scheme and
Equal Opportunities.*

*The Women's Committee's policy is to fund Women's Groups to a
maximum of £500 with a variety of aims and objectives.*

*A Joint Working Group with Lothian and Borders Police looking
into force guidelines on domestic violence has raised awareness and
has led to changes to force instruction as well as the development of
contacts with the local legal system.*

*Available from our Library are: Women's Committee Annual
Reports, Information Packs on Strip Searching, Cervical Screening,
Prosecuting Sexual Assault, See the Light Campaign and Women
and the Community Charge Leaflets.*

– – – oOo – – –

For further information contact:

**The Women's Unit, 12 St Giles Street, Edinburgh EH1 1PT
Tel: 031-229 9292 Ext. 3417/3871**

THE IMPACT OF THATCHERISM ON WOMEN IN SCOTLAND

Esther Breitenbach

It is commonly believed that the policies of Mrs Thatcher's governments have been an unmitigated disaster for women. Despite Mrs Thatcher's own achievement in what remains all too much a man's world, her indifference to the promotion of equality through legislative or institutional changes, and her attacks on the public sector, are regarded as having seriously undermined the progress towards equality of the 1970s.

In trying to assess the impact of Thatcherism on women in Scotland, the following should be borne in mind. The position of women in the late seventies in Scotland was far from ideal. What the seventies did achieve was a fairly thorough examination of just how bad women's position was, and just how much needed to be changed. Legislative changes such as the Equal Pay and Sex Discrimination Acts had come into effect, been scrutinised, and found wanting. Other needs had been identified, and practical action undertaken, as well as campaigning, to try to meet them. For example, campaigns against violence against women contributed to legislative changes that gave better protection to women than had previously existed. More importantly self help groups gave advice and support to large numbers of women who suffered violence in their home, or who had been the victims of rape, sexual assault, or incestuous abuse.

The threats to curtail the provisions of the 1967 Abortion Act had been fought successfully, and the labour movement had been won over to seeing this as an issue relevant to its members. The Employment Protection Act gave women a statutory right to maternity leave and pay, and the State Earnings Related Pension Scheme gave women the promise of better pensions by recognising the period of interruption to employment caused by childrearing, and basing pension levels on the twenty best years' earnings.

Whilst such changes were a step in the right direction, they were in many cases the minimum required to comply with EEC directives on equality. The Labour governments of the seventies were neither imaginative nor wholehearted in their commitment to women's equality. Thus, in the absence of Thatcherism, any progress towards equality would undoubtedly have been slow, and women would have had to fight for it every inch of the way.

The question being addressed here is whether or not women in Scotland have made progress towards equality since 1979, and whether or not they have a greater degree of autonomy (recognising that the two are not the same). Ideally, in order to answer this question a full statistical picture would be drawn charting the changes in Scottish women's position across a range of areas. Firstly, constraints of space and time prevent this. Secondly, and more importantly, the data that would allow such a picture to be drawn are simply not available. No-one regularly collates and publishes data on women in Scotland that would allow us to fully monitor the position of women in Scotland.[1]

What follows then is an attempt to describe the situation facing Scottish women in a number of areas which are crucial to their ability to participate equally in society, and crucial to the autonomy they can exercise in their lives. In particular, the article focuses on access to material resources e.g. income and housing, which are basic needs and concerns for all. The level to which we have access to these resources is a crucial determinant of our status in society. Discussion of access to these resources is set in the context of changes in family structures, and their implications for women.

Changes in family structures

Major long term demographic changes have been occurring in Scotland, as elsewhere in the industrialised west. In general these are an ageing population, falling birth rates, decline in family size, a rise in the divorce rate, and a rise in the number of single parent families.

The population of Scotland between 1979 and 1986 was as follows in Table 1.

Women continue to make up a majority of the population and 'although fewer girls are born than boys, women outnumber men by middle age and constitute a substantial majority of the elderly population.'[2]

The projected population for Scotland is as follows in Table 2.

As the Scottish Abstract of Statistics points out, 'By the year 2021 over 20 per cent of men and nearly 27 per cent of women are projected to be aged 60 or more compared with 16 per cent and 23 per cent respectively in 1984'.[3]

The birth rate in Scotland, which rose to a peak in 1964 then fell sharply to reach a low point in 1977, has in recent years fluctuated around 12-13 births per thousand population.

Despite the common argument that youth unemployment is likely to

TABLE 1

Estimated population and number of births.   Scotland 1979-86.

Year	Population (thousands)				Births (thousands)			
	All	Males	Females	Women as % of total	All	Males	Females	Females as % of total
1979	5203.6	2505.0	2698.6	51.86	68366	35351	33015	48.29
1980	5193.9	2500.9	2693.0	51.84	68892	35395	33497	48.62
1981	5180.2	2494.9	2685.3	51.84	69054	35283	33771	48.90
1982	5166.6	2489.5	2677.1	51.82	66196	33911	32285	48.77
1983	5150.4	2485.0	2665.4	51.75	65078	33656	31422	48.28
1984	5145.7	2483.5	2662.2	51.74	65106	33144	31962	49.09
1985	5136.5	2480.5	2656.1	51.71	66676	34120	32556	48.82
1986	5121.0	2475.0	2646.0	51.66	65812	33874	31938	48.52

Source: Report of the Registrar General for Scotland, 1986.

TABLE 2

Projected population by age groups at 30 June, Scotland, 1983-2023.

(thousands)

Year	0-4		5-15		16-19		20-29		30-44		45-59/64		60/6-74		75+	
	Male	Female	Male	Female	Male	Female	Male	Female	Male	Female	Male	Female	Male	Female	Male	Female
1983	168	160	412	392	186	177	407	393	490	492	545	448	185	404	92	199
1991	178	169	356	336	144	137	425	411	531	526	524	434	185	384	103	216
2001	176	166	391	369	130	122	309	297	565	556	564	473	177	364	109	219
2011	151	143	367	346	146	137	310	297	452	444	634	511	179	387	112	219
2021	157	148	328	309	128	119	327	312	395	386	612	485	210	420	121	226
2023	157	149	330	311	123	115	318	305	408	398	590	455	209	423	130	239
Change 1983-2023	−11	−11	−82	−81	−63	−62	−89	−88	−82	−94	+45	+ 7	+24	+19	+38	+40
% change 1983-2023	−7%	−7%	−20%	−21%	−34%	−35%	−22%	−22%	−17%	−19%	+8%	+2%	+13%	+5%	+41%	+20%

Age Group

Source: General Register Office for Scotland.

FIGURE 1
BIRTH RATES, SCOTLAND, 1900-86

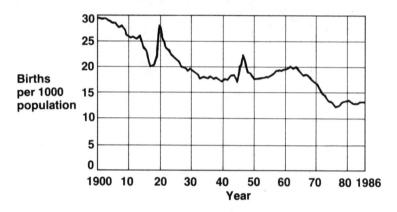

LIVE BIRTHS PER 1,000 WOMEN
BY AGE OF MOTHER
SCOTLAND, 1957 TO 1986

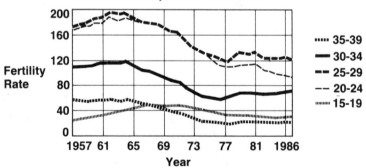

Source: Registrar General's Report 1986

result in an increase in teenage mothers, overall statistics up to 1986 do not bear this out. However, the overall statistics are likely to conceal considerable variations both in terms of locality and socio-economic status of mothers. For example, in 1986 the percentage of births to unmarried parents ranged from 10.8 in the Western Isles to 32.4 in Glasgow. Thus it may be that for certain categories of young women there is an increase in the birth rate.

What is clear, however, is a significant change in the marital status of teenage mothers.

'Pregnant teenagers are now much less likely to get married than in the past, with the result that in 1984, 1985, and 1986 there were more births to unmarried mothers than to married ones in this age group.'[4] More young mothers are choosing to stay unmarried, and to keep their babies (see Table 3).

A high proportion of births to married mothers under twenty occur within eight months of marriage. This rose from 68.3 per cent of all live births to married mothers under twenty in 1979 to 74.4 per cent in 1986. Marriages in these circumstances are the most vulnerable to failure, as divorce statistics show.

Abortion statistics show that whereas in 1975, almost as many married women as single women had abortions, by 1984 there had been a significant shift toward single women. Women most likely to have abortions are young single women in the 16-19, and 20-24 age groups. Though teenage pregnancies have not been rising, the statistics on teenage mothers and abortion suggest that there needs to be far better services for this age group, both in the provision of contraceptive facilities and advice, and in support for young mothers.

The Divorce (Scotland) Act 1976 made divorce in Scotland both easier and cheaper by providing for divorce on the grounds of non-cohabitation, after two years with the consent of both parties, and after five years if consent was withheld by one party. More recently divorce, for childless couples who agree to divorce and who have no disagreements over money, has been made easier still, and can be done through the local Sheriff Court.

Table 4 shows the numbers of divorces in Scotland between 1977 and 1986, and the grounds for divorce.

Divorces on the ground of non-cohabitation now account for over half of all divorces, compared to 40 per cent in 1979. About 1 in 4 marriages in Scotland end in divorce, compared with 1 in 3 in England and Wales. In 1986 6,912 divorces, or 52.9 per cent of all divorces in that year, involved women who had been married under the age of 21, and who had dependant

TABLE 3

Historical trends in teenager pregnancies in Scotland

Year	Number of live births to women under 20	Births to married women under 20	Births to unmarried women under 20	Births to unmarried parents as a % of all births	Births to teenagers as a % of all births
1949	4210	3422	788	18.7	4.4
1965-69	9087	7295	1792	19.7	9.5
1970-74	9037	6864	2173	24.0	11.4
1975-79	7399	5125	2274	30.7	11.3
1980	7226	4584	2642	36.6	10.5
1981	6871	4186	2685	39.1	10.0
1982	6885	3785	3100	45.0	10.4
1983	6341	3200	3141	49.5	9.7
1984	6342	2833	3409	54.6	9.6
1985	6518	2639	3879	59.5	9.8
1986	6381	2160	4221	66.0	9.7

TABLE 4

Divorces, by ground, Scotland, 1977 to 1986 – Divorce (Scotland) Act, 1976.

Year	Adultery	Behaviour	Desertion	Non-cohabitation (2 years and consent)	Non-cohabitation (5 years)	Other	All grounds of divorce	Nullity of marriage	Dissolution	Total
1977	935	1,743	433	563	1,030	3	4,707	8		4,715
1978	1,307	2,874	393	1,613	1,762	1	7,950	8		7,958
1979	1,486	3,454	235	1,931	1,576		8,682	7		8,689
1980	1,940	4,189	305	2,479	1,555	2	10,470	8	1	10,479
1981	1,703	4,133	230	2,438	1,369	2	9,875	6		9,881
1982	1,873	4,814	244	2,812	1,524	4	11,271	12	1	11,284
1983	1,789	4,674	200	4,214	2,350	8	13,235	3		13,238
1984	1,415	4,351	142	4,250	1,741	7	11,906	9		11,915
1985	1,760	5,020	120	4,665	1,791	15	13,371	2		13,373
1986	1,610	4,620	129	4,950	1,729	16	13,054	9		13,063

Grounds of divorce

Source: Registrar General's Report. 1986.

children. A further 29 per cent of divorces involved women who had been married between the ages of 21 and 24, and who had dependant children. This would suggest that women who marry young, and who have children are more vulnerable to marriage break-down, or, to put it another way, it raises questions as to the capacity of young men to deal adequately with the responsibility of marriage and a family, since inevitably in the vasr majority of cases, it is the woman who will shoulder the responsibility of bringing up the children on her own.

Since the early seventies the number of marriages has been falling. This trend continued between 1979 and 1986. Given the rising divorce rate, the proportion of marriages where one or both partners has been married before, is also rising. There is, however, a marked difference between the propensity of men to remarry and the propensity of women to remarry, as the table below shows.

TABLE 5

Marriage rates – Scotland. 1979 - 86

Year	First marriage per 1000 population		Remarriage per 1000 population	
	Male	Female	Male	Female
1979	60.8	67.1	52.7	16.1
1980	59.4	66.0	56.6	17.6
1981	54.9	61.6	55.5	16.2
1982	51.3	57.5	52.9	16.1
1983	49.0	55.2	54.8	17.3
1984	49.5	56.2	54.9	17.4
1985	48.0	54.9	55.7	17.8
1986	46.3	52.8	53.6	18.0

Source: Report of the Registrar General for Scotland 1986.

The number of single parent families in Scotland increased from 64,000 in 1976 to over 98,000 in 1981. The 1981 census showed that there were about 98,210 single parent families in Scotland (90 per cent of them headed by women) involving 152,380 children. Forward estimates put the figures for 1988 at 133,006 single parent families involving 174,459 children.

The figure on the following page shows the composition of single parent families in Scotland as revealed by the 1981 census.

FIGURE 2: LONE PARENTS IN SCOTLAND: SOME STATISTICS

Numbers, Sex and Marital Status, 1981 Census

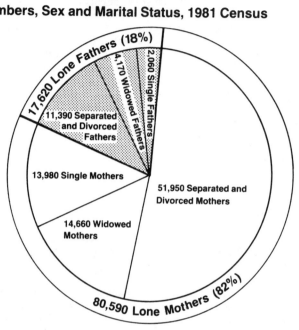

Source: 1981 Census, Household and Family Composition Tables (10% sample), with addition of estimated 5,000 single mothers.

In Scotland in 1981 14 per cent of all families with children were headed by one parent, ranging from 8.7 per cent in Shetland to 20.4 per cent in Glasgow.

These long-term demographic changes are a product, among other things, of rising living standards leading to greater longevity, advances in preventive and curative medicine and its provision and advances in the development of contraceptive drugs and devices. Social mores have also changed. Marriage is no longer seen as a permanent state, and is being replaced by cohabitation for a growing section of the population. A growing number of women are exercising the option of motherhood outside the state of marriage or cohabitation. Legislative changes have facilitated this process, in particular laws relating to abortion, divorce, protection against violent partners, and housing for homeless persons.

The signs are that many of these trends will continue e.g. the ageing of the population, rising divorce rates, rising numbers of single parent families. Such fundamental demographic changes are scarcely amenable to government policies, though how governments respond to such changes does of course have an impact on people's lives. For example, a deteriorating health service may result in a decrease in life expectancy and rising infant mortality rates, at least within the poorest sections of the population. Failure to develop appropriate social provision may result in an intensification of poverty, in particular for women, with consequent ill-effects on their health, and on the health of their children. Thus the challenge for government is to attempt to understand the implications of those changes, and to make provision accordingly, and this the Thatcher government has signally failed to do.

For women in Scotland, as in the rest of Britain, demographic changes have altered their relationship to the labour market, have rendered their poverty increasingly visible, and have created new social needs to which current social policies are an inadequate response.

Work and Pay

At the time of Mrs Thatcher's accession to power the general position of working women in Scotland was as follows. On the whole women in Scotland worked in low paid, low grade semi-skilled or unskilled jobs in the secondary sector of the economy. The majority of women workers in Scotland were concentrated in service industries, more than half of them were married, and over a third worked part-time. Women in Scotland had lower pay than women in England and Wales, they worked longer hours and had poorer childcare facilities. Women's employment was highly concentrated in the service sector of the economy – over 72 per cent of women workers worked in insurance, banking, finance, professional and scientific services, public administration, and the distributive trades. This contrasted with male employment which was much more evenly distributed throughout the economy.[5]

Since 1981 the tendency for women's employment to be concentrated in the service sector is likely to have increased, given the decline in employment in the manufacturing sector in Scotland.

In 1981 63 per cent of working women worked full-time and 37 per cent worked part-time. The trend towards part-time work has continued. By 1987 the proportion of women working part-time had increased to 43.6 per cent, with a corresponding decrease in full-time women workers to 56.4 per cent.

TABLE 6

Employees in employment by industrial sector, Scotland 1981.

Industrial sector	Men 000's	%	Women Full-time 000's	%	Part-time 000's	%	Total (=100%) 000's
Agriculture, forestry and fishing	34.5	87.1	3.0	7.5	2.1	5.4	39.6
Energy and water supplies industries	62.8	87.0	7.9	10.9	1.5	2.1	72.2
Extraction of minerals, manufacture of metals chemicals	53.4	82.5	9.4	14.5	2.0	3.0	64.7
Metal goods, engineering and vehicles industries	170.3	81.1	35.2	16.7	4.7	2.2	210.1
Other manufacturing industries	120.7	54.7	81.6	37.0	18.4	8.3	220.6
Construction	150.3	91.8	9.2	5.6	4.2	2.6	163.7
Distribution, hotels and catering, repairs	137.3	39.4	112.2	32.2	99.1	28.4	348.5
Transport and communication	105.0	81.0	19.5	15.1	5.1	4.0	129.6
Banking, finance, insurance, business services and leasing	59.7	48.9	46.6	38.1	15.9	13.0	122.3
Other services	233.8	39.4	217.3	36.6	142.9	24.1	593.9
Total	1127.6	57.4	541.7	27.6	295.8	15.1	1965.1

Source: Census 1981 Scotland: Economic Activity, Table 9.

The Census of 1981 showed an increase from 54.3 per cent to 61.7 per cent of economically active women between 1971 and 1981 (ie. the percentage of the female population aged between 16 and 59 either in work or seeking work). This increase is projected to continue. Women have consistently increased their share of the labour force – from 42.6 per cent in 1979 to 46.6 per cent in 1987.

In the decade between 1975 and 1985 the number of male employees in employment in Scotland fell by 183,000, whilst the number of female employees rose by 41,000. At the same time as women's employment has increased, women's unemployment has increased. According to official figures, 65,000 women were unemployed in 1979. This rose rapidly to 109,000 in 1982, and has since fluctuated somewhat.

TABLE 7

Employees in Employment in Scotland 1975-87

Thousands

Employees in Employment	75	76	77	78	79	80	81	82	83	84	85	86	87
Men	1219	1210	1198	1200	1209	1188	1128	1097	1069	1048	1036	1020	1006
Women	858	861	873	867	898	897	874	867	854	882	899	866	880
Total	2076	2071	2071	2067	2107	2085	2002	1964	1923	1930	1936	1886	1886
Women as % of total	41.3	41.6	42.1	41.9	42.6	43.0	43.6	44.1	44.4	45.7	46.4	45.9	46.6

Source: Scottish Abstract of Statistics. Department of Employment Gazette.

TABLE 8

Unemployment in Scotland 1975-87

Thousands

Unemployment	75	76	77	78	79	80	81	82	83*	84	85	86	87
Men	76	105	126	124	117	143	206	232	224	228	240	248	241
Women	23	39	60	63	65	80	99	109	100	101	106	111	103
Total	99	144	186	187	182	223	305	341	324	329	346	359	345
Women as % of total	23.2	27.0	32.2	33.7	35.7	35.9	32.5	31.9	30.9	30.6	30.6	30.9	29.9

* Figures collected on different basis from 1983
Source: Scottish Abstract of Statistics. Department of Employment Gazette.

In 1987 103,000 women were recorded as unemployed. In 1979 women represented 35.7 per cent of the total official unemployed in Scotland. This had declined to around 30 per cent by 1987. However, establishing the true figure for women's unemployment is impossible, for a number of reasons. From 1978 onwards the government encouraged married women to register as unemployed since, as a result of the new pensions regulations, this affected women's entitlement to pension rights. In addition new female entrants to the labour market were no longer allowed the option of the married women's stamp. The sharp increase in female unemployment after 1979 was due in part to the increase in registration. At the same time the pattern of unemployment was markedly different from other countries using different methods of registration and recording of statistics. One commentator, making a comparison with Belgium, Sweden and France, noted, 'The rising number of women entering the work force has been accompanied by rising female unemployment. Women in these countries have generally had higher unemployment rates than their male counterparts, except in the UK, where the official figures are believed to underestimate the number of jobless women by 50 per cent.'[6] There have been a number of changes subsequently in the method of collecting statistics. Married women not entitled to Unemployment Benefit were excluded from the count in 1982. In addition the availability for work test for people claiming Unemployment Benefit now includes the condition that women with children must have childcare arrangements made if they are to qualify as available for work. Again this will have had the effect of excluding many women. Whilst it is impossible to say how many women are actually unemployed, it can certainly be concluded that the recorded figure is a gross underestimate.

In 1975 the Equal Pay Act came into force, but progress towards equal pay for women seems to have ground to a halt. Immediately after the Act came into effect there was an improvement in women's pay relative to men's. By 1979 full-time women workers' pay was 62.5 per cent of men's. It then fell to 59.7 per cent in 1979, climbing back to around 62 per cent in 1981 and staying there.

Women non-manual workers' pay has increased at a faster rate than women manual workers' pay, but in both cases women's position relative to men's remains virtually unchanged. The New Earnings Survey, from which the above figures are derived, excludes part-time workers. Thus the true picture regarding differences between men and women's take-home pay will be much worse. In 1987 the average weekly pay of part-time women workers was £59.40.

As the Equal Opportunities Commission's statistical profile notes, 'women's economic activity is substantially influenced by the ages of any children in their families.'[7]

TABLE 9

Earnings – Average weekly earnings. Full-time employees. Scotland.

All Employees	79	80	81	82	83	84	85
Men	101.2	123.1	140.0	154.5	167.5	178.7	189.7
Women	60.4	74.7	87.1	95.0	104.0	111.1	119.1
Women's pay as % of men's	59.68	60.68	62.21	61.48	62.08	62.17	62.78
Manual							
Men	93.6	112.2	124.8	136.9	145.8	156.2	164.2
Women	84.3	66.3	73.3	79.2	86.4	91.3	99.4
Women's pay as % of men's	58.01	59.09	58.73	57.85	59.25	58.45	60.53
Non-Maual							
Men	113.0	139.8	161.8	179.9	196.6	208.6	224.0
Women	63.0	78.2	92.5	101.0	110.1	117.9	125.6
Women's pay as % of men's	55.75	55.93	57.16	56.14	56.00	56.51	56.07

Source: New Earnings Survey.

Despite declining levels of state childcare provision it is likely that the tendency of women to return to work is increasing. A recent report from the United States showed that the numbers of new mothers remaining at work has passed the 50 per cent mark.[8] In Scotland there is an increasing number of registered child-minders, which would suggest an increasing number of women returning to work soon after having children.

It is undoubtedly the case that women will have made progress in some respects, for example, some women will have gained access to traditionally male jobs, some women will have achieved higher rank in their occupations, others will have benefitted from the use of the Equal Pay Act to improve their pay. However, whatever progress has been made has not been enough to make a difference to the global picture. Women are still

TABLE 10

Economic activity of wives aged 25-44 years, by age of youngest child. Scotland 1981.

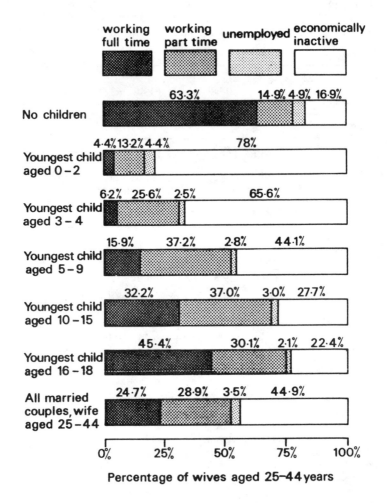

Percentage of wives aged 25–44 years

Source : Census 1981 Scotland : Household and Family Composition, Table 27.

likely to be concentrated in the service sector, their pay relative to men's has not improved, and more of them are in part-time jobs, which frequently lack security. More women have jobs than in 1979, but more of those jobs are part-time. Whilst access to an independent income will be a gain for many individual women, women's position as a highly exploited, flexible and expendable source of labour remains unchanged.

The rapid rise in women's unemployment is a reflection both of the job losses that have occurred to women, in particular full-time manual jobs in the manufacturing sector, and the growing number of women who are active participants in the labour market. This is a major historical change. Gone are the days when full employment meant full male employment. Economic change in the past decade has done little, if anything, to fulfil women's demands for work outside the home, nor to fulfil their aspirations for equality.

To what extent can this failure to make progress be laid at the door of the Thatcher government? The increase in women's participation in the labour force, and the increase in part-time work, are trends that are at work internationally. Likewise the industrial restructuring in which the old heavy industries are in decline and new production and distribution industries, relying on sophisticated microtechnology, are operating in quite a different way, can be seen at work internationally. The use of information technology is changing the way in which both production and distribution are being organised – in terms of size of plant, location, mobility, and structure of the labour force.

A significant rise in unemployment has also occurred in industrialised countries under the impact of world recession. However, it seems widely recognised that the depth of the recession experienced by Britain between 1979 and 1982 was directly attributable to the government's economic policies. Indeed, 'a variety of economic analysts have estimated the additional job loss attributable to the government at around half a million jobs.'[9] In addition, the recession has had differential effects in the south and the north of Britain. As John MacInnes points out, 'only the South has increased employment during the upturn in employment since 1983; the North is still losing jobs.'[10] In particular the impact for women has been that since 1983 part-time employment has increased dramatically in the North, but full-time employment for women has continued to fall, whereas in the South it has grown strongly. Thus it can be argued that Thatcherite economic policies, by intensifying the recession, and by aggravating the divide between North and South, have had a negative effect for women in Scotland.

In addition the government's refusal to actively promote equality through legislative measures has acted as an obstacle to progress. The government has had to reluctantly concede women's right to claim equal pay for work of equal value, an amendment to the Equal Pay Act forced on it by the EEC. This amendment will in the long term help to improve women's position. Creation of the Single European Market in 1992 also has implications for policy measures affecting women workers, such as better maternity and paternity leave arrangements, and childcare provision. The experience of the sixties and the early seventies suggests that women's position in the labour market relative to men's is likely to improve in a period of economic growth. But in addition to this an actively interventionist approach is needed to create the conditions in which women can equally participate in the labour market. Government policies since 1979 have blocked women's progress towards equality at work. The future however, offers some hope. Membership of the EEC is likely to enforce measures which will promote equality, and demographic change such as the decline in young entrants to the labour market may create opportunities for women.

Unemployment, Benefits and Poverty

The difficulties in assessing the level of women's unemployment have been discussed above. This lack of official recognition of women's unemployment is in turn intimately linked to women's disadvantaged position in relation to benefits. Despite the recent changes to the Social Security system, the system remains based on the conceptions of its founder, William Beveridge, who 'assumed the universality of the nuclear family with the husband and wife "working as a team" – the wife at home and the husband in employment.'[11] This led to a system in which married women's benefits were dependent on their husband's national insurance contributions. The consequence of this is that many married women have no access to unemployment benefit in their own right, nor to sickness or maternity benefits. It also delays their entitlement to a pension until their husband's retirement, and then only at the lower dependant's rate. In 1981 there were still 3 million women paying the reduced stamp. This means that 'this reduced entitlement to benefits will continue well into the next century unless contribution rules are changed.'[12]

For women currently of pensionable age, the majority remain dependant on their husband's contributions for their pensions. The numbers of women dependant on retirement pensions has also substantially increased.

Women's greater longevity and their dependence on reduced pensions means that they suffer a considerable degree of poverty in old age. Furthermore, dependence on a husband's contributions is becoming an increasing problem for women in an age where an increasing number of couples are choosing to cohabit, and where the rising number of divorces also means a loss of benefits to women dependant on their husband's contributions.

TABLE 11

Claimants receiving Unemployment Benefit 1974-85. Scotland.

Thousands

Figures taken from November each year except * May	74	75	76	77	78	79	80	81	82	83	84	85
Men	31	46	56*	57	46	44	79	N/A	76	68	78*	67
Women	8	16	20*	26	28	29	42	N/A	41	40	42*	38
Total	39	62	76	83	74	73	121	–	117	108	120	105
Women as % of total	20.5	25.8	26.3	31.3	37.8	39.7	34.7	–	35.0	37.0	35.0	36.1

N/A = Not available
Source: Scottish Abstract of Statistics.

TABLE 12

Recipients of National Insurance Pensions and Benefits, 1974-1985. Scotland.

Thousands

Retirement pension	74	75	76	77	78	79	80	81	82	83	84
Men	243	247	252	261	262	267	266	267	265	264	261
Women on own NI contributions	198	196	197	190	162	164	171	179	184	192	197
Women on husband's NI contribution	131	135	140	143	145	147	147	148	148	148	147
Widows on husband's NI contributions	137	145	152	157	189	192	194	195	194	192	191
Total Women	466	476	489	490	496	503	512	522	526	532	535
Total on retirement pensions	709	723	741	751	758	770	778	789	791	796	796
Women as % of total	65.7	65.8	65.9	65.2	65.4	65.3	65.8	66.1	66.4	66.8	67.2

Source: Scottish Abstract of Statistics.

The State Earnings Related Pensions Scheme (SERPS) introduced in 1975, did go some way towards improving the position of women, though inequalities in earnings still meant lower pensions for women, and many part-time women workers had no access to the scheme. Changes to the scheme made by the present government have, however, been to women's disadvantage. The encouragement to opt out of the scheme, and invest in personal pensions, offers no solution to women's poverty in old age. Personal pensions which are 'money purchase' schemes do not stand up well to inflation, and the eventual sum available for investment in an annuity, is unpredictable. The higher cost of annuities for women is a further disadvantage.

Ultimately equality of access to occupational pension benefits depends on equal pay. Whilst women's employment pattern continues to be interrupted by childbirth and childcare, there is need for a state pensions scheme that gives adequate recognition to this, and that is less tied to employment history. As Dulcie Groves comments, 'Given the inadequate levels of state pension provision and the limited opportunities most women have to save or invest for old age, their limited access to the benefits of occupational pension scheme membership has been a major factor in the construction of female poverty in old age.'[13] We have an ageing population in which women will continue to predominate. The changes in pensions legislation introduced by the Thatcher government are not good news for women. Not only do they cause greater poverty for women now, but they will do so for generations to come.

Just as married women have been disadvantaged in their access to Unemployment Benefit, married and cohabiting women have been disadvantaged as claimants of Supplementary Benefit, and now of Income Support. Until recently it was obligatory for the man in a married or cohabiting couple to claim the benefit for the couple. The complicated and poorly publicised Equal Treatment rules allowing couples some degree of choice as to who should be nominated as the claimant, have done little to change this situation. Couples' income is aggregated, and in most cases the man remains the claimant. Thus many women dependant on Supplementary Benefit, and now on Income Support, do not have access to benefit in their own right. In this situation there is no guarantee that income is equitably distributed amongst members of the household.

The general effect of the changes in the Social Security system is to have increased poverty. The government claims that economic growth has raised the living standards of the poor. Frank Field, writing in the Guardian, shows that between 1970 and 1978 benefit for the poorest increased by an average of 1.1 per cent per annum. But, 'in the 7½ years from November 1978 to April 1985, the scale rate rose by only 0.7 per cent in real terms. But this average takes no account of the changes in benefit regulations such as the 20 per cent rate contribution under the new Income

Support system. There have also been other losses, such as regular weekly additions, and the loss of single payments for most claimants,'[14] The true rate of increase in the rate of benefit since November 1978, Frank Field concludes, is only 0.4 per cent per annum. The new rules are particularly punitive in their treatment of young people, and effectively attempt to enforce dependency on parents up to the age of 25.

Women suffer from the changes to the system in particular ways, as well as from the general increasing degree of impoverishment. The flat rate maternity grant, albeit grossly inadequate, is no longer available to all mothers. Only women receiving Income Support will be entitled to assistance. The abolition of single payments will hit women particularly hard, since many single payments were given for maternity clothes, clothes and equipment needed for a new baby, children's clothes and for furniture and redecoration. The level of single payments in Scotland was also far more generous than elsewhere. The Social Fund, which is much more limited, basically involves giving loans to claimants, which they are expected to repay. Certain priority groups will obtain grants in some circumstances. One of these is the grant for essential baby equipment which will be paid, if a claimant can prove they have no other means by which to obtain the item. The inevitable consequence of these changes will be a deterioration in living standards, with ill-effects on the health of women and children. Child Benefit has not been uprated to keep pace with increases in the cost of living, and is potentially under threat from the government.

As long as married and cohabiting women are unable to claim benefit in their own right, it will be impossible to say how many women are dependent on benefits. Given the rise in unemployment for both men and women in Scotland it is inevitably far more than in 1979. A growing proportion of those dependant on benefits are long-term recipients. As Frank Field pointed out in the article quoted above, 1.5 million claimants have been drawing benefits continuously for over five years.

Another issue which must be addressed in considering the extent of poverty amongst women is that of the distribution of income within households. Whilst much research on poverty has examined the resources available to households or family units, there is no guarantee that women have equal access to these resources, whether they are at poverty level or above. Indeed, the evidence there is on distribution of resources within households shows that women can experience substantial poverty and deprivation in families whose family income takes them above the poverty line.

Perhaps the most significant change relevant to the growth of the visibility of women's poverty is the growing number of single parents, and the increasing proportion of single parents dependant on benefit. In

November 1987 of all families claiming Supplementary Benefit, 58 per cent were single parent families, a total of 77,389 families in Scotland. Single parents are the fastest growing group on benefits. The proportion of single parents dependant on benefit has also increased.

TABLE 13

Employment patterns of lone parents with dependent children

		Males 1. % of total 1981	Females 1. % of total 1981	Females 2. % of total 1984
i	Working full-time	66	25	17
ii	Working part-time	1	18	22
iii	Out of employment	24	7	
iv	Not seeking	9	49	61

Source: **1. Census 1981 Scotland Household and Family Composition (10% sample table 32).**
2. Labour Force Survey 1984.

In Strathclyde in 1985 almost two thirds of single parents in the region were on Supplementary Benefit. In 1981 70 per cent of single parents in Edinburgh were on Supplementary Benefit. This suggests a considerable deterioration in the position of single parents, many of whom are caught in a poverty trap, where any wages they might be able to earn are insufficient to offset the cost of childcare.

Over the period since 1979 there has been a growing number of elderly women dependant on state benefits, or inadequate pensions; a growing number of women dependant on benefits through unemployment; and a growing number of single parents dependant on benefits. In addition it must also be remembered that low pay is a cause of poverty, and has long term effects, in excluding women from occupational pensions, or at best bringing only a meagre pension. According to Frank Field the relative pay of the poorest non-manual working women has declined by 7.5 per cent since 1979.

The increase in women's poverty is partly a result of demographic changes, in particular an ageing population, and a growing number of single parent families. However, rising unemployment, changes in pensions legislation, restrictions on social security benefits, and reduction in state childcare facilities, have all played their part in intensifying women's poverty.

Women's poverty, however, is not a new phenomenon. It is arguable to what extent women are becoming poorer relative to the rest of society, and to what extent their poverty is becoming more visible. As Jane Lewis and David Piachaud point out, 'At the start of the century (1909) 61 per cent of adults on all forms of poor relief were women. Today 60 per cent of adults for whom supplementary benefit is paid are women'.[15]

Recently there has been a greater recognition of women's poverty, mainly because many more women are likely at some point in their lives to be household heads, either in old age or as single parents. This has meant that women's poverty has become statistically visible through their status as householders.

Whilst government policies since 1979 have undoubtedly aggravated the problem of women's poverty, a resolution of the problem will not come through merely tinkering with the current social security system. There is little sign that opposition parties have begun to seriously grapple with the development of new social policies in response to major demographic and social change in order to eradicate the problem of poverty in general and of women's poverty in particular.

Housing

As a result of the Thatcher government's commitment to transform Britain into a 'home-owning, share-owning, democracy' there has been a significant change in the distribution of housing tenure in Britain. Scottish housing has long been dominated by the public secor. Women are more likely to rely on public sector housing provision than men, thus the enforced privatisation of the housing stock has particularly serious implications for them. Distribution of tenure is markedly different for households headed by women, compared to all households in the population. Likewise distribution of tenure is markedly different for single parent families compared to other families with dependent children.

Of the relatively small proportion of women householders who are owner occupiers the majority are older women, often widows, who own their properties outright, but are likely to be at the bottom end of the housing market in the poorest quality housing. As the Women and Housing Sub-Committee of Edinburgh District Council have noted poverty and old age are closely associated, particularly for elderly women, and this is primarily a function of low income in earlier life. 'Thus many elderly women find themselves in a home which they dearly love, but which requires either maintenance or adaptation to suit their needs, which they

FIGURE 3: TENURE DISTRIBUTION

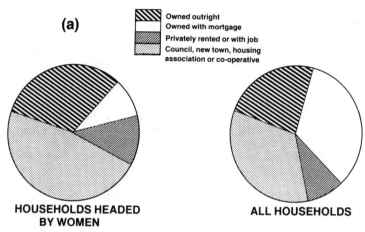

(a)

Owned outright
Owned with mortgage
Privately rented or with job
Council, new town, housing
association or co-operative

**HOUSEHOLDS HEADED
BY WOMEN**

ALL HOUSEHOLDS

Source: General Household Survey 1983, table 6.12

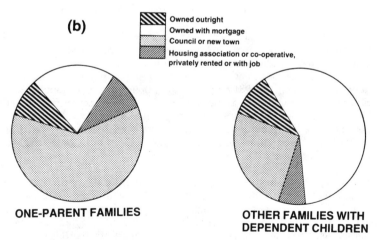

(b)

Owned outright
Owned with mortgage
Council or new town
Housing association or co-operative,
privately rented or with job

ONE-PARENT FAMILIES

**OTHER FAMILIES WITH
DEPENDENT CHILDREN**

Source: General Household Survey 1983, table 3.19

feel they are unable to finance.'[16]

The greater availability of mortgages through competition between banks and building societies, combined with the outlawing of discrimination on the grounds of sex and marital status in lending, is likely to have increased the number of women who are mortgagors. Nonetheless, women are still likely to be restricted to the lower end of the market by their lower pay. Overall, women householders, and in particular single parents, are far less likely to be homeowners than single men or married couples.

Women rely heavily on council housing and again this is particularly true of single parents. According to the 1981 Census 78 per cent of single parents in Scotland lived in council houses, compared to 41 per cent of two parent familes. Two per cent were in housing association properties compared with one per cent of two parent families. Women often end up in the least desirable council housing, and again this is particularly true of single parents. A national study, quoted by the Scottish Council for single Parents, showed that twice as many single parent families in council houses lived in poor areas compared with two parent families; 25 per cent of single parents lived in flats, compared to 10 per cent of two parent families; and 25 per cent of single parents shared with others, compared to 5 per cent of two parent families.

The major reason that women are allocated the least desirable housing is that many are seeking housing because they are leaving a relationship, and therefore are gaining access to housing through being defined as homeless. In the process many are, of course, becoming single parents.

The Housing (Homeless Persons) Act 1977 has undoubtedly provided women with a means of access to housing which they previously lacked. The number of applications under the Act resulting from disputes with spouses or cohabitees has consistently risen, and the vast majority of these are likely to be from women. In 1981 60 per cent of applications from families with children were from single parent families. The administration of the Act, however, often disadvantages women in terms of the quality of the housing offered, and the provisions of the Act are sometimes interpreted so narrowly that women are denied the right to housing to which the Act should entitle them.

Research conducted by Mary Brailey in four local authority areas in central Scotland, in 1981 and 1982, showed that 'almost a third of women applying for housing do so through the homelessness route, and women make up a far higher proportion of homelessness applicants than they do of waiting list applicants.'[17] As she goes on to point out there is plenty of evidence to show that homeless people tend to be rehoused in low demand housing in poor quality neighbourhoods.[18] Thus women tend to be allocated poorer housing than households headed by men. Being housed through the route of homelessness not only means for most women poor quality housing, it also means going through a humiliating process of investigation to establish whether entitlement is 'genuine', and often means spending months in poor standard temporary accommodatiion.

Many local authority housing departments tend to assume that the normal tenant is a man with a wife and children. In 1979 85 per cent of couples who were renting in Scotland had the tenancy in the man's name, and only 5 per cent were joint tenants. Whilst there has been a shift towards joint tenancies it is still likely to be the case that for the majority of couples the man is regarded as the tenant. This can pose serious problems for women wishing to be considered as eligible for housing in their own right because of marital breakdown. In some cases women who wish to end a relationship cannot obtain their own housing because they are already regarded as being adequately housed in the marital home. In addition some local authorities still impose conditions of eligibility such as physical separation, solicitor's letters, custody orders, and even legal separation or divorce.

There are councils, however, who take a far more enlightened approach, to problems of homelessness in general, and to women's homelessness in particular. Glasgow District council, for example, accepts relationship breakdown as a legitimate reason for homelessness (whether or not violence is involved), and it recognises that battered women have a priority need even if they have no children.[19] One of the authorities in Mary Brailey's study operated a system where staff could use their discretion to house single parents in areas of higher demand than they would qualify for under the normal points system. This was combined with a policy of offering accommodation of a standard equivalent to the marital home, and this resulted in a majority of single parents receiving housing of a similar or higher standard than their previous home.

Whilst it is clear that the Housing (Homeless Persons) Act of 1977 has given women in certain situations an entitlement to housing that they were previously denied, and whilst the changing consciousness about women's place in society has prompted some councils to change their policies to respond more adequately to women's needs, on the whole councils still tend to base their allocation policies on a model of the nuclear family and a 'conventional' life cycle which regards marriage as a permanent state. As Mary Brailey argues, this model is misguided. 'Many people do not follow the conventional life cycle pattern........For instance in 1984, 30 per cent of the applicants on Glasgow's housing waiting list were single people under 65.' But, 'Most importantly, the conventional pattern takes no account of the breakdown of relationships, and formation of subsequent new households through remarriage or cohabitation which growing numbers of people experience. Nowhere has this part of today's typical life cycle been successfully incorporated into council housing policies – it is still treated as an administrative headache.'[20]

Another piece of legislation which has increased women's rights in relation to housing is the Matrimonial Homes (Family Protection) (Scotland) Act 1981. In particular this Act confers occupancy rights to the matrimonial home, irrespective of whose name ownership or tenancy is in, and it empowers the courts to divide the value of a property between spouses on an equal basis, and it also empowers the courts to prohibit the sale of the matrimonial home on divorce and to award occupancy to a spouse bringing up dependant children under the age of sixteen. Whilst this is an improvement on the previous situation, divorced women who have lived in privately owned housing whilst married, may still face homelessness. Where a woman occupies the matrimonial home whilst bringing up children, the threat of homelessness is only being postponed till the youngest child is sixteen. A half share of the value of a house will seldom be enough to acquire another one, and if a women is on benefit or low pay she is unlikely to be able to get a mortgage. This leaves some women in the impossible position of having a sum of money which is in no way adequate to give them access to home ownership, but which is large enough to disqualify them from eligibility for council housing.

There is a growing mismatch between the pattern of people's life-cycles, and the composition of the housing stock. Not only does the existing housing stock need to be used differently and imaginatively to respond to changing social patterns, but new housing, which is tailored to these patterns, needs to be built. Where councils do recognise these changing patterns, they are prohibited by central government policy from building to meet needs.

Women, as we have seen, remain greatly disadvantaged in terms of income, many being reliant on low pay and benefits, and this is a crucial determinant of their access to housing, especially for single parents. What then are the implications for women of the extension of private housing through the Housing Scotland Bill (to become law in April 1989)? As the Women and Housing Sub-Committee of Edinburgh District Council notes, 'The combined effects of the Housing Bill and Scottish Homes will be to virtually end the role of local authorities as housing providers. Unless local authorities can persuade their tenants that alternative landlords will not provide a better service, local authority stock will dwindle. What will be left will be a "rump" of welfare-type housing and housing for social needs groups.'[21] In other words, those on the lowest incomes will be left in the public sector, housed in the least desirable housing. The likely result of the government's housing legislation will be the creation of a ghetto of public housing mainly occupied by vulnerable, poor, single parent and elderly women.

The Poll Tax too is likely to affect women's ability to pay for adequate housing. The disposable income of low income families will be further limited. Single parent families with teenage children are likely to be particularly hard hit, as, in the absence of work being available for young people, mothers will have to carry the burden of the Poll Tax for all family members. Elderly women will also be hard hit by the Poll Tax, since they are more likely to be poor. The Poll Tax for them is likely to be substantially higher than any rates for which they are currently liable, as they are more likely to live in poorer private sector housing or public housing.

Since 1979 more women in Scotland have gained access to housing in their own right. Legislation, which itself is a reflection of changing social patterns, has facilitated this. At the same time the stock of public housing is being reduced, and is deteriorating through lack of finance for adequate maintenance. New private building is for the most part beyond women's reach, and if women have become home-owners it is likely to have been at the lower end of the market. More women have more autonomy in relation to housing, but are more likely to have poorer housing conditions, particularly if they are separated or divorced. Insofar as the private housing sector has been extended there has been a reduction in the amount of housing to which women might have access. However, it seems that as far as the restriction on women's access to decent quality housing is concerned, the worst is yet to come.

The forward march of women halted?

If we are to ask the question whether women in Scotland have made progress towards equality in the decade since Mrs Thatcher came to power, then the short answer is that they have not. The overall picture for women in Scotland is that in terms of work, income and housing their position relative to men's remains grossly unequal. Whilst the global picture must conceal variations within particular sections of the population, for the majority women's pay remains the same relative to men's; more women have jobs but more of those jobs are part-time; and more women are unemployed. Increasing numbers of women are dependent on benefits, particularly the elderly, and single parents. More have gained access to housing in their own right, but are likely to be housed in poorer conditions.

To what extent has Thatcherism contributed to this situation? The sexual segregation of the labour force, the increasing economic participation of women, and the increasing proportion of jobs that are part-time are all long-term characteristics of the labour market, and are common to a number of industrialised nations. Thatcherism has allowed this process to continue unhindered, but cannot be said to have caused it. However, the high levels of unemployment in Scotland were partly caused by the government's monetarist policies, and to that extent Thatcherism can be blamed for the rise in women's unemployment.

Increased dependency on benefits of elderly and single parent women are likewise the result of long-term demographic change. However, the reduction in women's pension rights, and the squeeze on benefits resulting in an intensification of poverty for women, can be directly attributed to government legislation. Women's greater access to housing is largely a result of the Housing (Homeless Persons) Act 1977, enacted by the Labour government. But the growing restrictions on women's choice in terms of housing, and the deteriorating housing conditions in which they live, are a direct result of the government's determination to transfer housing to the private sector.

The inevitable conclusion is that the impact of Thatcherism on women in Scotland has been negative, and has arrested progress towards equality. The promotion of equality will not happen through the 'free' play of market forces, but only through positive action and social reform. It is consistent with Thatcherite philosophy that there should be no intervention to promote equality. It is also consistent with Thatcherite philosophy that there should be an attempt to reimpose so-called 'Victorian' values emphasising monogamy and parental responsibility, in direct contradiction to the changing life-cycles and patterns of relationships which constitute contemporary social reality.

Despite the general negative impact on women in Scotland of ten years of Thatcherism, and the lack of progress towards equality, it would be wrong to regard the situation as being either unchanged, or without hope. It is here that the distinction between equality and autonomy becomes crucial. For if women are not more equal, they are certainly more autonomous.

More women have jobs, and therefore have access to incomes in their own right, and to the social benefits associated with work outside the home. More women are choosing to leave relationships in which they are subject to violence, or other forms of oppressive behaviour, which they find intolerable. Many single parent women regard themselves as better off on their own, even though they may depend on lower incomes, because they at least have complete control of the income they do have. More women are gaining access to housing in their own right, and therefore more control over the way in which they live. Women have more control over their fertility, and more women are choosing single motherhood. All those factors add up to a gain in autonomy for women, and indicate a continuing change in women's consciousness of how they wish to live their lives. Thatcherism may have increased the odds against women in Scotland, but women have not given up the struggle.

Esther Breitenbach

Acknowledgements: I would like to thank the following for helping me find information for the article – Pat Stuart, Ann Stafford, Lynn Jamieson, June Fraser, Norma Jones, Sue Robertson. I would also like to thank Lynn Jamieson for her comments on an earlier draft. The views expressed are, of course, my own.

References

1. The EOC's 'Women and Men in Scotland – a statistical profile" – a digest of statistics produced in 1985 to mark the end of the Un decade for women is the only publication of its kind yety to appear in Scotland. Even this is limited in its range, since it is restricted to areas covered by the Equal Pay and Sex Discrimination Acts. It covers population, education, training, employment, earnings, and public life, but not social security and national insurance benefits, pensions or housing. Many published statistics do not give breakdowns by sex for Scotland, or do not ask questions in the first place that would solicit the desired information. Whilst a great deal of information is available from the census, the frequency with which censi are carried out does not-allow a detailed historical picture to be built up. There remains a desperate need for statistical information on women in Scotland to be collected, and for in-depth research to be carried aout.

2. *Women and Men in Scotland – a statistical profile.* EOC, 1985, p.1.

3. *Scottish Abstract of Statistics*, No.15, 1986, p.1.

4. Statistics on Young Single Mothers in Scotland. Scottish Council for Single Parents.

5. See, E Breitenbach, "Women Workers in Scotland", *Pressgang*, 1982.

6. Diane Werneke, "The Economic Slowdown and Women's Employment Opportunities", *International Labour Review*, Vol.117, No.1, 1978, p.39.

7. EOC, *op cit*, p.26.

8. Maggy Meade-King, "Those Who Made it Can't Take it", *Guardian*, September, 1988.

9. John MacInnes, "The North-South Divide: Regional Employment Change in Britain 1975-87". Centre for Urban and Regional Research, Glasgow University, *Discussion Paper* No.34, p.3.

10. MacInnes, *op.cit*, p.9.

11. Peter Esam, Robert Good and Rick Middleton, "Who's To Benefit?", *Verso*, 1985, p.19.

12. Esam, Good and Middleton, *op. cit*, p.60.

13. Dulcie Groves, "Occupational Pension Provision and Women's Poverty in Old Age", in eds. Caroline Glendinning and Jane Millar, *Women and Poverty in Britain*, Wheatsheaf Books, Harvester Press, 1987, p.217.

14. Frank Field, "Behind the Tory Rhetoric the poor still suffer", *Guardian*, August 1, 1988.

15. Jane Lewis and David Piachaud "Women and Poverty in the Twentieth Century", Glendinning and Millar, *op cit.*, p.28.

16. Report of Women and Housing Sub-Committee, Edinburgh District Council, 29 March, 1988.

17. Mary Brailey, "Women's Access to Council Housing", *Planning Exchange Occasional Paper*, No.25, p.47.

18. Mary Brailey, *op cit.*, p.65.

19. See Mary Brailey, *op cit.*, p.50.

20. Mary Brailey, *op cit.*, p.18.

21. Report of Women and Housing Sub-Committee, Edinburgh District Council, 29 March 1988.

BLACK WOMAN, WHITE SCOTLAND

(A Comment on the Position of Black Women with particular reference to Scotland)

Rowena Arshad and Mukami McCrum

Since the paper by Miles/Muirhead[1] in the *Scottish Government Yearbook 1986*, Scottish thinking has in general shifted from a stance of total complacency about racism to one that accepts, be that grudgingly or willingly, that racism is not a problem confined to areas of high black[2] populations eg: Birmingham, London. This has resulted in measures adopted by local authorities and the voluntary sector, ranging from implementing equal opportunities policies and commissioning studies[3] on the needs of minority ethnic groups to spasmodic attempts at racism awareness/multi-cultural/anti-racist training programmes for personnel and fieldstaff.

Despite all this, 'awareness-raising' has yet to occur across the board nor has it radically affected existing policies. This paper does not wish to enter into a 'numbers debate'; it is immaterial if there was none, one or one hundred blacks per square mile, as the issue of equality within policies and general combatting of racism still exists. We do not intend to reiterate historical reasons for racism in Scotland; these have been well documented elsewhere. Instead it is our intention to comment on our own perceptions of the position of black women in Scotland today, and to investigate further how the triple oppressions of race, gender and class determine the lives of black women. We have chosen the areas of employment and service provision as examples though this is by no means an exhaustive list of categories. Before commenting on these areas, a section on the general position of black women and their relationship with the women's movement has to be included and understood for the rest of the paper to be in context.

It is also important to add, that whilst we refer to the triple oppression in the paper, race, gender and class cannot be tagged to each other mechanically for, as concrete social relations, they are enmeshed in each other and the particular intersections involved produce specific effects. The need for the study of the intersection of these divisions has been recognised by other black feminists.[4]

Not just a question of visibility

When documenting black experiences and black history, the black man is commonly used to represent the entire black population. The black woman continues to be invisible. This invisibility occurs not just through patriarchy but through racism. The women's movement as we know it today is often used to represent all women. The truth of the matter indicates differently. Radical feminist Adrienne Rich, in attempting to eulogize the role of white women, asserts:

"...It is important for white feminists to remember that – despite lack of constitutional citizenship, educational deprivation, economic bondage to men, laws and customs forbidding women to speak in public or to disobey fathers, husbands, and brothers – our white foresisters have, in Lillian Smith's words, repeatedly been 'disloyal to civilisation' and have 'smelled death in the word "segregation" ', often defying patriarchy for the frist time, not on their own behalf but for the sake of black men, women, and children. We have a strong anti-racist female tradition despite all efforts by the white patriarchy to polarize its creature-objects, creating dichotomies of privilege and caste, skin colour, and age and condition of servitude."[5]

There is little historical evidence to support Rich's claim that white women as a collective group are part of an anti-racist tradition. In fact, white women anti-slavery advocates, motivated by religious sentiment, chose to work to free the slave. However, this moral reform did not extend to an attack on racism. The status of black women continued to be lower than white women in the racial hierarchy. This was well-illustrated when well-known American women's rights advocate Elizabeth Cady-Stanton expressed anger that inferior 'niggers' should be granted the vote while 'superior' white women remain disenfranchised.[6]

The reason for mentioning the above is not to advocate divisions within the women's movement but simply to show the reasons behind the growth of a black feminist movement and to illustrate how history affects the shape of the women's movement today.

Bell Hooks, the black American feminist, states:

"In much literature written by white women on the 'woman question' from the nineteenth century to the present day, authors will refer to 'white men' but use the word women, when they really mean 'white woman'. Concurrently the term 'blacks' is often made synonymous with black men."[7].

By natural extension, when we use the term 'Scottish', to whom are we referring - a white Scotland or multi-racial Scotland? It is a matter of the speaker's perception of what is the norm. Who do we therefore mean when we use the term 'woman'? Today, the political struggle for equality in Scotland has produced women's committees, women-only events, women officers within trade unions, women representatives on committees and so on, but how many of these represent the voices of black Scottish women? We quote the Scottish Black Women's Group, who in 1986, stated:

> ".. There is no platform in Scotland at present that provides us with a base from which to express our point of view. There is much need to bring a political dimension into an area that is plagued by pseudo-cultural and quasi-sociological interpretations, that have led to inappropriate measures eg: 'racism-awareness training' and 'cultural evenings' for ethnic minorities which have done little to allow black women and the black community to define for themselves a course of action.."[8]

It is still the case today that the onus is on the black woman to put her identity on the personal and political agenda. But surely the reverse should be true if authorities, institutions operate equal opportunities policies as most now do.

However, it is not just a question of visibility. Hazel V Carby states:

> "..In arguing that most theory does not begin to adequately account for the experience of black women, we also have to acknowledge that it is not a simple question of their absence, consequently the task is not one of rendering visibility.."[9]

Indeed if visibility was the solution, the problem would cease to exist. As Usha Brown[10], a black feminist activist from Glasgow, cynically reminds us, black women are very much in vogue. There are studies, films, novels, stories and plays about us, but very little support for radical action that black women take. We are needed to provide our experiences, to prove that passive acceptance of oppression is part of our culture, and that black men are more oppressive. She adds that black women are caught in a Catch 22 position. She writes:

> "...Our opportunity for liberation lies in coming to the West – we either do not take advantage of it and continue to suffer, and whose fault is that? Or we do, but lose our ethnic appeal and are no longer black and still continue to suffer and whose fault is that?.."[11]

This scenario exists as our oppression is often seen to be a result of our religions, cultures, ethnic patterns and history. Presupposing this is the case, in challenging it we run the risk of exposing ourselves and our communities to further discrimination by those who capitalise on negative aspects of any minority groups. This same group are also of the opinion that problems exist because of the presence of blacks and not because of racism and prejudice.

To therefore state that the needs of black women are not met due to their invisibility would be misleading for black women are visible, but in areas and guises acceptable to a society operating within a racist framework.

Communality or Camouflage

There has tended to be a constant highlighting of the communality between the 'woman' and the 'black' – both of whom are up against sexist and racist structures. We feel this has alienated attention from the specificity of the oppression and contributions of black women. To begin with, we are both black and women; secondly, black feminists have been and are still demanding that the existence of racism must be acknowledged as a structuring feature of relationships with white women. Sojourner Truth, US black feminist pointed to the ways in which 'womanhood' was denied the black woman:

> "...That man over there says women need to be helped into carriages and lifted over ditches, and to have the best place everywhere. Nobody ever helps me into carriages and lifted me over ditches, or over mud-puddles, or gives me any best place! And ain't I a woman? Look at me! Look at my arm! I have ploughed and planted, and gathered into barns, and no man could head me! And ain't I a woman? I could work as much and eat as much as a man – when I could get it – and I have borne thirteen children and seen most sold off to slavery, and when I cried with my mother's grief, none but Jesus heard me! And ain't I a woman?..."[12]

The dehumanisation of black womanhood during the years of slavery whether indentured or otherwise has influenced the power position and images of black women today whether they be in the Third World or in the West.

Concepts often advocated by the women's movement as sources of oppression can and do become problematic when applied to black women, in particular the concepts of 'the family' and 'patriarchy'. In the comprehensive study of feminist theory *Women's Oppression Today* by Michele Barrett[13], the contemporary family (effectively under capitalism) is cited as a source of oppression. We would not deny that the family can and is a source of oppression but it has also served as a refuge for political and cultural resistance to racism. For many black Scottish women, the family unit is often the only security in the face of negative and often hostile experiences that face most black people in Britain. In addition, language isolation has meant for some that they are often most secure within the home and contact with outside communities may be virtually non-existent, as is their take-up of certain provisions and local authority services such as provision for their children, cervical smear tests and so forth. The family has also been, for many, the only sources informing them of existing facilities, and is the forum to give black women the confidence to use these facilities.

For many white Scots particularly from the Highlands and Islands, the idea of individualism is a historically alien concept. How much more alien then for the black Scottish woman, particularly first generation Scots whose roots lie in countries where familial, caste, tribal or national interests are often dominant? For us, struggles out of poverty, from racism, from isolation, from a Eurocentric culture define our priorities and also represent the major sources of our oppression.

White feminists have also emphasized 'patriarchy' as a cause of their oppression. The matter is not so simple – racism both individual and institutional ensures that black men do not have the same relations to patriarchal/capitalist hierarchies as white men in Scotland. In the words of the Combahee River Collective:

"...We struggle together with black men against racism, while we also struggle with black men about sexism..."[14]

In addition to addressing themselves to the white feminist analysis of roots of oppression, black women must also address themselves to the role of the state in defining their position in society and its relationship to black people (see final section of paper).

Special attention for 'ethnic minorities'

The British state waives its concerns for black people into an extensive and intricate network of bodies like the Commission for Racial Equality (CRE) and the Community Relations Council (CRC). From the state's point of view it is money well spent providing essential agencies for the promotion of good 'race relations'[15] For these organisations, who face cuts in their funding, the reality is often the opposite.

Here in Scotland, a position of complacency is being replaced by explanations for the existence of racism, for example, that it is due to the effects of cultural difference. The institutions no longer simply ignore the needs of black people and particularly black women, but regards these needs as 'problems' requiring a solution.

The line of argument most favoured and supported is that of the provision for the needs of black women. Attention is focussed on special needs based on their culture, ethnicity, religion, language. But focussing attention is not necessarily the same as responding to these needs. These needs cannot be met within the mainstream services, as mainstream provision tends to provide for what is perceived to be the norm group, which is often the white bourgeoisie.

Two steps need to occur. First it is necessary to look at alternatives which may appear as a threat to the established ways of working with black women; and second to challenge and change the stereotype of black women. Professionals and fieldstaff need to be educated about different values and expectations of different cultures. The emphasis should also not be on the needs but rather the rights of black women. But two potential dangers exist in the 'needs' ideology. First, in deciding what these needs are; and second, in that the solutions and responses offered are often made from a white perception of needs based on stereotypical imagery.

SERVICE PROVISION

Recently local authorities and government departments have made tremendous changes and advances in service delivery despite resource constraints which have encouraged service administrators to streamline and restrict facilities. April Carter[16] argues that pressure and campaigns by women has changed, to a degree, the attitudes of institutions both private and public, decision and policy makers, as well as the public as a whole. This has created greater opportunities for some women to attempt entering areas previously dominated and controlled by men. These gains, however, are far from adequate for all women and particularly black and poor women. This section also provides a brief case study of a project we consider to be an example of good practice in the field of service provision.

Social services

Provision of social services to black people is still on the agenda for political debates and comments years after the initial recruitment of black people to work in Britain. Comments include – 'black people are lazy', here to drain the economy and 'sponge' on social services, to 'black people are resourceful, independent with strong family ties who need no outside help or interference'. Political arguments which pose black people and their culture as a threat to the economy and white British values create an uncomfortable atmosphere for administrators and black users of social services. However, there have been serious attempts made by some local authorities to shift emphasis from cultural differences and family inadequacies, as an explanation for poor take-up of services, to analysing the institutions and their accessibility to the black community. This, coupled with an analysis of structural pressures, both economic and political, and the experience of being black in Scotland has helped to challenge misunderstandings and misconceptions of the black community and work towards a service more in tune with the expectations of black people. It has also to be said that it is often ignored that black people are tax-payers too, and consequently are entitled to the same access to services as any other tax-payers and consumers in this society. Examples of how wrong assumptions and expectations of black people by social workers and educators in their assessment and decision making affects service provision is well-documented.[17]

Within the Scottish context, in our experience, the majority of black women who make use of the social services first come into contact with the department after a crisis, for example, the breakdown of marriage, when social workers, doctors, teachers or the police decide that their children are difficult and need special attention or help. According to SHAKTI Women's Aid (see case study), some women are aware of the various statutory departments such as the Department of Health and Social Security, Social Work, Children's Panels, but none are aware of how these departments operate, the range of services on offer and the relationship between different institutions and departments. Due to lack of information, many black women encountering social services lose out by often agreeing to accept what is offered without question. It must be remembered that these encounters tend to be of a problem-solving nature and as such can sometimes be confrontational. Though departments are now publicising their services in community languages, it is futile doing so if the leaflets do not reach the intended readers or if the intended readers cannot in fact read the language – very often, as in the case of Panjabi, spoken Panjabi is common but few read or write it.[18]

Housing

Housing-related problems are the commonest complaints levied by black people. Since the inception of the Sex Discrimination Act 1976 and the Race Discrimination Act of 1975, blatant discrimination is no longer practised officially. However some practices, regulations and procedures deny black women equal access to better housing.[19] For example, a policy to house black people apart based on the assumption that housing them together creates ghettos results in much hardship for single parents, divorced women and the elderly. This is further substantiated by Shahid Ashrif who writes in Network 21 that:

> "...There have been cases drawn to the attention of the Housing Department where single parents with young children have been housed in all white housing estates on the outskirts of Glasgow, far from places of worship or where Asian foods were available. These women have not only suffered isolation from support of the Asian community but have also been subjected to systematic racial harassment..."[20]

The assumption that black people tend to have large families often

213

results in their being housed in sub-standard houses which are difficult to heat and have previously been rejected by white people. The expectation that black people will take care of their single homeless and the elderly means that many authorities make no provision at all for these groups. The changing nature of black families and the economic and social pressures that have altered kinship patterns are not taken into account. Organisations such as Shelter Scotland echo this sentiment as applicable to the general situation in Scotland.

Finally the regulations and procedures are often complicated, even for the most fluent of English speakers. For black women, lack of information in simplified jargon-free format, or in mother tongue languages creates further problems. The attitude of staff when conveying information and advice can be off-putting to black people especially when they are treated as ignorant clients who should be grateful for being in this country and beneficiaries of the 'welfare state' meant really for the 'real' British.

Quoting Shahid Ashrif again: "...black people ought to be housed in accordance with their needs and if these be cultural/religious, these ought to be considered seriously.."[21] The whole issue of housing black families and in particular black women needs to be discussed within all housing departments taking into account the requirements of black families, recognising how factors like racial harassment, security and isolation play an important part when determining allocation policies and the awarding of points.

Health

Health services for women in Scotland are improving particularly for those who know how to take advantage of what is now available. Recent campaigns to promote breast and cervical cancer screening through Well Women clinics, women's groups and doctors' surgeries have increased the numbers of women going forward for screening. However, during a recent screening session organised by West Lothian District Council in Spring 1988, not a single black woman came forward. To understand this, we need to examine the manner and nature of publicity, the times of the sessions, the location, access and eligibility for screening. Obviously, it is also important to find out from black women why they did not attend the clinics. Times and dates of these sessions are arranged by organisers and health board staff who carry out the screening. Organisers are given a choice between morning or afternoon sessions and women are invited to book for a specific time. Locations are often held within towns thus making it difficult for women who live in more rural villages with little or no direct and regular transport. In the case of West Lothian, although publicity was carried out through leaflets, posters and local press, five black women we spoke to said they had not heard of the special screening sessions. They added that they would not have gone anyway unless they knew of other black women who would accompany them. This makes sense when we realise that suggestions for such screening sessions often originate within women's groups. The majority of black women are not part of established women's groups started by such organisations as Community Education, Churches and the National Housewives' Registers. Black women – even the most articulate, academic women – express concern at attending all white women's groups, as experience dictates they are often alienated, patronised and sometimes rejected.

In a similar screening session at the Roundabout International Centre, Edinburgh, fifteen black women came forward for screening. The session was publicised through black women's groups and through centres dealing with black people. The sessions were open to black women only and the times coincided with other women's activities at the Centre. A similar session is currently being arranged in West Lothian in consultation with black women and community workers.[22] These sessions should be preferably staffed by both black and white health workers. We have chosen recent cancer screening campaigns as examples but we do not expect it to be different in other services offered by the Health Board.

Contraception, maternity and depression are other areas of concern to black women. Communication and the relationship between patient and doctor are vital to ensure correct diagnosis. The inability of medical staff to speak community languages coupled with a black patient's inability to speak fluent English often result in a confusing, intimidating consultation session, with the patient leaving unsatisfied, and the staff harassed. Diagnosis of someone suffering from post-natal 'blues' can be magnified to 'post-natal depression' and so on. The use of interpreters are increasing but there should be further training of medical staff in language awareness and communication skills.

Regarding childbirth, women complain that they are not allowed to practice their traditional rites because hospital routines do not take such needs into account.[23] Questions are not asked as to why the number of black women who attend ante-natal clinics do not take-up Parentcraft classes offered by hospitals to assist labour. Another area of concern is depression. Depression in black women is often assumed to be linked to cultural deficiencies rather than to problems that cause depression in all people such as marital problems economic and social pressures, isolation and loneliness. In addition, counsellors are mostly white and cannot understand the added problems caused by racism.

Recommendations for good practice service delivery

1. Challenging the 'open door' policy: This policy operates on the basis that the door is open and the onus is on the individual to make use of the facilities. Questions should be asked if the atmosphere behind

the door is welcoming to the black community and relevant to their needs. This policy also assumes that the client is familiar with the range of services on offer. Such policy ignores potential communication barriers and assumes the environment is 'racism-free'. Administrators of services have a responsibility to find out why black women do not use services and to create avenues for them to gain access. For example, it is a step in the right direction to have women-only sessions at public swimming pools, but there should also be female life-guards on duty.

2. Increasing language awareness among staff: The provision of better information in community languages is important because it indicates that the service offered is for all. Knowledge of one's rights to services helps a great deal.

3. Accessibility: Large imposing offices very often with no disabled or pushchair access are by their aura intimidating. These are often in busy city centres daunting to people who live on the outskirts where many housing estates are situated, or to people from rural areas. Access can be improved by holding local surgeries, or workshops or by sending representatives to rural areas and to places where black people meet, such as Gurdwaras (Sikh temples).

4. Eligibility for services: The whole area of criteria and eligibility needs to be examined with an anti-racist perspective, for example, the criteria for the allocation of daycare places within social services.

5. Recruitment of black workers has to be a priority to create a multi-racial workforce. These workers should not be employed to deal only with black issues but should be integrated into all aspects of service provision. It is often assumed wrongly that being black means understanding universally all other black people. Matching of black staff and black users should depend on whether staff and user desire it and share a common tradition. It is necessary to recognise the diversity of black people.

6. Training of present staff should continue. It is often easier to continue to depend on the Interpreting Service, goodwill among black volunteers or to pass the 'case' on to organisations such as CRC, CRE, Shakti, All this amounts to is an abdication of responsibility. Training should not be of a reflective, navel-gazing nature, but should allow workers to decide which good practice models to adopt.

This is by no means a comprehensive list, but represents, in our opinion, key areas. Changes are often slow to come about because of disbelief and resentment by service providers that their own institutions designed to help the vulnerable can fail black people, due to racism and discrimination. The following case study of a black women's refuge is an indication that improvements can be made when policy makers take positive action.

Case Study: Shakti Women's Aid

Shakti is a refuge for black women and their children (if any) who wish to escape domestic violence from husbands, partners or families. The need for a separate refuge was recognised because other refuges and statutory institutions were not equipped to give appropriate support and shelter for black women. Shakti was started by a group of black women supported by Edinburgh Women's Aid in 1985. The project was funded in 1986 by Edinburgh District Council.

Shakti refuge became operational in 1987. The project is run by a collective of women backed by a support group who share the aims and objectives of the project. They employ two full-time staff and have a team of volunteers. Since the refuge became operational, the demand for spaces has been regrettably high.[24]

Within a short time of starting, Shakti realised that it was impossible to remain a single issue project given the nature of the problems that women brought to them. Issues such as racism, health education, housing, welfare benefits and coping with and understanding the system were major problems that were identified. Shakti, with the help of the rich and varied experiences of women from different backgrounds, has embarked on a programme of publicity, education and consciousness-raising, liaison with statutory and voluntary agencies such as social work, police, schools and housing departments. Also Shakti liaises with women's groups all over Britain.

Finally, Shakti disproves the assumptions and expectations society holds for black women. Pramila Sachidharan argues that "...Separate refuges have allowed black women space to define their own terms in fighting racism and sexism, which would not have been possible in the mainstream women's aid movement..."[25] Shakti offers such a space to black women in Scotland and enables them to counteract socialisation which through male ridicule and aggression has intimidated women.

The challenge to all policy makers is to take positive action and introduce new ways of working with black women and the black community.

EMPLOYMENT

"The bulk of writings on women's employment falls into three categories: political, educational books and pamphlets, theoretical writings and empirical case studies. Of the wide variety of 'educational' material available, much of it is devised for women trade unionists and activists: material on employment legislation, legislation on women's place in the workforce and on women in trade unions. The more academic writings about women's paid work have veered between theoretical analyses and empirical case studies.."[26]

Statistics on black women in mainstream employment in Scotland, in fact statistics on black women on any category, is virtually non-existent. Monitering is often based on ethnic or gender origins, and there is no mechanism to allow for cross-referencing. When we approached the Equal Opportunities Commission (EOC), Glasgow, requesting information and statistics, we were sent a publication titled *Women and Men in Scotland*, a statistical profile published in 1985 representing the latest figures for Scotland. This digest of statistics was prepared to depict the relative position of women and men in Scottish society. This did not breakdown to ethnic groups. We were also informed that the EOC did not deal with matters on 'race' or 'colour', as this was the responsibility of the CRE. The CRE informed us that it was already an up-hill struggle for them in their attempts to get employers to monitor ethnically. They were unable to help beyond that. There is little or no collaboration between the two organisations. This raises the indeterminable question of the position of black women within statistical studies.

As April Carter states in her book *The Politics of Women's Rights*:

"..Women have suffered particularly from the cumulative effects of 'Thatcherism' and from unemployment. Black women have come out worse in this, since they have to contest both racism and sexism, and in addition the majority of them are the poorest sector of society. They have therefore been particularly vulnerable to unemployment – for example the unemployment rate for all women under 25 between 1980 and 1981 rose by 58% but for black women, it rose by 64%..."[27]

There are no more recent statistics, and the figures above represent Britain as a whole. Research is being updated currently, but we are unable to quote from it as materials are very much in first draft stages. The situation is changing, through pressure from women's committees and women's officers within government, but the pace of this change has been modest. There is still no requirement to monitor equality of access to employment in many areas. Where there has been monitoring, such as the civil service and within local government, the information is not easily obtainable or easy to decipher, and may be published for some but not all government departments.

Again the figures do not breakdown to show the number of black women. It is also important to add that statistics can be biased, depending on how and where the survey was carried out. For example, surveys based on heads of households may well under-record households headed by black women or are likely to miss the poorer households. Bias in representation and response has therefore to be considered.

Potential Obstacles facing Black Women in Employment

D J Smith states that "...Women are already discriminated against as women, and this tends to restrict them to more junior and less well-paid jobs: they are therefore not regarded as a threat, and there is less need for employers to discriminate against them on the ground of colour as well in order to keep them in a subordinate position..."[28] We would be wary of accepting these comments uncritically as some authors have done.[29] It cannot be denied that black women face dual discrimination. Moreover, some employers are now women, predominantly white women, and racial discrimination can be a bigger obstacle than sexual discrimination for black women gaining employment – as for instance, black mothers often face greater obstacles with regard to childminding than do white mothers.[30] A report on working mothers and childminding in 'ethnic minority communities'[31] confirmed that Asian and West Indian women face a particular disadvantage in this sphere. The study presented a number of other factors. Firstly, black women are less able to get access to the day-care provision they most desired than white mothers. Secondly, they had less access to subsidized or free services ie: day nurseries and nursery schools. Thirdly, they had greater difficulty finding childminders near their home; and finally, some white minders refused to take black children.

The whole area of black single parenthood whether through divorce or otherwise, has not been studied. The number of black single parents is on the increase. The issues of having good childminding provision, being kept informed of employment opportunities, crossing the language barrier, become all the more vital for black women in this category.

In our discussions with Scottish black community workers and black women seeking jobs in professional areas, we found that age, family circumstances and education affect the type of jobs women aspire to or are channelled into. The internal gender divisions of each ethnic group will also affect the participation of men and women of the group in the labour market. In Scotland, the majority of Afro-Caribbean men are professionals, most coming as students in the last decade or post World War Two. Afro-Caribbean women continue to be employed as service workers – in particular auxilliaries within the National Health Service. Older Asian women, particularly the Chinese women over the age of 30, tend to be employed in the family catering industry such as take-aways and supermarkets. The younger women seek jobs outside family businesses in the financial sector such as banking. It is often felt that parental influence and some career guidance staff often channel the young women to work within their community because of racism and discrimination in mainstream employment.[32] This ideology is further substantiated by research carried out by the Training, Education and Employment for Minorities Project (TEEM)[33] which highlights not only the constraints on black teenagers in seeking the employment of their choice, but as expressed by TEEM researcher Abdou Said Bakar, 'protective channelling' into safe jobs often occurs. Though this is often done with the best intentions, it sidesteps two issues, one that young blacks are not allowed for whatever reason to gain equal access to mainstream employment, and two, a recognition by employers of the factors preventing access, one of which is racism. It is right at this point to raise the question of the effectiveness of equal opportunities policies. Equal opportunities is about changing the environment so that black people can be employed equally; it should also be about ensuring the current workplace environment is ready to accept black workers.

The continuing assumptions about black women, in particular 'Asian female domesticity' and cultural constraints have affected black women's ability in gaining employment. It is often ignored that black women like any other have always borne the multiplicity of roles, as carers, mothers, consumers, providers, objects of desire and abuse. They too tend to be at the bottom of the pay and power scales, employees not employers, and unpaid sowers, reapers and breadmakers, not recognised to be breadwinners. As Pratibha Parmer suggests: "what is new about their situation in Britain is that they have not worked in an industrial situation. It was the experience of working outside the home in a non-agrarian industrial capitalist enterprise that was different rather than the experience of working to subsidize the family.."[34]

Aid agencies and development education researchers have for a long time supported the illusion that Third World women who are involved in subsistence work, do not really 'work'. As a result, black women's experience as workers attained in the so-called Third World are often marginalised, as are the qualifications they obtain. A stark example is that of an experienced teacher of 28 years experience, trained with a British University, who was not given recognition when settling in Britain and ended her working career as a catering assistant and cleaner (one of the author's parents). This was not because of incorrect paper qualifications, but that teaching in a foreign country and the methodologies used there are unrecognised. Black women due to their lack of appropriate qualifications, and often due to the inequality of the education system, have not always been best prepared for the labour market. We argue that 'on-the-job training' must return as common provision by employers in order to assist the redressing of the current imbalance. This, of course, applies not only to black women, but is generally applicable for all people who have been discriminated against because of gender, race, class and disability.

On the other hand, many employers can claim that black women have entered semi-professional and professional jobs, such as the authors of this paper. On closer examination, these women have more often than not, ended up in race-related fields, such as multi-cultural education, community relations councils, or projects sponsored to work with multi-racial communities. Women in this category are often used to provide anti-racist training, and to lend credibility by acting as token blacks on committees and other forums. Their opinions are requested on draft policy papers, to assist in areas unrelated to their job descriptions, and many are over-worked and underpaid for the amount of work and advice offered. Other black women beaver away at the grassroots level for the community again without status, recognition or financial remuneration. We would perhaps understandably adopt a more cynical view of this but would like to add that there have also been genuine attempts made by policy makers and management to include the black woman's perspective.

Images, labelling, assumptions and false expectations have been most influential in shaping the attitude of employers to the black community and black women. Usha Brown argues that the assumption that black girls will marry young or enter family businesses is not only damaging but misleading. It ignores the fact that there is a large number of black working class families who do not have family businesses or corner shops. Women in these situations do not have real choices. The economic pressures that affect most for example, high-mortgage repayment, high rents, increasing cost of living, result in women going into the 'informal' economy as a result of the recession (homeworking is an example), or remaining wageless due to the absence of access to mainstream employment either because of imappropriate or lack of qualifications, language barriers, institutionalised racism, lack of good childcare provision or a combination of all these factors. Others enter part or full-time employment in service industries where they remain invisible; as cleaners they enter offices after dark, as cooks they remain in the kitchens, and as seamstresses, they stay at home.

Another question to be answered must be that of the number of black youngsters who enter further education. Universities in Scotland have a large black population made up of overseas students which often misleads and allows the educational establishments to ignore the growing black Scottish population. If black youngsters are not entering further education colleges, skills training centres, we need to find out the reasons.

Recommendations for Equality in Employment

Most of these recommendations have been suggested by the Scottish Ethnic Minorities Research Unit (SEMRU) report[35] and many are expressed by the minority ethnic communities. In addition, we would add,

221

that policy makers and employers committed to equality and change must first shake off what has for so long been regarded as the common-sense image of black women (in particular Asian women) that the reasons for their low position/numbers in the labour force and low participation in trade unions are due to language difficulties and cultural constraints. Black women are aware that there is an unspoken assumption that they are dumb and inferior because they cannot speak English. Without entering another field of debate, we merely wish to state that more awareness of language as a specific form of oppression is required.

1. Active recruitment of black people, especially women. These should include personnel with bi-lingual skills. Employment of black staff is particularly crucial to the fields of health, social work and education. Employment of black women should not be limited to jobs such as hospital auxilliaries, cleaners, administrative officers, and junior clerks.

2. Training of current staff, particularly senior and middle management to the insidious workings of institutionised racism and discrimination.

3. A review of evaluation procedures and criteria for acceptance onto training schemes, and jobs in general. Systematic ethnic monitoring will also show up gender differences.

4. Better information exchange between potential employers and the black community. Information about loans and grants available to allow self-employment, business enterprise schemes, and better use of the Careers Advisory Service. On-the-job training should be a considered option. The establishment of training centres for women, with active recruitment of black women.

5. Improved childcare facilities for all women. Making sure information of the full range of options is accessible for black women. Leaflets should be produced to cover community languages.

6. Making sure the equal opportunities policies are not farcical. Challenging the 'open door' policy. (see recommendation 1 in the Service Delivery section). Advertising of jobs should not be via 'word of mouth' as this would discriminate unintentionally against the black community. Jobs should be advertised in minority ethnic press and magazines.

Radical or Cosmetic Change?

"...Over the past ten years, we had seen the appearance of volumes of material documenting our struggles as Black people, and of course we welcomed this for we had relied for too long on the version of our story put forward by white historians and sociologists. And we have seen the women's movement follow suit, documenting 'her story' from every angle except our own. But despite the efforts of Black men and white women to ensure we were no longer 'hidden from history', there was still a gaping silence from Black women..."[36]

These sentiments were expressed in a publication by women in England in 1985. We agreed to contribute to this Yearbook as we felt the voices of black Scottish women still remain unheard. A case in point is the difficulty we had in writing this paper due to the lack and non-existence of information regarding the position of black women in Scotland. Most research carried out on black women has been done south of the border and mainly from a white perspective, be that male or female, middle or working-class. This has allowed an assumption that black women's experiences are uniform and coupled with the popoular view that Scotland has 'good race relations because there is no racism here' has meant that not only is the position of black Scottish women been ignored, it is actually worse. It also raises the question as to why the majority of research has been carried out by white academics. Organisations like the EOC assume they represent all women, but the reality is somewhat different. Most organisations, both governmental and non-governmental, cater for the status quo, (the white population in Scotland) many do not automatically include the black viewpoint. This is further highlighted when we examine the recently published findings of the Low Pay Unit in Edinburgh.[37]

The Unit Report has been welcomed by low-paid workers and campaigners against low pay. Though the report highlights occupations that are poorly- paid, one wonders if workers in take-aways, restaurants or even homeworkers have been considered. It can be argued by the researchers that these areas were included under the general occupations of chefs/cooks, waitresses or shop assistants. In an 'all being equal' situation, this explanation would be acceptable. However, the current perception of the Scottish reader of the report would not extend to black low-paid workers or homeworkers. Therefore these areas do merit a mention to ensure that readers do incorporate them into their sphere of understanding and analysis. Secondly, the report includes an Employment Rights Checklist, but how many black groups know of its existence?

This invisibility of black women and their communities will continue as long as access to decision and policymaking bodies remains unequal. The political arena in Scotland is white, male-dominated, and in general more interested in strategies for obtaining the black/woman vote, but less committed to adopting policies that would either allow the black or white woman an active role within politics, or to policies that represent social change rather than reform. The women's committees and the existence of women's officers will continue to be farcical as long as their existence is dependent on the whims of the ruling party, their ability to respond to women's demands is limited, and the constraints of having to operate within male-defined structures are not removed. In addition, as we would argue that women do organise differently to men, it must be recognised that black people have different priorities too. It is often assumed that the forum exists for individuals to participate equally and that the black person can join and fit in. This concept of integration has in practice been that of assimilation. It is a sad fact that the first black woman Member of Parliament (MP) in Britain was only elected in the last general election. When, if ever, will Scotland send a black woman MP to Westminster or the Scottish Assembly, should it exist?

One area that is common to all black women and is often specific to the black community is that of Immigration. Pratibha Parmer documents instances of how racist immigration laws affect black women (in particular Asian women from the Indian sub-continent): long periods of separation from husbands and/or dependent children, being subjected to humiliating medical examinations for diseases or strip searches reminiscent of virginity tests at ports of entry all create a great deal of mental stress and tension to women. As Sivanandan puts it "...successive British governments, whether Tory or Labour have used Nationality Laws and Immigration Acts to adjust intake of labour in Britain...".[38] However, primary immigration is now down to a trickle and has been so for many years, and existing control in the main is now affecting families waiting to be reunited. For many black people, two messages are clear; if you want family life, go home; if you want to live in peace, go home. A case of immigration control has become 'induced repatriation'. When approaching Community Relations Council officers, the subject that most worries the first-generation black in Scotland is one of immigration. This is particularly acute for black women who have to depend on husbands for their right to reside in this country. Many of these women often have to put up with brutal treatment rather than face deportation and separation from, or worse, losing their children. These abuses have been further documented elsewhere.[39] We do not have the space to acknowledge fully the extent of damage this form of state control has over black lives. This area merits a paper of its own.

Real change would mean accepting that racism does prevent black women's full participation on equal terms in the political, social, economic and cultural life of Scotland. Instead of taking black women as objects of research or groups in 'need', it is more advisable for politicians and policymakers to uncover class and gender specific mechanisms of racism amongst the white society. Finally, we would ask, when the term 'Scottish' or 'Woman' is used, who do you mean?

Rowena Arshad, Co-ordinator, Multi-Cultural Education Centre.
Mukami McCrum, Senior Development Worker, SHAKTI, Women's Aid.

References

1. Miles R & Muirhead L, 'Racism in Scotland: A Matter for Further Investigation' in *Scottish Government Yearbook 1986*, Unit for the Study of Government in Scotland, Edinburgh 1986, pp.108-136.

2. We have chosen the word 'black' to refer to all people of colour who are discriminated against by racist structures and attitudes within Scotland's white dominated culture.

3. Ethnic Minorities Profiles: *A Study of Needs and Services in Lothian Region and Edinburgh*, Vol.I, II, III, by Scottish Ethnic Minorities Research Unit (SEMRU), Edinburgh College of Art/Heriot-Watt University, Edinburgh, 1987.

4. Anttias F and Yuval-Davis N, 'Contextualizing Feminism – Gender, Ethnic and Class Divisions' in *Feminist Review*, Winter 1983, London, pp.62-75.

5. Hooks Bell quotes Adrienne Rich in *A'int I A Woman: Black Women and Feminism*, Pluto Press, London, 1981, pp.125.

6. *ibid*, pp.125-128.

7. *ibid*, pp.125-128.

8. *Edinburgh Women's Liberation Newsletter*, No.41 Scottish Black Women's Issue, Edinburgh, Nov. 1986.

9. Carby H.V., 'White Women Listen, Black Feminism and the Boundaries of Sisterhood' in *The Empire Strikes Back; Race and Racism in 70's Britain*, Hutchison & Co., London, 1982, pp.183-211.

10. Brown U, 'What The Shouting Is About' in *Edinburgh Women's Liberation Newsletter*, Scottish Black Womens' Group Issue, Nov. 1986, Edinburgh.

11. *ibid*.

12. Carby HV, quotes Sojourner Truth, *op cit*. pp.214.

13. Barrett M, *Women's Oppression Today*, Verso 1980.

14. Combahee River Collective, 'A black feminist statement' in Moraga

and Andzaldua (eds) *This Bridge Called My Back: Writings by Radical Women of Color*, Persephone Press 1981, p.213.

15. We remind the reader that the term 'race relations' is an ideological construct rather than a given reality – as stated by R Miles and A Dunlop in 'The Racialisation of Politics in Britain: Why Scotland is Different' in *Patterns of Prejudice*, Vol.20, No.1, 1986 – a view the authors of this paper support.

16. Carter A, 'Women in the Eighties' in *The Politics of Women's Rights*, Longman Group UK Limited, 1988, pp.107-8.

17. *Employment, Education and the Community*, Unit 15 and 16, Open University Press, Milton Keynes, Reprinted edition 1985.

18. Further information can be obtained from Shakti Women's Aid, Edinburgh.

19. Black women fleeing domestic violence often find they cannot be housed easily in certain districts as they are deemed to lack a 'local connection criteria' required by some local authorites. Edinburgh District Council and SHAKTI have a special arrangement to overcome this problem.

20. Ashrif, S, 'Developing an Antiracist Approach to Welfare and Social Services' in *Network 21*, Winter 1988, Moray House College of Education, Edinburgh.

21. *ibid*.

22. Since this article was written, the screening session in West Lothian had taken place. In this instance over 14 black women came forward.

23. Oral evidence from Chinese Community Worker, May Fong, based at the Lothian Community Relations Council.

24. More information available direct from SHAKTI Women's Aid, Edinburgh.

25. Sachidharan P, 'Separate Refuges for Black Women: Ghettos or Power Houses' in *Leeds Black Women's Newsletter*, Issue No.1, Jan.1987.

26. Beechey V, 'What's so special about women's employment? A review of some recent studies of women's paid work', in *Feminist Review*, Winter, 1983, No.15, London.

27. *op cit*, pp .

28. Smith D J, in *Racial Disadvantage: The PEP Report*, Penguin, 1977.

29. Phizacklea A, & Miles R, in *Labour and Racism*, Routledge and Kegan Paul, p.9.

30. Parmer P, 'Gender, race and class: Asian women in resistance', in *The Empire Strikes Back: Race and Racism in 70's Britain*, Centre for Contemporary Cultural Studies, Hutchison & Co. London 1982, p.248.

31. *Who Minds*, Report on working mothers and childminding in 'ethnic' minority communities, Community Relations Council, 1975.

32. *op cit*, May Fong.

33. *op cit*, pp.99-126.

34. *op cit*, p.249.

35. *op cit*, Vol.11, Appendix IV, pp.1-6.

36. Bryan B, Dadzie S, Scafe S, in *The Heart of the Race: Black Women's Lives in Britain*, Virago Press Lit. 1985, p.1.

37. *Low Pay in Edinburgh*, published by Edinburgh Low Pay Project, 1988.

38. Sivanadan A, 'From Immigration Control to Induced Repatriation' in *A Different Hunger: Writings on Black Resistence*, Pluto Press Ltd, London 1982, pp.133-135.

39. See back copies of *Race Today* and *Spare Rib*. Also: T Wallace and R Moore, in *Slamming The Door*, Martin Robertson, 1975.

WOMEN IN TRADE UNIONS IN SCOTLAND

Yvonne Strachan and Lesley Sutherland

Introduction

An assessment of women's participation and locus in the trade unions in Scotland requires to be prefaced by a brief analysis of their position in employment.

As much of this has been dealt with under other sections of the Yearbook it is only necessary to outline the matter here. A cursory glance at women in and indeed out of paid employment suffices to show that they continue to be treated differently and less well than men, and that employment policies and strategies which fail to recognise the different employment experience of women discount over 50% of the population. One of the significant aspects of women's involvement in the trade union movement is that women are beginning to change how they and their work are perceived within the trade union movement.

The mainstream perception of women's employment is that it is peripheral to the individual and to the economy. This is despite the fact that women are frequently the sole wage earner, head the vast majority of single parent families and provide essential income in a substantial number of households. The notion that women's work is peripheral in terms of the economy is also questionable if one considers the rate and density of female employment and the hidden contribution of women's unpaid labour. Women bear the major burden of domestic responsibility and do the bulk of community and voluntary care. The myths about women's employment are fuelled by the fact that women's employment is often ignored in employment and economic strategies, and limited statistics and analyses are available on women in the labour market.

From what is available we are able to glean that women's participation in the labour market has increased over the last few years. The 1984 Census of Employment shows that the rate of female participation in employment is higher in Scotland at 44.2% than in Great Britain as a whole at 43.9%. The difference was solely attributable to a higher rate of female part-time employees in Scotland.[1]

The part-time nature of much female employment is another feature. Women also experience interruption to work through maternity and childcare or the care of other dependants. Women's employment tends also to be concentrated in certain sectors – e.g. the public services/caring services; component manufacture; retailing and clerical; and because women's work is so segregated, it has been undervalued and regarded as unskilled. This in turn creates the conditions for low and unequal pay. (see Table 1).

Women by the nature of their employment are much more vulnerable to being used as a reserve labour force – being drawn in and discarded from the labour market as expediency dictates. Government policy and employers' strategies, (such as, employing workers for fewer than 16 hours a week and thereby excluding them from such employment rights as are left, or paying less than £41 per week so as to avoid paying employers' National Insurance), conspire to make women a particularly vulnerable and exploited section of workers. Employers tend not to invest in part-time workers when it comes to training and indeed it is true that women generally have much less access to training and skills acquisition. To compound the situation, women's wages, on average, still remain (despite legislation) substantially below that of men's. In fact the General Municipal Boilermakers and Allied Trades Union (GMBATU) neatly summed up the position of women with regard to earnings in a recent publication.[2] They argued that sex bias is robbing women of some £15 billion per year and quoted the following statistics:

> Whilst men who constituted 55% of the total employees in employment worked 64% of the hours, and had 72% of the total income from employment: women, who constituted 45% of employees, worked 36% of the hours, and took home only 28% of the income.

From current economic and employment trends, it seems unlikely that the position of women in employment is going to improve. The increase in part-time employment which ought ostensibly to provide greater opportunities for women, more often provides opportunities for greater exploitation, as such expansion has not been matched with the employment rights accorded to full-time employees. The trend towards the development of so-called 'green field' sites signals more low-skill employment in, for example, component assembly, in which women are presumed to be more competent. The Government's concerted attempts to strip the nation of its assets through the sale of the nationalised industries and the wholesale privatisation of local and public services has, and is having, a devastating effect on women's employment, in terms of lower wages and even fewer employment rights.

How then has the trade union movement responded to the predicament of women in the labour market?

TABLE 1   Employees in employment by occupational group, Scotland 1981.

Occupational group	Men		Women Full-time		Part-time		Total (= 100%)
	000's	%	000's	%	000's	%	000's
Professionals supporting management	44.8	77.7	11.2	19.4	1.6	2.8	57.6
Professionals in education, welfare and health	56.6	30.0	94.6	50.1	37.6	19.9	188.8
Literary, artistic and sports	6.1	58.3	2.9	28.1	1.4	13.6	10.5
Professionals in science, engineering, technolgy	73.6	91.9	6.0	7.4	0.5	0.7	80.0
Managerial	87.3	79.8	19.9	18.1	2.2	2.0	109.4
Clerical and related	75.6	23.8	186.2	58.6	56.2	17.7	318.0
Selling	43.2	32.4	42.5	31.9	47.7	35.8	133.3
Security and protective service	48.7	91.0	3.0	5.6	1.8	3.4	53.6
Catering, cleaning, hairdressing and other personal service	43.7	17.6	77.2	31.3	127.6	51.4	248.5
Farming, fishing and related	40.6	91.9	2.3	5.1	1.3	3.0	44.2
Materials, processing, making and repairing (excl metal & electrical)	97.2	64.1	45.0	29.6	9.5	6.3	151.7
Processing, making, repairing etc (metal & electrical)	222.4	96.7	7.0	3.0	0.5	0.2	229.9
Painting, repetitive assembling, product inspecting, packaging etc	38.9	54.7	28.2	39.6	4.0	5.7	71.2
Construction, mining etc	69.8	99.5	0.3	0.5	–	–	70.2
Transport operating, materials moving and storing	130.5	94.6	6.0	4.4	1.4	1.0	137.9
Miscellaneous	40.6	89.6	4.1	9.0	0.7	1.5	45.4
Inadequately described	8.1	53.3	5.5	35.9	1.6	10.8	15.2
Total	1127.6	57.4	541.7	27.6	295.8	15.1	1965.1

Source: Census 1981 Scotland: Economic Activity, Table 3.

Over the past ten years or so the unions have become more sensitive to the experiences and needs of women. In the following sections the representative aspects of women's participation and their impact on policy and campaigns is examined. It is important, however, not to omit or disregard less tangible aspects such as changes in the perceptions and attitudes towards women in the trade unions. This shift, it may be argued, emanates from three main sources. The first is from women in trade union themselves. Women's involvement in trade unions is not a new phenomenon. Indeed Esther Breitenbach identified a reference to women's union action as early as 1852 by the Edinburgh Maidservants Union Society.[3] Moreover, women engaged in industrial disputes and campaigns have frequently shown themselves to be committed, tenacious and inventive in their strategies. For example at Lee Jeans the women occupied the factory in the face of closure and subsequently set up a co-operative to maintain production. This spirit was refreshing when other closures in the central belt had met with little resistance. The women at Plessey had wholeheartedly defended their factory at Bathgate and were instrumental in generating widespread community support for the campaign against closure. The factory did in fact close but several of the women activists continue to work and campaign in the West Lothian area. Women against Pit closures which emerged from the combined efforts of women in the mining communities during the miners strike, demonstrated to the movement how women, hitherto not involved in political activity, could effectively organise solidarity and generate widespread national political and financial support. So successful was the organisation of women that in many areas it was their support which sustained the strike. The impact of the women's organisation was felt, not only on the strike but in the domestic relationships of the women and indeed in the relationship of the women's groups to the NUM itself. Consideration was given to the women's demand for associate membership, a demand which had been agreed in the Scottish Area, but did not take effect nationally.

Women have, therefore, come to demand more from their unions, in terms of recognition of their status and a responsiveness to their needs as women workers. This development is linked in its evolution to the second source – the growth of the women's movement and feminism together with the movements for equality and civil rights. These movements highlighted the subordinate role of women in society. Thirdly, the trade unions themselves have been forced to review their organisation, their structures and their traditional recruitment policies – particularly those unions whose industrial base was most affected by the onslaught on traditional manufacturing industries perpetrated through the Government's economic policies. Unions have had to examine how to sustain their membership and indeed expand it. As part-time and temporary workers are notoriously ill-organised, unions have seen them as a potential source of new members. Moreover the changes in employment patterns mentioned above are engaging more women in the labour market and altering the profile of 'a worker'; no longer so readily identifiable as a white, semi-skilled, male, working full-time in a large factory and sole family wage earner. It would be improper to conclude, however, that unions are involved only in a cynical recruitment exercise. While undoubtedly unions are anxious to recruit, they also have to meet the articulated demands of their women members. Unions have, therefore, also given attention to their image and considered seriously how they might increase their attraction and responsiveness to women members.

Trade unions constitute the means of collective representation and protection at work and this applies to all workers whether male or female. It is encumbent on the unions to ensure that they are capable of embracing the needs of all members. The attempt to weaken unions through legislation and the judicial process, as we have witnessed in the 1980/82 Employment Acts and the 1984 Trade Union Act and in the removal of legislation on recognition rights, has made the job of organising workers more difficult, particularly in areas of low unionisation, such as part-time employment. The situation for vulnerable groups of workers, including women, is aggravated by the erosion of employment protection such as maternity and unfair dismissal rights, and is most certainly not helped by the strategies of some employers. These include employing people at sufficiently few hours so that earnings fall below the threshold at which it is necessary to pay National Insurance contributions; and employing more part-time workers because this reduces costs in the areas of pensions, holidays, overtime, and even the basic rate of pay. Furthermore the Government's White Papers entitled 'Lifting the Burden' and 'Building Businesses not Barriers' give some indication of its attitude towards employment protection. The Government see protection as a barrier to job creation and a burden on employers. Part-time workers can expect their pay and conditions to deteriorate further if the proposals contained in these papers come into effect. The proposed increase in the number of hours required to be worked before a worker is covered by employment protection is an area of major concern, and the effects would be felt by a considerable number of women part-time workers. Women therefore have been playing, and must continue to play, a significant role in sustaining and developing trade unions to meet the challenges of the times.

Membership and Participation in Trade Unions

The capacity to influence change depends very much on the influence one exerts on the instruments of change – in this case the trade union movement. The degree of influence is often commensurate with the degree of participation, representation and extent to which one's views are considered. For women then it is crucial that they are represented in and enabled to participate fully in the trade union movement.

It is virtually impossible to provide an accurate statistical statement of the size and extent of women's involvement in the trade union movement in Scotland. Very few studies have been done on the subject and there is a lack of relevant data. Many unions do not differentiate between men and women in their membership returns and in turn are unable to register the number of women members with the Scottish Trades Union Congress (STUC). Furthermore, there are few singularly Scottish unions and of the British unions, not all will keep membership figures for Scotland. It has been known for some unions to estimate their Scottish female membership based on national percentages. This, however, is inaccurate and does not take account of regional variation which can be quite substantial. (For example, the Transport and General Workers Union (TGWU) has a national figure of women workers of 16% whilst the Scottish figure is 22%.) this means that the STUC figure of 300,000 women members out of a total of 910,000 may well be an underestimate.

Two studies have been helpful to those interested in this area of women's involvement. Esther Breitenbach in her book 'Women Workers in Scotland' (1982) provides the fullest examination of women at work and in trade unions in Scotland (this study is referred to in John Leopold's paper – 'Trade Unions in the 1990s'). The statistics are drawn from 1979 figures and clearly there have been changes since then, but our experience would indicate that many of her conclusions remain valid today. The second study, conducted by the Trade Union Research Unit (TURU) in 1986 for the STUC, attempts to provide details of the participation and representation of women in the trade union movement in Scotland.

Although a number of unions did not respond to the survey, the information provided demonstrates very clearly that women are still not proportionately represented within their unions and confirms our experience that women still face barriers to their fullest participation, see Table 2.

To a certain extent we should not be surprised, if disappointed, that this section of the working population has been neglected for so long. Historically trade unions have given scant attention to the needs of women. Indeed several unions debarred women from membership for a considerable time. Despite the crusading efforts of women who, at the turn of the century and into the 1920s, laid the foundations for women in trade unions – and of course the impact of the active role of women during the war years – women generally were not regarded as key workers, but rather as cheap labour, peripheral to the economy. Women were primarily seen as houseworkers, responsible for the children and the domestic maintenance of the man/men of the house, and whenever domestic or national circumstances dictated, they could be drawn into the labour market. Once in paid employment they occupied low status, low paid jobs and the opportunity for improvement often eluded them as domestic commitments and employers' attitudes rarely opened up access to training and

TABLE 2 Representation of Women within a sample of Unions in Scotland 1985/86.

Union	Total Memb.	Female Memb	% of Women	Total FTO	Female FTO	
TGWU	132,564	30,416	23	54	3	(10)
GMB	115,941	44,750	39	29	3	(11)
AEU	95,000	15,000	16	19	0	(3)
NUPE	71,443	48,581	68	16	2	(11)
USDAW	45,396	29,103	64	20	1	(13)
EIS	45,559	29,150	64	14	3	(9)
COHSE	24,600	20,172	82	5	0	(4)
BIFU	22,000	11,500	52	4	1	(2)
NUR	12,376	693	6	2	0	–
APEX	6,117	3,485	57	4	0	(3)
NUJ	2,251	475	21	1	0	–

TURU Survey 1986

The figures in brackets denote the number of female full-time officers (FTO) posts which should exist in relations to the number of women members.

(The pattern of under-representation is repeated if one examines the decision-making committees of trade unions and the leading lay positions.)

---

promotion. As trade union members, women frequently found that they were regarded as second class members.

They were often, in the early days, regarded with suspicion and treated as inferior because they paid lower union contributions. Few women participated in the management of unions and, as is the case today, women did not find it easy to get involved in union activities. In 1920 Barbara Drake, in a study commissioned by (LRD), highlighted the problems faced by women in trade unions and the obstacles to their participation. She observed that most women were employed in a limited number of occupations which were largely unskilled and low paid. Most women had a broken term of industrial life and women's work was widely undervalued. In most industries women did not receive equal pay. The work status of women was reflected in their status within the trade union movement. Most women found it hard to participate in union activities; and the reasons cited were the burden of home duties, the comparative lack of experience, and the long tradition of women's social and economic dependence on men. These problems mirror the situation today. Women were not being considered and did not have the power, control or influence within trade unions to bring about the necessary changes.

The last two decades have begun to alter this situation. As we described in the Introduction, several factors have shifted the perspectives of trade unions. The 1970s witnessed the construction of a legislative framework to begin to combat discrimination against women in employment, such as the Sex Discrimination Act, Equal Pay Act, and Employment Protection Act (viz. maternity rights). A corresponding shift in emphasis on women has taken place within most political party programmes, and trade unions have taken up the issue, not only with respect to policy and campaigns but in terms of internal structures and representation. Conference agendas began to reflect the demand for increased rights/representation, the call for positive action programmes and more imagination in the areas of recruitment and organisation. An examination of the facts led trade unions to accept that the lack of women involved in decision-making and policy formulation meant that their perspective was missing. This was particularly evident in the field of pay bargaining where claims reflected the concerns of the male full-time workers – percentage increases, bonus payments, guaranteed minimum hours and overtime payments. Pay claims were very rarely loaded in favour of the low paid or part-time workers. Further issues like maternity/parental agreements were rarely confronted. At the same time unions recognised that to expect the situation to change without an intervention was naive. Hence the move to positive action programmes and internal change.

Several unions established Women's Advisory Committees (Union of Shop, Distributive, and Allied Workers (USDAW), National Union of Public Employees (NUPE),Transport and General Workers' Union (TGWU), General Municipal Boilermakers and Allied Trades Union (GMB)) others like the Association of Professional, Executive, Clerical, and Computer Staff (APEX), established Equal Opportunities Committees. The purpose was to feed the views of women directly into the decision making committees of the Unions. Some unions introduced special seats on their leading committees to enable direct representation. NUPE had a particularly successful experience of this where, by creating five reserved women's seats, they were able to generate the environment for more women to seek election. Now more women sit on the executive committee through the traditional route than occupy the women's seats. Several unions hold women's conferences through which policy development can take place and one or two unions have appointed women's officers to try and concentrate attention on the needs of women workers. So, it might be argued, if all this change was taking place over the last decade, how is it that the statistics present such a grim picture? Have any of these measures changed anything? We believe they have.

Several unions in Scotland have increased the proportion of women members (TGWU, Amalgamated Engineering Union (AEU), NUPE, MSF, Confederation of Health Service Employees (COHSE), National Union of Tailors and Garment Workers (NUTGW))[4]; others have increased the number of women full time officers in Scotland (EIS, TGWU, GMB, USDAW). NUPE, TGWU, NUTGW all report increases on their leading national committees and EIS over the last three years has increased the representation of women on its Council and Executive by 6% and 4% respectively[5]. NUPE also state that up until 1983 it had not had a woman President; since then there have been four.[6]

Delegations to union and political conferences have been improved in favour of women in some unions for example, the TGWU has eleven reserved places for women on its delegations to both the Trades Union Congress (TUC) and the Labour Party Conferences; and in Scotland, the TGWU regional delegations to both the STUC and Scottish Labour Party conferences have three reserved places for women. Furthermore, at the STUC level, the number of reserved seats for women has increased from two to three.

Statistics are, of course, important but they cannot give a complete picture of the progress being made by women in trade unions in Scotland, nor indeed do we measure the involvement of women members solely in terms of the number of women occupying official positions in the Unions. Other changes indicate the movement taking place within trade unions.

Unions have recognised that if women are to be recruited into unions, and indeed if they are to stay and participate, then unions must be relevant, and attractive to women and capable of delivering the demands of women. To this end, recruitment is high on the agendas of all unions and for some, most notably, TGWU, USDAW, and the GMB, there is a particular emphasis being laid on part-time and temporary workers. This has meant that unions have not only attempted to improve their official representation, but they have also attempted to improve services, published materials, education, benefits, organisation, policy and campaigns.

To illustrate, some unions have introduced a reduced rate of contribution for part-time workers and for women on maternity leave; others are considering whether the benefits they offer are discriminatory. Most unions have begun to publish special material for women members and publications for general use which highlight the areas of concern for women workers. For example, USDAW have produced some excellent pamphlets on equal pay and cervical cancer screening; NUPE have recently launched a very impressive pack on women's health; TGWU have a useful set of shop stewards' handbooks on equal pay/sexual harrassment/part-time working and maternity rights; GMB have comprehensive pamphlets on a range of issues dealing with women's working lives; and many unions, including the STUC Women's Committee, produce bulletins especially for women members. Perhaps the most significant indication of the change in the types of produced materials was during the Alton Bill campaign at the beginning of 1988. At least two unions, NUPE and Civil and Public Services Association (CPSA) produced national material on abortion rights and several unions including NALGO produced local material. Such a situation would not have been possible a few years ago.

One area where women have been particularly critical of unions has been in terms of branch organisation. It is clear that overly formal meetings, conducted in jargon, on issues of selected interest, held in the evenings, have rarely inspired women to attend. Furthermore, the fact that previously fewer women occupied branch official positions in many unions or that childcare arrangements were almost non-existent compounded this lack of appeal to women. When women did not attend branch meetings a charge of apathy was often levelled rather than a concerted effort made to discover why women did not attend and measures taken to rectify the problems. The attendance at branch meetings generally is a problem for trade unions and has heightened the resolve of many unions to investigate, and where necessary improve, branch organisation and activity. Such an examination is opportune because the organisational requirements of part-time workers and temporary labour are different from those of full-time workers in large single site factory or office complexes. A recent survey conducted for Labour Research Department has indicated that more women are occupying branch positions and this may augur well for a change in branch attendance by women.

A further aspect of organistion which was deemed to be very important for women is the whole area of childcare facilities. As is indicated later, many unions have strong policy on childcare and indeed the STUC is engaged in highlighting the importance of childcare to women's participation in the labour market and the economy. Meanwhile trade unions themselves have recognised that the lack of childcare arrangements can be a barrier to women participating fully in the union's activities. It is therefore an issue being discussed by many unions. Provision is patchy as getting the right level and type of arrangement has been difficult to deliver. To a certain extent there is still resistance – bringing women into the trade union domain is tolerable but children are just too much! But more often than not there are practical hurdles to be overcome and matching what is practical and possible to what is expected. EIS and the Society of Graphical and Allied Trades (SOGAT), have child minding allowance schemes and this is gaining currency as a viable alternative to creche facilities where appropriate. The STUC and most unions have facilities at their national conferences, residential schools and women's events.

Education has made a major contribution to increasing the confidence of women to take part in their unions and to develop the skills and knowledge to become active within it. Most unions provide specialist courses for women members and endeavour to incorporate the problems facing women workers in their general education programmes. The STUC

Women's Committee runs four weekend schools a year and these are very well attended.

Some unions have taken the question of women's participation so seriously that they have conducted special surveys to determine precisely the situation. The GMB surveyed their national and local agreements and in conjunction with national statistics compiled a report and programme for equality.[7] NUPE has initiated a major review of women's participation in the Union and the data for this will be collected by late 1988. It is intended that this information will pave the way for implementing further strategies to increase women's participation in the future.

The STUC Women's Committee and Women's Conference have both undergone change in recent years. The conference gets larger every year and the attendance is an indication of the interest it now attracts. It is now very rare to see delegations led by men and indeed very few unions actually have men on their delegations. More members of the General Council attend as observers and the report of the Conference now goes to Congress. Changes have occurred within the Women's Committee. The title of 'advisory' has been dropped and the Committee now has the right to report directly to Congress on the activities of the committee. Internal communication between the committee and the General Council has improved and the influence of the committee has grown. There has been an increase in the number of women delegates attending the STUC Congress but the proportion is still very disappointing. Happily efforts from the STUC Women's Committee have improved the number of motions, relating to areas of interest for women, that appear on the agenda of Congress.

The importance of the change in the representation and participation of women is not just about numerical improvements, nor indeed only about policy develoment and changed campaigning priorities, it is also about a different way of doing things. Women recognise the need for structure and organisation but attach less importance to formality. Many meetings of women in the movement are relatively informal and tend to be organised to maximise involvement and build up confidence. Essentially women are trying to find ways to get more involved, to have a greater voice in union affairs and to change things. Some men, on the other hand, already are involved and have a voice, but have less impetus to change. Of course, many men do recognise the need to change to accommodate the needs of women. It is, however, women who are the catalysts for organisational change. For example, union meetings where women have had some influence have undergone a process of 'Glasnost'. Greater concern has been given to the use of language and attempts made to demystify the procedures; the timing of meetings and the accessibility of venues has been considered; agenda items are more carefully selected to be more relevant to women; branch officers are charged with the responsibility of encouraging members to participate in debate; childcare facilities are now given due consideration; and even the seating at meetings is organised to create the most productive environment. One spin off from the impact of women on branch meetings has been that meetings are more relevant and easily understood by everyone – male and female – and this it is hoped will assist the revitalisation of union branch life in some quarters.

Policies and Campaigns

Women's impact on the trade unions and union's desire to be more attractive to women can be readily seen in the policies unions and the STUC adopt.

The STUC Women's conference debates the whole gamut of trade union issues including those which particularly affect women. It does so because all matters which affect women in employment are, by definition, trade union issues. At the 1987 STUC Women's conference issues such as the economy and industrial development encompassing debate on the manufacturing base, iron and steel and the coalfields, were discussed. If it may seem that such issues are remote from women given their numbers in the industries, it is argued forcibly that the economic wellbeing of the community is tied to the success of wealth-creating industry. In adopting a wide perspective, women have been a progressive force within unions. Reference has been made to the role of women against pit closures and the women's support groups during the Miner's strike. They evolved new means of organising, constructed new alliances and forged new links, not only organisationally but also in how we interpret the relationships between employment, economy and community. Women within the unions, benefiting from that experience and drawing on their own, are feeding a similar kind of perspective, analysis and organisation into their own representative bodies.

Being capable of adopting a broad-based approach to what are legitimate areas of concern has ensured that women's organisation and campaigns are not sidelined. There have been those who subscribe to the idea that women should organise separately, not as a means to an end but as an end in itself. The force with which this was advocated by some in the early 70s served to dissuade many women from taking part in women's activities for fear of marginalising their concerns/demands and undermining the concept of trade unionism – the unity of the workforce. However, the majority of women within the trade union movement now accept the necessity for women to organise together to achieve change in the movement. They do not see such organisation as a replacement for the movement. Hence the tension of the early 70s has lessened and a consensus has developed that women's organisation provides the base from which women can increase the impact they have on their own union and the movement as a whole.

One area in which this impact on policy and campaigns may be observed is in the profile given to pay and conditions – at the heart of trade union concern. Women, as we have said, are concentrated in low paid jobs frequently associated with poor conditions, for example in holiday pay, sick pay and pensions. Women constitute the bulk of part-time workers who in turn experience low pay, poor conditions or exclusion from employment protection rights by virtue of the number of hours they work. Recognising this, several unions have launched campaigns to combat low pay, such as TGWU's Living Wage Campaign and those of NUPE and USDAW. Other unions, the large general unions among them, have analysed the trend in work patterns, identifying them as predominantly female and have developed recruitment campaigns accordingly. GMBATU has targetted hotels, catering and distribution whilst the TGWU has given priority to recruitment amongst part-time and temporary workers in both private and public sectors. All unions recognise that the law as it currently stands offers very little to the worker and that improvements will be best achieved by collective organisation and bargaining. However, unions also recognise now that with respect to low pay, there is a need to enhance the bargaining process through statute and the movement is committed to a policy of a statutory minimum wage (SMW). Indeed the TGWU, long opposed to the SMW, shifted its policy in 1987. This reflects the impact of women, who make up the bulk of low paid workers, within the movement.

Equal Pay is a significant area of union action. The evidence is plain that women are not equally rewarded for their labour, and some of the reasons have been referred to above. A Government which had to be dragged unwillingly into line by a European Directive is not likely to bring in protective legislation of its own accord nor to put pressure on employers. Unions have taken up the cudgels despite the protracted nature of the procedures and have achieved successes. After seventeen years, the women at Ford won equal pay; Julie Hayward, supported by her union GMB, succeeded after five years; the TGWU recorded successes with the fish packers in Hull, Freemans (Pickstone) and Walter Alexander (Falkirk) to name but a few. The task is difficult not only because the law is so complex, but because apprehension and even hostility sometimes exists amongst male union members. This has to be tackled as indeed the built-in bias of collective agreements should be challenged, where the underlying assumption is that the worker is male, white, full-time and employed in heavy manufacturing.

Despite the difficulties, a growing number of cases are being taken up, for example Apex has ten cases at Industrial Tribunal and a further twenty cases under negotiation. This is good news for women members.

Women rightly give a high profile in what might be loosely described as 'social policy'. This concern is not only historical but a reflection of women's experience. The quality of the social wage is very important for women not only because women are frequently employed in the industries which deliver the social wage – local authorities, the National Health Service (NHS) and other caring and service industries – but also because they are expected to deliver through their unpaid labour wherever there are shortfalls.

Two areas reveal the overlapping concerns of women and social policy in unions. No doubt because of recent changes in pension provision, the impoverished position of women has been highlighted. Not only are women themselves disadvantaged in terms of pensions, but also it frequently falls on them to care for elderly relatives. The other area is in women's health. Many trade unions have produced specialist information relating to women's health. Several unions have highlighted cervical cancer screening as a priority and have conducted campaigns both to raise awareness and to establish it as a negotiating issue. As women have been and are becoming more prominent in the workforce the effect of employment on women's health has become an issue for trade unions.

Perhaps even more significant in revealing the changing status of women and the issues that are relevant to them within unions are those that relate to women's control over their own bodies. Sexual harrassment is one such issue and no matter how hard unions may find it to deal with, at least at policy level, the fact that it exists is now acknowledged. This is indeed a significant change in union's perceptions. Some unions have stated quite explicitly that the victim should be supported and that apart from ensuring fairness and justice in terms of procedure, they will not support the harasser. Others have been less explicit but recognise sexual harassment as a genuine grievance. It would be naive to assume that sexual harassment does not continue to be a widespread industrial problem nor that it is not perpetrated, on occasion, by one union member on another. Notwithstanding this, acknowledgement of this issue as valid for union action and concern is a progressive development. Further evidence of unions' growing reflection of women's perspectives manifested itself during the recent campaign against the Alton Bill. The position achieved within the trade union movement that it was a woman's right to choose and that any dilution of this was a component of regressive social policy, held firm and the STUC and its affiliates played an active and committed role in the Fight Alton Bill campaign.

Returning to those aspects of policy which more directly affect women at work, one of the reasons why women continue to occupy lowly paid, low status jobs is their unequal access to education and training which in turn afford access to different sectors of work. There has been a long-running campaign to achieve improved access to quality education and training particularly in science and technology. Effort has also gone into pointing out where schemes, whether Government inspired or other, discriminate against women's participation through restrictions, location, timing or other factors.

Progress needs to be made in the field of childcare where the promised nursery expansion has still to take place and statutory maternity rights are the worst in Europe. For example Belgium, Denmark, France, West Germany, Spain and Sweden all have less restrictive periods of qualification for benefits and all have better maternity pay arrangements than Britain. The Government has little desire to increase rights in this area as can be seen from the loss of maternity rights which took place through the Employment Act (increasing the period of qualification from one year to two years); and the loss of the maternity benefit through the Social Security Act. The implementation of the proposals in the Employment White Papers will also increase the number of women who will no longer qualify for maternity rights. Similarly it was the British Government which vetoed the introduction of the EEC Directive on Parental Leave which would have given every parent three months off in the first two years (five years in the case of handicapped children) to meet parental responsibilities.

Unions have managed to negotiate better maternity agreements in some areas and the demand of women in the trade unions has been for an expansion in provision not only in maternity arrangements but also in paternity and parental leave agreements. Here in Scotland, the trade unions have been vocal in highlighting the importance of childcare in terms of the contribution of women in the economy and a number of developments are taking place. The STUC Women's Committee is currently examining a trade union strategy on childcare. The Standing Commission on the Scottish Economy has considered this question seriously and discussion is taking place around the feasibility of partnership in provision between local authorities, employers and the community. Internally, unions are looking at how best to provide facilities to meet the needs of women members.

Whilst all of these issues are debated and acted upon, it should not be assumed that women's aims have been achieved. There are few policy makers who would deny that women should have equality, getting it put into practice however is more difficult. Progress is slow. Discrimination exists at all levels even in the language of the movement. However, where there was ignorance or neglect, there is at least now sensitivity and awareness and indeed acceptance that the concerns of women are the concerns of the whole trade union movement. The trade unions can no longer ignore their women members nor fail to see that women are vital to the future of the trade union movement. It is also to be hoped that unions recognise that the trade union movement gains from the participation of women not only numerically but in terms of a wider vision, a more comprehensive perspective and enhanced democracy.

Conclusion

As we can see there have been a number of improvements in the position of women within the trade unions in Scotland. Movement has taken place in the scale of representation although this has been small for the most part. Much needs to be done to improve the level of representation of women on leading committees, in official positions and particularly on negotiating committees. This question is most certainly on the agenda of union Women's Committees. The changes which have taken place on the recruitment and campaigning fronts are more positive. Here, resources, and attention are being deployed to address the recruitment of part-time and temporary workers, and unions have seen the necessity of focusing on campaigns specifically relevant to women. As a consequence of this change in the campaigning and recruitment profile, the image of trade unions is beginning to change. Unions are recognising the need to communicate in a modern way; to give attention to how attractive the union is to potential members; and to look at how it projects itself. Some change has, therefore, taken place in the number of women who are represented in the advertising of unions; in the union's resource materials; and indeed in the personnel endeavouring to get the union message across. However, this approach is still young, and we still have some way to go in dispelling the 'male, grey' image of trade unions.

Of course, there are those who have a vested interest in tarring the image of trade unions. It could be argued that some employers and the Government are intent on presenting trade unions as obsolete – dinosaurs in a modern world. We know that unions are not obsolete, but we have to convince an increasingly non-unionised workforce that to gain improvements in their working lives and to maintain and extend employment rights, we need a strong and active trade union movement. The importance of this question is emphasised for women when we consider that women will make up an increasing part of the workforce in the coming years, and the forecast is that the proportion of part-time workers will also increase. The demographic trend is that by the 1990s there will be a substantial reduction in the number of 15-24 year olds in the labour market and employers have already begun to experience a skill shortage. This situation is spurring some employers into action to recruit/retain women workers. We understand for example: the Royal Bank of Scotland is looking at mortgage facilities for its part-time workers; is developing its equal opportunities policy; and considering the question of parental leave.

The prospect therefore that women will have greater bargaining power in the coming years is dependent on trade unions successfully recruiting and organising women workers. The potential is there and the unions should grasp the opportunity presented to us.

At the same time, however, the trade unions recognise only too readily that this Government has a clear employment strategy which does not wish to extend the protective and employment rights of workers, least of all part-time workers. There is unlikely to be any positive change to the legislative framework for employment in the lifetime of this Government although the impact of the Single European Market in 1992 may result in some legislative improvement in the future. This is possible because, as discussed above, other countries in Europe have tended to have more progressive legislation on women than Britain.

The demand of the trade union movement is, however, to continue to seek legislative change in the areas of low pay, equal pay, part-time work, parental leave, maternity rights, childcare provision, employment protection and of course in trade union rights. The latter is crucial. The improvements to women's working lives will not be assisted by an emasculated trade union movement or indeed by the inability of trade unions to effectively organise and represent their members.

Whatever the difficulties, there is growing recognition that women are a significant part of the workforce with a key role to play in the Scottish economy. The steps taken to improve our representation and organisation within the trade union movement may seem small but they mark progress. Women in the trade union movement do get frustrated and tired of the time it takes for many of our demands to gain recognition, but we are optimistic. Because change *must* come for the survival of the trade union movement and indeed the betterment of the movement, it *will* come.

Yvonne Strachan, Women's Officer, Transport & General Workers' Union.
Lesley Sutherland, Education and Research Officer, Transport and General Workers' Union.

References

1. Standing Commission on the Scottish Economy, *Interim Report*, February 1988.

2. GMB, *Winning a Fair Deal for Women*, 1988, p.3.

3. E Breitenbach, *Women Workers in Scotland*, Pressgang 1982, p.40.

4. TURU, *Trade Union Women in Scotland: A Statistical Report*, 1986, passim.

5. EIS, *Response to WCOTP questionnaire on women's issues*, 1988, passim.

6. NUPE, Vice-Presidential Address – Ina Love, May 1988.

7. GMB, *op cit*.

8. TUC, *Survey of TUC Course participants*, 1988, quoted Labour Research, September 1988, Vol.77, Number 9, pp.19-20.

WOMEN'S COMMITTEES IN SCOTLAND

Sue Lieberman

Preface

The growth of Women's Committees has been one of the more striking developments in Local Government in the past decade. From the first, established by the Greater London Council in 1982, the spread has been rapid. There are now approximately 32[1] full standing Women's Committees or sub-committees throughout the UK, of which five[2] are in Scotland with at least two more pending; not to mention a comparable number of Equal Opportunities Committees. All represent an attempt to tackle the inequality which women experience in relation to local government as an institution and to the services which it provides.

In common with other positive action initiatives in local government, in particular those on race and disability, Women's Committees have grown in part from a specific political base, referred to variously as the 'New Urban Left'[3] or as 'Local Socialism'.[4] This represents a conscious attempt by a new generation of more radical Labour councillors to redefine political affiliations in terms of a coalition of various groups experiencing different forms of disadvantage, and no longer purely class ones; what, in Gramscian terms, is often described as 'the urban dispossessed'. This attempt is by no means a phenomenon common to all Labour councils, but has more clearly emerged in those areas where there has been an occupational shift of power in local Labour party politics towards a professional often university educated class. Not surprisingly, the first six Women's Committees were in London, where the Labour Party has a stronger numerical following from within the middle-class intelligentsia than in the industrial heartlands.

This provides the *political* context in which Women's Committees were first set up. It still remains a distinct strand in the establishment of many Women's Committees. But the trend has now spread to the more traditional Labour heartlands, of which Scotland may be considered an example. The experience of Women's Committees in Scotland is therefore of interest in that it allows for a contained look at an area where the conflict between fashionable ideas and established interests may be more overt, and in this sense can offer a more variable commentary on the ups and downs of Women's Committees than may be the case 'down south'.

Of course, even allowing for the contextual changes in which Women's Committees have been allowed to develop, it goes without saying that the major thrust behind their being set up in the first place has been the impact of the women's movement. Women's Committees represent the first specific attempt to translate into institutional terms action to meet the needs of a discrete group within the population whose demands were underpinned by a distinct body of ideology. In this sense, Women's Committees were in advance of similar efforts on race, disability and homosexuality, where coherent theories as against the practical effects of disadvantage were either less clearly formulated or popularised. So Women's Committees also act as a commentary on the difficulties and conflicts involved when theory meets reality; that is, when a body of ideas which are essentially at variance with institutional norms are translated into the institutional setting.

Not surprisingly, the establishment of any Women's Committee is almost invariably accompanied by controversy. I say not surprisingly, because such a venture challenges simultaneously a number of interests and structures within local government: political, economic, institutional and personal. The overriding task of the Women's Committee has to be to cope effectively with these conflicts and to achieve some recognisable progress. Unfortunately, the job is often made considerably more difficult by a lack of clarity from the outset as to the complex nature of these conflicts and as to what realistic objectives there might be. The fact that, despite the difficulties, Women's Committees are not only spreading but in most cases achieving important results is a tribute to the dedication of those involved. It should not blind us to the fact that many of the difficulties they face are unnecessary. If the same degree of care and thought was given to the establishment of a Women's Committee as, say, to a programme of decentralisation of services, responsibility for success or failure would depend less heavily on the abilities and efforts of a few individuals. Realpolitik, however, dictates that marginalisation is an essential component of seemingly positive responses to movements which fundamentally challenge the distribution of power and wealth in society.

This chapter does not purport to be a detailed examination of the work of Women's Committees in Scotland. Neither time nor resources permit such an exercise. The intention is to provide a general background as to the context and thinking behind the setting up of Women's Committees; to describe some of their achievements in Scotland; and to discuss some of the political and organisational problems affecting them. The focus is specifically on Women's Committees, rather than on the more broadly titled Equal Opportunities Committees[5], since the former are more politically and publicly exposed and act more as a focus, variously, of support and opposition. The experience of Women's Committees *qua* Women's Committees therefore provides more of a statement on the impact of controversial experiments on established institutions. The chapter concludes with an assessment of the principle of a Women's Committee. The emphasis throughout should be understood as applying to Scotland, except where otherwise stated.

THE ORIGINS OF WOMEN'S COMMITTEES

Women's Committees began in London, in circumstances of particular political and ideological change. These circumstances will be briefly described. But the spread of Women's Committees to Scotland, and possibly to more 'conservative' councils in parts of England, has taken place against a somewhat different background. It is important to acknowledge these distinctions. At the end of the day, different political ideologies may be less important than a deeply-rooted sexism in explaining the difficulties all Women's Committees seem to face. However, we have to recognise that both factors – and others – exist and interact, affecting both the climate of opinion and events. There is no blueprint for success. But unravelling the issues which affect and influence may help those involved in the setting up of Women's Committees to understand realistically what action they may need to take or to avoid in order to maximise their chances of succeeding.

In London, Women's Committees seem to have broadly emerged from a combination of two dominant factors. One was the growth, during the 1970s, of a new left-of-centre movement in the Labour Party which had its feet, for want of a better word, in community politics and the politics of protest. The 'generation of '68', having found that there were limits to the effectiveness of direct action moved systematically into mainstream politics during the next decade in order to influence and change from within. Others still stayed on the outside, preferring to channel their political energies through independent movements, such as the tenants' movement, or more formalised pressure groups such as Gingerbread and Child Poverty Action Group. Nevertheless, there remained considerable movement between the two.

The relationship between community action and formal political change is a fascinating area of study, and one quite relevant to the issue of Women's Committees. Are women better off continuing to organise outside of mainstream structures? Or should they join power structures in order to effect change? In reality, these choices are not mutually exclusive. But they form a continuing dilemma for feminists in trying to decide the best means of achieving change, and the experience of Women's Committees has not necessarily resolved this dilemma.

The other major strand in the evolution of the first Women's Committees was the growing articulacy of the Women's Movement. This had also in part developed from the radicalisation of politics in the late 1960s and 1970s in which many of the women involved, influenced by the growth in feminist ideas, began to recognise that 'gender-blind' political action in effect left women's social and economic position unchanged. During the 1970s, a wealth of feminist theory and writing developed, analysing patriarchy, language, marxist theories of reproduction, the family, sexuality and other major issues associated with the complexities of women's position in society. This profoundly influenced the development of the Women's Movement and of particular women's interest/action groups. Some groups – notably, Women's Aid groups – even began to gain tenuous access to resources, to set up refuges for women experiencing domestic violence. Although in truth such initiatives could be unconsciously dismissed by those in power as *merely* meeting the requirements of a particular form of social deviance, they were important for giving women themselves a recognised basis from which to analyse and challenge the social meaning of violence towards women in general.

This growth in confidence and awareness underpinned the thinking of those women now moving into mainstream politics at the local level. They began to see – often from their own experience – that the under-representation of women in politics and attitudes towards childrearing and domestic roles were closely intertwined. The work of the Women's Movement pointed them to a realisation that systematic discrimination, intended or unintended, affected women's opportunities in every sphere of local government activity. The question was, what to do about it? And the answer, to Valerie Wise, elected to the new Labour administration at the Greater London Council in 1981, was to set up a committee specifically devoted to the promotion of women's interests.

This move was tremendously attractive to London feminists. Hundreds turned up to each of the GLC Women's Committeess open meetings. Undoubtedly, it spurred women on to call for similar moves in their own borough councils. By the end of 1982, no fewer than five other councils in London – all Labour-controlled – had established full standing committees or sub-committees of central committees. The GLC's became by far the biggest, with a staff approaching 100 at abolition in 1986. It also continued to set the pace, establishing norms such as popular consultation, strategy working parties and high grading of staff.

This rapid growth was very influential in other areas. Women in the Labour Party up and down the country, who had perhaps been struggling for years to get women's issues onto the agendas of their local parties, saw the establishment of a Women's Committee as an immediate vehicle for getting women's concerns addressed. Younger men councillors, who increasingly were coming to dominate local political scenes, began to see women's committees as a hallmark of what a 'right-on' new Labour left council should be doing – along with initiatives on race, disability, and socialist enterprise. In this way, the impetus to set up Women's Committees shifted from having a fairly strong popular feminist base to being more heavily determined by party caucuses.

The crucial issue in all this seems to be the extent to which 'fashionable' political causes reflect and relate to the needs and interests of the electorate. The Women's Movement has often been accused of being white, middle-class and able-bodied. It is often – in my view, correctly – argued that whereas *some* issues are common to all women, others – particularly the effects of race and class – have distinct effects.[6] Women's Committees in London were greeted with enormous enthusiasm by organised white women's groups, but they soon ran into conflict with black women's groups over issues of race. This is symptomatic of the frequent gap in experience between promoters of Women's Committees and the communities they are intended to serve. In London, the general absence of black women from the mainstream Women's Movement and of black people from the Labour Party meant that this separation could initially be overlooked. In the industrial areas of the north, where working class experience still underpins the Labour Party, and therefore local politics, to a much greater extent, the gap between 'middle-class theory' and 'working class experience' could not be so overlooked. In Scotland, there were no great calls from an organised women's movement outside of the Labour Party for Women's Committees to be set up. Most of the initial battles have been fought purely within the confines of the political structures, and can crudely be characterised as being between men (and sometimes women) on both the traditional right and the far left of the Labour Party, in opposition to women activists supported by middle class men in the centre left ground.

Thus, of the five women's committees currently in existence in Scotland, only one – Stirling's (which was the first in Scotland) – came about as the result of a decision by the Labour *Group* running the council. This decision, crucially supported by the influential leader of the council, Michael Connarty, came as a result of direct influence from the GLC in the person of Valerie Wise. The others were all the result of manifesto commitments, made through the party *membership*. This difference is important. It creates the possibility of an initiative being imposed on a potentially hostile ruling group. Not only, therefore, does this mean that the Women's Committee has to establish its credibility with women outside the council; not only has it to find a way of tackling discriminatory practices and perceptions throughout the administrative structures of the council; it may have to do this in the face of obstruction within the ruling group. This may in part explain, for example, why there was a year's delay between the establishment of a Women's Committee in Edinburgh, and the setting up of a unit to service the committee.

This extremely unpromising starting point is not inevitable; nor does it undermine the case for a Women's Committee initiative *per se*. But it does call for better reflection by those responsible for the initiative as to the subsequent strategies that will be needed to overcome those barriers. Too often, the achievement of a Women's Committee is seen as an end-product in itself, with insufficient thought as to the continuing support it needs. This can result in a feeling that the Committee has been abandoned to its own fate, and this is an inauspicious atmosphere in which to begin work.

It should be said that continued reference to the Labour Party in relation to Women's Committees is not a sign of partisanship. It is simply the fact that the vast majority of all Women's Committees, and all of the ones in Scotland, have been set up by Labour Councils. The other major political parties do not tend to display the same interest. Indeed, the position of Conservative councillors in Scotland can generally be described as one of overwhelming hostility to the concept and existence of Women's Committees. The SLD, on the whole, is more supportive – indeed, the previous Alliance parties demonstrated much the best track records, pro rata, in encouraging women into active politics. However, it has to be pointed out that in Aberdeen, the Women's Committee set up under a Labour administration was abolished when the Liberal Party took control in 1986, and was replaced by an Equal Opportunities Committee, an ideologically different vehicle that blurs the distinction between different forms of disadvantage and oppression.

All this may look somewhat invidious. After all, the women's movement is non-partisan, and the ideology of feminism is often antagonistic to the theories underpinning mainstream political parties. For example, conventional Marxist theory pays no attention to the role of women in the production of wealth or the reproduction of labour: consequently, women's work becomes invisible. Thatcherite ideology is explicitly geared to the exploitation of women in their domestic roles, although individual women may escape this through personal access to the benefits of the free market. The concept of gender equality is not specific to a class perspective; in fact, it sits well within a Liberal ideology. Be that as it may, for better, for worse, the development of Women's Committees is, at present, closely tied up with Labour party politics, and it is within that framework of class, race, gender, populism and radical town hall politics that Women's Committees currently exist.

THE WORK OF WOMEN'S COMMITTEES IN SCOTLAND

"For too long, within the Council and the local community, decisions about how money was spent, and what the priorities were, were in the hands of committees that were largely made up of men. The Women's Committee is trying to change this, because women have an important contribution to make in decisions.....

The District Council set up the Women's Committee to make sure that the voice of women and the interests of women were well represented and are made to count....."[7]

Broadly speaking, the work of Womens' Committees falls into three distinct fields of operation. I shall define these as:

a) providing a direct service or support to women, often a new/ experimental service, or support in an area outwith the council's own direct interest;

b) working with other departments and committees of the council to modify existing service delivery in women's interests; and

c) tackling the council's employment practices and conditions of service

All of these function within a broader framework still, viz. to raise awareness and to ensure that women's issues are placed on the local authority agenda, as the above quotation suggests. Nor are the three fields mutually exclusive; for example, provision of a workplace creche or a cervical cancer screening programme for women employees intrudes into both (a) and (c). However, some kind of categorisation is helpful in order to identify patterns and the ones I have used offer a reasonable starting point.

It also has to be observed that there may be a difference in level of operation between a Women's Committee functioning at Regional level, and one at District level. Of the five Women's Committees presently operating in Scotland, three are district committees (Stirling, Edinburgh and West Lothian), and two are regional (Lothian and Central). If generalisations can be drawn from such small samples, the more localised nature of district councils tends to result in more direct contact work with women in communities outside the council; whilst the much larger size of regional councils, geographically, as employers of women, and as responsible for the two largest of council services (education and social services), suggests the more strategic importance of focussing on work internally.

Looking at the three areas outlined above, it is immediately noticeable that activities associated with the first, ie. providing a direct service or support to women, have received by far the most attention. Childcare, health, and violence recur the most frequently until now as issues to which Women's Committees in Scotland and their units have addressed themselves.

Childcare stands out as the single biggest concern. All three District Councils have operated Christmas shopping creches; Stirling with such success that a permanent shoppers' creche has now been established, with over 35,000 registrations in its first year of operation. Creches at Women's Committee meetings both inside and outside the council have also been established as a norm, and the provision of workplace creches pursued with varying degrees of interest, if with no practical outcome to date. Some committees/units have initiated discussions with other sections of their councils with a view to improving childcare provision associated with leisure or educational opportunities, although progress is inevitably slow.

That childcare should receive so much attention from Women's Committees is hardly surprising. The restrictions imposed on women's lives through their responsibility for childrearing are such that to talk of opening up opportunities for women in any field of activity is meaningless unless alternative childcare provision is made. Even to consult with women in the community is affected: preschool children have to accompany their mothers to meetings; women have to leave activities at 3 o'clock to pick up their children from school; single parents cannot leave their children to go out at night. "Who cares for the children?" is one of the key questions in a feminist analysis of societal organisation. It is inevitable that Women's Committees will at an early stage address themselves to this issue in some way.

To a lesser extent, it is also inevitable that, at some level, Women's Committees will take an interest in health issues. Women's health has been a major area of interest and activity in both the women's movement and in community work with women for the past ten years. This is for three reasons: one, women have particular health needs associated with their reproductive system; two, again as a result of their role within the family, they have greater contact with health services; and three, the health service is dominated by men in crucial areas of diagnosis and resource allocation, hence power is perceived to be misused in various ways to subordinate women's personal and collective interests. Health has also become one of the most highly politicised of public service issues over a long period; not only in relation to the NHS, but also as a result of various forms of government propaganda: on smoking, alcohol and drugs, for example. Public consciousness of health as an issue is high, and it is therefore not surprising that it is an area in which women are readier to mobilise. The promotion of cervical cancer screening, the support given to hospital and other women's health action groups, and the organising of women's health events, all of which have featured in the work of Women's Committees, can be viewed to a large extent within this context.

Violence against women is another theme which echoes around Women's Committees. Violence, or the fear of violence, whether physical or sexual, affects women's lives to a quite remarkable extent, for example, restricting women's freedom of movement at certain times or in certain areas. The law, the police, physical planning, public transport, street lighting and specialist support services are all involved. Women's Committees in Scotland have variously organised local conferences on the issue of violence, sought dialogue with police forces, supported Women's

Aid and Rape Crisis Centres, and lobbied for improved public safety measures.

That these three issues – childcare, health and violence – have received such particular attention from Women's Committees in Scotland tells us something about the processes through which the committees operate. All these issues have gained emphasis as a result of the contact Women's Committees have had with women and women's organisations in the community. They are major issues for women, as already explained. It is therefore of particular importance for the credibility of Women's Committees that they are seen by women to achieve something in these areas. The very newness of Women's Committees, quite apart from their political vulnerability, means that they will be heavily scrutinised; thus raising a positive public profile for the committee, and one which can not only generate active support from women in the community but may serve to deflect or moderate criticisms and hostility from other quarters, becomes closely tied up with the need to "deliver some goods" in areas which women have identified are of special concern. Another clear example is the provision of grant-aid to women's groups and organisations. At least two Women's Committees (Lothian and Edinburgh) have made grant-aid an important point of contact with women's groups, and one which features significantly in their publicity. It may be pertinent that both these committees are in councils with established traditions of grant-aid.

The second area of activity is by far the most complex, and one, correspondingly, in which there are fewer examples of specific achievements to point to. The reasons for this will be discussed further on. In many respects it is the most fundamental purpose of Women's Committees to change the unconsciously discriminatory norms by which councils have hitherto functioned in their policies and service delivery; therefore all Women's Committees/Units, however tentatively at first, must take this on.

Many early initiatives are patchy. Subsequently, most Women's Committees recognise that more time has to be devoted to building structures and systems of communication internally before real change can be achieved. After two years, for example, Edinburgh established a Women and Housing Sub-Committee, jointly serviced by officers from the Housing Department and the Women's Unit, to look more systematically at women's housing needs and council responses. Stirling determined in its fourth year to focus on leisure and recreation services as a main service area where gender analysis and positive action measures would be needed. Central Region has prioretised the development of good communication systems within the Council, whilst Lothian has looked to the provision of childcare in all educational establishments as an initial major service objective. Edinburgh provides another example of a different approach. In its first year, the Women's Committee gained the agreement of the

Recreation Committee to employ two specialist fieldworkers within the Recreation Department to develop women's involvement in sports and recreation activities. This is a logical – and, one may argue, a more natural – extension of the Women's Committee's own grassroots work, as it provides for more consistent contact and development work with women, whilst freeing the Women's Committee to focus more on policy issues.

These examples – none of them earth-shattering – indicate a variety of approaches which can be taken to changing service delivery. All are equally valid, and which approach suits which situation will depend on a variety of circumstances, not least of which is what will gain cooperation and support from others. It is often a source of considerable frustration to Women's Committees and their officers that it is relatively easy to gain contact and response from women directly, and relatively difficult to tackle the local authority itself. However, it has to be recognised that a local authority is a large organisation and change will tend to occur slowly, especially with the minimal resources at the disposal of most Women's Committees. In this sense, it is unwise to expect – or to fear – too much of Women's Committees; the setting of modest attainable objectives and a realistic timetable is a far more useful approach.

To a large extent, this is also true of work on the council's own employment practices. Work on this area is central to Women's Committees' concerns, for local authorities are major employers of women and for the most part of women at low grades. In Lothian Regional Council, for example, some 20,000 women are employed out of a total of 28,000 within the workforce. Of these the majority are employed in low grade, low paid jobs with only a small proportion of women attaining top management posts. It is well recognised that women on the whole will continue to predominate at the low-paid, part-time level of the employment market without attention being paid to improved maternity rights, childcare, career breaks, training and confidence building, and a variety of other issues. An Equal Opportunities policy is an essential corollary of a Women's Committee, and Women's Committees will usually enter into this area of work in response to developments – or sometimes lack of developments – in the personnel arena.

Two Women's Committees in particular have prioretised this area of work. In Stirling, the Women's Committee was involved with Personnel in producing an Equal Opportunities policy; and in Lothian, issues such as equal pension and sickness rights, and improved maternity conditions, have been the focus. Prioretising employment matters requires a similar approach to working on service delivery, with two important differences. One is that it is a more concentrated area of work than the council's entire service operation, and one in which it may be possible to achieve consolidated results more quickly. The other is that it brings a third party onto the scene: viz, the trade unions. Depending on circumstances, the latter can be a source of support or obstruction, for they reproduce many of the same conflicts over the importance of gender issues to be found within the Labour party, both being movements which have evolved in a society and a class based on the gender division of labour.

This section has not set out to document every activity undertaken by Scottish Women's Committees to date. The purpose has been to indicate the kind of approaches and priorities Women's Committees have adopted, and to suggest the rationale for this. The range of work touched on by most Women's Committees is merely reflective of the tacit expectation that they should tackle all issues of gender disadvantage. Almost any issue of interest to a local authority has relevance to women; realistically, choices have to be made, and the early years of a Women's Committee's life are as much about choosing the most effective directions as they are about being able to point to a list of achievements.

Problems & Issues

"If the combined job descriptions of most local authority women's officers were boiled down to one sentence it might read something like this:

'To change the world within 37 hours a week, but to do so using minimal resources, with due care not to attract adverse publicity and preferably without causing any discomfort to the deep-seated beliefs and traditions of the public, the council as a whole and the Labour Group in particular'."(Anon)

The setting up of a Women's Committee is almost invariably accompanied by two reactions: support and hostility. As already suggested, support tends to come in the first instance from women within the Labour Party, from some (but not all) women councillors and from some, usually younger, male councillors and party members who aspire to non-sexist practice. By contrast, hostility, frequently quite overt, comes at a political level both from opposition parties (especially the Conservative party) and from within the ranks of older, male party members, and at an administrative level from within the machinery of the local authority itself. Women's Committees usually spend much of their early years in treading a delicate line between wanting to convince supporters of their worthiness, whilst assuaging some of the hostility. As the above quotation suggests, they do so with minimal resources and with maximum expectations, and it is therefore within the difficult area of idealism and theory versus realism and practice that so many problems tend to arise.

The origins of these problems are both confused and complicated. At a political level, leaving aside the simplistic and largely uniform hostility of the local Conservative party, Women's Committees stand at the crossroads of socialism and feminism, and they are vulnerable on both fronts. The power struggle that has been waged within the Labour Party for the past 10 years or more, between, broadly speaking, the old right guard, the hard left and the centre left directly affects Women's Committees both before and after their establishment. Crudely speaking, the 'old right' of the party, which dominated it until the 1970s and which is still very strong in the old Labour heartlands, depends on a traditional membership which is heavily dominated by working class, male trade unionists. Both their personal *and* political position is bound up with a set of family relationships in which women have always been subordinate, for example, by providing the appropriate domestic arrangements by which men can, at a much earlier age and to a far greater extent than women, enter actively into politics or trade unionism. While this still applies in large measure to the whole of society, it has been challenged by the Women's Movement; and given that the latter is generally speaking middle class and educated, it allows traditionalists to dismiss it as irrelevant to a working-class party.

This attitude has found more clearly articulated echo from within the ranks of the hard left. To a large extent, the latter is a reworking of the traditional Labour base, albeit with a refined sense of Marxist purism. In the ideology of the hard Left, the class struggle is supreme, while 'positive action' whether on gender, disability, sexual orientation or race is seen as a diversion from the main task (although racial initiatives are sometimes coopted). The most obvious example of this in practice in a council is in Liverpool, where, in contradistinction to other Labour authorities where a 'new Left' group had ousted a traditional one, the hard Left leadership after 1982 successfully opposed any call for the establishment of a Women's Committee.

Women's Committees gain the majority of their political support from the 'middle left' ground, where they are part of a reworking of socialist concepts, and of efforts to reach out to a new, mixed audience of voters. But support may only go so far, and they are not infrequently caught up in some of the wider power struggles between left and right in which compromises and changes of allegiance are often made. The sheer lack, in numerical terms, of women councillors is a serious disadvantage when it comes to the Labour group holding firm to an anti-sexist course of action.

In Scotland, whilst things are changing, much political power still resides with the traditional sector of the Labour Party. In some areas, this means that a Women's Committee simply will not be set up; in others, that if one is set up, it will have considerable difficulty in challenging certain political norms within the Labour Group. A brief story, not from Scotland, will illustrate both the difficulty in separating the personal from the political, and the tensions that can result. In the early 1980s, I helped set up a local community health project, funded through the Urban Programme, in the north-east of England, in a traditional working-class area, where there was a close relationship between local male trade unionists and the local male councillors. This project concentrated substantially on work with women, including helping women to become more conscious of their own needs and more assertive. The resultant change in family politics led many of their husbands to lobby the councillors to withdraw funding from the project, which they held responsible for their wives' new attitudes. The project survived, but largely because the old right wing were no longer in the ascendancy in the council itself.

This example also illustrates another problem for Women's Committees: that of control. In traditional Labour areas, there is often a reluctance to support 'independent' groups, and a corresponding tendency to steer all new developments directly from the council. Even in areas where financial support is given to independent community groups, it is usually accompanied by a requirement that the council, in the person of local councillors, is strongly represented on the group. This may create difficulties for women's organisations who may view this as incompatible with their own aims and structures – for example, the inclusion of men in their decision-making. Where Women's Committees, therefore, may aim to work with and support women's groups in the community, they may find themselves on the horns of a dilemma between encouraging independence and conforming with group policy on control. It is noticeable, for example, that in the two areas, Edinburgh and Stirling, where councils have supported the establishment of new technology training centres for women, both centres have included male representatives of the funding councils in their management arrangements. There is no suggestion that this in itself has been a source of conflict in either situation, but it is certainly an area in which purist feminist ideology has to meet the political requirements of the ruling party.

One particular arena in which political battles are always waged is that of the budget. The combined weight of political opposition to a Women's Committee usually means that compromises are made over the size of budget the committee can wield, including how many staff it can appoint, whether it gives grants, and what direct powers are at its disposal. A great deal of significance is attached to this – some real, some symbolic. The Women's Committee need a reasonable budget in order to appoint sufficient staff and to undertake some initiatives, like a shoppers' creche, or consultation meetings. Most of the Scottish Women's Committees are resourced to the bare minimum, most evidently in their staffing. But arguments in favour of apportioning a budget to reflect the size of the female population are somewhat simplistic. The Women's Committee is not the only committee to deal with women, and its initiatives are as much to do with demonstration as actual provision. If the Women's Committee is successful, it is arguable that the effect will be apparent in other committees of the council 'bending' their programmes; if it is not, a substitution budget will not tackle institutionalised sexism in the long run. Whilst the size of the budget is important, it is not necessarily in having a large budget that the Women's Committee will be most successful. Success will lie more importantly in the way in which the Committee and its officer(s), interface with the rest of the council.

So far I have dwelt in some detail on the political constraints affecting Women's Committees. However, there is an equally, if not more, important arena of conflict to be found within the bureaucratic complexities and subtleties of the local authority as an institution. Here, the puny resources invariably allocated to a Women's Committee, coupled not infrequently with a lack of clarity as to realistic objectives, priorities and means, are a crucial factor.

A local authority is a large organisation, with a complex structure and a well-established system of decision-making and implementation. Almost all main service committees have large departments with substantial staff at their disposal; advice, in the form of reports, is presented to these committees in time-honoured ways, and decisions having been made, the result is handed back to officers for implementation. Overall policy direction is given to a central Policy and Resources Committee, which in more sophisticated councils is serviced from a relatively small Chief Executive's Department, whose job it is to coordinate and corporately manage the individual service departments.

In contrast, a Women's Committee is often serviced by one Women's Officer, charged with the unenviable task of taking forward work in the interests of women in all areas of the Committee's interest: publicity and campaigning, forging links with women in the community, setting up new initiatives *and* introducing non-sexist policies and practice throughout the council. It is a job demanding a high level of commitment, and frequently characterised by burnout within the space of 2-3 years. In Scotland, four of the five established Women's Committees are serviced by one Women's Officer, who in turn may have the support of some clerical and administrative assistance.

A whole host of questions attach themselves to this situation. What background, skills and expertise will the Women's Officer be expected to have? What grade will she be paid on? Who will she report to? And, most important of all, how will she be supported to make sense of the quite unrealistic expectations attached to her job, to define achievable priorities, and to deal with the hostility and obstacles placed in her way? All of these questions have surfaced at some stage in the life of all Women's Committees in Scotland; not all of them have been satisfactorily answered.

It is worth examining some of the issues at stake here. To begin with, the background and skills of the Women's Officer herself. The choices here are as wide as the choices of the work of the Committee. A Women's

Officer may have a background in the women's movement, in community work, in adult education, in trades unionism, in local politics or in local government. She will seldom have experience in more than two or three of these areas. Selecting an officer with a particular background or interest inevitably means predisposing the work to take a certain direction, at least initially; it also means that a considerable amount of learning will have to take place to cope with the other areas of the Committee's interest. For example, an officer with experience of local government will understand how to go about building bridges with departments, but may have less experience in 'outreach' work with women in the community. Neither background is of itself more appropriate, but the unavoidable result of having only one post to fill is that of having to give a certain preference to one set of skills, which may or may not be in accordance with the requirements of the situation once the officer is in post.

Here the issue of management support becomes of central significance. Most Women's Units are placed in a central department – usually that of Administration or of the Chief Executive. The strengths and weaknesses of this decision need to be carefully considered. An officer, part of whose job it is to persuade the rest of the council to modify its policies in the interests of women, needs access to policy structures. Some councils do not have those structures; or do not have effective ones. Or a more senior officer may take the view that, because the Women's Officer reports directly to the Women's Committee, she is either outside his (usually his) jurisdiction or does not need supervision. This results in a failure to integrate the Women's Officer within the power structures of the council, and thus in her marginalisation. It will make her job of working to change the council considerably more difficult and may reinforce a pressure to concentrate more on working directly with women outside the council or within the council's workforce.

Linked to this is the issue of pay. The grading of Women's Officers is in itself quite a contentious issue, with those opposed to the initiative seeking a lower grade of pay, and supporters arguing for a salary scale commensurate with the responsibilities of the post. Here again, the hierarchical nature of local government is a factor. Power and responsibility are measured in terms of pay; the lower the grade, the less access the officer will have to certain layers of decision making. As it happens, this is one area in which, under the influence of Stirling, Scotland has succeeded in establishing a better norm than amongst the early Women's Committees in England[8], with the majority of Women's Officers graded on PO2/3 – a reasonable position within the echelons of lower management.

A reluctance to appoint more than one Women's Officer inevitably restricts the work a Women's Committee is able to undertake. However, even where a decision is taken to appoint a number of officers, other questions arise. In Edinburgh, three Women's Officers were appointed simultaneously. Under pressure from the district women's party, and in contrast to the proposal by the Personnel Department, they were appointed on the same grade and as a collective. Now this raises some very interesting issues. Collectives are a hallmark of feminist ideology. They are adopted as working arrangements deliberately to counterpose traditional hierarchical systems which are perceived as being male and oppressive. Even in autonomously-run organisations, they experience difficulties inherent in the nature of collectivity, and it is not uncommon for members of a collective to feel frustrated, abused or similarly oppressed. The advantages of a collective are usually considered to be that they equalise responsibility for decision- making, and therefore are democratic, and that they share out all the tasks. This process is almost always more time-consuming than conventional forms of decision-making.

But local government is of its very nature a hierarchical institution. Creating collective arrangements for Women's Units may make a decisive political statement about challenging oppressive 'male' structures. They may achieve less decisive political reality in terms of effective functioning and change within the norms of the organisation. The time, necessary to collectives, spent on discussion, sharing information, agreeing on priorities and tasks, and overcoming disagreement, does not sit easily in an institution where management is by results and where the requirements of the committee cycle are pre-eminent. Moreover, any conflict, which as indicated is far from uncommon in collectives generally, within a unit as politically exposed as a Women's Unit, may reinforce a prevailing scepticism within the authority's officer corps towards the whole initiative.[9]

These issues all revolve around the difficulty of reconciling theory with reality. As such, they are not confined to Women's Committees, but have relevance to any situation in which new concepts, especially politically vulnerable ones, are applied to local government traditions. What Women's Committees demonstrate is that feminist ideology cannot revolutionise local government overnight. Indeed, the very act of setting up a Women's Committee suggests a tacit acceptance of the need to conform to some extent in order to work and to change from within. The choice is not between feminising local government and betraying all feminist principles by being coopted wholesale; rather it is about selecting forms of action that will advance women's interests as broadly, and at the same time as specifically, as possible, taking account of the culture, history, organisational systems and political realities of the authority.

In this section, I have discussed some of the political and structural issues affecting Women's Committees as a commentary on their need to look realistically at the strengths and weaknesses of their situation. The clearest message is that limited resources and internal opposition constrain what can be achieved; therefore time and thought need to be given to the most effective ways of achieving structural change. In the last section, I will consider what future lies in store for Women's Committees and whether there are alternatives for improving women's lot in relation to local government.

THE ONLY WAY?

Women's Committees have now been in existence for rather less than ten years; in Scotland for less than five. Already in parts of England there are signs of a shift away from Women's Committees, even where they have been established. Does this suggest revisionism on the part of radical left politics? Or is it indicative of a legitimate reappraisal of how women's equality may be best achieved?

Women's Committees have undoubtedly made a mark on local government politics and have achieved a great deal, both practically and in raising women's profile and awareness. Yet they are still very much on the margins of local government, still subject to political controversy, and still struggling, in an unfavourable financial climate, for better resources. The question therefore has to be asked: are Women's Committees the only or even the best way of achieving change for women in local government?

I am not going to provide any simple answers to this question. Uncritical defence in a sensitive area is as unhelpful to an initiative's consolidation as unremitting attack. The mistake, in my view, lies in the unhesitating pursuit of one sole goal, regardless of possible alternatives. The key question for any council should not be, "Shall we set up a Women's Committee?", but "How can women's equality best be achieved within this council?", and underlying this, "What priority do we give to tackling gender disadvantage?" The answer to this may well be a Women's Committee; equally it may not, and I say this without in any way wishing to detract from the achievements existing Committees have made.

The advantage to setting up a Women's Committee is that it makes a decisive political statement – at least in the public mind – about a council's commitment to gender equality. It acts as a focus around which women can mobilise, and it should also act as a positive influence on other sections of the council. The disadvantage is that a Women's Committee can be a very empty gesture; it can lack political strength and real political support, can be poorly resourced, can raise unrealistic expectations, and can distract from other arenas of action. Thus in some ways it is a mixed blessing rather than an unequivocal good.

In one sense, it is impractical to take the view that a Women's Committee is the *only* means of achieving change for women. Many councils will never, for political reasons, set up a Women's Committee.

Though often these will be Conservative-controlled councils with little or no interest in women's equality, it would be short-sighted to write off all councils as incapable of positive action. Initiatives of specific benefit to women can and do take place in councils without Women's Committees, or outside a Women's Committee's jurisdiction. East Lothian District Council, for example, which lacks a Women's Committee, has for many years had some housing policies more sensitive to women's needs than some councils with Women's Committees. In Edinburgh, the decision to set up a women's new technology training centre came independently of the Women's Committee, though the decision to appoint specialist staff in the Recreation Department did not. Further, equal opportunities policies and programmes can as – or sometimes even more – effectively be pursued through mainstream Personnel functions. Each local authority's starting point varies, and what works in one cannot automatically be transferred to another.

It is likely, however, that the establishment of a Women's Committee gives greater impetus to such initiatives, since it establishes a body with a specific interest in ensuring that they continue and spread. The benefits of this, however, have to be weighed up: in some authorities, a lower profile may be considered to be a more effective route so as not to raise powerful antagonisms. Underlying tensions within the ruling group can easily be exposed by a confrontational attitude on the part of a Women's Committee, and this may actually harm certain proposals that may otherwise have gone through. Judgements have constantly to be made over the balance to be struck between ends and means.

Women's Committees, are not the only mechanism through which work of benefit to women can develop. In some cases, they may for quite valid reasons be thought to be less appropriate than other methods. The unique value of a Women's Committee is that it provides a focus and a direction for women and for work on women. But – and it is an important but – Women's Committees are not a substitute for action by the council; their role is to draw attention, to pioneer, and to promote change within the council as a whole. If this is not recognised and accepted by the rest of the council, the restrictions on the Women's Committee will be such as to provoke legitimate questioning of the purpose in setting it up.

Since the early days of Women's Committees, things have changed quite markedly. Some councils have consolidated the establishment of a Women's Committee by setting up in addition specialist Women's Units in service departments. Others have abolished their Women's Committee, reduced its powers or have merged it into a broader Equal Opportunities Committee. London boroughs with severe financial crises are particularly evident in the latter course, and this completes a rather depressing circle. If Women's Committees, which proliferated in the south in the heyday of radical town hall politics, are so vulnerable to financial pressures, has their existence seriously tackled an inherent sexism in local authorities, or done other than to confirm women's marginalised position in an economy and a society dedicated to other priorities? Indeed, what future is there for Women's Committees under the continued onslaught on local authorities by central government?

The prospects for Women's Committees may now be bleak. Yet for all this, Women's Committees have made gains for women. They have increased women's access to resources, and have legitimised their demand that their needs be taken seriously. They are still on the increase in Scotland, and the longer that each Committee is in existence, the more chance it will have to consolidate its work and to influence other sections of the Council. As one Scottish Women's Officer has put it: "The face of local government has been changed beyond recall. Women have been put on the agenda, and that can never go back." Women's Committees may be under-resourced; they may be subject to political whims; and there may be alternative routes towards gender equality. But, for as long as local government continues in its present form, Women's Committees remain a valid and a viable option to begin tackling the disadvantage that women experience in their everyday lives.

Sue Lieberman works part-time for Lothian Regional Social Work Department and part-time as a freelance writer. From 1985-87 she worked as a Women's Officer in Edinburgh District Council.

References

1. This figure excludes lower status structures such as Women's Forum, Officer Women's Unit only, Women's Panel and Women's Working Party. Details obtained from the National Association of Local Government Women's Committees, Pankhurst Centre, Manchester.

2. During the course of writing this chapter, the Women's Committee in Aberdeen was restored, bringing the total number in Scotland to six.

3. John Gyford, "The new urban left: a local road to socialism?", *New Society*, 21 April 1983.

4. Martin Boddy & Colin Fudge (eds), *Local Socialism*, Macmillan.

5. Equal Opportunities Committees usually refer to equal *employment* opportunities within the Council for a range of disadvantaged sections in Society: Women, black people, people with disabilities, and gay people. They do not therefore provide the same political focus on gender disadvantages, though they may be less diffuse in their field of operation.

6. See, for example, Hazel Carby and Pratibha Parmar, separately, in CCCS, *The Empire Strikes Back*, Hutchinson, 1982. Also various other writings by Parmar in, for example, *Feminist Review*, No.17, Autumn 1984.

7. Stirling District Council Women's Committee *Newsletter*, Spring 1986.

8. As evidenced by Isabella Stone in *Equal Opportunities in Local Authorities*, Equal Opportunities Commission, March, 1988.

9. Edinburgh District Council has now abandoned collective arrangements within its Women's Unit.

SOCIAL WORK IN SCOTLAND: PROBLEMS AND PROSPECTS

Margaret Yelloly

Introduction

Recent years have seen social work taking on a new and unenviably high profile in the media. In large part this interest has concerned a series of tragic deaths of children – Jasmine Beckford, Heidi Koseda, Tyra Henry, Kimberley Carlile. Not all of those children were in care, but all were in some way the responsibility of social workers, and in each case qualified workers failed to act effectively to prevent a child death. Paradoxically criticisms of social work and other professionals in the more recent Cleveland case ran the other way; here it was overzealous protection of children thought to have been sexually abused which was the focus of attack. It is important to note at the outset that all of them took place in England and Wales; in Scotland the system for dealing with child abuse is significantly different and the independent role of the Reporter and the Children's Panels in reviewing social work decisions, ought to act as a powerful check on these decisions, and render mistaken or negligent actions less likely.

This is not the place to examine the substance of those inquiries; the article by Lorraine Waterhouse and James Carnie elsewhere in this *Yearbook* deals with child sexual abuse. The *effect* of them, however, has been to 'open the files' and to expose every aspect of social work practice and training to public scrutiny in a way experienced by no other profession. This has had both negative and positive effects. While work in situations of risk has become even more hazardous and stressful through fear of censure, a more positive consequence has been the development of a much more informed and temperate debate in the serious media, and a greater public awareness of the responsible role given to social workers under statute. If there is a demand for more effective training and demonstrable competence, there is also growing recognition that this must be accompanied by a clear public mandate, underpinned by the resources and the legal and administrative systems which enable it to be properly discharged. 'We are concerned', commented the Cleveland Inquiry Report, 'about the misplaced adverse criticism social workers have received from the media and elsewhere. There is a danger that social workers...will be demoralised. Some may hesitate to do what is right. Social workers need the support of the public to continue in the job the public gave them to do. It is time the public and press gave it to them.'[1]

This article will examine some of the issues presently facing the social work profession, and the implications for social work education and training. Since the discussion must take account of these criticisms, it is right to acknowledge that there is much dedicated and often skilled social work being undertaken every day; sadly, it is failures that hit the headlines, while successes go unsung.

Social Work in Scotland

Social work is a relatively new profession, which only began to achieve a recognition and status as an occupational group for which training and qualifications were essential after the Second World War, with the development of a new structure of personal social services, – in particular the new Childrens' Departments, which clearly required trained personnel. Social work and welfare functions were divided between a number of different departments (childrens', health, welfare, education, and probation and aftercare) which led to a fragmented and inconsistent service. Scotland took the lead in creating new comprehensive Social Work Departments in 1969, which included within their brief social work and other services for children, elderly people, those with a mental illness, mental or physical handicap, and the functions of the probation and aftercare service. In England and Wales, Social Services Departments providing 'a community-based and family-oriented service...available to all' were established in 1971, on broadly similar lines though governed by different legislation.

There were significant differences between the functions of the departments in Scotland and those in England and Wales. Under the Social Work (Scotland) Act 1968 local authorities were given a broad brief to promote social welfare together with wider discretionary powers than their English counterparts. Further, the probation and aftercare functions undertaken by Social Work Departments in Scotland are in England the province of a separate Service. In Scotland, therefore, departments have important functions in relation to adult offenders and the penal system which are absent from those in England and Wales. Despite these considerable differences of origin, function, and legal mandate there is little evidence of major substantive difference between the departments in Scotland and those in England and Wales, and their organisational structure and day to day practice do not differ markedly. Social workers north and south of the Border complete a common training validated by the Central Council for Education and Training in Social Work, and there is very considerable mobility of staff.

The advent of the new departments was far more than a territorial reorganisation, and it opened up new career prospects for social workers. Carried along by the tides of economic growth in the 1970's, the departments grew in size and relative power. In the Scottish departments the total number of staff doubled from around 15,000 in 1971 to 28,000 in 1979, with a proportionately smaller increase of 2,000 to 1985[2]; in England and Wales the number of social workers employed by local authorities increased by 43% between 1974 and 1984[3]. For field staff there are now prospects of promotion from basic grade social worker to senior practitioner posts with specialist responsibilities, or to supervisory and middle management posts as team leaders; beyond that, there can be progression to managerial posts as Principal Officers, Area managers, or senior headquarters staff. As an indication of the size and scale of Social Work Departments, the Director of Social Work for Lothian (Scotland's second largest Region) controls a budget of £70 million, a staff of 5,000 and commands a salary of £40,000. While local authorities are by far the major employers of social work, there are also opportunities in the voluntary sector – with the large child care organisations such as Barnardo's and National Childrens Homes, in the Church of Scotland, and with a range of voluntary and community projects of various kinds.

To define social work is not straightforward. It is not synonymous with 'staff of social work departments'; these include an enormous range of staff for whom a social work qualification would not necessarily be appropriate – home helps, occupational therapists, residential care staff, instructors in training centres among many others. Further, the title is not protected, as it is in France; it can be used by anyone engaged in charitable endeavours in an informal way without qualifications or agency mandate. In practice, however, employers have defined certain posts as requiring a social work qualification and the term has a clear connotation. For present purposes, the term 'social worker' will refer to those holding a social work qualification, or those occupying a post for which such a qualifcation is normally required; a distinction will therefore be made between social work and the broader range of social service and social care functions for which a social work qualification is not necessarily the most appropriate

The range of tasks social workers carry out is extremely wide – they may be found in Social Work Department area teams, in community projects, working with drugs victims and AIDS sufferers, in prisons, hospitals and in residential and day care facilities such as family centres and homes for elderly people. For many of these posts, despite their heterogeneity, a social work qualification is required. While in part the wide currency of such a qualification reflects some lack of clarity as to what kind of training is appropriate for particular jobs, it also indicates a recognition that a social work training does confer a certain level of knowledge, competence and, perhaps even more significantly, a common approach and value base (best described as person-centred) acquired through the professional acculturation process of training.

The responsibility for the promotion and validation of social work training throughout the United Kingdom lies with a statutorily established body, the Central Council for Education and Training in Social Work. At present the Council awards two qualifications, the Certificate of Qualification in Social Work, and the Certificate of Social Service; its remit extends to staff in residential, day and domiciliary settings, and in training centres for those with a mental handicap. Until 1987 only the CQSW was recognised as a social work qualification, but the CSS now has formal recognition as a social work and not merely a social service qualification, and for the Central Council (though not necessarily for employers) is equivalent to CQSW for salary purposes. Courses leading to the CQSW are located in universities and the higher education sector; they last for a minimum of two years, with the possibility of a year's exemption for some graduates with relevant degrees and prior experience. The UK is unusual in that the same professional award is made whether the course is at graduate or non-graduate level, and whether it leads to a Certificate, a Diploma, or a Masters' degree. Unlike the United States, therefore, social work in Britian is not a graduate profession, though about half of those gaining a CQSW do so on graduate and undergraduate courses.[4] But unlike most European countries, social work training in Britain was established in the universities from 1911 and has maintained a strong presence ever since.

CSS schemes began in 1975 and were set up to meet the training needs of a range of occupational groups *other than* social workers (field workers were specifically excluded) and were modular in form. They were not a preliminary to CQSW, nor were they intended to provide a qualification in social work; they were said to be 'equal but different.' However the relationship between the two qualifications was never made explicit. As time has passed, CSS has become a major qualification route for those working in residential and day care services, particularly senior staff, and it has become increasingly apparent that the similarities between the two qualifications are stronger than the differences. Despite the different structures, patterns and location of training (CQSW courses are mounted in higher education, mainly in universities and polytechnics, while CSS courses are employment-based, modular, and jointly mounted by employers and [mainly] colleges of further education) there is considerable overlap in content; further, the entry qualifications of two-year nongraduate CQSW students and CSS students do not differ markedly. The distinctions have been particularly untenable in Scotland where, unlike England and Wales, universities, central institutions and colleges of education engaged in CQSW training have also been closely involved in CSS schemes. While CQSW and CSS are less 'different' than was originally envisaged, they are very far from 'equal' as far as status and career opportunities are concerned and this has become a major source of frustration for CSS holders. While CQSW trained staff are to be found both in residential and day care and field work, CSS holders have not had the same freedom of movement into field services; the effect has been to limit career mobility and progression and to increase separation and differences in status between residential and field work.

CQSW courses are the major qualification route; 67% of students entering qualifying courses in 1986 were on CQSW courses, and 33% on CSS[5]. The proportions have however altered significantly; CQSW intakes have declined by 10% between 1980 and 1987, while the proportion of CSS students increased by the same proportion; CSS programmes now produce a third of the total output of qualifying students. (Table 1).

TABLE 1
Student Intakes by Type of Course, 1980, 1987

	1980		1987	
CQSW	3970	(78%)	3364	(67%)
CSS	1100	(22%)	1642	(33%)
TOTAL CQSW/CSS	5070		5006	

[Derived from CCETSW, *Data on Training*, 1987, Table 1]

In Scotland the proportion of trained field social workers is high – far higher than in England and Wales. In 1986, 93% of those occupying basic grade social worker posts and above in Scotland held a social work qualification (the CQSW or CSS), as compared with 84% in England, Scotland and Wales together[6]. Importantly, this level of qualification relates only to those occupying fieldwork posts. Among senior staff in local authority residential work in Scotland, 17% have a social work qualification and altogether 58% hold this or another relevant qualification, for example, in nursing or teaching; 42% have no qualification for the work.

TABLE 2
Qualifications of Senior Staff in Residential Homes and Hostels

Officer/Assistant Officer in Charge	No.	CQSW/CSS		Related Qualification		None	
Residential, establishment, children	313	88	(27%)	123	(39%)	104	(33%)
Homes for the elderly	869	116	(13%)	405	(46%)	348	(40%)
Other homes and hostels	259	47	(18%)	72	(27%)	140	(54%)
TOTAL	1441	249	(17%)	600	(41%)	592	(41%)

[Derived from SED/SWSG Statistical Bulletin, 1987]

In childrens' homes the numbers of qualified senior staff are very much higher – 27% have a social work qualification, and two thirds hold this or a relevant qualification. The above figures relate only to officers and assistant officers-in-charge; taking staff in residential work as a whole, there are enormous numbers in direct caring roles who have no form of social work or social care qualification – no less than 85% of houseparents in childrens' homes, for example and 94% of care staff in homes for the elderly have no such qualification[7].

Specialist and Generic Training

The inception of unified social work departments with their broadly based social work and welfare functions mirrored changes which had already taken place in social work training. In the 1950's and 1960's social work training courses abandoned their existing specialist and separate programmes for psychiatric social workers, child care officers, medical social workers, probation officers, and family caseworkers, and switched to a pattern of generic training, largely patterned on the innovative Carnegie course established at the London School of Economics and Political Science in 1954. The assumption underlying generic training was that the knowledge and skills required by social workers in any area of practice were largely common ones, and that the core of training should be these common elements. To this generic base could be added some degree of specialist knowledge to equip students for practice in particular settings, for example, the knowledge of law and criminology needed for work with offenders. The introduction of (and indeed the teaching on) generic courses was powerfully influenced by American models; the development of a substantial occupational group with a common training, identity and professional culture was a necessary basis for the professionalisation of social work on American lines. It was believed that genericism need involve no loss of specialist expertise.

The generic principle was strongly endorsed by the Seebohm Committee, which believed it desirable that 'a family or individual in need of social care should, as far as possible, be served by a single social worker....with a comprehensive approach to the social problems of his clients.'[8] 'The kind of social worker we expect to emerge', said the Report, 'will be one who has had a generic training aimed at giving him competence, after experience, to cope with a whole range of social need...'[9] Specialism would still be needed, but as backup to the 'general practitioner' of social work, and the kind of specialisms expected to develop would not be along traditional client-group lines.

Generic training was also the policy of the Central Council for Education and Training in Social Work, which permitted but did not encourage specialism, within courses, except in broad areas such as residential and community work. Basic courses which were clearly specialist and trained only for a particular branch of social work such as probation or mental health were phased out in the 1970's. The Council has 'continued to assert that training for social work should be generic, although it did not assume that it necessarily followed that any one social worker carry the full range of the employing agency's functions. It did not oppose the development of particular emphases within CQSW training, and encouraged further specialised training in social work at post-qualification level.'[10] Increasingly, however, as social work training has adapted to the requirements of the major employers for the broad range of knowledge and competence required by area teams (which cover most aspects of work within a local area) specialism in training has been eroded and has been replaced only to a limited extent at post qualification level. The expansion in knowledge and research relevant to social work practice, contained in a burgeoning literature, together with the need for comprehensive grounding in the social sciences, social policy, law and psychology (as well as social work theory and practice itself) has meant that curricula have become overloaded and it has been increasingly difficult for social workers at the point of qualification to be equipped both with broad background knowledge and with a real sense of competence in some area of work.

The Review of Qualifying Training

In 1982 the Central Council instituted a review of qualifying training and solicited the views of professional, employer, union and educational interests both on the CQSW/CSS issue, and on broader questions relating to the future structure of training. There followed a process of consultation, examination and debate lasting six years and generating mountains of paper. It culminated in the presentation to the Government of *Care for Tomorrow* containing proposals for a new form of qualifying training which would extend to three years and would incorporate within it both of the existing routes.[11] Proposals were also included (at a late stage) for a new lower level qualification, a Certificate in Social Care, allowing for progression to the higher level Qualifying Diploma in Social Work. While there were differences on particular aspects of the Council's proposals the foundation of a basic three-year qualifying training was (and is) undoubtedly right educationally, and enjoyed the support of all major interests.

Since the inception of the review of qualifying training the initial agenda has altered and expanded. A number of reports have made serious criticisms of existing training, first and most publicised the Report of the Inquiry into the Death of Jasmine Beckford (the Brent Report) published in 1985.[12] The Report (largely the work of Louis Blom-Cooper) commented adversely on almost all the professional workers involved, but most especially the social workers, as those holding statutory responsibility. Blom-Cooper endorsed a qualifying minimum of three years as 'the very least that the profession itself should require in order that its members can shoulder the immense responsibilities which society puts upon them'[13]; further, qualifying training should lead to a greater degree of competence in specialist areas, such as child care; and in the understanding and performance of statutory duties where the social worker acts with legal authority.

That the weaknesses highlighted in the Brent Report could not be dismissed as tragic aberrations has been confirmed by other reports. Of particular concern were the findings of the DHSS Children in Care research initiative detailing the shortcomings of local authorities in England and Wales in caring for children, and revealing a dismal picture of the level and adequacy of social work practice. The message of these nine studies was 'that social workers and their seniors are not offered the opportunity to acquire the sophisticated skills, knowledge and qualitative experience to equip them to deal confidently with the complex and extremely emotive issues raised by work with children and families'[14], despite their key position in decision-making, planning and service provision.

The extent to which specialism should be incorporated into qualifying training remains a major issue, and a more specific focus on particular areas of practice in the third year of training was a key feature of the QDSW proposals. Child care is a priority for all social work departments, and nearly a quarter of newly qualified workers have a caseload in which work with children at risk predominates.[15] There are therefore strong pragmatic arguments for greater specialisation within qualifying training, accompanied by the introduction of a requirement that those working with children at risk have undergone approved training for the purpose, on the lines of that now required of mental health officer training. It is likely that a greater degree of specialism in relation to the major client groups (elderly people, and those with mental illness or mental handicaps) will be included in basic training (in line with existing practice on CSS schemes), though this may well be on the basis of a two-stage qualification.

In April 1988 the proposals for three-year qualifying training were rejected by the Government. No doubt cost factors played a part (the estimated cost of the changes was just under £50 million) but it is evident that its assessment of priorities and that of the Central Council were greatly at variance. CCETSW's concerns about two-year programmes were evidently not shared by the Minister who did not accord qualifying training a high priority in relation to other competing claims, not least those needed to improve the skills of existing social care staff in the residential care of the elderly and children. Work on the Certificate of Social Care is rapidly going ahead and is intended to provide the qualification for some 13% of staff in Social Work Departments.[16] Whatever the reasons for the Government's refusal to fund the changes, commitment to them from most other major interests has remained undiminished; CCETSW is continuing to pursue the implementation of QDSW in limited improvements consonant with its principles. The ultimate aim, as set out by the Association of Directors of Social Services in a recent Manifesto[17], is to achieve 'a continuum of training including a common generic core of study, flexible links with pre and post qualifying training and systems of exemptions to enable staff movement from pre-qualifying levels to the QDSW process'. New initiatives can be anticipated in postqualifying training which will be targetted on areas of greatest training need and attract direct Government funding. Examples are the recent Scottish Office initiative in funding a substantial programme of training in Child Abuse Studies at the University of Dundee; and in England and Wales, direct funding from the DHSS for training in work with elderly people.

Training for Competence: SCOTVEC and NCVQ

At the same time, the whole agenda for training has changed with the advent of the National Council for Vocational Qualifications in 1986, to establish a coherent national framework for vocational qualifications in England, Wales and Northern Ireland. Scotland is already energetically reforming the field of vocational qualifications through SCOTVEC (The Scottish Vocational and Educational Council) though for the future mutual recognition of qualifications approved by SCOTVEC and NCVQ will have to be ensured. Primary tasks for NCVQ are to implement a national framework – the National Vocational Qualification – and to get agreed standards of competence within this framework. An award which carries the NVQ hallmark will indicate: that the qualification is awarded for a defined level of competence in a nationally recognised system; that it is of acceptable national standard, and that it is based on skills, knowledge, understanding, and ability in application; that there are no unnecessary barriers to entry; and that there are routes to progression.

At present NCVQ is mainly concerned with levels 1 to 4 of the national framework: however, government approval has already been given to an extension of work to level 5 (professional qualifications) and upwards.[18] Social work and social care fall within the remit of a United Kingdom Lead Industry Body, the Care Consortium, which has representation from COSLA and the trades unions. In addition, a Care Sector Liaison Group for Scotland has been formed to ensure that particular Scottish interests are taken account of in the Care Consortium. The Consortium will develop a recognised pattern for all forms of vocational training within the sector, in line with the NVCQ framework; as work proceeds it will not only bring a new clarity as to the kinds of training and qualification needed to develop specific task competencies, but it will also generate new forms of provision, with possibilities of career progression between them.

The importance of these bodies can hardly be exaggerated; although they will work with and through professional bodies and educational institutions making awards, for the first time the level, content and shape of these awards will be powerfully influenced by a national body which is employment-led, and in which the traditional autonomy of professional bodies in determining their own awards will be challenged. Whatever the debates about the professional status of social work training in past years, the effective decisions for the future will lie neither with the profession itself nor with the CCETSW, but with NCVQ. Profound changes will almost certainly occur in the whole structure, pattern and provision of social work and social care training in the next decade, and many cherished assumptions of social work education (for example the preference for integrated rather than modular educational patterns as a medium of personal growth and learning) may be jettisoned. The new emphasis on linking awards to the definition and assessment of competence rather than to the completion of particular courses brings an entirely new dimension to the training debates. It allows for a qualification to be built up gradually in a number of different ways, and for new skills to be added. The significance of *length* of course as a determinant of an award is therefore greatly diminished; for the future there is likely to be a greater variety of qualification routes, and a sharpening both of the areas of competence to be assessed, and the process by which it is done.

The Status and Effectiveness of Social Work

Despite the wide currency of the term professional and CCETSW's commitment to a professional level award, it is clear that social work does not enjoy comparable status with established professions such as medicine or the law. It is one of a number of professional groups, like nursing, teaching, occupational therapy, occupying a middle ground and clearly requiring particular training and skills, but unable to command a protected status and title, or to lay claim to a unique body of knowledge and skills. They are sometimes termed 'semi-professions' or 'para-professions' but neither is satisfactory, since they define these occupational groups in terms of what they are not rather than what they are. Clearly there is considerable element of overlap in knowledge and expertise between social work and other established professions, but the defining characteristic of social work is its particular statutorily defined purposes. It is not possible to conceive of social work in isolation from the functions of the agencies within which it is practised. Nevertheless, to discharge these responsibilities effectively, social workers also develop distinctive and systematic working methods (or theories and models of practice). Traditionally, these lie in two directions. First, *direct casework* or *counselling*, ranging from simple advice to behavioural treatment and family therapy; second, *indirect work* or intervention aimed at changing or alleviating the situation in some way, often by the marshalling of resources. These two aspects are termed respectively counselling and social care planning in the Barclay Report.[19] Both these elements are invariably present though the balance may shift in the ebb and flow of ideological tides and according to the professionals' (and their employers') perception of the nature of the needs and problems which confront them, and of the most effective way of dealing with them.

The substantial literature on social work effectiveness has been reviewed elsewhere[20] but it is worth remarking that a very substantial body of research now exists which identifies factors associated with positive outcomes and which can serve to give clearer direction to social work practice and to curriculum development within social work education. These evaluative studies are not new – the seminal work of Reid and Shyne was published in 1968[21] – but have been built upon in the UK by Goldberg, Gibbons and Sinclair[22], by the Personal Social Services Research Unit at the University of Kent[23], and by numerous evaluative studies of different projects concerned with specific groups – those with a mental handicap and very old (particularly confused elderly people) in the community. These relate both to direct social work intervention and to social care planning. In terms of direct practice, for example, there is strong evidence that effective work is most likely to occur where short- term, focussed approaches are employed, where clear and modest goals are established and targets for change are agreed and explicit (often in the form of a written contract).[24] There is now a formidable body of evaluative research of very direct relevance and significance for social work practice, on which social work curricula should be based, and an incontrovertible arguments for a much stronger empirical basis for social work training. This of itself would do much both to increase social workers' competence and enhance their standing – with the medical profession in particular, which is trained to a respect for evidence.

The question remains: effective in what? Distinct and often competing ideologies have characterised recent debates about the nature of social work and its central tasks and were heightened rather than laid to rest by the Barclay Report. Professional ideologies are consensual belief systems which enable purposeful action to be taken in situations which are uncertain, confusing, and incompletely understood. They tend to assume particular significance where, as in social work, action can rarely be decided on empirical or scientific grounds alone, and where ethical and moral considerations are important determinants. Two such positions can be discerned in the Barclay Report, represented succinctly in the Appendices to the main report. The first of these, adopted by Brown, Hadley and White, placed primary emphasis on community-oriented social work, necessitating a major shift in thinking and current practice in social work. This involved quintessentially a focus on the support of informal systems of care within the community (which undoubtedly make up by far the bulk of 'care provision'). On this view, the account of informal caring networks and of community social work in the main report was overly conservative and failed to recognise 'the over-riding importance of locally-based informal relationships in providing care for most dependent people, and the significance of locally-oriented services in strengthening and reinforcing such networks when they need support'.[25] To enable social service departments and social work to relate effectively to these networks requires local 'patch-based' neighbourhood teams, consisting of front-line generalists (with specialist backup) engaging in social care planning, a role which calls for a strong community oriented stance; an ability to work collaboratively with and through a wide range of people, particularly lay (or non-professionals); and a degree of entrepreneurialism in developing and supporting caring networks.

While there is a place for skilled social work assessment and counselling and (outwith the patch team) specialist backup, Hadley and his colleagues see this as much less central than 'frequent, reliable, practical, sensitive contact' with informal carers, which relies less than hitherto on direct social worker/client contact and face to face work, and mediates assistance through others. This is clearly very much in line with Seebohm thinking, though further developed and elaborated, and is influenced strongly by notions of local accountability, choice, and participation.

An alternative view advanced by Robert Pinker is critical of the community social work model of the main report, as well as the neighbourhood model of Hadley, and defends the existing client-centred or casework model of practice (in its broadest sense) as basically sound. In Pinker's view the community social work model is too broad, too wide-ranging, too ambitious, too unspecific and too little determined by the statutory responsibilities and institutional imperatives which govern social work to be viable. 'The efficient and humane discharge of social work duties,' he argues, 'calls for specialised legal, psychological and social knowledge.'[26] He believes that the enormous complexity of the needs which social workers in area teams are called on to address is underrated by the proponents of community social work, and that a far greater degree of specialist knowledge and skill is needed at the qualifying stage and by basic grade social workers.

There is considerable validity in Pinker's argument. The influx of systems approaches in the 1970's and the extension of conceptualisations of social work intervention to include work with individuals, groups, communities, and indeed the social system itself – coupled with the universalist vision of the Seebohm Committee – created impossible expectations and a widening gap between aspirations and actual competence in these varied arenas. The functions of Social Work Departments as the dominant employers of social workers must be central to any analysis of social work practice, which is increasingly dominated by the requirements of statutory duties and a case-based approach. However, it may be that the community social work model is particularly well-suited to Scotland, with its strong community roots and established local cultures and traditions, and there is some evidence that the organisation and practice of area teams is moving that way.[27] The implications of developments in community care also seem to point in that direction.

Community Care

The face of social work and social care provision is changing very rapidly. Of particular significance in the next decade will be the effects of demographic changes (particularly a dramatic rise in the numbers of elderly and very old people) combined with a policy of community care. The development of community care has been endorsed by successive governments, and points to a major shift in the balance of care from institutional or residential care to care in the community for priority groups such as elderly people, and those with mental illness, mental handicap, or physical disabilities. The creation of a range of community-based services is intended to enable even very vulnerable people to have choice in where they live and to be supported in it. Community care, as the DHSS describes it, 'is a matter of marshalling resources, sharing responsibilities and combining skills to achieve good qualify modern services to meet the actual needs of real people, in ways those people find acceptable and in places which encourage rather than prevent normal living.'[28]

Both the *SHAPE* Report of 1980[29] and the *SHARPEN* Report[30] of 1988 support increased provision for community care, but *SHARPEN* recommends that the *priority* for service development for older people and those with a mental handicap or mental illness lies in care in the community. At the same time, there is evidence that community care has developed more slowly in Scotland than elsewhere in the UK (albeit in the context of higher per capita spending on both health and personal social services) and hospital and institutional options have figured more strongly.[31] If the recommendations of *SHARPEN* are accepted, a new impetus will be needed in the next decade.

As the Audit Commission points out, staff are the key resource for community care. 'Appropriate buildings provide a suitable environment...But it is people who do the caring. Sound manpower planning and effective training are essential'.[32] It argues that work in the community calls for particular skills – the ability to work autonomously, to make decisions and adjust patterns of working to the needs of those served, flexibility and judgement. Further it suggests that there is a common core of community care skills which could be developed for all those involved in community-based care based on shared training.

In the implementation of community care policies, social workers will be a key resource. Common training (particularly at the postqualification stage) needs to be developed for professionals of different disciplines working in the community – community nurses, occupational therapists, social workers – which will provide the understanding, common approaches and shared skills necessary to effective interdisciplinary working. Though there is much rhetoric about joint approaches and shared working, the reality of interdisciplinary work in the community is little understood and shared training minimal. The Griffiths Report comments that 'an overriding impression on training is the insularity of training for each professional group.'[33] The development of new forms of training with national recognition requires action at the national level, particularly between the General Nursing Councils and CCETSW and there is little evidence as yet of a strong concerted approach, though a new initiative for the joint training of nurses and social workers for work with people with learning disabilities is at the planning stage in Scotland. The training implications of recent successful community care initiatives need to be assessed, and incorporated in a common national training strategy.

Within this strategy, the social work role is likely to change markedly; it will involve less direct work, and more of a case management function in identifying and assessing needs of individuals and families, constructing care packages building on informal care and neighbourhood support, providing or buying in other services as needed, but in such a way that people are so far as possible fully involved in all decisions and enabled to retain maximum control over their own lives. The values and attitudes underlying this client-oriented approach have long been a key aspect of social work training, but the case management role has not. There are therefore new skills to be identified and learned, not least the capacity to tolerate and work with risk. Not all these aspects of community care require a social work training, and other forms of training for auxiliary community support workers (community carers as Griffiths terms them) providing a range of personal, nursing and domestic care will need to be devised. Social work with these priority groups has generally attracted low status in social work departments in comparison with work with children, and tends to be allocated to social work assistants or unqualified staff. If community care is to develop imaginatively and in innovative ways, the *SHARPEN* priorities must also be reflected in the training and deployment of social workers, so that skilled staff are attracted to this field of work.

Within the social care field as a whole, the private and voluntary sectors are already playing an increasingly significant part – private care homes for elderly people, private mental health care, private childrens' homes, private personal care services (possibly in the future private prisons) – with a corresponding reduction in public care provision. Welfare pluralism accords ill with the primacy given to public sector social services in Scotland[34], but is the implication of Sir Roy Griffiths' view on the role of local authorities. These he sees as 'designers, organisers and purchasers of non-health care services, and not primarily as direct providers, making the maximum possible use of voluntary and private sector bodies to widen consumer choice, stimulate innovation and encourage efficiency.'[35] In future the role of the social worker in local authorities may focus more sharply on child protection, and on assessment and coordination of care;

while career opportunities for direct counselling and therapeutic work, attracting the most able staff, may come to lie (as they do in the United States) with the private and voluntary sectors. The constriction of the role of local authority social worker to that of 'street-level bureaucrat' concerned with people-processing is not, it may be said, a scenario likely to hold much appeal for Scottish social workers.

Social Work as Politics

Considerable attention has been paid above to the need for clearly defined skill and competence. While of particular importance to social work (whose credibility depends upon it) vocational relevance and competence are now the name of the game for all vocational programmes. However, this is in no sense an argument for the abandonment of the broad base of social work education, and it is notable that nursing training is shifting firmly in this direction, with the establishment of Departments of Nursing Studies within the Universities. There are three major reasons why the educational base of social work needs to be safeguarded.

In the first place, social work in Britain has always had a firm commitment not only to person-centred practice, but to social justice; its work lies characteristically with the poorest and most disadvantaged members of society, and practically speaking, much of the social worker's time is spent in enabling people to get the resources they need, either by assisting them to develop a corporate power base from which to articulate and take action on their own behalf, or by advocacy for them. If this characteristic of social work is to survive, it is vital that the understanding of the socially and politically constructed world within which social work moves (and indeed the political role of social work itself) should feature strongly in qualifying training. In Scotland there are distinctive emphases in social service provision and social work practice which reflect the way that practice is politically shaped; for example, the strong emphasis on public sector rather than private sector care, and on welfare rights aspects of social work.

In the second place, social needs and our perception of them are constantly changing; there are new problems (AIDS for instance) which require new responses. A capacity for flexibility and innovative response to as yet unforeseen events is an essential requirement but one which goes beyond the task-specific purview of training, and calls for 'reflective practitioners',[36] educated to cope with uncertainty, and to use whatever resources of skill and knowledge they may have in new and unique situations.

Lastly, the *way* in which people get what they need may be as important as *what* is provided. In other words, great importance has to be attached to the processes involved in social workers' interactions with people and local communities, and to the development of practice models which stress democratic accountability and openness of decision-making. Services have to be provided in ways which maximize choice and participation, and which aim to strengthen and enable people to take action for themselves in ways which enhance and do not undermine their rights and wishes as persons and as citizens. There is abundant evidence that the social workers clients value are those who listen, try to understand their point of view, do not judge or condemn, and ensure they are fully involved in decisions which are made – values which are traditionally at the heart of social work practice

Margaret Yelloly, Professor of Social Work and Director of Social Work Education, University of Stirling.

References

1. *Report of the Inquiry into Child Abuse in Cleveland*, HMSO, London, 1988, Cm 412.

2. SED/SWSG, *Statistical Bulletin*, 1985.

3. Audit Commission, *Making a Reality of Community Care*, HMSO, London, 1986.

4. CCETSW, *Data on Training*, 1987, Table 10.

5. *ibid*, Table 1.

6. SED/SWSG, *Statistical Bulletin*, 1987.

7. *ibid*.

8. *Report of the Committee on Local Authority and Allied Personal Social Services*, HMSO, London, 1968, Cmnd. 3703, para. 516.

9. *ibid.*, para. 527.

10. Letter from Director of CCETSW to Heads of Department of CQSW Courses, 18 January 1982. (My italics).

11. CCETSW, *Care for Tomorrow*, 1987.

12. *A Child in Trust*, London Borough of Brent, 1985.

13. *ibid.*, p.204.

14. DHSS, *Social Work Decisions in Child Care*, HMSO, London, 1985.

15. CCETSW, *Data on Employment of Newly Qualified CQSW Holders*, 1988, p.7.

16. CCETSW, *Care for Tomorrow*, Table 1.

17. Association of Directors of Social Services, *Competeance for Caring: Manifesto*, July 1988.

18. NCVQ News, April/May 1988.

19. *The Role and Tasks of the Social Worker*, Report of the Barclay Committee, National Institute for Social Work, 1982.

20. For example, Webb, A. and Wistow, G. *Social Work, Social Care and Social Planning*, Longman, London, 1987; Sheldon, B. 'Social work effectiveness experiments: review and implications.' *British Journal of Social Work*, 16, 1986, pp.223-242.

21. Reid, W. and Shyne, A *Brief and Extended Casework*, Columbia University Press, New York, 1968.

22. Goldberg, E.M., Gibbons, J. and Sinclair, I. *Problems, Tasks and Outcomes: The Evaluation of Task-Centred Casework in Three Settings*, George Allen and Unwin, London, 1985.

23. Davies, B.P. and Challies, D.J., *Matching Resources to Needs in Community Care: An Evaluated Demonstration of a Long-term Care Model*, Gower, Aldershot, 1986.

24. Goldberg, E.M. et al, *op cit*.

25. Barclay Report, p.220.

26. *ibid*, p.240.

27. *Directory of Community Social Work Initiatives*. National Institute for Social Work, 19876.

28. Quoted in Hunter, D.J., and Wistow, G. 'The Scottish Difference: Policy and Practice in Community Care.' *Scottish Government Yearbook 1988*, Edinburgh, Unit for the Study of Government in Scotland.

29. SHHD, *Scottish Health Authorities' Priorities for the Eighties*, Edinburgh, HMSO, 1980.

30. Scottish Health Service Planning Council, *Scottish Health Authorities' Review of Priorities for the Eighties and Nineties*, HMSO, 1988.

31. Hunter, D J., and Wistow, G., *op cit*.

32. Audit Commission, *Making a Reality of Community Care*, London, HMSO, 1986, p.60.

33. *Community Care: Agenda for Action*. Report by Sir Roy Griffiths, London, HMSO, 1988, p.ix.

34. Parry, R., 'Privatisation and the Tarnishing of the Scottish Public Sector', *Scottish Government Yearbook 1986*, Edinburgh, Unit for the Study of Government in Scotland.

35. Griffiths Report, para, 1.3.4.

36. Schon, D A., *The Reflective Practitioner*, Temple Smith, London, 1988.

THE MISSING SCOTTISH DIMENSION IN SOCIAL CARE POLICY: A COMMENTARY ON THE GRIFFITHS REPORT ON COMMUNITY CARE AND THE WAGNER REPORT ON RESIDENTIAL CARE

Mike Titterton

The policy fields of community care and residential care for the priority groups of the elderly and the mentally and physically disabled have witnessed a flurry of recent official and independent reports of late.[1] The publication of two reports in particular, the Griffiths report on community care and the Wagner report on residential care, in March 1988 has done much to galvanise the policy debate south of the border.[2] Though the Wagner review was restricted to England and Wales, and the Griffiths review to just England, there are clear implications for the policy debate in Scotland. This article presents the main findings of these reports, along with a brief assessment of the implications of each. In particular, the article focuses upon the failure to articulate and acknowledge the Scottish experience of community and residential care within the national policy debate.

Sadly, the gap between policy intent and policy outcome in the area of community care could, as a number of critical studies have shown,[3] scarcely be wider. Much of the policy debate, moreover, appears to have been focused around a particular construction, or rather set of constructions, of 'community care policy'. Three problematical aspects of this debate may be singled out. Firstly, community care policy often contains highly ideological assumptions about the family, and about the role of women as carers. It has been argued, for example, that community care policy serves to reinforce the caring burden placed upon women.[4] Secondly, there is often a curiously limited understanding of how policy and service variables interact in social care, producing an unduly narrow 'top down' view of policy development. The wide scope for interpretation of policy by professionals in the field is often neglected; a recent Scottish study has shown that the determination of policy outputs in the delivery of social care is often more complicated than has so far been assumed.[5] Thirdly, large assumptions are often made about policy uniformity within the United Kingdom, so that variations in the implementation and interpretation of 'community care' tend to be glossed over. It has been shown, for example that policy outputs in community care can vary substantially between Scotland and England.[6] This 'unholy trinity' of analytical problems has produced unsatisfactory and partial explanations of policy development.

In this review of the Wagner and Griffiths reports, the third of these problems is considered in terms of the 'missing Scottish dimension' in social care policy. After the background to the reports is presented, the key recommendations of each are discussed in turn, with a brief consideration of how relevant each report is to the Scottish context.

Background to the reports

The Griffiths review was set up by Social Services Minister Norman Fowler following the disquiet over the findings of the Audit Commission for England and Wales.[7] Though principally concerned at first with the effectiveness of funding mechanisms in community care, particularly the operation of joint funding schemes, the Audit Commission team under David Browning and his colleagues assembled evidence which suggested that government policy as a whole was contradictary and unclear. Griffiths was invited at the end of 1986 to undertake a review, with the emphasis very much on a small scale inquiry which could report fairly quickly. Sir Roy, with a small team of eight advisers, set about gathering evidence, including occasional field trips. The review was restricted to just England, with Wales, Northern Ireland and Scotland excluded. The reasons for this were partly pragmatic and partly political. The emphasis was on a speedy and flexible response to growing concerns about the deployment and effectiveness of initiatives with resource implications such as joint financial undertakings, and DHSS ministers were reluctant to commit themselves to a large and possibly unwieldy inter-departmental exercise. Furthermore, the Audit Commission report which had led to the setting up of the review had itself been restricted to England and Wales. However there was evident disappointment in Scotland that the Griffiths review would not extend north of the border and some groups made efforts to send evidence to the review, as will be seen below.

Reactions to the appearance of the report were overshadowed by the dismay at its low key presentation; it appeared on the day after a controversial budget, with no comment from the government. MPs complained that they had trouble getting hold of early copies, and there was an element of farce as copies to bodies such as the Association of Metropolitan Authorities went to the wrong address. Sir Roy Griffiths was to later deny that his report was buried; his entry into hospital prevented his appearance at any press conference.[8] Nonetheless, the government had succeeded in raising suspicions and in producing a good deal of speculation as to the reasons for the low key reception.

The Wagner report is the Independent Review of Residential Care which was commissioned by the Social Services Secretary in December 1985. Like Griffiths, Scotland was excluded from the review. Wagner was in part intended as a complement to the reviews conducted for the DHSS by the joint central and local government working party, the second of which, under Joan Firth, was published in July 1987, and looked more narrowly at the question of financial support for residential care.[9] The Wagner review was set up at a time, as the report notes, when there was 'widespread agreement' that residential services, especially in the statutory sector, were suffering from combined problems of low status within the social services, low morale among staff, and perceived as a last resort.[10] The report also mentions the impact of the scandals at the Nye Bevan Lodge in Southwark and concern about public homes in Camden and private homes in Kent. In many ways Wagner represents the residential follow-on from the Barclay report on social work practice.[11] Like Barclay, there is an emphasis on pulling together current thinking in the area in order to influence the conventions of social services practice.

Both reports reveal what Olive Stevenson has called 'tiptoeing through the political tulips'; as she noted in her critical response to the Wagner report, the working group is noticeably coy about the widespread concern over the massive growth in private homes for the elderly, and the contradictory role that the use of supplementary benefits has played in social care policy, but openly attacks certain trade union attitudes towards the division of labour in residential care.[12] Griffiths, to pursue the metaphor further, manages to grasp a few fearsome looking nettles, such as the location of political responsibility for the development of community care, as we will see below. It is too early to judge how successful either report has been in this political balancing act; both reports are presently before government interdepartmental committees and ministers have promised to bring forward their own proposals in due course.

The Griffiths Report: 'Community care: an agenda for action'

The remit given to Griffiths was a restricted one, namely, 'to review the way in which public funds are used to support community care policy' and the options for action to improve use of these funds. To his credit, Griffiths interpreted this broadly and made a number of wide ranging suggestions and recommendations which touch the very foundations of community care policy itself.[13] One pair of commentators have declared that the report is the 'most significant statement about community care since the Seebohm report'.[14] The principal aim of the report is the specification of a clear policy framework for the development of community care; but there is a subsidiary aim which strives to effect a profound change in the very attitudes of social service providers. The latter are to assume the new management role as buyers and organisers of care, rather than as direct providers of care as such, coordinators of individually tailored 'packages of care'. According to Griffiths himself, social workers require a new set of skills, so that they may become social 'care managers'.[15]

The key recommendations of the report are:

1. that local authorities are best placed to take the main responsibility; 'the major responsibility for community care rests best where it now lies: with local government';[16]

2. social services departments should be able to assess the community care needs of their locality, identify individual needs, arrange the delivery of packages of care and adopt a more enabling role;

3. a Minister should be placed in charge 'clearly and publicly identified as responsible for community care';[17]

4. a new financial basis for community care is needed, with specific grants (up to 50% of costs) to be made to local authorities;

5. collaboration between social services agencies and health, housing and other related agencies is essential and should continue within a clear policy framework.

Those who were looking for a more radical agenda, one which challenged the prevailing conventions of social care, such as those based on certain ideological perceptions of the relationship between gender and care, were doubtless disappointed. However such a disappointment is based on a misunderstanding of the nature of the report. Griffiths provides two essential missing ingredients: firstly it provides clear and sensible recommendations for a policy framework, which many of those working in the personal social services will endorse; and secondly, it attempts to provide a management lead for the development of community care, in an area notorious for the lack of clear management responsibilities. As such it provides a practical agenda for change, which many 'radical' prospectuses do not.

There are problems with the Griffiths agenda: space constrains us to highlight one central difficulty in particular. This is the problem of the changing roles of social service agencies and social workers. Firstly, the roles allocated to social service departments as 'buyers of care' rather than direct providers will simply not work in many cases, as Sir Roy has admitted elsewhere.[18] Different localities have different service and resource mixes. Secondly, the role of social workers as 'care managers' has still to be firmed up; this clearly overlaps with the issue of training, which many would regard as the basic stumbling block to any meaningful reform. The failure of the government to respond to CCETSW's plea for three years' training for social workers was a bitter disappointment to the profession. Sir Roy Griffiths is clearly more concerned, however, to have such topics firmly on the agenda, for discussion between central government and local authorities, rather than a centrally imposed blueprint for management. Nonetheless, as the briefing paper on Griffiths produced by the Kings Fund Institute noted, something approaching a 'cultural revolution' will be required among those responsible for providing services, if the agenda for reform is to work.[19]

A number of commentators suggested that the emphasis on local authorities was unwelcome and that funding basis would be equally unwelcome to ministers; still others pointed to more fundamental issues of policy mechanisms and style of policy development within the government.[20] On the whole the report was welcomed by such local authority bodies as the Association of Metropolitan Authorities, Association of County Councils and the Association of Directors of Social Services (who have recently set up a Griffiths Implementation Group), from voluntary groups such as National Council of Voluntary Organisations and employee groups like the British Association of Social Workers and the National Association of Local Government Officers. Many added their own qualifications however. The emphasis on local authorities has provided a fillip to many in the local authority sector, but two issues in particular were singled out; concern about resources, and the emphasis on the role of the private sector in contributing to the 'welfare mix'.[21] Concern over privatisation was strongly expressed by union bodies such as NALGO.

Some pressure groups, such as MIND, have been less enthusiastic about the general shape of the recommendations; stiff criticism has come from Chris Higginbotham of MIND, who argued that Griffiths missed the opportunity to pull together health and social services.[22] Perhaps the most serious criticism, however, has come from the health services themselves; for example, Peter Millard, Professor of Geriatric Medicine at St George's Hospital London, has argued that Griffiths' plans would have a 'disastrous' effect on the long term care of the elderly, since it was the failure of social service agencies, with GPs, to provide care which led to the transfer of services in 1948.[23] This criticism is somewhat misplaced, since Griffiths is certainly not arguing that health inputs should be replaced by social services, merely that local authorities are best placed to coordinate the package of care which is to be provided to individuals in need of help. Nonetheless, it does show that resistance can be expected from those in the health services who feel that their input should remain firmly under the control of health authorities.

Griffiths: how relevant to Scotland?

While initial reactions to Griffiths north of the border were tinged with disappointment that Scotland was not included in the review, the consensus of opinion among those in the social services has been generally favourable. The Care in the Community Scottish Working Group, representing some

22 agencies, while criticising the fact that Scotland was excluded, has described it as a 'valuable aid' for those campaigning for community care.[24] The Group had also sent a submission to Griffiths, outlining a number of points of concern regarding the state of community care in Scotland, such as the adverse effects of the poll tax.[25] Similarly, the Convention of Scottish Local Authorities (COSLA) sent a report which, while welcoming the review, argued forcefully that progress towards care in the community in Scotland has been slow, and expressed concern about the lack of proper resources.[26] The Association of Directors of Social Work, like its English counterpart, has generally condoned the contents of the report; new president Fred Edwards has praised Griffiths for providing a pragmatic managerial framework, paving 'the logical way forward.'[27] Dennis Gower, Scottish Secretary of the British Association of Social Workers, has declared that Griffiths has 'enormous and far reaching consequences' for social workers, and that further study is called for.[28] For the voluntaries, spokespersons such as Lord McCluskey for Scottish Association for Mental Health, also hailed the appearance of the report, suggesting that it presented an opportunity to look at 'why so many Scots are locked up in large Victorian institutions'.[29] Griffiths is also being considered by policy advisers in the Social Work Services Group and the Scottish Home and Health Department but Scottish Office ministers are not expected to comment on the relevance of the report before the new Department of Health in Whitehall has signalled its intentions on action over its proposals.

While Scotland shares many problems with England and Wales in 'making a reality of community care', evidence is accumulating that the Scottish experience is highly distinctive, and that community care is less developed than in England and Wales, particularly for priority groups such as the mentally disabled.[30] Joint planning and joint working mechanisms appear to be less well developed, hindering progress in the field. Other barriers to the development of community based care have been cited, such as the less than forceful policy lead by the Scottish Office, the balance of care to be found in Scotland, the dominance of the hospital oriented approach in areas such as care for the mentally handicapped, and as the quote from Lord McCluskey suggests, the cultural legacies of high levels of institutional provision. However there are recent signs that things are picking up north of the border. The appearance of the updated priorities document, known as SHARPEN, has at least emphasised a renewed policy commitment by the centre to move away from the dominance of hospital care in the balance of care, towards greater community based provision.[31]

The last few years have seen a notable growth, on the ground, of interesting initiatives in such vital fields of service development as supported accommodation, often led by Scotland's large voluntary sector. Critics of the slow pace of community care development must also recognise that health boards have been understandably reluctant to embark on ambitious schemes of transfer of vulnerable groups into the community, where few facilities may be available and follow-up is poor and funding mechanisms are ill-defined. The unfortunate experience of closure of long-stay mental illness wards south of the border have not been lost in Scotland.

While Griffiths is a welcome addition to the policy debate on care in the community, a 'supplementary agenda for action' may well be required in Scotland. [32] For example, in Scotland it is the health side which has been traditionally seen as the leader in developments, partly as a result of the dominance of the hospital sector in the balance of care. Social work departments will have to be prepared to assume a more forceful role in joint planning. Griffiths is unlikely to work north of the border without a conscious recognition of the political, administrative and cultural barriers which stand in the way and without a significant increase in investment in the infrastructure of community-based forms of care.

The Wagner Report: 'Residential Care: A Positive Choice'

The terms of reference given to the Independent Review of Residential Care were to 'review the role of residential care and the range of services given in the statutory, voluntary and private residential establishments' and to consider 'what changes, if any, are required to enable the residential care sector to respond effectively to changing social needs'. [33] This was clearly a broad remit, in contrast to the one given to Griffiths; the working group which was set up was also granted a longer time for the compilation of its findings, allowing them to consider a large body of evidence and submissions, and to produce some wide ranging proposals for change. The central aim of the working group was an ambitious one: the group was seeking to 'promote a fundamental change in the public perception of the residential sector and of its place in the spectrum of care'. [34] In a bold move, the working group, evidently influenced by the submissions it received, attempted to redefine 'residential care' itself and rejected traditional understandings of the notion. The group embraced the 'challenging concept' that the traditional model of residential care should be discarded in favour of the dual concepts of 'accommodation' and 'support services'. [35] The novelty of this approach is that it allows the group to do two things: firstly, to locate 'residential care' firmly within the spectrum of community care – 'residence must be seen as an element in a range of community care services' [36]; and secondly, to place an emphasis on a 'package of care' which should be delivered to the individual. Both these emphases allow for a convenient tie-in with Griffiths.

On this basis, the working group decided to elucidate general principles of care, as well as put forward recommendations. Its two key principles are: firstly, people who move into a residential establishment should do so by a positive choice; no one should have to change their permanent accommodation in order to receive services which could be made available to them in their own homes. Secondly, living in a residential establishment should be a 'positive experience', with rights as citizens protected. Together these principles bolster the stress on the recipient of care as consumer; again this fits in well with Griffiths.

The key recommendations of Wagner are:

1. local authorities 'should take the lead in the strategic planning of accommodation and support services'[37];

2. a statutory duty should be placed on local authorities to propose a 'reasonable package of services, enabling a person to remain in their own home if that is their choice and it is reasonable for them to do so'[38];

3. nominated social workers should act as agents of users;

4. an across-the-board independent system of registration and inspection should be developed, with national guidelines;

5. community care allowances should be introduced for those with special needs, to help them choose services they want;

6. the grading of care staff as manual workers should cease, and all senior posts should be filled by staff with social work qualifications.

The overlap with Griffiths – the emphasis on the role of local authorities, on 'packages of care', on consumer choice – is not accidental. Though Griffiths was set up well after the Wagner working group, there was a conscious effort by the group to liaise with Sir Roy, as Lady Wagner has pointed out.[39] Indeed, she has gone on record as saying that Griffiths provides a 'main plank' for the successful implementation of the recommendations of her working group.[40] This overlap has not been lost on the professional bodies, some of whom have demanded the immediate implementation of both reports.

On the whole, Wagner has been widely welcomed by the professional bodies and others involved in residential care. Though there have been a few dissenting voices, the majority have felt that Wagner has pulled together and distilled the latest and best elements in recent thinking on residential care.[41] Most have welcomed the emphasis on the user of care, and on the principles of 'positive choice'. The trade union bodies welcomed the proposals concerning the upgrading of staff, although concern was expressed by representatives of private home owners about the cost of this. While the working group was relatively successful in collecting evidence from elderly persons and their carers, with some evidence gleaned from the child care sector, very little was heard from the mentally handicapped and the mentally ill, a failure which the group openly acknowledged. Again the issue of resources was frequently mentioned by those commenting on the report; like Griffiths, many have emphasised that investment will be needed if the recommendations are to be implemented. Lady Wagner has responded to such criticisms by arguing that the report was intended to 'select the right menu rather than to up the bill'.[42]

Wagner: how relevant to Scotland?

Most of Wagner's main proposals are of direct relevance to Scotland. Very few would take issue with its central recommendations on the need for a 'positive choice' and on consumer rights. Many would accept the statement from the Scottish branch of BASW that Wagner embodies 'commonsense and progressive measures' which have often been called for in recent years.[43] The proposals of the report are viewed as being rather less contentious than those contained in Griffiths, though its fate is often seen as being intertwined with that of the Griffiths report.

There are, however, a number of distinctive features of residential care in Scotland which may well call for a 'Scottish emphasis' in the implementation. There are contrasting trends to be found in the Scottish care scene at present; while there is a reluctance by some health boards to move away from traditional models of residential based care, other agencies such as Fife Social Work Department have shown a good deal of impatience with the conventional models, particularly with respect to children and mentally handicapped adults. Scotland differs significantly from England and Wales in its balance of provision across the caring sectors; it has relatively higher levels of community based provision for the elderly and relatively lower levels of residential provision, and lower levels of provision overall for the physically and mentally disabled.[44] The 'welfare mix' within residential care is also rather different. The Scottish voluntary sector has a much higher profile than its counterparts in England and Wales; in the case of the elderly, nearly 30% is voluntary, with agencies such as the Church of Scotland heavily involved in provision. Private sector provision, while it has grown in recent years, is still much less prevalent than in the south. However the Scottish experience would seem to suggest that the components of 'consumer choice' are quite distinctive in UK terms. Before Wagner could be properly implemented in Scotland, further investigation of the specific characteristics of residential care in Scotland and of the unique combination of problems which beset the development of community-based forms of care north of the border is essential.

The missing Scottish dimension

There are clear implications for the policy debate in Scotland arising from both the Griffiths and Wagner Reports, but there are a number of fundamental problems which would make the implementation of both reports in a coherent policy package difficult. It was noted above that Scotland lags behind England and Wales in community care and joint planning and joint working, though there are encouraging signs of initiatives of late. There is evidently a serious gap in Scottish community care policy, with few official policy documents in existence and with few signs in past years of a coherent and forceful policy lead by the Scottish Office. Thus COSLA has complained of 'minimal leadership' in the promotion of community care. This has meant that 'the important policy debate leading to the progressive introduction of more radical models of community care has not happened'.[45]

The relative absence of this debate in Scotland has also meant that, sadly, Scotland has tended to contribute little to the formation of UK national policy in the important fields of community and residential care. This stands in sharp contrast to the experience in Wales, where the Welsh Office has done much to lead the way in respect of mental handicap policy.[46] Of the 200 odd submissions considered by the Wagner review group, only 6 were from Scottish bodies; the working group itself consisted entirely of members from England and Wales. Griffiths accepted some Scottish submissions, such as from COSLA, but the Scottish experience itself was not directly considered. At a conference on joint planning and community care, organised by the Care in the Community Scottish Working Group in January 1987, Lord Glenarthur, then Minister of Health and Social Work at the Scottish Office, hinted that representations would be made to the Griffiths review, but there is little evidence of this in the report itself. Yet if Scotland has some rather gloomy lessons to report, it also has much of positive value to contribute to the national policy debate, and its social service and health agencies can provide numerous interesting examples of the 'good practice' which the ADSS and the Audit Commission would like to see advertised more widely. This is, moreover, a far cry from the Scottish social policy of the 1960s, when the Scottish Office forged ahead in areas such as juvenile justice and the organisation of social work with imagination and flair. It would be less than fair to expect Scotland's hard-pressed policy advisers to emulate this vision in a time of profound resource uncertainty. Nevertheless, it is reasonable to hope that the appearance of the Griffiths and Wagner reports, along with the recent publication of SHARPEN, might begin to stimulate a long overdue debate in Scotland.

Mike Titterton, Lecturer, Department of Social Dministration and Social Work, University of Glasgow.

References

1. Audit Commission for England and Wales, *Making a Reality of*

Community Care, HMSO, London, 1986; *Public Support for Residential Care*, Report of a joint central and local government working party chaired by Joan Firth, HMSO, London, 1987; National Audit Office, *Community Care Developments*, London, 1987; House of Commons Committee of Public Accounts *Community Care Developments*, Session 1987-88, HC 300, HMSO, London, 1988; Scottish Health Service Planning Council, *Scottish Health Authorities Review of Priorities for the Eighties and Nineties*, HMSO, Edinburgh, 1988.

2. *Community Care: Agenda for Action*, A Report to the Secretary of State for Social Services by Sir Roy Griffiths, HMSO, London, 1988 and National Institute for Social Work, *Residential Care: A Positive Choice*, Report of the Independent Review of Residential Care chaired by Lady Wagner, HMSO, London, 1988.

3. See, inter alia, House of Commons Social Services Committee, *Community care with special reference to adult mentally ill and mentally handicapped people*, Second Report, Session 1984-85, HC 13, HMSO, London, 1985; N Drucker (ed), *Creating community mental health services*, Scottish Association for Mental Health, Edinburgh, 1987; J Gulstad, *The Right to be ordinary: a study of obstacles and achievements in community care in Scotland*, Glasgow Special Housing Group, Glasgow, 1987; N Malin (ed), *reassessing Community Care*, Croom Helm, London, 1987.

4. See G Pascall, *Social Policy: a feminist analysis*, Tavistock, London, 1986.

5. D J Hunter, N P McKeganey and I A MacPherson, *Care of the Elderly: Policy and Practice*, Aberdeen University Press, Aberdeen, 1988.

6. D J Hunter and G Wistow, *Community Care in Britain: Variations on a Theme*, King Edward's Hospital Fund, London, 1987; M Titterton, *Policy Outcomes in the Mental Health Services in Scotland and England*, unpublished paper, 1987.

7. Audit Commission for England and Wales, *op. cit.*

8. Sir Roy Griffiths, interview in *Community Care*, 19 May 1988, p. 7.

9. DHSS, *Public Support for Residential Care*, *op. cit.*

10. Wagner report, p 1.

11. National Institute of Social Work, *Social Workers: their roles and*

tasks, Report of inquiry chaired by Peter Barclay, Bedford Square Press, London, 1982.

12. O Stevenson, 'Will it've been worthwhile for the old people?', *Community Care*, 21 April 1988, pp.28-9.

13. Griffiths report, para. 2, p. ii.

14. D Hunter and K Judge, *Griffiths and Community Care: meeting the challenge*, Briefing Paper No. 5, King's Fund Institute, 1988, p.4.

15. Sir Roy Griffiths, interview in *Community Care*, *op. cit.*

16. Griffiths report, para. 5.2, p.11.

17. *Ibid.*, para 22, p. vi.

18. Sir Roy Griffiths, interview in *Community Care*, *op. cit.*

19. Hunter and Judge, *op. cit.*, p.19.

20. M Titterton 'Disability and community care: is the debate being suppressed?' in *Disability Today*, Vol. 2, No. 2, 1988, p. 10.; M Henwood and G Wistow, 'Making a reality of care in the community – really!', *Social Services Insight*, 1 April 1988, pp. 6-7; T Harris, 'All quiet on the government front', *Social Services Insight*, 22 april 1988, pp. 14-15; see also M Titterton, *Life after Griffiths? A Scottish Perspective on Community Care*, Unpublished Paper, April 1988.

21. See, for example, A Walker, 'Paradoxes and possibilities', *Community Care*, 28 April 1988, pp. 32-3.

22. Cited in an article on the conference on 'Partnership in Care', *Community Care*, 2 June 1988, p.3.

23. See the article 'Griffiths plans for old rejected', *Community Care*, 5 May 1988, p.4.

24. Care in the Community Scottish Working Group, *Overview of Community Care Policy: Griffiths Report*, Briefing Note, Scottish Council for Single Homeless, Edinburgh, March 1988.

25. Care in the Community Scottish Working Group, *All but the Rhetoric!*, Submission with appendix to Griffiths Review, Scottish Council for Single Homeless, Edinburgh, November 1987.

26. Convention of Scottish Local Authorities, *Care in the Community in*

Scotland, Submission to Griffiths Review, Edinburgh, September, 1987.

27. Cited in S Nelson, 'Uncertainty in Scotland over report', *Community Care*, 24 March 1988, p.2.

28. British Association of Social Workers (Scottish Committee), *Rostrum*, supplement on the Griffiths Report, Edinburgh, February, 1988.

29. Cited in S Nelson, *op. cit.*

30. See, inter alia, F M Martin, *Between the Acts: community mental helath services 1959-1983*, Nuffield Provincial Hospitals Trust, London, 1984; D Hunter and G Wistow, 'The Scottish difference: policy and practice in community care' in D McCrone and A Brown (eds) *Scottish Government Yearbook 1988*, USGS, Edinburgh and *Community Care in Britain*, *op. cit.*; Drucker, *op. cit.*; Gulstad, *op. cit.*; Titterton, *Life after Griffiths? A Scottish perspective on community care*, *op. cit.*

31. Scottish Health Service Planning Council, *op. cit.*

32. See Titterton, *Life after Griffiths? A Scottish perspective on community care*, *op. cit.*

33. Wagner report, p.1.

34. *Ibid.*, p.3.

35. *Ibid.*, passim, pp.17-8.

36. *Ibid.*, para. 13, p.11.

37. *Ibid.*, para. 1, p.115.

38. *Ibid.*, para. 2, p.115.

39. Lady Wagner, 'A positive choice', article in *Community Care*, 10 March 1988, pp.22-3.

40. Address by Lady Wagner to joint NISW/Community Care conference, cited in *Community Care*, 21 April 1988, pp.2-3.

41. See the special articles on Wagner in *Community Care*, 14 April 1988 and 21 April 1988; also *Social Work Today*, 10 March 1988.

42. Lady Wagner, interview in *Community Care*, 14 April 1988, p.16.

43. British Association of Social Workers (Scottish Committee), *Rostrum* supplement on the Wagner Report, Edinburgh, June, 1988.

44. See Hunter and Wistow, *Community Care in Britain, op. cit.* and Titterton, *Life after Griffiths? A Scottish perspective on community care, op. cit.*

45. Convention of Scottish Local Authorities, *op. cit.*, p.9.

46. Welsh Office, *All Wales Strategy for the development of services for mentally handicapped people*, Cardiff, 1983.

CHILD SEXUAL ABUSE: A SCOTTISH PERSPECTIVE

Lorraine Waterhouse and James Carnie

Perhaps more than any other issue, with the obvious exception of the emergence of AIDS, child sexual abuse has been the social 'discovery' of the 1980s. Until the early part of this decade very few people were aware of child sexual abuse as it is now understood. This is not to suggest that the problem did not exist prior to this, simply that reporting rates were no where near their current levels. Over the last few years the media attention paid to the sexual abuse of children has been quite extraordinary, resulting in a massive increase in public awareness of the problem. What, though, underlies this spread of concern, and what are the Scottish perspectives on the issue?

I. The Political Context

The 'politics' of the issue can be traced back to the early seventies and even before when the emergence of the physical abuse of children, combined with the acknowledgement that domestic violence was more widespread than had previously been thought, catapulted the activities of social workers into the political spotlight.[1] This was particularly so in cases where so-called 'mistakes' in social work practice had led to tragic outcomes. The resulting enquiries, and especially the one into the death of Maria Colwell in 1974 in England received widespread publicity and stunned an incredulous public into recognising that such problems existed in modern times.

National interest in the Colwell Inquiry recommendations can probably be attributed to a timely coincidence between its occurrence and the advent of newly organised social work and social service departments in Scotland, England and Wales. Never before had there been this unprecedented access to information about social work practice. Public loss of faith in the state's ability to protect children, together with growing social anxiety about the decline of the family and the growth of violence, provoked political concern about the nature and direction of social work practice and about the accountability of social workers themselves. Poor inter-agency communication was identified as one of the major problems in dealing with child abuse, and the debate on improving inter-agency co-operation has continued unabated ever since.

The political impetus was given further weight by the campaigning activity of established pressure groups such as the National Society for the Prevention of Cruelty to Children (NSPCC), the Royal Scottish Society for Prevention of Cruelty to Children (RSSPC) and the British Medical Association (BMA). In addition to these traditional bodies, emergent feminist organisations like Rape Crises and Women's Aid began to set up helplines and refuges during the 1970s. Public attention was brought to the experiences of those women who 'spoke out' about their childhood ordeals of sexual abuse. Their experiences clearly challenged the myth that women and children were at risk mainly from strangers; instead it was becoming increasingly apparent that most sexual abuse occurred within the confines of the family.

II. Changing Values

The use of children sexually has existed throughout history and across cultures, but whether such behaviour was conceived of and defined as abuse has been dependent on the societal values of the period.[2] Particular sexual behaviours have been defined as normal at one period in history while later these same behaviours are defined as immoral and later still as criminal and then as psychopathological. In both ancient Greek and Roman civilisations an acceptance of sexual practices between adults and children prevailed. Child prostitution was commonplace as was the practice of anal intercourse between teachers and boy pupils. Other ancient civilisations such as the Incas of Peru, and the Ptolemaic Egyptians also permitted certain types of incest in isolated, privileged classes.

In Western society, it is being increasingly recognised that child sexual abuse is the expression of the perpetrator's need for dominance. This is accomplished by the exertion of the perpetrator's authority over the subordinated child. Thus, it is an act of exploitation committed in complete disregard of the harm inflicted on the child. Moreover, the harm is compounded because child sexual abuse is an abuse of power and a betrayal of trust.[3] Originally identified in feminist writings but now absorbed into mainstream thought, the acknowledgement of the innocence of the child victim and the abuse of power and trust by the offending adult, is central to a proper understanding of the problem.[4]

Further, the idea that child sexual abuse is something which is only to be found in 'dysfunctional' families is increasingly also being challenged. The notion that the problem is somehow confined to socio – economically deprived groups or to ethnic or cultural minorities has been dispelled and it is now commonly accepted that the problem is much more widespread than had hitherto been imagined. That child sexual abuse can happen in otherwise perceptibly 'ordinary' families is disturbing and unsettling to many members of the general public, threatening as it does their belief in traditional family values and their conception of the family unit as the lynchpin of liberal democratic society.

III. Definition and Incidence

Any attempt to define 'sexual abuse of children' is fraught with difficulties. Rather than referring to any specific type of sexual behaviour, the term "sexual abuse" may mean anything across a range of activities from exhibitionism to genital manipulation to intercourse to child pornography. With no standardised definition of the subject matter, the common usage of the label 'child sexual abuse' conceals the different meanings which may be attached to it.[5]

It is, therefore, extremely difficult to produce a neat, accurate and all-inclusive definition of child sexual abuse. However, many experts in the field have offered their working definitions and one of the most widely cited, to which we would subscribe, describes sexual abuse as 'the involvement of dependent, developmentally immature children and adolescents in sexual activities that they do not fully comprehend, are unable to give informed consent to, and that violate the social taboos of family roles'.[6]

The sexual abuse of children is surrounded by such secrecy that it is virtually impossible to obtain a truly accurate picture relating to the scale of the problem. Estimates of both the incidence (number of cases per year) and prevalence (proportion of the population affected) vary considerably. From the dramatic increases in reported cases of child abuse over the last few years it would be easy to conclude mistakenly that there is a current epidemic of child molestation which is getting worse. However, it is generally acknowledged that this increase is related more to greater public awareness and acceptance of the existence of the phenomenon, rather than to any great explosion in the actual number of acts of sexual abuse.

Estimates of the scale of the problem tend to come from one of two sources – either cases reported to various agencies, or survey studies of adults that ask about previous experiences of abuse. There are limitations to both these sources. Of the first, it is recognised that large numbers go unreported each year. Some of the reasons for this involves difficulties in documenting abuse – without physical evidence, a child may not be believed, or the suspicion is so vague that it is not reported. Additionally, the possibility of separation from parents or other disruption of the family may cause a child to give a false retraction or to deny a valid complaint. In addition pre-school children may not be able to communicate effectively events or may be unaware that the behaviour of the abuser is anything unusual.[7]

There are also difficulties with the second source of information – survey studies. Here there are problems concerning the representativeness of the survey sample, the design of the questionnaire and its administration and the under-reporting of abuse. Also, since such surveys ask adults for their childhood experiences, they cannot give a current incidence or prevalence rate of the sexual abuse of children as each individual is reporting on the past. A review of available research material (overwhelmingly American) reveals widely conflicting prevalence rates – anything from 6% to 62% for females and from 3% to 30% for males.[8] Notwithstanding the fact that it is impossible to identify a consensus prevalence rate, the one important conclusion that can be drawn from this data is that the level of child sexual abuse is far from trivial, even if one were only to accept the very lowest rate.

Difficulties, then, still persist in accepting child sexual abuse as a real issue, in defining the problem coherently, in understanding its true nature and in estimating the extent of its prevalence. How then are professional front-line practitioners supposed to recognise the problem of child sexual abuse and how do we expect them to react when it confronts them in the course of their daily work? Recognition is, of course, intrinsically connected to definition, but even those professionals who have a working definition with which they are confortable still have problems in identifying sexually abused children.

IV. The Cleveland Controversy

In July 1987, a statutory inquiry chaired by Lord Justice Butler-Sloss was established to investigate the arrangements for dealing with suspected cases of Child Abuse in Cleveland because of concern expressed by parents, nurses, police and Members of Parliament at the sharp rise in cases in the county.[9] The recognition of child sexual abuse was one of the main issues in the Cleveland controversy. Of course, the irony in this instance was not that highly trained professionals had failed to identify cases of sexual molestation, but that they had identified 'too many' in too short a space of time. It has been said that recognition of sexual abuse in a child is entirely dependent on an individual's inherent willingness to entertain the possibility that the condition may exist.[10] In Cleveland key figures certainly became involved in a determined effort to detect abused children.

Like enquiries before it, the debate is set within the context of English laws, policies and practices. Perhaps paradoxically one principle recommendation of the inquiry, to establish a new Office of Child Protection, derives in part from the Childrens' Hearing system in Scotland and in particular the role of the Reporter. The proposed Office of Child Protection would perform a similar function to that of Reporter, namely provision for assessment independent of the local authority as to whether the intended proceedings are well founded and in the best interest of the child. By adapting the Scottish precedent the hope is to introduce an impartial check and balance in the professional identification of child abusers before such cases go to Court. Whether it would prove efficient or effective simply to graft one dimension of the Scottish legal system onto the otherwise very different legal arrangements for dealing with child sexual abuse in England and Wales merits more attention than Lord Butler-Sloss was able to allow.

V. Some Research Findings

Our current research into the professional identification of, and response to, child sexual abuse in Scotland is tending to shed some light on a number of the issues raised thus far.[11] This research has focussed on tracing the history of a sample of referrals for child sexual abuse which have come to the attention of the professional services of four Scottish Regions participating in the study. The premise which has underpinned the study is based on the idea that the professionals' perceptions of the problem, denoted by their definitions and explanations of child sexual abuse, will influence their actions in the early stages of a referral and will affect their judgements regarding the degree of intervention required and the types of solution sought. As the research has been carried out at a time of growing public and professional awareness of the problem, it has provided an opportunity to study the emergence of policy and its impact on the practice of relevant professionals.

The information being presented here is based on an early and partial content analysis of the responses of front-line practitioners involved in our sample of cases. Details on some 50 cases drawn from social work records in late 1986/early 1987 were examined, and the principal professional participants involved in dealing with each case identified. It was decided that as social work and the police were the agencies most frequently involved in the early stages of investigation, the bulk of the interviews should focus on them as key informants and around 100 such interviews were therefore undertaken (50 social work; 50 police). This narrowing of focus has the advantage of allowing more detailed exploration of the ideas and practices of two professional groups but at the same time the disadvantage of failing to encompass the range of different perspectives and influences which make up the professional assembly.

VI. Definition and Identification in Practice

Reference was made earlier to the idea that the label 'child sexual abuse' concealed the different meanings which could be attached to it. Moreover, it was suggested that the way in which 'child sexual abuse' was defined or described could have an effect on the way in which the problem was identified and responded to. Two somewhat different styles of definition were noted in our research.

In the first category respondents offered 'functional' answers which described different types of acts which might represent child sexual abuse together with a depiction of a set of circumstances in which it could arise and a set of common symptoms to be found in the child. A majority of both social workers and police tended to adopt this style, making reference to a wide range of activities from the comparatively mild to the very serious which could comprise sexual abuse. One social worker, for instance, remarked that 'there are lots of levels of abuse', while another simply said 'any use of a child by an adult for sex'. Very often the tendency would be to list things such as voyeurism, exhibitionism, petting, intercourse and rape and many of the police officers, perhaps not surprisingly, favoured legal terms or specific crime categories as a means of conveying the types of activity they had in mind.

In the second category respondents offered more 'abstract' answers. These involved a conceptual analysis of child sexual abuse in which 'dysfunctional' family dynamics, adult-child power relationships and male psycho-sexual motivation, were given greater prominence. There was often only a fine dividing line between these definitions and the first category, but the distinguishing feature lay in the use of a key word or expression which revealed a deeper understanding of the causes of abuse and of the betrayal of trust which abuse necessarily involved. Quite a sizeable minority of social workers and police used this descriptive style making reference to the power element within sexual abuse, the lack of informed consent, the emotionally immature child, the secrecy and fear involved and the adult male's need for sexual gratification and dominance.

What difference, if any, the two types of definition make in the early stages of identifying child sexual abuse referrals is not yet clear. The functional definition focuses on manifestations of sexual abuse in the child without reference to causation; whereas the abstract definition concentrates on the actions of adults towards dependent children and the motivation for such acts. An over-reliance on the former can lead to difficulties in interpreting symptoms which by themselves are usually not discrete enough to discriminate sexual abuse from other childhood conditions. Too great an emphasis on the latter can involve difficulties in differentiating between permissible and impermissible behaviour in the context of different family settings, and in ascribing moral values to particular actions arising therein. Of course, this is not to suggest that there can be permissable sexual behaviour with children, rather that the limits of the acceptable at different ages concerning such things as nudity, embracing and horseplay are not easy to draw. The very varied nature of allegations of sexual impropriety in the home calls for sensitive assessment and a flexible response.

In practice, however, the distinction between defining the problem and identifying it was not so clear cut and in the minds of many of the respondents the two were virtually the same thing. Indeed, it is perhaps surprising to learn that only a few respondents indicated that identification itself was a major problem. This was because the majority of both social workers and the police felt that their role was not so much to identify child sexual abuse per se, but to *respond* to it when the problem was brought to their attention through a referral. One WPC in a Female and Child Unit remarked – 'I think by the time we're involved it's already known that sexual abuse has occurred, so we're not really the ones who are identifying that this girl or this boy has been sexually abused'; while her colleague confirmed 'we tend to act on information given to us either by a parent or social worker or teacher usually'.

Sometimes though, social workers could be faced with delicate decisions – 'from our point of view we tend to be responding to referrals coming from elsewhere and it's difficult to know if they are accurate'. Therefore, social work often had to be doubly cautious, concerned not only about the accuracy of referral by others, but also about their own professional competence to decide which were the discriminating indicators – 'There are no clear hallmarks', said an experienced Senior, 'invariably what we are talking about is a number of factors coming together of which disclosure (by the child) is in my view certainly the single most important'.

Provisional examination of the case material in our sample reveals that the main source of information regarding child sexual abuse emanated from within, or very close to, the family itself. We have found that around 60% of disclosures came from victims themselves, from the non-abusing parent or relative, or from a close family friend. Approximately 30% of the sample disclosures came, perhaps not surprisingly, from those professions most closely associated with the day-to-day care of children – namely schools and the medical profession. Being in almost daily contact with the children, teachers were in an ideal position to monitor any suspicious changes in a child's behaviour and to alert the relevant welfare agencies should a case continue to give cause for concern. Whether teachers actively sought this role in the frontline, given their many other varied responsibilities was, of course, another question.

What then becomes apparent, both from the sample figures and from respondents' comments, is that those agencies most directly involved in the investigation and subsequent management of child sexual abuse cases – social work and the police – are not themselves very prominent in identifying their own case material. In only a small percentage of cases, some 10%, did social work or the police 'discover' the problem on their own, that is, appear as the first link in the referral chain. It was far more common for them to appear later in the 'chain of referral' in a reactive role to information received from outside sources. Uncertain whether abuse has occurred, social work and police enter the arena to investigate, while other professionals, to some extent, give way. The complaint almost invariably depends on allegations, usually against existing family members and consequently involves for all concerned a provocative and disturbing encounter whether or not abuse exists.

VII. Changing Priorities

Widespread agreement existed amongst both police officers and social workers that reporting rates in Scotland had increased quite dramaticaly over the last two years. Publicity given to the issue on television and in the press had opened up the subject – 'it makes us more aware that this problem does exist and probably to a greater extent than we first thought'. Few could quote figures, but there was an understanding that the perceived increase related to reporting *rates* and did not necessarily reflect an increase in actual numbers in the community at large. It was simply that more cases were coming to the attention of social work and the police as a result of the growing public awareness of the problem. The underlying feeling amongst many was, however, that the reported cases only represented 'the tip of the iceberg'. As one experienced social worker commented, 'there are far more incidents taking place than come to our knowledge and far more youngsters are involved than we know about at the present time; hence there is a very active concern to make channels available for youngsters to confide'.

It was thus acknowledged that the issue had to be accorded the very highest priority in order to ensure protection of the child and to a lesser extent to combat the very newness of the issue itself. Social workers indicated that when a child sexual abuse referral came into the team it would be given top priority, over-riding all other work. 'No matter what you have on, it is dropped for the child sexual abuse referral and investigated!'. The police too were aware of the increased workload caused by the rise in reporting rates and expressed their determination 'to get to the bottom of the problem'.

What this 'drop everything else' ethic implies for day to day practice is probably less straightforward than the policy intention may suggest. With an increase in child sexual abuse referrals coming at a time of tight fiscal restraint not all cases of sexual abuse necessarily can be treated with the same seriousness and urgency. Not only then must these cases be pitted against other pressing issues facing social work and police but also they may have to be ranked against each other. Perhaps the reality of the situation is that 'everything else' is not, and cannot be, dropped by the social worker, but merely relegated in the hierarchy of priorities. While it may be comparatively easy to conclude that the potential threat to a child's life and health deserves timely attention, how are those children most at risk to be identified?

The difficulty, of course, lies in deciding what constitutes a sexual act or a sexual intention. Often police and social workers are being forced to act as moral arbitrators about what constitutes reasonable behaviour between adults and children. This can leave individual practitioners feeling vulnerable:-

'There is so much anxiety around currently that either individuals or in terms of representing their profession or their department, people are feeling they have to make sure they are not liable, if you like. The problem about that is you are nearly always dealing with a range of uncertainties and if you are going to go for certainty you can usually make only very crude decisions.'

One of the problems in Cleveland lay in this failure to differentiate between the seriousness of cases. Once a child manifested particular symptoms thought to be consistent with sexual abuse, its removal to a place of safety followed as a matter of course. Not only did this all inclusive approach draw some questionable cases into the net, causing for the families concerned much emotional upheaval, it also overloaded the system and created for the social workers a similar strain.

Despite the high priority given to child sexual abuse, rarely, it seems, is a social worker's existing case load lightened to accommodate the practical and emotional burdens of having to cope with such work. Some social workers did complain of the expectations, that more work would have to be fitted into the available time and existing schedule. As one respondent· commented 'it takes an awful lot of time to do it properly, time is the big factor'. Thus it seems straightforward to suggest that if social workers are being expected to carry the burden of a child sexual abuse case in addition to the demands of their existing caseload, then the additional work (in some instances) will lead to greater pressure with its attendant problems of heightened anxiety and stress.

The 'discovery' of child sexual abuse as a 'new' crime has also placed new burdens upon the police who, like social work, face a similar growth in service demand. Such demand has been responded to in part by creation of specialist Female & Child units in many Forces. These units comprise female officers trained to investigate crimes of violence and abuse against children and women, sensitively and authoritatively. The public expect child abuse cases to be investigated and 'cleared-up' quickly. As a consequence many of the Female and Child Units are working to capacity, with specialist officers under pressure to deal with an ever increasing workload. If child abuse reporting rates continue to rise at their present levels then inevitably there will be further repercussions for the police's operational strategy on the matter.

Both the police and social work were unanimous in placing the interests and welfare of the child victim above all other considerations. On this there was absolutely no equivocation. Where doubt and uncertainty did arise was in the *form* that intervention should take. Concern was expressed about whether the decisions and actions being taken in the short term as a result of the 'crisis' were necessarily in the longer term interests of the child. Also, it was often difficult to weigh in the balance the 'rights' of the child to be protected against the 'rights' of the parents not to be subjected to the unnecessary intervention of the welfare agencies.

Given the sensitive nature of the problem, both police and social workers were quick to point out that they could not just 'jump in' when a case was referred. Matters certainly had to be investigated promptly but over-anxiety had to be guarded against. The impression was conveyed that front-line practitioners faced a considerable dilemma in this capacity. What was the appropriate response time in each particular case? How long for instance, could a social worker, afford to reflect on matters before deciding to act? One summarised this difficulty neatly commenting, 'I think there is a danger of over-reacting at times – OK, we've got to protect the child in the first instance, but we have to be very, very sure of what we're doing'.

VIII. Policy Trends

Scotland's system of Children's Hearings, with their regular reviews and parental involvement, may offer certain safeguards against the lack of communication which precipitated the Cleveland controversy. Although it was not strictly within the remit of Butler-Sloss to compare directly policy and practice in Scotland and England, the Report, somewhat equivocally, states that 'the relative advantages and disadvantages of the two systems in the Cleveland perspective would not be easy to evaluate'.[12] While England is now looking to adopt certain Scottish precedents into its child care system, for instance, the proposed Office of Child Protection, it would be prudent for those north of the border to acknowledge some of the more general themes of the Butler-Sloss Report as being applicable to the Scottish context, especially those recommendations which spell out the need for those investigating child abuse to make a *conscious effort* to ensure they act in the best interests of the child.[13]

The advantages of a multi-disciplinary approach are now commonly acknowledged by front-line practitioners – shared information, shared responsibility, shared accountability. Most people seem to endorse the *idea* of inter-agency co-operation; yet the traditional adherence to professional autonomy is notoriously difficult to overcome, and in Scotland, as elsewhere, problems still remain in creating a truly integrated approach.

There seems to be a widespread belief amongst many that the Scottish system affords more opportunities for professionals to make contact in a multi-disciplinary way. This belief stems from the notion that Children's Hearings provide the catalyst for both practitioners and lay personnel to come together to address each particular case from a collective perspective. Whether such an assumption is entirely justified is perhaps open to question, for it tends to overlook the fact that many important decisions can be reached by individual agencies prior to a case coming before a Children's Panel. The decision-making nexus between individual agencies, N.A.I. Case Conferences, the Office of the Reporter and Children's Panels is still far from clear.

Yet a forceful endorsement of the Scottish system was given in a submission to the Cleveland Inquiry by John Forfar, President of the British Paediatric Association. He comments:-

'The Children's Panels in Scotland appear to be a better way of dealing with the problem of suspected child abuse than the system which pertains in England and Wales. They provide a means by which, in conjunction with selected informed lay advisers and under the chairmanship of a professional assessor, paediatricians and other doctors dealing with children can interview parents and children (jointly or separately) along with representatives of social work departments and the law. This provides a means of appreciating and assessing a multi-disciplinary problem in a multi-disciplinary way. It reduces the risk or arbitrariness and provides a means of achieving a more co-operative and flexible approach.'[14]

The key word in the passage is 'appear' which gives some credence to the idea that the belief in the system is possibly greater than its actual strengths. The belief, therefore, may become a self-fulfilling prophecy which can make both practitioners and independent observers less critical of structural flaws and weaknesses. This in turn may lead to a dangerous complacency.

The very 'newness' of the problem of child sexual abuse has obviously caught many agencies off-balance. Only a few years ago it would be rare for sexual abuse to be considered as the possible cause of a child's or family's difficulties. It has taken time for senior policy-makers to assimilate the issues involved and to respond with new initiatives. Some might argue though, that many of the problems, particularly those pertaining to inter-agency co-operation, have been known for long enough. However, this may underestimate the very real problems that sexual abuse creates for those trying to respond to it.

Perhaps what needs to be better understood is that professionals act within different operational frameworks and difficulties and conflicts can arise between agencies because their respective frameworks often do not match. Indeed, there is no reason why they should, for in many ways they represent an agency's separate identity and perspective. However, in finding common ground for collaboration it will be necessary to have a more realistic appreciation of such frameworks in order to understand where the compromises over practice lie.[15]

Certainly, significant advances have been made in improving the understanding between professionals about child sexual abuse issues in a number of areas throughout Scotland in the last few years. At management level multi-disciplinary Area Review Committees met in most regions to discuss policy and co-ordinate activity, with N.A.I. Guidelines being revised to cope with the new demands being placed upon professionals. The police too have responded positively to the problem by creating in a number of Forces new specialist Female and Child Units comprising women officers trained to deal with sexual abuse investigations compassionately and discretely. And at grassroots level many local initiatives are emerging, ranging from ad-hoc joint training seminars to more permanently established weekly or monthly discussion groups involving various disciplines.

Thus, the 'policy response' to child sexual abuse in Scotland has been in a sense both revisionist and innovative. Revisionist, because such was the upsurge in public awareness and reporting rates that existing policies formulated with other forms of physical abuse in mind had to be swiftly updated and modified in order to take account of the sudden new demand for service. Innovative, because with the passage of time a fuller appreciation of the nature of the problem has emerged and this has led to a number of significant breakthroughs in multi-disciplinary co-operation and co-ordination at the local level.

What effect these latter developments in local response will have on central policy-making remains to be seen. A balance may eventually have to be struck between implementing uniform policy guidelines applicable to all, while accommodating a certain measure of responsible devolved autonomy to allow for local practice. In theory, this degree of flexibility is already built into one Region's Guidelines:-

"Any procedures must admit to the possibility that, for very good reasons, certain sections of them will not be followed in certain circumstances. However, it is imperative that any course of action which deviates from the procedures are fully justifiable..."

There are, paradoxically, dangers in developing an effective local network system in that those involved can become victims of their own success. The more effective they are at uncovering the problem the more their work load increases. Also they can begin to find themselves labelled 'experts' in the field, with the result that fellow professionals in adjacent localities start to rely on them for advice and help, further increasing their burgeoning workload.

Ultimately, of course, the objective of the inter-agency approach should be to enable front-line professionals to understand more fully their different perspectives and operational roles in order to promote trust, communication and collaboration. The difficulties in achieving this, however, even in today's enlightened climate, should not be underestimated.

Lorraine Waterhouse, Lecturer, and James Carnie, Research Fellow, Department of Social Policy and Social Work, University of Edinburgh.

References

1. N Parton, "Politics and Practice" in *Community Care*, September 26 1985, pp.22-24.

2. P B Mrazek and C H Kempe, *Sexually Abused Children and Their Families*, Oxford, Pergamon Press, 1981, p.5.

3. M McLeod and E Saraga, "Abuse of Trust" in *Marxism Today*, August 1987, pp.10-13.

4. K Edwards, "Probing the Power Struggle" in *Nursing Times*, April 29, 1987, Vol. 83, No. 17, pp.47-50.

5. J LaFontaine, "Child Sexual Abuse", *ESRC Research Briefing*, January 1988, p.2.

6. M D Schechter and L Roberge, "Sexual Exploitation" in *Child Abuse and Neglect: The Family and Community*, (edited by R E Hefler and C H Kempe) Cambridge, Mass., Ballinger Press, 1976.

7. K McFarlane et al, *Sexual Abuse of Young Children*, New York, Guildford Press, 1986.

8. D Finkelhor et al, *A Sourcebook on Child Sexual Abuse*, London, Sage, 1986, Ch.1.

9. *Report of the Inquiry into Child Abuse in Cleveland 1987*, HMSO, Cm 412, 1988, (The Butler-Sloss Report).

10. S Sgroi, cited in Mrazek and Kempe, *op.cit.* p.14.

11. For reasons of confidentiality, comments and extracts taken from this research must remain unattributed.

12. Report, *op.cit.*, p.239.

13. *ibid.*, pp. 243-254.

14. *ibid.*, p.302.(N.B. The reference to "the chairmanship of a professional assessor" is incorrect.)

15. H Keville, "Joint Venture" in *Insight*, April 8, 1988, pp.12-14.

A BOOK O' PAIRTS

Grant Jordan

The preface to Andrew McPherson and Charles D. Raab *Governing Education: A Sociology of Policy Sincr 1945* (Edinburgh, EUP, 1988), opens with a quotation from Bruce Millan which claims that Government Ministers feel powerless; they indicate their preferences but policy nonetheless means consultation and such change as is effected cannot just be achieved by administrative or Ministerial fiat. Millan says, 'I sometimes wished that I could just make up my mind about something and say that that would be the end of it...'

McPherson and Raab establish this is the point of interest in studying politics in a sophisticated and mature democracy. We have the machinery that allows elected dictatorship but that is not our practice.

Some might argue that the ground rules have changed as this book took its stately passage from field work to print. Would Michael Forsyth give the same impression? However the onus is still on those who believe that we have transformed our practices to make their case. Politicians and analysts have always believed that a consensus existed just long enough ago for past controversies to become covered in the syrup of nostalgia.

This book will be subject to very different reviews – not only through the inevitably varied views of those doing the reviewing but because the book is addressing different constituencies. The teaching profession will clearly be interested in explanations of the derivation of policies over buildings, examinations, career structure and the like. There is clearly a rather different thrust to the book in terms of the sociology of educational administration. There is a political science aspect of understanding how things happen. Before the inevitable quibbles and reservations are rehearsed it is worth establishing that this is a serious contribution to these various literatures.

The doubt remains however as to whether the parts have not been allowed to multiply in a somewhat self indulgent manner. That this is a long book (555 pages) can be construed negatively as well as positively. Length can represent lack of control rather than thoroughness. A problem with these different clienteles for this work is that some sentences (and pages) are written in a style that may be valuable in establishing the authors credibility for a particular readership but will simply glaze the eyes, if not shut them, of the reader who simply wants to discover who exercised power, over what. For example the authors suggest, 'In these ways, therefore the myth was institutionally biased and constituted a third dimension of power in the sense identified by Lukes.' (p477)

In attempting to be a work for all markets the book spreads itself too thinly even at this length. For example, it uses as one of its dimensions of analysis partnership versus centralisation. It is not really clear how this scale is to be measured. Rod Rhodes' account of the power dependence approach is surely worth more than a mention in the footnotes and a passing nod on page 197.

The authors make the point that it is possible that power has moved from society to government and from the educational professionals and officials to officials acting as agents of government. This point seems to be about the decline of the 'professional bureaucratic complex' in the face of a repoliticising of education. This seems a hypothesis worth exploring but the authors surely lead us astray when they suggest that such an argument has affinity with corporatist theory. Instead of discussing their evidence they start reviewing and attempting to apply the theory of others – principally Philippe Schmitter.

The Big Names of Theory

They suggest later that corporatism was a means of the government absorbing leaders of producer groups into the decision process in stable and long lasting relations in which demands could be bargained and conflict contained. The authors thus saw corporatism as being not much more than consultation,

> '...governments that seek predictability may incorporate the leaders of interest groups in decision-making procedures, and thereby drift towards corporatism.'(p22)

They describe the difference between pluralism and corporatism as depending on the degree of conflict between the groups and Government – with corporatism holding that there is collaboration between groups and government in policy formulation and implementation. (p473). This ignores too much literature on Government/group relations that not only preceded Schmitter's corporatism but was specifically rejected by Schmitter. The authors quote Grant's suggestion that corporatism is a possibility of arriving at *effective* bargains but this is not a sensitive enough criterion. It cannot be the case that effective bargains = corporatism and failed = pluralism. (p473) They cite Colin Crouch's warning that individual pieces of behaviour should only with great care be labelled as corporatist. Crouch was emphasising that corporatism is a system of organising society and if there is no system we are not left with partial corporatism but non corporatism.

One can see why the authors would want to relate their particular fragment of the social picture to wider theories but unfortunately pluralism and corporatism have not been constructed as clearly specified and easily applied theories. It is tempting to see them as alternatives but unwise. Pluralism and corporatism are discussed at various points in the book but nonetheless the sum of the various passages is still too thin for the specialist. We seem to be introduced to the big names of theory to prove that the authors have done their homework, rather than to carry that debate much further.

McPherson and Raab say (p474), 'Perhaps after Brunton the Department was still trying to perfect and extend a corporatist strategy..' But were civil servants not in fact trying to do something less grand? They were trying to fit in as many pieces of the puzzle as they could while minimising conflict.

The terms of that academic debate have changed substantially in the past couple of years and their theoretical discussion seems beached by a tide that has turned. The book proves that really there is not much future in studying empirical events with a toolkit of *either* pluralism *or* corporatism (or even with a couple of varieties of these.) It is a pity that the book tries to do so before concluding on page 482 that it is not 'on'. And why do they need to invent the term 'coordinated pluralism' rather than discuss the concept of sub-governments and corporate pluralism that predominate in the non-corporatist literature on interest groups? Everything Phillippe Schmitter has said has not been wrong and he warned somewhere of the dangers of creating a Tower of Babel of the social sciences.

From a perspective of 1988 the analysis cries out for discussion in terms of 'networks' – and seems to demand an exploration of the term policy community. The academic fashion for corporatism is as dated as bell bottom trousers.

The Interviews – the Big Names in Education

If the book is not most favourably judged in terms of theoretical innovation it does much better in terms of research methodology. What McPherson and Raab have done is to open up – in a self conscious manner – a research approach that attempts to exploit 13 on-the-record interviews with key policy making individuals (and 12 unattributable interviews). The book is therefore studded with verbatim extracts. Some will think that the authors have been given too much of the raw material and too little interpretation. It is in all honesty difficult to maintain enthusiasm for the 'colour of their socks' detail of someone else's case study. But we should respect that McPherson and Raab were pursuing a method of using oral history. It is pointless to gather the fine print and subsume it in sweeping generalisations.

This method worked for them because they were lucky enough to break into the network of relevant individuals (and skilled enough to establish their credibility when working within that network.) However it is a method and not the method.

In using such interview material there is the danger, well recognised by the authors, of a discrepancy between actions and recollections. Even where the respondent has no intention to mislead, memory is, as McPherson and Raab admit, mortal. There is a more subtle danger in using interviews in that the more successfully one penetrates the world of the policy makers, the easier it is to accept their world view and the more seduced one becomes by their explanations. There is thus a social dynamic in using interviews that makes the researcher less free than his colleague working as an archive rat. We need to note the special feature of these interviews was that the authors transcribed the whole interviews and secured an agreed text with the subjects. These transcripts ranged from 40 to 320 pages. The authors were then free to make their own use of the material.

One respects the creation of a new on-the-record data source that others can use, but it is likely that in the future new questions will suggest themselves – questions on which the McPherson-Raab interviews will be mute. Moreover it is not clear that the argument of this book would have been materially affected had the authors not, more conventionally, done their interviews and then cleared the relevant passages. Certainly the authors would have been spared much effort; spared of that effort they could have extended their pool. They may have encouraged less unanimity in their sources if they had sessions with the gloves and the tape recorders off. The attributable interview has great advantages but it may restrict rather than encourage frankness. The Heclo and Wildavsky precedent of 'off the record' comments in *The Private Government of Public Money* is surely positive.

Reservations aside, the interview-based material gave some important data. The material from Bruce Millan and others on the Scottish Office position in the PESC negotiations filled a hole and was a nice Scottish supplement to our general knowledge about the operation of PESC.

Again the material is particularly interesting on the role of Parliament. Rodger (p169) pointed out that it was only those members of the Opposition briefed by the EIS or by their local Directors of Education, that could make much of a contribution. Even more stage managed was when the Opposition asked the civil servants for headings for their speeches and even before the speech was made the civil servants could provide their

Ministers with a reply. Rodger was equally scathing about the interventions by MPs through Question Time where the questions were only loosely connected to the live issues that the teachers and authorities were discussing, 'He wasn't really asking the guts and substance of the thing at all.' The only thing that stops us including Parliament as one of the dignified elements of the Constitution is the fact that it is often not...

The degree of methodological introspection with which the authors approached their on-the-record interviews was both a strength and a weakness. It is important for researchers to consider the implications of their approaches, but life is difficult for empirical researchers with a highly developed sense of the lack of objective human reality. The authors agonised,

'...the nature of reality is itself contested, not only between historians and social theorists, but also between theorists of different persuasions. At the heart of these debates lie fundamental disagreements over which persons and events should figure in an explanation, and how they should be described. Thus data may arbitrate theory, but they may also be created by theory, insofar as theory finds a particular significance in events and redescribes them accordingly.'

Worse, they go on '...the view that 'reality' is constituted by an ideographic complexity is itself a conjecture.' (p9)

Apart from the obscurity of these passages – and even with a dictionary in hand I cannot understand whether they meant ideographic or idiographic as both seem equally irrelevant – there is the sense that some academic snobbery is slipping out – against what are seen as the crude mechanical efforts of empirical discovery.

The authors may be right in saying that (p499) there is a disputed nature of reality. The fact that there are different 'truths' to be told by different participants is a point that can be made without the hand wringing.

Their arguments brought to mind one of W J M Mackenzie's throw away comments, 'Empirical politics is no longer an intellectual slum: perhaps some philosophers would care to visit us?' (See *Explorations in Government*, 1975, p206)

Mackenzie is a strangely neglected figure in these chapters. We have few enough major thinkers in the fields of administration and policy making that we can afford to ignore them because they published in the wrong decade. Later is not necessarily better. Mackenzie would have been particularly useful for McPherson and Raab because he cheerfully admits to being part of the great and the good – though he seemed to use his entree taling down information to be used in evidence against his colleagues. He was of the generation of McPherson and Raab's subjects and was steeped in the Scottish academic tradition. To look at the first few pages of his Introduction to the above work we find that his first paragraph claims that the study of politics involves the myths of power as well as legitimate authority and of rational human collaboration. A couple of pages later he is discussing *The Democratic Intellect*. He describes his attendance at Edinburgh Academy, '...lying in the heart of the Scottish bourgeoisie'. The self sufficiency of the Scottish educational system is confirmed when Mackenzie was telephoned to be told that as a seventeen year old he had won a scholarship to Balliol. As everyone seemed to think it 'a good thing', he had to mask the ignorant question, 'What was Balliol, please?'

It is praise to say that the mixture of reflection and detail, personalities and theories in *Governing Education* would please Mackenzie who avoided setting up different approaches as competitors. The book was very much his kind of party. He should have been invited.

The Myth of the Lad of Pairts

One of the key chapters discusses 'The Kirriemuir Career'. This sets out to discuss the 'Scottish Myth'. Presumably the term myth implies some untruth. In the Preface we are told that a particular, selective, and demonstrably incomplete picture of Scotland and its education system was represented as the empirical reality.(pxxi) This one assumes was the myth. It is not clear to this hopelessly biased product of Forfar Academy where the myth lies. It may be true that the sort of community school of Forfar and Kirrie's own Webster's Seminary is not in a statistical sense 'normal'. But their value to the educational policy makers could have been considerable in giving a standard of what a good school looked like. They could have provided a target. The authors on nearly their final page say that myths can celebrate values. In this sense the myth can be accurate even if the classroom experience of every pupil does not accord with it. One suspects that the authors have for so long accepted in their own minds that there was a myth here, that they presented their thesis in too cryptic form and have failed to cater for the reader who does not share their particular 'assumptive world'.

In the conclusion the authors deal with high level generalisations about authority, representation, legitimacy and the like. This is one kind of answer to the question, 'What was it really like?' but the novelty of the material was the horses' mouth detail about what people did and the conclusion was perhaps thin on these less abstract matters.

This is then a book that suffers by the standards it set for itself. It cannot quite deliver in all the areas in which it attempts to contribute. But it will be part of the dialogue in all these areas and perhaps the notion that books can resolve arguments is naive. The best thing about the book is the quiet manner in which the book explores the undramatic politics of policy making through the creation of authority structures that in time look as if they are 'givens'. It shows how networks can operate by subconsciously selecting participants with particular values. It shows that civil servants can be more important to decisions than manifestoes and party posturing. Too often the assumption appears to be that there is a contest between democracy and the sort of politics of consultation among civil servants and interested parties. But to reduce that input of expertise and to reject the views of the affected is hardly to enhance the operation of a practical democracy. The book shows that our understanding of a democratic society is enhanced by on the record interviews from the main participants. They are no friends of democracy those who attempt to protect us from the facts of our democratic life. The Scottish Office deserve credit for their tolerant non-intervention.

Grant Jordan, Department of Politics and International Relations, University of Aberdeen.

Reply to Jordan

Andrew McPherson and Charles D Raab

Jordan warns of Babel but claims that different 'truths' cannot be arbitrated. He cannot intend this self-contradictory position. Nor does he maintain it when he prefers his account of the Scottish myth to ours. Again, he says, rightly, that we show 'how networks can operate by subconsciously selecting participants with particular values'. Thus Jordan concedes that there can be logical grounds for preferring a particular account of others' views and behaviour. Were there not, Babel would multiply and we would indeed 'wring our hands' over reality.

Description is practical politics. Does 'vocational education' describe a liberating or an enslaving curriculum? The Labour Party has never decided. Description is also academic politics. Can the reality of educational governance be adequately expressed by the vocabulary of one academic discipline? One must look to other social sciences as well, and also to educational practice. Is this 'self-indulgent'? No, but it risks self interest. Hence our concern with the safeguards of theory, method, and evidence.

Jordan writes that 'pluralism and corporatism have not been constructed as clearly specified and easily applied theories. It is tempting to see them as alternatives but unwise'. We say the same (pp. xii, 12, 22, 473, 482). We discuss big ideas, not big names. A pervasive theme of the book is the effect of educational expansion on power-dependencies in government. This is more than a 'nod' in Rhodes' direction (see p.472). Jordan's own work equates the concepts of 'subgovernment' and 'policy community'. The latter is a second pervasive theme, *pace* Jordan. We do indeed conclude that educational governance since 1945 fits no theory tidily. But how could a reader conclude the same before we presented the story (nine-tenths of the book)? Is Jordan really content to write for a reader who 'simply wants to know who exercised power'? Simply indeed! Incidentally, Jordan's preferred account of myth is ours too. We explicitly rejected the view, wrongly attributed to us, that myth is merely false belief (see pp.407, 498- 501).

SCOTTISH LEGISLATION 1987

Hamish McN Henderson

Although 1987 may not be described as an *annus mirabilis* for Scottish legislation, it must be admitted that several remarkable Acts were passed. In a year with a general election, it was something of an achievement that nine out of the fifty-seven Acts passed were *Scotland only* ones, although several were brief private members' Bills obviously planted by the government. Eight of the nine completed their Parliamentary course before the election.

The *Animals (Scotland) Act* and the *Debtors (Scotland) Act* brought long-awaited reforms. The *Criminal Justice (Scotland) Act* is devoted mainly to adding to the powers of the courts and of various officials in the fight against drug trafficking and serious fraud. Finally, the *Abolition of Domestic Rates Etc (Scotland) Act* did much more than that. It introduced several varieties of machinery for collecting community charges, but before it is fully operative it will have undergone many amendments to keep it in step with the corresponding English legislation of 1988.

Chapter Number
9. *The Animals (Scotland) Act.* The gestation period of this Act was a full quarter of a century. In 1963 the Law Reform Committee for Scotland recommended that the common law rule of strict liability based on knowledge of the vicious propensities of an animal should be replaced by the ordinary rules of liability based on negligence or *culpa*(Cmnd 2185).

However, following the Report of the Royal Commission on Civil Liability and Compensation for Personal Injury in 1978 (Cmnd 7054) under the chairmanship of Lord Pearson, the Scottish Law Commission published a consultative memorandum (No 55) in 1982, and then in 1985 its report, "Obligations: Report on Civil Liability in Relation to Animals" (Scot Law Com No 97, 1985-86 HC4). As usual, a draft Bill was annexed to the report, and this is closely followed in the present Act.

The Act imposes strict liability on the keeper in certain circumstances. "Keeper" is defined at length. Basically a keeper is the owner or possessor of the animal, or a person who has actual care and control of a child under the age of 16 who owns or possesses the animal.

A person looking after an animal temporarily for its or any other person's or animal's protection is not regarded as having possession, while a person abandoning or losing an animal continues to be regarded as its keeper until someone else acquires ownership or possession. (The Crown does not become owner of abandoned animals.)

For the keeper to be liable for injury or damage caused by an animal, the animal must belong to a species or be a hybrid, or be of a variety, age or sex, which, unless controlled, because of its attributes and habits is likely to injure severely or to kill people or animals, or to damage property. The injury or damage must be directly referable to these attributes or habits.

Animals scheduled in the *Dangerous Wild Animals Act 1976 (c 38)* are expected to injure or kill by biting, savaging or harrying. These range from emus to adders. Four-footed farm animals (including deer) are considered to be likely to damage land and crops materially.

If you happen to catch bovine tuberculosis from innocent contact with an infected cow, it seems that there is no liability under this Act, but if you are bitten by a rabid dog and contract rabies, you will have a claim against its keeper.

The keeper is not liable when a person injured by an animal is the author of his own misfortune, or is an intruder and the keeping and use of the animal was reasonable, for purposes of protection of persons and property. If the animal is a guard dog, within the meaning of the *Guard Dogs Act 1975 (c 50)*, there must be compliance with the provisions of that Act – these include the need for warning notices at each entrance to the premises.

The occupiers of land may detain any animal straying on to land without anyone apparently in control of it, in order to prevent its causing injury or damage.

Perhaps it will be regretted by some readers that the Act does not apply to injury or damage caused by the mere presence of an animal on the road or elsewhere. In these circumstances the ordinary law of negligence will apply. There is therefore no change in our law where, for example, a pedal or motor cyclist collides with a black labrador in an ill-lit street at night.

It appears that on the continent, in jurisdictions whose law is based on the Napoleonic Code, there is strict liability, which may be covered cheaply by insurance.

This liability may be based, theoretically, on the principle that the person who enjoys the economic or social benefits derived from owning an animal, or who creates a risk to others because of such ownership, should face up to the consequences of any harm caused by the animal, irrespective of fault.

Where a person kills or injures an animal, it will be a defence to prove that the act was done in self defence, or for the protection of another individual or livestock (so long as that person was the keeper of the livestock, owner or occupier of the land on which it was present, or was authorised by any of these). However, self defence and protection are limited to cases when the defender has reasonable grounds for believing that there are no other practicable means of dealing with the situation, whether or not the animal is under the control of any individual.

The Crown (ie "the state") is expressly bound by this Act, but not the Queen in her private capacity. So the hapless hiker who has an unpleasant encounter with the royal corgis on Balmoral estate will have to look elsewhere for his remedy.

Chapter Number
18. *Debtors (Scotland) Act.* The Scottish Law Commission's Report on Diligence and Debtor Protection (Scot Law Com No 95, 1985-86 HC 5), published in November 1985, provides the basis of the *Debtors (Scotland) Act.* This Act repeals a dozen pre-Union statutes, the oldest going back to 1503, as well as part or all of about 30 others. The Act is divided into seven parts.

Formerly the Sheriff could order payment by instalments in decrees from summary causes only. Now Part I of this Act provides for the making of time to pay directions or orders, as explained below, in all cases, in favour of an individual debtor, who owes money personally or in a representative capacity (such as a tutor or curator bonis), or as a partner of a firm. These directions or orders give the individual time to pay by slowing down the usual procedures for enforcing a court decree, known as the "execution of diligence", by unsecured creditors by way of arrestment of money due to the debtor or poinding of his goods and their subsequent sale. ('Poinding' is pronounced 'pinding', and means to empound.) However, secured creditors may continue to call up their standard securities over land (popularly called "mortgages") or exercise their liens, etc., over goods or documents of a debtor, but these directions or orders may not be made where a time order has been made under the *Consumer Credit Act 1974* (C39).

Part I enables the Court of Session or the Sheriff, on an application by the debtor, to make a "time to pay direction" when granting decree for payment of any principal sum of money – the sum awarded (including any already quantified pre-decree interest) or expenses or both. Payment may then be by instalments at regular intervals or as a lump sum at the end of a specified period of time. Interest on the principal sum will also be payable by instalments, after payment of the principal sum. Time for making these several payments is calculated only from the date when the creditor has intimated the court's decree to the debtor, and specified the amount of interest due, if it is claimed.

At first a time to pay direction will be competent only when the debt (not counting interest and expenses) does not exceed £10,000. This may be increased by regulations made by statutory instrument by the Lord Advocate.

The making of a direction is not competent in relation to the award of a capital sum following divorce, nor for any of the extensive list of periodical allowances or alimentary payments awarded by Scottish courts or by other jurisdictions, collectively described as "maintenance orders", which are covered by earlier legislation. Similarly, payments of certain taxes, rates, and the community charges, and of civil penalties for failure to give a registration officer information under the *Abolition of Domestic Rates Etc. (Scotland) Act*, are excluded. The direction may be recalled or varied by the court which granted the decree, on the application of either party, in the event of any change of circumstances, if it appears reasonable to the court to do so.

So long as a time to pay direction is effective, the ordinary forms of diligence open to an unsecured creditor are in suspense. The creditor may follow the usual enforcement procedures if the direction lapses. It may lapse through default by the debtor, as when he is two instalments in arrears when a third is due, or if he is 24 hours overdue with a lump sum payment. It will also lapse if his estate is sequestrated (normally, on the petition of other creditors), or if he grants a voluntary trust deed for the benefit of his creditors generally, under the *Bankruptcy (Scotland) Act 1985 (c66)* or alternatively if he enters into a non-statutory composition contract with them.

Somewhat similar to a time to pay direction is a time to pay order. Once diligence has been commenced against him, after the granting of the original decree, he may apply to the sheriff. The sheriff may make an order in respect of any outstanding debt, or interest claimed by the creditor. The order is subject to limitations similar to those hedged about the making of a time to pay direction. The order may not be made if diligence has proceeded so far that goods belonging to the debtor have been poinded, or his goods have been otherwise arrested, and a warrant for their sale been granted but not yet executed, until the diligence is completed. Otherwise the progress of the diligence might be jeopardised. A debtor who has already had the benefit of a time to pay direction may not be granted a time to pay order.

On the application's being made, the sheriff must normally make an interim order, which, on intimation to the creditor, advising him of his opportunity to object, partially freezes the execution of diligence against the debtor, so that the creditor may not proceed to a warrant sale, gain possession of goods previously arrested in the hands of third parties, nor arrest earnings of the debtor.

The making of the full order effectively freezes the execution of most forms of diligence against the debtor. Like a time to pay direction, a time to pay order may be recalled or varied by the sheriff on the application of either party. An order similarly lapses on the default of the debtor, or on the occurrence of any of the insolvency processes mentioned above in connection with the termination of a time to pay direction.

Part II remedies some of the problems associated with poinding and warrant sales. Formerly, the goods exempted from poinding were limited to simple items such as clothing, beds and tools of trade. But the valuation put on poindable items tended to be much below their market value.

The new rules are much more liberal in leaving the debtor with most of the articles to be found in a reasonably affluent household.

Clothing, medical aids, books and other educational items up to £500 in value, toys and other articles reasonably required for the use of the debtor or any member of his household or the upbringing of children of the household, no matter where situated, are exempt from poinding. So are tools of trade, books and other equipment up to £500 in value, reasonable required by the debtor or a member of his household for their profession, trade or business.

Also exempt is an extensive list of items, so long as they are in the dwelling house of the debtor and are reasonably required for use there by the household.

The Lord Advocate may vary the above financial limits and any of the items in the latter list.

Caravans, houseboats, being moveable, may be poinded, but if they are the debtor's, or another person's, only or principal residence, either of these may apply to the Sheriff who may order no further steps to be taken for a specified time.

In addition, although articles in the common ownership of the debtor and a third party may be poinded, the co-owner may, inter alia, buy out the debtor's interest in the article, or require the creditor to reimburse him.

Poinding, which is carried out by an "officer of the court", that is a messenger-at-arms or a sheriff officer, may be executed only on weekdays, and normally only between 8 am and 8 pm. The powers of forced entry to execute a poinding in a dwelling house are restricted.

Traditionally the value attributed to poinded goods has been notoriously low. Now the officer of the court must value them at their open market value, or call in the aid of a professional valuer if he considers this to be advisable. As second-hand modern furniture has a relatively low market value, the new rule may not make much difference (if indeed there is anything worth poinding after taking all the exemptions into account apart from, say, a second TV set and a microwave oven).

The debtor has 14 days after poinding to apply to the sheriff to release an article from the poinding, if the sheriff considers it would be unduly harsh in the circumstances to include it in the poinding and in any subsequent warrant sale.

Detailed rules of poinding procedure reproduce existing rules, with modifications. For example, the debtor will now have 14 days within which to redeem any poinded article at the appraised value, instead of the former on-the-spot "offer back", when he was unlikely to have much ready cash.

A poinding lasts a year from the date of execution.

The poinded goods may be sold only after a warrant of sale has been granted by the sheriff, following an application within the year to him by the creditor or an officer of the court.

Sale is by auction; if it does not take place in an auction room where the appraised value of the poinded articles does not exceed £1,000, an officer of the court appointed by the staff may conduct the warrant sale. The sale may not take place in a dwellinghouse without the written consent of the occupier or debtor. The creditor and debtor may agree to cancel the sale twice to give the debtor time to pay.

There are provisions protecting the interests of third parties whose goods have been poinded while in the debtor's possession, and to deal with the situation when goods are owned in common by a debtor and a third party. Formerly, the latter class of goods could not be poinded for the debtor's debts.

Part III contains detailed provisions replacing arrestment of wages with three new diligences against earnings. "Earnings" is defined in detail, to include bonuses, commissions, pensions other than most public sector pensions, social security pensions or allowances, and various other periodical payments.

The new diligences are "earnings arrestment", "current maintenance arrestment" and "conjoined arrestment orders".

Earnings arrestment is for enforcing payment of any ordinary debt actually due at the date when diligence is executed, not for future debts.

Current maintenance arrestment is for enforcing payment of current maintenance due to be paid after execution of the arrestment. ("Maintenance" has the extended meaning mentioned above in discussing Part I.)

A conjoined arrestment order is to enforce payment of three or more debts owed to different creditors against the same earnings. The debts may be of different kinds, eg arrears and current maintenance due to a wife, and an unpaid electricity bill.

Part IV consists of a single section, which gives life to two schedules to the Act. These deal with the procedure for obtaining a summary warrant for enforcement of payment of central and local government taxes, and the associated new uniform procedure for poinding and sales following the issue of such a warrant. This new procedure is very similar to ordinary poinding procedure, and incorporates the new safeguards, especially as to the extensive range of household goods which may not be poinded.

Imprisonment for failure to pay rates and taxes is abolished, having been virtually unused for the past two decades. Imprisonment to enforce payment of arrears of aliment and fines for contempt of court survives.

Part V enables the Court of Session, by Act of Sederunt, to regulate the activities of officers of court and the procedure for their appointment, while continuing the system whereby they act as independent contractors. They have to obtain the permission of the sheriff principal if they wish to undertake for pay "extra-official" activities which are not actually prohibited by Act of Sederunt. These must not be incompatible with their official function. This is designed to allow flexibility, so that debt collection might be permitted in a rural area, where the official load was relatively light.

The Court of Session is advised on the making of these Acts of Sederunt by the Advisory Council on Messengers-at-Arms and Sheriff officers, appointed by the Lord President. It consists of a Court of Session Judge as chairman, two sheriffs principal, two officers of court, two solicitors, the Lord Advocate's nominee and the Lord Lyon King of Arms.

The applications of sheriff officers for appointment as messengers-at-arms are vetted by the Court of Session, but the actual commission is granted by Lyon.

There are detailed rules for inspection of the work of officers of court, the investigation by a solicitor of alleged misconduct by them, and subsequent disciplinary proceedings before the relevant court.

Parts VI and VII deal with sundry procedural matters. Perhaps the most important points for the debtor-in-the-street to note are that money recovered goes first to pay the costs of poinding and sale, or of arrestment, interest following the decree of the court, and lastly the principal debt, interest thereon, and expenses of the court action. It is no longer necessary for the creditor to raise a further action to enforce payment of unpaid diligence expenses.

Chapter Number
23. *Register of Sasines (Scotland) Act.* This is a brief statute, enabling the Secretary of State to make regulations laying down methods of operation in the Register of Sasines. These are the manner in which deeds are recorded, and the making available of the Register to the public for inspection.

The Act and regulations made under it do not affect the law as to the contents of the Register, nor the evidential value of the Register or of extracts from it.

The somewhat opaque language of the Act means that the records in the Register may be kept in any format prescribed by the Secretary of State in regulations. It was explained in Parliament that the immediate intention is to switch records of deeds to microfiche. Searchers will be provided with several microfiche copies, and so not have to wait until bound volumes are free, as at present.

The Secretary of State already had extensive rule-making powers to regulate the making up and keeping of the Land Register of Scotland under the *Land Registration (Scotland) Act 1979 (c 33)*.

Chapter Number

26. *Housing (Scotland) Act*. This Act consolidates housing legislation derived from over forty Acts passed between 1914 and 1986. As there has been at least one Act on this topic in all but two of the past twenty-one years, this is most welcome to the user. However, within less than four months of its coming into force, yet another Housing (Scotland) Bill had been introduced in the House of Commons.

Chapter Number

36. *Prescription (Scotland) Act*. This Act contains a minor amendment to the Act of the same name, passed in 1973 *(c 52)*, designed to correct an anomaly resulting from the combined effects of the *Bankruptcy (Scotland) Act (c 66)* and the *Insolvency Act 1986 (c 45)*. It retroactively restores the rights of creditors, lost on 29 December 1986 (when the relevant provisions of these statutes came into force), whereby the presentation if, or the concurring in, a petition for the winding up of a company, or the submission of a claim by a creditor in the liquidation of a company, interrupt the running of prescription (that is, the time limits) on the debt claimed.

Chapter Number

40. *Registered Establishments (Scotland) Act*. This Act consists of a series of textual amendments to the *Social Work (Scotland) Act 1968 (c 49)* and the *Nursing Homes Registration (Scotland) Act 1938 (c 73)*. It brings Scottish arrangements into line with those applying to England and Wales, now consolidated in the *Registered Homes Act 1984 (c 23)*.

The Act modifies the definition of establishments that are required to register with the local authority, that is, a regional or islands council, or the Secretary of State, as may be directed under the 1968 Act. The test is that the whole or a substantial part of the function of a residential or other establishment is to provide people with personal care or support, with or without board, and whether for reward or not.

The definition does not apply to an establishment already controlled or managed by a central or local government authority or required to be registered with them under any other enactment.

Grant-aided and independent schools which provide the care or support as mentioned above as well as education may now also apply for registration under the 1968 Act, but are not required to do so. Formerly, if registered as schools they could not be registered for social work purposes.

The certificate of registration does not relate to any part of the establishment used exclusively for educational purposes.

Details of the appointment and departure of the manager, if he is not the owner, must be notified to the local authority within 28 days. Similarly, 28 days' notice of the intention of a registered person to cease to operate a registered establishment must be given to the local authority.

The local authority may cancel registration on any ground that would have justified refusal of registration in the first place, for failure to notify change of manager or to pay the annual registration fee, or if the owner or anyone else involved in running the establishment has been convicted of any offence relating to the conduct of an establishment.

Registration requires compliance with conditions for operating the establishment laid down by the local authority, which may be varied from time to time.

There are provisions for making representations to the Secretary of State or the local authority against proposed, new or varied conditions followed by a hearing. Following the eventual decision, there may be an appeal to an appeal tribunal established under the *Social Work (Scotland) Act 1968*.

Independent establishments which provide both nursing and residential care, to be known as "jointly registrable establishments", must be registered under both the 1938 Act and the 1968 Act, that is, with both the local Health Board and the local authority.

Local authorities will recoup the cost of administering registration and inspection of premises by charging fees for applications for registration or variations of conditions, and renewal of registration. Maximum fees to be charged are fixed by the Secretary of State. He will also fix the actual fees to be charged by local Health Boards.

Chapter Number
41. *Criminal Justice (Scotland) Act*. This Act falls into two parts. Part I stems from the Fifth Report of the Home Affairs Committee: "Misuse of Hard Drugs – Interim Report" (1984-85 HC 399), published in 1985, and follows similar provisions applicable to England and Wales under the *Drug Trafficking Offences Act 1986 (c 32)*.

Somewhat unusually for what purports to be a "Scotland only" Act, several sections apply to England and Wales, and a few to Northern Ireland, in order to secure a United Kingdom-wide system of enforcement, to deprive traffickers of their ill-gotten gains.

When a person is convicted in the High Court of trafficking in "controlled drugs" as listed in Schedule 2 to the *Misuse of Drugs Act 1971 (c 38)* and associated offences, the prosecutor may, when he moves for sentence (or, where the accused is remitted to the High Court for sentence, before sentence is pronounced) apply to the Court inviting it to make a confiscation order. This orders the accused to pay whatever the Court considers appropriate out of the proceeds of his drug trafficking activities. This may be in addition to a fine, imprisonment or other form of penalty.

Perhaps exceptionally, the accused's drug trafficking activities taken into account by the court may include some which have not been the subject of criminal proceedings, and the intention of the Act appears to be that they need not be restricted to Scotland. Overseas activities would be relevant.

The making of a confiscation order may be postponed by the Court for up to six months after conviction, to enable further information to be obtained before it comes to a decision.

The Act lays down rebuttable assumptions that the Court may make in assessing the sum to be paid, and sets out in detail what property is realisable, basically (subject to qualifications) his whole estate worldwide and also that of recipients of what are perhaps somewhat ambiguously termed "implicative gifts". These are gifts made within six years prior to the granting of a warrant to arrest, or of a constraint order against,the accused, as well as gifts made at anytime, if tainted in virtually any way by drug trafficking. The formulae for valuing the gifts, or gifts disguised as sales, is designed to inflate their value in favour of the realising authorities.

Failure to make the payment required under a confiscation order may lead to imprisonment. Where a confiscation order is in excess of a million pounds, the term of imprisonment for default is 10 years. This period of imprisonment will run from the expiry of any other period of imprisonment imposed on the trafficker originally, or itself imposed for default of payment of a fine.

At the very beginning of proceedings against a suspected trafficker, the Lord Advocate may apply to the Court of Session for a "restraint order". This order interdicts the suspect from dealing with his realisable property, and also any third party named in the order as appearing to the Court to have received an "implicative" gift from the suspect, from dealing with that property.

As a belt and braces operation, the Court of Session is further empowered to interdict a person not subject to a restraint order from dealing with realisable property.

Realisable property will be dealt with by an administrator appointed by the Court of Session on the application of the Lord Advocate.

Since this is an international problem, there are provisions for the enforcement of confiscation orders made in the rest of the United Kingdom or in countries designated by Order in Council, following registration by the Court of Session. Similarly there are provisions for enforcement of Scottish orders furth of Scotland.

In very limited specified circumstances, compensation is payable by order of the Court of Session on an application's being made by the holder of realisable property who has suffered substantial loss or damage and satisfies the Court that there has been serious default by an investigator, namely, a police constable (or a constable under any other authority, eg Railway police), a procurator fiscal or agent of the Lord Advocate, or Customs and Excise officers.

The Act Contains provisions to avoid conflicts between the procedures discussed above and those laid down under personal bankruptcy and company insolvency legislation.

Anyone doing "anything which is likely to prejudice the investigation" (*sic*) is guilty of an offence and liable to a fine or up to five years' imprisonment, or both. Anyone helping a trafficker to hold on to the proceeds of his trafficking in virtually any conceivable way may suffer a fine or up to fourteen years' imprisonment, or both. Where the trafficker himself is sentenced to imprisonment, the Court must also impose a fine unless it is satisfied that it would be inappropriate to do so; if it makes a confiscation order, it has discretion to add a fine.

Part II of the Act is rightly headed "Miscellaneous".

A customs officer may detain an individual suspected of offences punishable by imprisonment for up to six hours for questioning and search. The suspect must be informed that he is not obliged to give any information other than his name and address, and of the officer's suspicion, the general nature of the alleged offence and the reason for detention. Details of the whole proceedings must be recorded.

The suspect must be told that he is entitled to have a solicitor or one other person "reasonably named by him" notified of his detention with as little delay as is necessary. In the case of a child under 16 the officer must similarly advise the child's parent, who must be given access to the child, except when the parent is also a suspect, when access is discretionary.

For suspicion of certain drug smuggling offences, an individual may be detained for up to 24 hours. This period may be extended by the sheriff, on the application of the procurator fiscal, to seven days. During this detention the individual may be required to provide specimens of blood or urine and submit to intimate body searches carried out by a registered medical practitioner.

Fixed penalties are well-known in relation to motoring offences, as an alternative to prosecution. The procurator fiscal is now given discretion, in the case of offences triable in a district court, to make a conditional offer to the alleged offender. Under this offer, which will indicate the fixed penalty offered, and details of alternative instalment payments, the alleged offender will normally have 28 days to decide whether to accept the offer by paying the full amount or the first instalment. If he does so, any liability to conviction will be discharged. If he falls down on his instalments, recovery of the balance will be by means of civil diligence.

The fixed penalty for these offences will be not more than level 1 on the standard scale, set by an order of the Secretary of State subject to annulment by either House of Parliament.

The limit of the sentencing power of sheriffs for offences punishable on conviction on indictment (ie with trial by jury) to two years' imprisonment is now raised to terms of up to three years.

Children found guilty in summary proceedings before the sheriff, where imprisonment may be imposed on persons aged 21 or more, may be detained (by order of the sheriff) by the appropriate regional or islands council in residential care anywhere in the United Kingdom, as seems appropriate to that council, for up to one year.

Certified transcripts of recordings of interviews between a police officer and an accused person will be receivable in evidence and (subject to challenge as to their making or their accuracy by the accused at least six days before the trial) they will be sufficient evidence of the making and accuracy of the transcript.

The Act concludes with a miscellany of further relatively minor amendments to both substantive and procedural criminal law.

Chapter Number

47. *Abolition of Domestic Rates Etc. (Scotland) Act*[1] Since the early days of this century there have been investigations into and comments on the problem of finding acceptable techniques for financing local

government expenditure. A Royal Commission reported in 1902 (Cd. 1067). In 1926, Whyte, in *Local Government in Scotland*, commented on the unpopularity of the existing rating system. It has undergone modest variations since then, and in the lifetime of the present government the path to change was paved by two Green Papers, *Alternatives to Domestic Rates* (Cmnd 8449 (1981)) and *Paying for Local Government* (Cmnd 9714 (1986)).

The Bill to introduce similar legislation for England and Wales that was making its way through Parliament in the first half of 1988 underwent so many amendments that by the time this present Act is fully in force it will undoubtedly also be much amended in order to harmonise with the provisions to be applied south of the Border.

The Act opens with the proclamation that domestic rates are to be abolished with effect from 1st April 1989. The term, as a technical legal expression, is in fact created in this Act for the first time, only to die within less than two years.

The abolition of domestic rates is achieved by the simple device of providing that "domestic subjects" (another neologism) shall cease to be entered in the valuation roll from 1989-90 onwards. The definition of "domestic subjects" is minimal. Since the contents of the definition may be added to and subtracted from by regulations, any attempt at present to obtain a picture of its precise meaning is like trying to photograph Lewis Carroll's Cheshire Cat.

The Secretary of State will be able to prescribe by regulations according to a statutory formula the maximum non-domestic rate for each authority. This rate will be levied not only on entirely non-residential subjects, but also on "part residential" (sic) subjects, as defined in the Act and as to be further defined in regulations. There will thus be non-domestic regional, district and islands rates.

Various aspects of compensation for compulsory purchase, eligibility for house improvement grants, the apportionment of liability for repairs to roofs and common stairs in tenements, and other schemes, are affected by valuation for rating, whether expressed as assessed rental, gross annual value, net annual value or rateable value. Accordingly, the valuation rolls existing before 1st April 1989 are to be kept alive, and if necessary amended to take account of changing circumstances, and the creation of new domestic subjects, as if they had been in existence before that date. In twenty years' time, allowing for inflation, they should look very out of date.

Although the media have persisted in talking and writing about "the Community Charge" – described abusively by its critics as "the Poll

Tax" – the new charge which replaces domestic rates in fact comes in a multiplicity of guises. There are regional community charges and district community charges, for which the levying authority will be the regional councils, and the islands community charges, levied by the islands councils. These charges are then subdivided into the personal community charge, the standard community charge and the collective community charge. They will normally be payable in 12 equal monthly instalments.

The personal community charge is to be levied on persons aged 18 or over who are or become solely or mainly resident in the area of a local authority, payments being adjusted *pro rata* as their names move into or out of the relevant register.

Persons undergoing a full-time course of education are to be deemed to reside in the area of the local authority where they reside during *term time*. These students will be entitled to a discount on the personal community charge for which they would otherwise be liable. The meanings of these italicised phrases and the measure of the discount are to be prescribed in regulations.

Spouses living together and couples cohabiting in a heterosexual relationship will be jointly and severally liable for the personal community charges. This means that if one of the spouses or one member of the couple does not pay up, the other will be liable.

There are rules granting exemption from liability, some of which are likely to be somewhat difficult to understand and apply. Those exempt are persons aged 18 in respect of whom child benefit is payable, and severely mentally handicapped persons. Also exempt are persons other than full-time students mentioned above who are solely or mainly resident in premises in respect of which a collective community charge is payable, and persons whose sole or main residence is subject to non-domestic rates, other than those who are solely or mainly resident in part residential subjects. Some clarification was attempted by the government spokesman in the House of Lords, but further elucidation will have to await the effect of the "Cheshire Cat" regulations mentioned above.

Local authorities will fix their personal community charges after the non-domestic rate has been determined and the new revenue support grant order has been made, and taking into account the revenue from the standard and collective community charges.

The standard community charge will be payable in respect of second homes by the owner, or, where the property is let or sub-let for 12 months or more, by the tenant or sub-tenant. The amount of the charge will be between one and two times the personal community charge, according to the multiplier determined by the relevant local authorities. If the person liable to pay the standard community charge lets or sub-lets the property, he has a right of relief against the tenant or sub-tenant calculated by apportionment on a daily basis. Where premises are unoccupied or unfurnished, the charge is not payable for up to three months in any financial year.

Variations on this theme can be played by the Secretary of State, because he may prescribe in regulations a class or classes of premises to be exempt from this category; the criteria for so doing are themselves to be laid down by him in separate regulations.

Faimilies may apparently reduce their collective charge liability should one or more members elect to regard the second – or, for that matter, third – home as their sole or main residence.

The collective community charge is targetted by way of somewhat obscure rules – naturally to be supplemented by regulations – at those persons who are likely to fail to come within the earlier provisions of the Act, by residing in the relevant premises, such as a women's refuge, normally only for a short time. On the other hand, long-staying guests in a boardinghouse would be liable to the personal community charge.

The collective community charge will be payable by the owner or by a tenant or sub-tenant of the premises with a lease of at least 12 months, that is, the person normally in effective control of the premises. For any given premises, the collective community charge will be the product of the personal community charge and a collective community charge multiplier fixed by the registrar in relation to these particular premises. It will be fixed by estimating the number of persons who are solely or mainly resident in these premises, and who would otherwise be liable to pay the personal community charge, and by reference to factors to be prescribed in regulations. The payer of the charge will recoup it by charging individual residents a collective community charge contribution *pro rata* on a daily basis.

The Community Charges Registration Officer is the regional or islands area assessor, thus guaranteeing a measure of professional independence. (This office is combined for the Highland region and the three islands areas).

The register is required to show the name and address of the payer of each of the several community charges, and in particular the date of birth of each natural person registered. This last item has been a matter of perhaps surprising concern to some people, but, now that the date when individuals reach the age of majority appears on the voters' roll, eventually the diligent researcher will be able to establish the date of birth of virtually anyone he or she pleases who lives to adulthood. Objectors appear to overlook the fact that individuals using a driving licence as a means of establishing identity reveal their date of birth.

Rights of access to the register are limited. Various officials will have fairly extensive rights of access, but most limited will be those of the general public except for inspection of the entry relating to oneself.

In addition to the above community charges, and much less publicised, are the personal, standard and collective community water charges, which will operate in tandem with the other community charges. There will also be a non-domestic water rate. Sewerage services are to be paid for out of the community charges and non-domestic sewerage rates.

There are provisions enabling the Secretary of State to secure reductions of the community charges imposed by any authority and for schemes to provide rebates on community charges, but not on community water charges.

There are complicated rules for the fixing of the maximum non-domestic rate which each local authority may impose. They will be linked to the retail prices index, but subject to reductions to take into account revenue attributable to water and sewerage services.

Just as local authorities could not delegate the rate-fixing power to a committee, sub-committee or an official, so they may not delegate the determining of any of the new charges or rates.

The rate support grant is to be replaced by a revenue support grant, consisting essentially of a "needs" grant and a *per capita* amount.

Most commentators indicate that the new system of local taxation will be considerably more expensive to administer than the collection of rates which it replaces.

Chapter Number
56. *Scottish Development Agency Act.* This Act increases the total permitted borrowings of the Scottish Development Agency and its subsidiaries from £700 million which was fixed in 1981 by the *Industry Act 1981 (c 6)*, to £1,200 million.

These borrowings come in a variety of forms, such as borrowing from the National Loans Fund, loans guaranteed by the Treasury, loans from the European Investment Bank and the European Coal and Steel Community, and also by way of payments from the Secretary of State consisting of grants-in-aid (less administrative expenses plus public dividend capital issues).

The original limit set by the *Scottish Development Agency Act 1975 (c 69)* was a mere £200 million.

Hamish McN Henderson, Department of Scots Law, University of Edinburgh.

References

1. The recent history and many other aspects of the background to this Act were discussed by Archie Fairley in "The Community charge and Local Government Finance in Scotland", *Scottish Government Yearbook 1988*, pp 46 -61.

OPINION POLLS IN SCOTLAND
July 1987 - September 1988

David McCrone

We are indebted to System Three and their sponsors, the Glasgow Herald, and to MORI and The Scotsman, for permission to use their polls. This year, we are using their data more extensively to make sense of political and public opinion in Scotland. While we will maintain continuity with previous presentations in the *Yearbook*, greater use will be made of the opinion polls in what promises to be an important era in Scottish politics.

Voting Intention

Despite the ructions within the erstwhile 'Alliance' (a.k.a. Social and Liberal Democrats, Social Democrats, Democrats, Liberal Democrats), the opinion polls of the last twelve months show considerable surface calm (figures 1-2). Labour and Tory fortunes have shifted little, probably to the disappointment of the government and the surprise of Labour. The S.N.P. appears to be the main gainer in the polls, and it now stands in third place behind the Tories with a healthy 17 or 18 per cent. Since the General Election of June 1987, the old Alliance parties have seen their vote halved, so that they barely share 10% between them. We cannot be sure, of course, what shifts of support have been occurring beneath the surface, and there is likely to have been considerable shifting across parties over the last year or so.

The MORI polls for *The Scotsman* cross-tabulate voting intention against key social variables such as sex, age, class, housing tenure, trade union membership and pensioner status. The 'gender gap' in Tory voting has all but disappeared, although more men proportionately than women vote Labour (on average 4 percentage points difference) and for the S.N.P. (on average 5 percentage points difference). The former probably is explained by the continuing (but diminishing) differential in employment participation rates in employment, and by the fact that women live longer than men (age remains a political discriminator). The failure of the S.N.P. to attract women voters remains one of the conundrums of Scottish politics. The Tories do best among the over 55s (though still outvoted by Labour), and the S.N.P. among the under 24s (attracting 20% of the age category 18 to 24 according to the April poll), although Labour is supreme in all age categories.

FIGURE 1: VOTING INTENTION (SYSTEM THREE POLLS)
1987-88

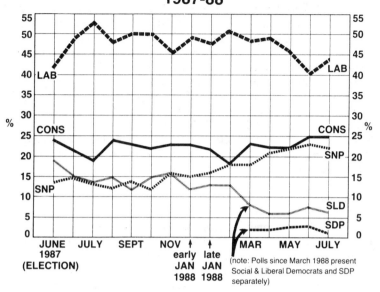

(note: Polls since March 1988 present Social & Liberal Democrats and SDP separately)

FIGURE 2: VOTING INTENTION (MORI POLLS) 1987-88

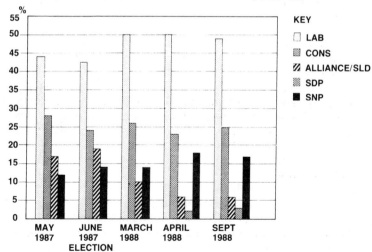

As expected, the top 'social class' (accepting for the moment the AB to DE scheme) votes Conservative, but only in a ratio of less than 2 to 1 over Labour (36% to 20%). The capacity of Labour to attract sufficient of Scotland's 'middle classes' (and Labour almost matches the Tories in the C1 category - the lower professionals and managers) is reinforced by the party's success among the owner-occupiers. Twenty four per cent of home owners express an intention to vote Labour, only 4 percentage points behind the Tories. So much for the political 'property gap', although it is very much in evidence among council tenants where Labour has a lead of 5 to 1. The class character of the other parties is less striking, albeit the Alliance etc. parties still draw their support from the middle class. The S.N.P., interestingly, does better among manual workers than among the AB/C1 groups, a feature in contrast to the 1970s when it appealed to broadly equal sections of all classes.

Constitutional Options

The polls continue to show strong support for constitutional change (figure 3), although the pollsters persevere in using the supremely ambiguous category 'completely independent Scottish Assembly from England' as a surrogate for Independence. It has been plain for some time that the term 'Assembly' is equated with some version of Devolution, and that the distinction between this and the second option 'Scottish Assembly as part of Britain but with substantial powers' is far from clear. We hope in the interests of clarity that the polling companies will make the distinction more obvious, perhaps by using the word 'Parliament' rather than 'Assembly' in the first category.

Nevertheless, we would be correct in concluding that around three-quarters of Scottish public opinion desires constitutional change (September poll). Even Tory supporters seem to be demanding change – 47% want 'devolution' (compared with 42% of all respondents) – though 42% are happy with the status quo. Undoubtedly there is a groundswell for constitutional reform in Scotland, which runs across party affiliation and across social class. Sixty seven per cent of people in the AB category want change compared with 79% in class DE.

Political Attitudes

Scots remain unconvinced that the government is doing a good job. Just over a quarter of voters claim to be satisfied with its performance, broadly in line with support for the Conservatives north of the border (September 1988).

FIGURE 3: PREFERRED GOVERNMENT for SCOTLAND
1987-88
(MORI POLLS)

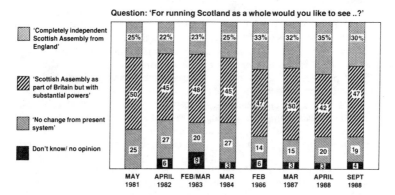

Question: 'For running Scotland as a whole would you like to see ..?'

Unemployment remains the issue worrying Scots most, fully two-thirds citing it as their foremost concern (September poll). This varies little by sex, age, class and even voting intention, for 65% of putative Tories mention it. Between March and September 1988, the N.H.S. receded in salience (from 46% to 21% of mentions), and the Poll Tax rose from 25% to 30%. Education and housing remain on the agenda at between 8 to 14%. All sectors of Scottish society share a similar view of the main issues facing Scotland today.

'State dependency': MORI asked in March 1988 whether Scottish people were too dependent upon State provision, as members of the Government have suggested. Only 27% thought so, and 63% disagreed, a fairly unsurprising finding north of the border. The government could take some comfort from the fact that 23% thought that there was too much reliance on the state for housing, but could take little solace from the view that, as regards education and employment, there was too little (34% and 48% repectively).

While a mere 27% of Scottish households were not in receipt of any benefits, much of the rest held child benefit (32%), or the old age pension (24%) according to the April poll. Changes in the benefit system left more losers than winners. While 12% claimed they would be better off, 33% thought they would be worse off, while 42% said it would make no difference. Fewer still thought the changes were 'fair' (8%) compared with 62% who thought them 'unfair'. Even Conservative voters viewed them as unfair (30%) rather than fair (26%). All in all, changes in the system of social benefits were winning few friends in Scotland.

Privatisation: The commitment to public provisioning remains strong among Scottish public opinion across a range of issues. The privatisation of *electricity* would bring a better service, thought only 11% of respondents (March poll), and only 27% of Conservative voters agreed with the policy. The privatisation of *local authority rubbish collection and public parks* was more popular (April poll), but still a minority taste. Forty four percent thought that services would improve, but 32% that they would deteriorate. A majority of Tories (52%) took the optimistic line, but the rest were unconvinced. Extending *private health insurance* was supported by only 20% of people, and Conservatives were roughly evenly divided between those who supported the measure (49%) and those who opposed it (43% in March 1988). Fifty eight percent of respondents thought that privatising *hospital services* would make things worse; 21% that they would improve. Nor does Scottish public opinion believe that there is too much reliance on state provision in health (a mere 14%). Equal proportions (38%) viewed it as 'too little' or 'just right'. The generally gloomy view of health provision in Scotland is manifested by the fact that only 8% believed that the standard of health care had improved over the last two years. Since 1986 when MORI asked the same question, seven percent fewer (37%) thought it had remained the same, and seven percent more (45%) that it had deteriorated.

Education: Despite the disruption in Scottish schools over the last few years, the education system remains well thought of (April poll). Sixty five percent thought that their local secondary schools did a very good or fairly good job, and only 10% that they performed poorly or badly. This ratio of over 6 to 1 favourable to the schools performance was remarkably stable across social class, housing tenure, and even political preference. Among Conservatives, the secondary system was judged to be performing well by 64%, and only 9% took a negative view. The Government's own performance in education was quite another story. Only a quarter thought that it was doing a good or fairly good job, and 51% that it was performing badly. Even professional and managerial workers (ABs) were fairly positive, although half of Conservative voters approved of their party's handling of education.

The opportunity to *'opt out' of the state education system* was supported by 31% of people, and opposed by 51%. Fully 49% of social class 'AB' and the same proportion of Tories opposed the opt out option. Asked if they would send their children to private schools if they could afford it, only 34% said 'yes', and 58%, 'no'. Even a majority of Conservatives (51%) said they would not, and class AB was evenly split 44% each. These results seem to reflect the abiding commitment of Scots to their education system, and suggests that plans to privatise the service has little support north of the border. The government can take some comfort from the finding that testing in schools at the ages of 8 and 12 has some support. Forty six percent approved, and 39% disapproved. Perhaps old attitudes to education in Scotland die hard.

Another maligned institution, *local government*, also received some support. In the poll in April 1988 prior to the District Council elections, respondents were asked to indicate how satisfied they were with their council. Fifty six percent expressed satisfaction, and 32% dissatisfaction. As regards the policy to transfer council houses, the main resource of the Districts, to private enterprise, 29% were in agreement, and 46% opposed, although a quarter were unaware of the policy.

The *Poll Tax or Community Charge* was carefully monitored by the pollsters. In March 1988, 17% approved and 75% disapproved. One month later, 21% were giving their approval and 72% were opposed. In September of 1988, 24% supported the policy, and 70% opposed it. Government supporters increased their approval from 47% in March to 61% by September.

Asked whether people themselves would be better off under the system, the figures were constant at 18%, with 52% saying they would be worse off, and 22% that it would make little difference. Interestingly, of those who would gain financially, 47% said they approved of the Tax, and 46% that they did not. Would they be prepared to withhold the money? In April, 42% said they would (44% would not); but by September, 37% were still prepared to resist (54% would pay).

Conclusion: What, then, are we to make of these polls of public opinion? Firstly, Scots are very reluctant Thatcherites. Even Scottish Conservative voters have considerable doubts about the more radical of government policies. The Poll Tax, education, privatisation of electricity, health care, local government services – all seem to indicate a reluctance to toe the government line. If the Scottish Conservatives believe that their task is merely to explain policies more fully so that people will believe, then they should pay more attention to what Scottish opinion, as reflected in these polls, is saying. Scots, the polls show, are not among Mrs Thatcher's natural bedfellows.

Technical Details:

MORI carried out three representative quota samples as follows:-

March 1988: 1,119 adults aged 18 in 55 constituency sampling points throughout Scotland;
April 1988: 1,108 adults aged 18 in 55 constituency sampling points throughout Scotland;
September 1988: 1,085 adults aged 18 in 54 constituency sampling points throughout Scotland.

System Three Scotland carry out monthly quota samples of around 1,000 adults in 40 constituency sampling points in Scotland.

SECTION 1

SCOTTISH OFFICE MINISTERS

Private Secretary*

Secretary of State   Rt Hon Malcolm Rifkind MP   D J Crawley Ext 4011
                                                 Assistants:
                                                  Mrs M S Jones DH Ext 6738‡
                                                  Miss U M Jamieson Ext 4021

Minister of State   Lord Sanderson (Lords)   A C MacLaren Ext 4023
                     (Agriculture, Fisheries,
                     Forestry, Highlands and
                     Islands and Tourism)

Minister of State   Ian Lang MP (Commons)   D C Henderson Ext 4015
                     (Minister for Industry
                     and Local Government
                     Finance)

Parliamentary   Lord James Douglas-Hamilton MP   M B Foulis Ext 4012
Under-Secretaries   (Minister for Home Affairs
of State   and the Environment)

                     Michael Forsyth MP   D B Binnie Ext 4107**
                     (Minister for Education
                     and Health)

*   at New St Andrew's House, Edinburgh EH1 3SX
     (031-244 ext) except
** at St Andrew's House, Edinburgh EH1 3DE
‡   Dover House, London (01-270 3000)

SECTION 2

REGIONAL COUNCILS

Names and Addresses of Convenors and Chief Officers

	Convener/ Population	Chief Executive	Director of Administration	Director of Finance	Director of Education	Director of Social Work	Director of Planning	Director of Roads
BORDERS Newton St Boswells TD60SA 083523301	Tom Hunter (Ind) 102,000	K J Clark		P Jeary	J McLean	A Cameron	P Gregory	R I Hill
CENTRAL Viewforth Stirling FK8 2ET 07863111	Charles Sneddon (Lab) 272,000	J Broadfoot	P W Buchanan	S Craig	I Collie	J A Ross	F Bracewell	G I McCrindle
DUMFRIES & GALLOWAY Council Offices Dumfries DG1 2DD 038753141	John Jameson (Ind) 147,000	N W D McIntosh		J C Stewart 038769191	W C Fordyce 30 Edinburgh Rd Dumfries 038763822	T McMenamay 8 Gordon St Dumfries 038763022	G L Mann	H D B Murray
FIFE Fife House North Street Glenrothes KY75LT 0592754411	Robert Gough (Lab) 344,000	J A Markland	W Breslin	A E Taylor	M More	A J Bowman	W Taylor	J T Rowson (Engineering) 0592754411

Convener/Population	Chief Executive	Director of Administration	Director of Finance	Director of Education	Director of Social Work	Director of Planning	Director of Roads
GRAMPIAN Woodhill House Westburn Rd Aberdeen AB9 2LU 0224 682222 — Geoffrey Hadley (Ind) 503,000	J D Macnaughton	A Campbell	A McLean	J A D Michie	Miss M Hartnoll	T F Sprott	G Kirkbride
HIGHLAND Regional Buildings Glenurquhart Road Inverness IV3 5NX 0463 234121 — Alexander Russell (Ind) 201,000	R H Stevenson	H Farquhar	J W Bremner	C E Stewart	J Dick	R Cameron	G K M Macfarlane
LOTHIAN George IV Bridge Edinburgh EH1 1UQ 031-229 9292 — James Cook (Lab) 742,000	G Bowie		D B Chynoweth	W D C Semple 40 Torphichen St Edinburgh EH3 8JJ	R W Chant Shrubhill House Edinburgh EH7 4DP 031-554 4301	D M Jamie 1 Parliament Sq Edinburgh EH1 1TU	P J Mason 19 Market St Edinburgh EH1 1BL
STRATHCLYDE Strathclyde House 20 India Street Glasgow G2 4PF 041-204 2900 — James Jennings (Lab) 2,345,000	R Calderwood		A Gillespie	E Miller	F E Edwards	R G Maund	W S McAlonan
TAYSIDE Tayside House 26-28 Crichton St Dundee DD1 3RA 0382 23281 — Ron Tosh (Lab) 392,000	J A Wallace		I B McIver	D G Robertson	P Bates	H Ramsay	J F White

346

	Convener/ Population	Chief Executive	Director of Administration	Director of Finance	Director of Education	Director of Social Work	Director of Planning	Director of Roads
ISLANDS COUNCILS ORKNEY County Offices Kirkwall KW15 1NY 0856 3535	Edwin Eunson (Ind) 19,000	R H Gilbert	R McCallum	R H Gilbert	R L Henderson	H MacGillivray	T W Eggeling	
SHETLAND Town Hall Lerwick ZE1 0HB 0595 3535	Edward Thomason (Ind) 24,000	M Gerrard	R S Lisk 31 Commercial St Lerwick	M Green 4 Market St Lerwick	R A B Barnes Brentham Ho Harbour St Lerwick	P Malcolmson 64 St Olaf St Lerwick	J Anderson Victoria Bldgs Explanade Lerwick	
WESTERN ISLES Council Office South Beach Stornoway PA87 2BW 0851 3773	Sandy Matheson (Ind) 32,000	G Macleod	R Barnett	D G Macleod	N R Galbraith 0851 3992	Mrs N E Macleod 0851 3664	J R Haworth	

SECTION 3

DISTRICT COUNCILS

Names and Addresses of Conveners and Chief Executives

	Convener/Provost/ Chairman	Chief Executive (unless stated)
BORDERS		
Berwickshire	J Evans	R Christie District Offices, Duns TD11 3DU (03618 2600)
Ettrick & Lauderdale	A L Tulley	C Anderson, PO Box 4 Council Chambers, Paton St., Galashiels TD1 3AS (0896 4751)
Roxburgh	G Yellowlees	K W Cramond District Office, High St. Hawick TD9 9EF (04507 5991)
Tweeddale	M A R Maher	G H T Garvie District Offices, Peebles EH45 8GH (0721 20153)
CENTRAL		
Clackmannan	W G Watt	I F Smith The Whins, Alloa FK10 3SA (0259 722160)
Falkirk	D Goldie	J P H Paton Municipal Buildings, Falkirk FK1 5RS (0324 24911)
Stirling	J Hendry	R Black Municipal Buildings, Corn Exchange Road, Stirling FK8 2HU (0786 79000)
DUMFRIES & GALLOWAY		
Annandale & Eskdale	F Park	J A Whitecross High Street, Annan DG12 6AQ (04612 3311)

Nithdale	E D Gibson	W W Japp Municipal Chambers, Dumfries DG1 2AD (0387 3166)
Stewartry	J Nelson	J C Howie Council Offices, Kircudbright DG6 4PJ (0557 30291)
Wigtown	J Brown	A Geddes Sun Street, Stranraer DG9 3JJ (0776 2151)

FIFE

Dunfermline	J Cameron	G Brown City Chambers, Dunfermline KY12 7ND (03837 22711)
Kirkcaldy	R King	J M Smith (Director of Administration) Town House, Kirkcaldy KY1 1XW (05922 61144)
North-East Fife	C R Sneddon	R Brotherton County Buildings, Cupar KY15 4TA (03345 3722)

GRAMPIAN

City of Aberdeen	R A Robertson	J J K Smith Town House, Aberdeen AB9 1AQ (0224 642121)
Banff & Buchan	W R Cruickshank	R W Jackson (Director of Administration and Legal Services) St Leonards, Sandyhill Rd., Banff AB4 1BH (026 12 2521)
Gordon	J Lawrence	M C Barron Gordon House Blackhall Rd., Inverurie AB5 9WA (0467 20981)
Kincardine & Deeside	D J MacKenzie	T Hyder Arduthie Rd, Stonehaven AB3 2DQ (056 92 62001)

Moray   E Aldridge   J P C Bell
High Street, Elgin
IV30 1BX (0343 3451)

HIGHLAND
Badenoch &   J A McCook   H G McCulloch
   Strathspey   Council Offices, Ruthven Road
Kingussie, Inverness
PH21 1EJ (054 02 555)

Caithness   J M Young   A Beattie
Council Offices, Wick
KW1 4AB (0955 3761)

Inverness   A G Sellar   B Wilson
Town House, Inverness
IV1 1JJ (0463 239111)

Lochaber   D P MacFarlane   D A B Blair
Lochaber House, Fort William
PH33 6EL (0397 3881)

Nairn   S A Macarthur   A M Kerr
(Director of Law and
Administration)
The Courthouse,
High Street, Nairn
IV12 4AU (0667 52056)

Ross & Cromarty   G D Finlayson   Douglas Sinclair
Council Offices, Dingwall
IV15 9QN (0349 63381)

Skye & Lochalsh   J F Munro   D H Noble
Park Road, Portree
IV51 9EP (0478 2341)

Sutherland   D I MacRae   D W Martin
District Office, Golspie
KW10 6RB (040 833192)

LOTHIAN
City of Edinburgh   Mrs E McLaughlin   A Hepburn
City Chambers, High St.,
Edinburgh EH1 1YJ
(031 225 2424)

East Lothian	G M Wanless	Malcolm Duncan Council Buildings, Haddington EH41 3HA (062 082 4161)
Midlothian	D Lennie	T Muir 1 Eskdaill Court, Dalkeith EH22 1DJ (031 663 2881)
West Lothian	D McCauley	W N Fordyce South Bridge St., Bathgate EH48 1TS (Bathgate 53631)

STRATHCLYDE

Argyll & Bute	W R Hunter	M A J Gossip Kilmory, Lochgilphead PA31 8RT (0546 2127)
Bearsden & Milngavie	Mrs J Cameron	I C Laurie Boclair, Bearsden G61 2TQ (041 942 2262)
City of Glasgow	Mrs S Baird	S Hamilton City Chambers, Glasgow G2 1DU (041 221 9600)
Clydebank	D S Grainger	J T McNally District Council Offices Clydebank G81 1TG (041 941 1331)
Clydesdale	Mrs E Logan	P W Daniels District Offices, Lanark ML11 7JT (0555 61511)
Cumbernauld & Kilsyth	Ms R McKenna	J Hutton Bron Way, Cumbernauld G67 1DZ (02367 22131)
Cumnock & Doon Valley	J Hodge	D T Hemmings Lugar, Cumnock KA18 3JQ (0290 22111)
Cunninghame	J Carson	B Devine Cunninghame House, Irvine KA12 8EE (0294 74166)

Dumbarton	W Petrie	L MacKinnon Crosslet House, Dumbarton G82 3NS (0389 65100)
East Kilbride	Mrs H Biggins	D Liddell Civic Centre, East Kilbride G74 1AB (035 52 28777)
Eastwood	Mrs J Y Macfie	M D Henry Eastwood Park, Rouken Glen Road, Glasgow G46 6UG (041 638 6511)
Hamilton	R Gibb	Alister Baird 102 Cadzow Street, Hamilton ML3 6HH (0698 282323)
Inverclyde	F A McGlone	I C Wilson Municipal Buidings, Greenock PA15 1LY (0475 24400)
Kilmarnock & Loudon	J Mills	R W Jenner Civic Centre, Kilmarnock KA1 1BY (0563 21140)
Kyle & Carrick	D MacNeill	I R D Smillie Burns House, Ayr KA7 1UT (0292 81511)
Monklands	E Cairns	J S Ness Dunbeth Road, Coatbridge ML5 3LF (0263 24941)
Motherwell	J Armstrong	J Bonomy P.O. Box 14, Motherwell ML1 1TW (0698 66166)
Renfrew	G Murray	Miss M C Thomson (District Administrator) Cotton Street, Paisley PA1 1BU (041 889 5400)
Strathkelvin	R M Coyle	C Mallon P.O. Box 4, Kirkintilloch G66 4TJ (041 776 7171)

TAYSIDE

Angus	B M C Milne	Patrick B Regan County Buildings, Forfar DD8 3LG (0307 65101)
City of Dundee	T Mitchell	J F Hoey City Chambers, Dundee DD1 3BY (0382 23141)
Perth & Kinross	A Murray	J E D Cormie 1-3 High Street, Perth PH1 5JU (0738 21161)

Source: Scottish Development Department

SECTION 4

DISTRICT ELECTIONS
MAY 1988

Seats won: Percentage of vote in brackets

	CON	LAB	SLD	SDP	SNP	OTHERS
BORDERS	12 (20.8)	2 (6.4)	2 (3.5)	0 (0)	4 (16.1)	33 (53.5)
Berwickshire	9 (52.6)	0 (0)	1 (15.6)	0 (0)	0 (5.4)	1 (26.3)
Ettrick & Lauderdale	1 (13.1)	1 (10.7)	0 (0)	0 (0)	1 (18.3)	13 (58.1)
Roxburgh	1 (23.2)	0 (0)	1 (3.7)	0 (0)	2 (15.8)	12 (57.3)
Tweeddale	1 (6.3)	1 (17.0)	0 (0)	0 (0)	1 (20.5)	7 (56.4)
CENTRAL	14 (18.1)	40 (45.8)	2 (2.0)	0 (0)	11 (28.8)	3 (5.5)
Clackmannan	1 (6.5)	10 (52.2)	0 (2.3)	0 (0)	1 (38.2)	0 (1.1)
Falkirk	3 (8.2)	20 (48.9)	0 (0)	0 (0)	10 (35.3)	3 (7.9)
Stirling	10 (39.8)	10 (37.6)	0 (5.0)	0 (0)	0 (13.7)	0 (4.1)
DUMFRIES & GALLOWAY	4 (13.9)	15 (26.6)	8 (14.3)	0 (0)	7 (12.4)	36 (33.1)
Annandale & Eskdale	0 (1.3)	2 (16.8)	8 (37.7)	0 (0)	0 (3.9)	6 (40.6)
Nithsdale	4 (25.5)	12 (39.2)	0 (1.7)	0 (0)	6 (17.0)	6 (16.9)
Stewartry	0 (0)	0 (0)	0 (0)	0 (0)	0 (0)	12 (100.0)
Wigtown	0 (0)	1 (8.4)	0 (20.3)	0 (0)	1 (20.6)	12 (51.0)

Seats won:
Percentage of vote in brackets

	CON	LAB	SLD	SDP	SNP	OTHERS
FIFE	9 (18.4)	58 (44.1)	16 (16.0)	0 ( )	5 (15.2)	4 (6.5)
Dunfermline	3 (11.9)	25 (52.7)	3 (11.1)	( )	3 (17.8)	0 (6.9)
Kirkcaldy	2 (15.0)	33 (58.6)	1 (2.5)	( )	2 (18.6)	2 (5.5)
North-East Fife	4 (34.7)	0 (5.4)	12 (47.4)	( )	0 (5.4)	2 (7.5)
GRAMPIAN	12 (13.4)	28 (24.8)	27 (18.9)	0 (0.7)	19 (22.1)	30 (20.3)
City of Aberdeen	9 (18.3)	28 (45.1)	14 (25.7)	(1.5)	1 (9.4)	0 (0.3)
Banff & Buchan	0 (1.0)	0 (5.7)	0 (2.3)	(0)	8 (46.7)	10 (44.5)
Gordon	0 (22.2)	0 (3.5)	10 (49.7)	(0)	0 (5.0)	6 (15.8)
Kincardine & Deeside	1 (14.6)	3 (8.1)	3 (21.3)	(0)	2 (11.2)	6 (45.1)
Moray	2 (8.1)	0 (8.5)	0 (1.4)	(0)	8 (45.4)	8 (36.9)
HIGHLAND	1 (1.0)	20 (17.6)	3 (3.0)	0 ( )	2 (10.0)	81 (68.7)
Badenoch & Strathspey	0 (0)	0 (0)	0 (0)	(0)	1 (30.3)	10 (69.8)
Caithness	0 (0)	2 (7.6)	0 (0)	(0)	0 (0)	13 (92.5)
Inverness	0 (0)	12 (30.7)	2 (7.7)	(0)	0 (7.9)	15 (53.9)
Lochaber	0 (0)	4 (35.0)	0 (0)	(0)	0 (5.4)	11 (59.8)
Nairn	1 (12.7)	0 (7.9)	0 (0)	(0)	0 (0)	9 (87.4)
Ross & Cromarty	0 (0)	2 (7.9)	1 (2.0)	(0)	1 (18.6)	8 (71.7)
Skye & Lochalsh	0 (0)	0 (0)	0 (0)	(0)	0 (0)	2 (100.0)
Sutherland	0 (0)	0 (0)	0 (0)	(0)	0 (0)	13 (100.0)

Seats won:
Percentage of vote
in brackets

	CON		LAB		SLD		SDP		SNP		OTHERS	
LOTHIAN	28	(29.3)	73	(42.3)	4	(8.3)	0	(0.3)	9	(17.9)	4	(2.2)
City of Edinburgh	23	(36.6)	33	(36.6)	4	(12.2)	0	(0.3)	2	(14.1)	0	(0.5)
East Lothian	4	(30.5)	12	(55.0)	0	(1.7)	0	(0)	0	(6.9)	1	(6.2)
Midlothian	1	(14.7)	14	(56.1)	0	(4.5)	0	(0.7)	0	(22.2)	0	(2.1)
West Lothian	0	(8.6)	14	(47.0)	0	(0)	0	(0.3)	7	(38.5)	3	(2.4)
STRATHCLYDE	55	(16.1)	280	(50.4)	20	(6.9)	0	(0.6)	30	(21.1)	32	(5.2)
Argyll & Bute	3	(11.5)	0	(9.3)	3	(10.1)	0	(0)	2	(13.2)	16	(56.2)
Bearsden & Milngavie	6	(40.2)	1	(15.7)	2	(30.5)	0	(0)	1	(8.9)	1	(5.0)
Clydebank	1	(6.0)	10	(57.2)	0	(0)	0	(0)	1	(32.1)	0	(5.0)
Clydesdale	1	(14.2)	9	(45.2)	0	(0)	0	(0)	4	(28.8)	2	(12.0)
Cumbernauld & Kilsyth	0	(0)	6	(51.6)	0	(0)	0	(0.7)	6	(47.9)	0	(0)
Cumnock & Doon Valley	0	(3.6)	8	(61.3)	0	(0)	0	(9.4)	1	(10.6)	1	(15.4)
Cunninghame	4	(20.0)	24	(52.3)	0	(2.6)	0	(0)	0	(18.3)	2	(7.0)
Dumbarton	4	(24.1)	7	(38.6)	0	(1.9)	0	(3.2)	3	(22.8)	2	(9.9)
East Kilbride	2	(9.7)	14	(51.6)	0	(6.2)	0	(0.7)	0	(30.4)	0	(1.8)
Eastwood	8	(47.8)	1	(11.7)	1	(17.8)	0	(2.8)	0	(6.8)	2	(13.4)
City of Glasgow	4	(14.3)	60	(58.0)	2	(6.5)	0	(0.1)	0	(19.7)	0	(1.8)
Hamilton	1	(10.0)	15	(54.7)	2	(7.8)	0	(0)	1	(19.9)	1	(7.9)

Seats won: Percentage of vote in brackets	CON		LAB		SLD		SDP		SNP		OTHERS	
Inverclyde	1	(6.9)	12	(45.3)	7	(35.4)	0	(0)	0	(12.4)	0	(0)
Kilmarnock & Loudoun	3	(18.8)	12	(48.3)	0	(0)		(1.1)	3	(31.8)	0	(0.2)
Kyle & Carrick	7	(33.8)	16	(45.2)	0	(5.7)		(0)	0	(10.0)	2	(5.6)
Monklands	0	(9.6)	18	(62.4)	0	(0.4)		(0.3)	2	(26.8)	0	(0.9)
Motherwell	2	(7.1)	23	(59.1)	0	(0.4)		(0.8)	3	(23.3)	2	(9.6)
Renfrew	6	(18.4)	32	(48.6)	2	(6.0)		(1.1)	4	(25.0)	1	(1.2)
Strathkelvin	2	(22.6)	12	(49.0)	1	(12.6)		(0)	0	(16.1)	0	(0)
TAYSIDE	28	(30.3)	34	(28.3)	3	(5.3)	0	(0.1)	26	(32.5)	3	(3.8)
Angus	6	(32.5)	0	(9.8)	1	(3.9)		(0)	13	(49.8)	1	(4.3)
City of Dundee	10	(22.5)	29	(47.3)	0	(3.3)		(0)	5	(25.3)	0	(1.9)
Perth & Kinross	12	(40.0)	5	(13.8)	2	(9.2)		(0.2)	8	(30.9)	2	(6.3)
SCOTLAND	162	(19.5)	553	(42.6)	84	(8.4)	0	(0.4)	113	(21.3)	242	(8.1)

Source: Election Studies, University of Dundee.

SECTION 5

MAJOR POLITICAL AND SOCIAL ORGANISATIONS IN SCOTLAND

1. **Political Parties**
   Communist Party, 44 Carlton Place, Glasgow G5 9TW
   (041-429 2558)

   Scottish Conservative Party, 3 Chester Street, Edinburgh EH3 7RN
   (031-226 4426)

   The Labour Party (Scottish Council), Keir Hardie House,
   1 Lynedoch Place, Glasgow G3 6AB (041-332 8946)

   Scottish Democrats, 4 Clifton Terrace, Edinburgh EH12 5DR
   (031-337 2314)

   Scottish National Party, 6 North Charlotte Street,
   Edinburgh EH2 4JH (031-226 3661)

   Social Democratic Party, 5 Royal Exchange Square, Glagow
   G1 3AH (041-221 8871)

   Scottish Green Party, 11 Forth Street, Edinburgh EH11 3LE
   (013-556 5160) and 113 West Regent Street, Glasgow G2 2RU
   (041-221 7142)

2. **Government Agencies**
   Crofters Commission, 4-6 Castle Wynd, Inverness IV2 3EQ
   (0463 23731)

   Highlands and Islands Development Board, 27 Bank Street,
   Inverness IV1 1QR (0463 234171)

   The Housing Corporation, Scottish Head Office, Rosebery House,
   9 Haymarket Terrace, Edinburgh EH3 7AF (031-226 3153)

   Manpower Services Commission for Scotland, 4 Jeffrey Street,
   Edinburgh EH1 1UU (031-556 0233)

   Scottish Development Agency, 120 Bothwell Street, Glasgow G2 JP
   (041-248 2700)

   Scottish Special Housing Association, 37-41 Manor Place,
   Edinburgh EH3 7EE (031-226 4401)

3. **Industrial and Social Organisations**
   Church of Scotland, 121 George Street, Edinburgh EH2 4YN
   (031-225 5722)

Confederation of British Industry (Scottish Office), 5 Claremont Terrace, Glasgow G3 (041-332 8661)

Scottish Consumer Council, 314 St Vincent Street, Glasgow G3 8XW (041-226 5261)

Scottish Council (Development and Industry), 1 Castle Street, Edinburgh EH2 3AJ (031-225 7911)

Scottish Council for Community and Voluntary Organisations, 18/19 Claremont Crescent, Edinburgh EH7 4QD (031-556 3882)

Scottish Trades Union Congress, 16 Woodlands Terrace, Glasgow G3 6DF (041-332 4946)

SECTION 6

SCOTTISH PARLIAMENTARY BY-ELECTION 1988
10 November 1988

Glasgow Govan (resignation of Bruce Millan)

		%	% Change since 1987
James Sillars (SNP)	14,677	48.8	+38.4
Bob Gillespie (Lab)	11,123	36.9	−27.9
Graeme Hamilton (Con)	2,207	7.3	−4.5
Bernard Ponsonby (Dem)	1,246	4.1	−8.1
George Campbell (Green)	345	1.2	
Douglas Chalmers (Comm)	281	0.9	+0.3
David Sutch (MRLBP)	174	0.6	
Fraser Clark (RASZP)	51	0.2	
SNP maj	3,554	11.8	Turnout 60.2%

Campaign polls

	Lab	SNP	Con	Dem	Others	
MORI (25-27 Oct)	59	23	13	4	1	
Stirling Univ (late Oct)	63	24	10	2	1	DK 14
System 3 (5-6 Nov)	53	33	8	2	3	DK 27
NOP (10 Nov exit poll)	38	51	6	2	2	

RECENT PUBLICATIONS IN SCOTTISH GOVERNMENT AND POLITICS

C H Allen

The list below covers material omitted from previous listing, and material published since the last list in the period 1.6.87 to 31.5.88. Where a publisher is not specified, the publisher and author are the same. I would be grateful to be told of any errors or omissions.

To make it easier to obtain theses on inter-library loan, I have included where possible the British Library (Lending Division) or University Microfilm numbers; these should be quoted when applying for a loan copy.

As there now exists a current index to the *Scotsman* (contact Ted Lloyd-Gwilt, Scotsman Index Project, 21 Buccleuch Place, Edinburgh) I no longer cite newspaper feature articles in the index. I also do not list reports of investigations by the local Government Ombudsman.

1. AGE CONCERN *Poverty and older people.* Edinburgh, 1987, 48pp.
2. AGNEW, J A "Nationalism: autonomous force or practical politics?" *Community conflict, partition and nationalism,* ed. C H Williams & E Kofman (London: Croom Helm, 1988).
3. AGNEW, J A *Place and Politics: the Geographical Mediation of State and Society.* London: Unwin Hyman, 1987, 288pp.
4. ALEXANDER, D *Report on a housing survey – Isle of Eigg.* Inverness: Shelter, 1986.
5. ALEXANDER, K et al *Standing commission on the Scottish economy: interim report.* Glasgow, 1988, 179pp.
6. ALLEN, C H "Recent publications in Scottish government and politics", *Scottish Government Yearbook 1988,* 344-71.
7. AL-QADDO, H & RODGER, R "The implementation of housing policy: the SSHA", *Public Administration,* 65, 3 (1987) 313-29.
8. ANON "Agricultural change in Grampian 1972-86", *Grampian Quarterly Economic Review,* Spring 1988, 1-20.
9. ANON "Alternative employment in Scotland", *Third Sector: Focus on Fact Supplement,* 3, 1987.
10. ANON "Edinburgh: city of finance", *Edinburgh District Council Economic and Employment Review,* Autumn 1987, 17-22.
11. ANON "Employment in Scotland and the Scottish regions", *Scottish Economic Bulletin,* 36 (1987), 13-29.

12. ANON "Out of work", *Edinburgh District Council Economic and Employment Review*, 5 (1988) 12-17.
13. ANON "Scotland's best hope", *Spectator*, 13.2.1988, 13- 14.
14. ANON "The manufacturing sector in Edinburgh", *Edinburgh District Council Economic and Employment Review*, Autumn 1987, 23-28.
15. ANON "Time to mourn the loss of our greatest company", *Scottish Business Insider*, 5, 2 (1988), 4-5.
16. ASH, J "Glasgow's housing achievements". *Housing Review*, Jan/ Feb 1988, 32-34.
17. ASHCROFT, B "Scottish economic performance and government policy: a north-south divide?", *Scottish Government Yearbook 1988*, 238-58.
18. ASHCROFT, B & LOVE, J "Evaluating the effect of external takeover on the performance of regional companies: the case of Scotland 1965-80." Glasgow: Strathclyde University, 1987.
19. BAILEY, S J "A poll tax for Scotland?", *Critical Social Policy*, 20 (1987) 57-65.
20. BAILEY, S J (ed), *The role of the Accounts Commission*. Glasgow: Glasgow University Centre for Urban and Regional Research, Discussion paper 27, 1986, 63pp.
21. BALFOUR, A "Can the backroom boy become a front man?", *Scottish Business Insider*, 4, 9 (1987), 8-10.
22. BAYLEY, R "Miles better?", *Housing*, October 1987, 14-17.
23. BEAUMONT, P B & CAIRNS, L "New Towns – a centre of non-unionism?", *Employee Relations*, 9, 4 (1987), 14-15.
24. BEAUMONT, P B & HARRIS, R "The government case against national pay bargaining: an analysis for Scotland", *Scottish Government Yearbook 1988*, 123-49.
25. BEGG, T *50 special years: a study in Scottish housing*. London: Henry Melland, 1987, 301pp.
26. BOCHEL, J M *An analysis of party support in Scottish parliamentary constituencies based on the 1986 regional election results*. Dundee: Dundee University Dept. of Politics and Social Work, 1987.
27. BOCHEL, J M & DENVER, D "The 1987 general election in Scotland", *Scottish Government Yearbook 1988*, 24-35.
28. BOYLE, R "Glasgow's growth pains", *New Society*, 8.1.1988. 15-17.
29. BOYLE, R "The price of private planning: a review of urban planning policy in Scotland", *Scottish Government Yearbook 1988*, 183-99.
30. BOYLE, R "Urban initiatives in Scotland: measuring the tartan factor", *Planner*, June 1987, 27-30.
31. BROTHERSTON, J "The NHS in Scotland 1948-84", *Improving the common weal*, (ed.) G Maclean (1987).
32. BROWN, D A & LEAT, P M K *Developing Grampian and its rural*

economy. Aberdeen: North of Scotland College of Agriculture, Agricultural Economics Division, 1988, 65pp.

33. BRUCE, S "Sectarianism in Scotland: a contemporary assessment and explanation", *Scottish Government Yearbook 1988*, 150-65.

34. BUTT, J "The Scottish economy", *Contemporary Review*, 250 (1987) 281-85.

35. CAIRNS, J A & HARRIS, A H "The experience of Scottish firms in the North Sea oil supply industry: a guide to the future?", *Quarterly Economic Commentary*, 13, 1 (1987) 71-76.

36. CALLANDER, R *A pattern of landownership in Scotland (with special reference to Aberdeenshire)*. Finzean: Haughend, 1987, 155pp.

37. C.B.I.(SCOTLAND) *Rate watching: a CBI guide to business/local authority consultations in Scotland*. Glasgow, 1985, 41pp.

38. C.E.S.Ltd *Local authorities and worker cooperatives. Report and case studies*. London, 1987 (Vol.2: Glasgow case study).

39. CHAPMAN, T "Class and social mobility: patterns of employment in rural and urban Scotland", *Deprivation and welfare in rural areas*, ed. P Lowe, T Bradley & S Wright, (Norwich: Geo Books, 198), 175-92.

40. CHURCH OF SCOTLAND *Housing Scotland's people*. Edinburgh: St Andrew's Press, 1988. 75pp.

41. C.I.P.F.A. (SCOTTISH BRANCH) *Guide to local government finance in Scotland*. Edinburgh, 1988.

42. CLAPHAM, D & KINTREA, K "Public housing", *Regenerating the inner city*, ed. D Donnison & A Middleton, 93-116.

43. CLAPHAM, D, KEMP, P & KINTREA, K "Cooperative ownership of former council housing", *Policy and Politics*, 15, 4 (1987) 207-220 (Glasgow).

44. CLEMENT, K J *Heavy objections? Problems in assessing major energy facilities in Scotland and Germany*. Glasgow: University of Strathclyde, Centre for the Study of Public Policy, 1988, 26pp.

45. CLEMENT, K J *The nuclear inquiry: a Scottish-German comparison*. Glasgow: University of Strathclyde, Dept. of Urban and Regional Planning, 1987, 29pp.

46. COHEN, A P *Whalsay: symbol, segment and boundary in a Shetland island community*. Manchester: Manchester University Press, 1987, 236pp.

47. COLLIER, A "Grampian shrugs off recession", *Scottish Business Insider*, 5, 5 (1988) 48-50.

48. COLLIER, A "Will Scottish Bus Group be allowed to take the high road?", *Scottish Business Insider*, 5, 4 (1988) 14-15.

49. COMMISSIONER FOR LOCAL ADMINISTRATION IN SCOTLAND, *Report ... for the year ended 31.1.1988..* Edinburgh: HMSO, 1988, 30pp.

50. COMMISSION FOR LOCAL AUTHORITY ACCOUNTS IN SCOTLAND *Accounts 1986/87*. London: HMSO, 1987, 12pp.

51. COMMISSION FOR LOCAL AUTHORITY ACCOUNTS IN SCOTLAND *Twelth report*. Edinburgh, 1987, 43pp.

52. COMMISSION OF THE EUROPEAN COMMUNITIES *European regional development fund: UK regional development programme 1986-90 – Section 9 Scotland, Section 10 Northern Ireland*. Luxembourg, 1987, 214pp.

53. CONNARTY, M & H "The conflict option", *Radical Scotland* 30 (1988) 11-12.

54. COOKE, P "Political regionalism: a critique and alternative proposal", *Community conflict, partition and nationalism*, Ed. C H Williams and E Kofman (London: Croom Helm, 1988).

55. C.O.S.L.A. *Forestry in Scotland: planning the way ahead.* Edinburgh 1987, 38pp.

56. C.O.S.L.A. *Submission on the SDD consultation document 'Scottish Homes'*. Edinburgh, 1987, 21pp.

57. COSTELLO, A "Rehabilitation in a rural context", *Rural housing in Scotland*, ed. B D MacGregor et al, 119-29.

58. COUNTRYSIDE COMMISSION FOR SCOTLAND *Forestry in Scotland: a policy paper*. Perth, 1986, 44pp.

59. CURRAN, J H *Public and the police in Scotland*. Edinburgh: Scottish Office Central Research Unit, 1987, 56pp.

60. DAVIDSON, P S *Widdicombe Committee evidence on local authority business: annexes to report giving evidence by Cllr. P S Davidson (Fife Regional Council)*. Dunfermline: Scientific Documentation Centre, 1987, 42pp.

61. DE MELLOW, R A "Trends in employment in industrial R&D in Scotland", *Scottish Economic Bulletin* 37 (1988) 9-12.

62. DEPARTMENT OF AGRICULTURE AND FISHERIES FOR SCOTLAND, *An agricultural development programme for Scottish islands: a five year programme*. Edinburgh, 1986, 61pp.

63. DEWAR, D "Scotland, the way forward", *Labour's next moves forward*. (London: Fabian Society, Fabian Tract 521, 1987).

64. DONNISON, D "Conclusion", *Regenerating the inner city*, ed. D Donnison & A Middleton, 272-91.

65. DONNISON, D & MIDDLETON, A *Regenerating the inner city*. London: Routledge Kegan Paul, 1987, 322pp.

66. DONNISON, D V et al *GEAR Review: social aspects*. Glasgow: Glasgow University Department of Town and Regional Planning, 1982.

67. DOWLE, M "The year at Westminster", *Scottish Government Yearbook 1988*, 12-23.

68. DRAPER, P et al *The Scottish financial sector*. Edinburgh: Edinburgh University Press, 1988, 347pp.

69. DRIEUX, J P *Les Lothians depuis la seconde guerre mondiale*. Doctorat d'etat, Universite de Strasbourg, 1988, 907pp.

70. DUMFRIES & GALLOWAY R.C., *Transport policies and programme 1985-90: second supplement 1987-92*. Dumfries, 1987,

55pp.
71. DUNCAN, S & GOODWIN, M "The Scottish solution", pp 171-76 of their *The local state and uneven development* (London: Polity, 1988).
72. DUNCAN, T *Community councils in Glasgow: the first ten years.* Glasgow: Strathclyde University Department of Politics, 1987, 9pp.
73. DUNCAN, T "Housing conditions in the rural areas: a commentary" *Rural housing in Scotland*, ed. B D MacGregor et al, 105-111.
74. DUNDEE D.C. *Industrial strategy review 1987.* Dundee, 1987, 48pp.
75. EAST LOTHIAN D.C. *Housing plan review 1987-92.* Haddington, 1987, 25pp.
76. EAST LOTHIAN D.C. *Housing plan review 1987-92: background information.* Haddington, 1988, 64pp.
77. EDINBURGH COUNCIL FOR THE SINGLE HOMELESS *Home ground: a survey of young people's housing needs in Muirhouse, Edinburgh.* Edinburgh, 1988, 32pp.
78. EDINBURGH D.C. *Decentralisation strategy document.* Edinburgh, 1986.
79. EDINBURGH D.C. *Poverty in Edinburgh: the other side of Festival City.* Edinburgh, 1987, 44pp.
80. ECOTEC *Report of the survey of Wester Hailes residents: needs, opportunities and ideas.* Edinburgh: SDA Joint Unit for Research on Urban Environments, 1986, 79pp.
81. EDWARDS, R "Beware the Tories, promising devolution", *New Statesman*, 17.7.1987, 15-16.
82. ELLIOTT, A & FORRESTER, D B (Eds), *The Scottish churches and the political process today.* Edinburgh: Edinburgh University Centre for Theology and Public Issues/Unit for the Study of Government in Scotland, 1986, 94pp.
83. ENGLISH, B "A taxing life", *Housing*, October 1987, 38-40.
84. FAINI, R & SCHIANTARELLI, F "Incentives and investment decisions: the effectiveness of regional policy", *Oxford Economic Papers*, 39, 4 (1987) 516-33.
85. FAIRLEY, A "The community charge and local government finance in Scotland", *Scottish Government Yearbook 1988*, 46-61.
86. FARRINGTON, S & MACKAY, T "Bus deregulation in Scotland. a review of the first six months", *Quarterly Economic Commentary*, 13, 1 (1987) 64-70.
87. FIELDER, S *Low cost home ownership in Glasgow 1977-83.* Glasgow: Glasgow University Centre for Housing Research Discussion Paper 7, 1985.
88. FINDLAY, P "Resistance, restructuring and gender: the Plessey occupation", *The politics of industrial closure*, ed. T Dickson & D Judge (London: Macmillan, 1987).
89. FINN, G P T "Multicultural anti-racism and Scottish education",

Scottish Education Review, 19, 1 (1987) 39-49.
90. FORBES, E & MUNRO, D *The SDA: an example to the nation?* London: Tory Reform Group, 1988, 28pp.
91. FOX, P "Collecting the poll tax in Scotland", *Public Finance and Accountancy*, 4.9.87, 8-10.
92. FRANKLIN, G "Towards the year 2000", *Radical Scotland* 30 (1988) 13-14.
93. FRASER, N A & MOAR, L *Compilation, analysis and updating of occupation by industry matrices for Scotland 1961-77.* Edinburgh: Industry Dept. for Scotland, ESU Research paper 8, 1983, 99pp.
94. FRY, M "Tories on the rocks", *Spectator*, 25.4.87, 47 & 49.
95. GAAB, M "Scotland's high and low roads", *Management Today*, Dec. 1987, 85-93.
96. GALLACHER, T *Glasgow: the uneasy peace. Religious tension in modern Scotland 1819-1987.* Manchester: Manchester University Press, 1987.
97. GARNER, C, MAIN, B & RAFFE, D "The distribution of school leaver unemployment within Scottish cities", *Urban Studies*, 25, 2 (1988) 133- 44.
98. GARNER, C, MAIN, B & RAFFE, D *School leaver employment and unemployment within Scottish cities.* Edinburgh: Edinburgh University Centre for Educational Sociology, 1987.
99. GIBSON, J S *Review of the Scottish Council of Voluntary Organisations.* Edinburgh: Scottish Office, 1987, 38pp.
100. GIBSON, T "Third term flagship; a description and evaluation of the poll tax", *Local Government Policy Making*, March 1988, 18-23.
101. GILCHRIST, J A *Devolution, federalism and industrial development: intergovernmental relations in industrial development under the Scotland Act 1978 and in the practice of Canadian federalism.* Glasgow: Strathclyde University Department of Politics Paper 56, 1987, 62pp.
102. GILLANDERS, E "Buchan: a region for sale?", *Farmers Weekly*, 5.2.1988, 44-47.
103. GLASGOW D C *City profile: facts and figures about Glasgow 1988.* Glasgow, 1988, 75pp.
104. GLASGOW D C *The condition of Glasgow's housing, Vol 1: house condition survey report 1985.* Glasgow, 1987, 82pp.
105. GLASGOW D C *GEAR local plan: written statement.* Glasgow, 1987, 112pp.
106. GLASGOW D C *People and households in Glasgow: current estimates and expected changes 1986-93.* Glasgow, 1988, 23pp.
107. GLASGOW D C *Research memorandum: unemployment within Glasgow by local area (July 1987).* Glasgow, 1987, 55pp.
108. GRAEME ROBERTSON, J *The Western Isles IDP: further lessons in human ecology.* Portree: Habitat Scotland, 1988, 64pp.
109. GRAMPIAN R C *Strategic forecast: employment, population, housing – 1987 update.* Aberdeen, 1987, 43pp.

110. GRANT, J S "Government agencies and the Highlands since 1945", *Scottish Geographical Magazine*, 103, 2 (1987) 95-99.

111. HARRISON, R J & PULLEN, W T *Bus deregulation in Scotland: a study of the early effects*. Edinburgh: Scottish Office Central Research Unit, 1988, 54pp.

112. HENDERSON, J *Semiconductors, Scotland and the international division of labour*. Glasgow: Glasgow University, Centre for Urban and Regional Research, Discussion paper 28, 1987, 55pp.

113. HIGHLANDS AND ISLANDS DEVELOPMENT BOARD *Guide to regions, islands and district councils*. Inverness, 1987, 21pp.

114. HIGHLANDS AND ISLANDS DEVELOPMENT BOARD *Annual report 21*. Inverness, 1987, 68pp.

115. HIGHLANDS AND ISLANDS DEVELOPMENT BOARD *Annual report 22*. Inverness, 1988.

116. HOOD, N *Future of the multinationals in Scotland*. Glasgow: Strathclyde International Business Unit, conference on Scotland and the Multinationals, 1986.

117. HOOD, N & YOUNG, S, "Note on exchange rate fluctuation and the foreign owned sector in Scotland", *Scottish Journal of Political Economy*, 35, 1 (1988) 77-83.

118. HOUSE OF COMMONS LIBRARY *Scottish White Paper on housing and the Housing (Scotland) Bill*. London, 1987, 58pp. (Ref.sheet 87/9).

119. HOUSING CORPORATION *Response to Scottish Homes consultation paper*. London, 1987.

120. HOUSTON, G *An interim assessment of the IDP for agriculture and fish farming in the Western Isles*. Inverness: HIDB, 1987, 67pp.

121. HUGHES, J J "Housing and rural development", *Rural housing in Scotland*, ed. B D MacGregor et al, 28-36.

122. HUME, M & OWEN, D *Is there a Scottish solution? The working class and the Assembly debate*. London: Junius Publications, 1988, 127pp.

123. HUNTER, D J & WISTOW, G "The Scottish difference: policy and practice in community care", *Scottish Government Yearbook 1988*, 82-102.

124. HUNTER, E *The Scottish women's handbook*. Glasgow: Stramullion, 1987.

125. HUNTER, T D "Close encounters of a bureaucratic kind", *Political Quarterly*, 58, 2 (1987) 180-90.

126. INDUSTRY DEPARTMENT FOR SCOTLAND *Aspects of the employment structure in the electronics industry in Scotland in 1985*. Edinburgh: IDS, Statistical Bulletin C3.1, 1987, 15pp.

127. INDUSTRY DEPARTMENT FOR SCOTLAND *The electronics industry in Scotland*. Edinburgh: IDS, Statistical Bulletin C1.2, 1988, 9pp.

128. INDUSTRY DEPARTMENT FOR SCOTLAND *New life for urban Scotland*. Edinburgh, 1988, 24pp.

129. INDUSTRY DEPARTMENT FOR SCOTLAND *Regional development: encouraging enterprise in Scotland.* Edinburgh, 1987, 7pp.

130. INDUSTRY DEPARTMENT FOR SCOTLAND, *Review of the HIDB. Economic and social change in the Highlands and Islands.* Edinburgh: IDS (ESU Research paper 13), 1987, 141pp.

131. INDUSTRY DEPARTMENT FOR SCOTLAND *Summary of review of the HIDB.* Edinburgh, 1987, 12pp.

132. JACKSON, A "Scottish ethnography", *Edinburgh Anthropology* 1 (1987).

133. JONES, H "Incomers to peripheral areas in Northern Scotland: some housing considerations", *Rural housing in Scotland*, ed. B D MacGregor et al, 37-47.

134. KEATING, M "Swings and roundabouts for COSLA", *Municipal Journal*, 21.8.87, 1550-51.

135. KEATING, M & CARTER, C "Policy making in the Scottish Office: the designation of Cumbernauld New Town", *Public Administration*, 65, 4 (1987), 391-405.

136. KEATING, M & MITCHELL, J "Scottish politics", *Yearbook '87* (Modern Studies Association), 27-38.

137. KELLAS, J "Scotland faces the 'doomsday scenario'", *Social Studies Review*, 3, 1 (1987) 34-35.

138. KELLAS, J "The Scottish political system", *Social Studies Review*, 3, 5 (1988), 180-83.

139. KEREVAN, G & SAVILLE, R *The economic case for deep-mined coal in Scotland.* Edinburgh: Napier College, 1985, 110pp.

140. KEREVAN, G & SAVILLE, R "Privatising electricity", *Radical Scotland* 28 (1987) 11-14.

141. KEREVAN, G & SAVILLE, R *Privatising the SSEB: a report on the consequences for Scotland.* Edinburgh: Scottish Coal Project, 1987.

142. KERNOHAN, R D "The condition of Scotland debate", *Contemporary Review* 251 (1987) 126-30.

143. KILGOUR, L & LAPSLEY, I *Financial reporting by local authorities in Scotland.* Edinburgh: CIPFA/Institute of Chartered Accountants (Scotland), 1988, 68pp.

144. KINSEY, R "The politics and ideology of the prison crisis", *Scottish Government Yearbook 1988*, 103-22.

145. LAWSON, A "Mair nor a rouch wind blawin..", *Scottish Government Yearbook 1988*, 36-45.

146. LAWSON, A "STUC take the high ground", *Radical Scotland* 27 (1987) 8-10.

147. LAZAROWITZ, M "Interview", *Left Review* 1 (1987) 9-10.

148. LINDSAY, I "Divergent trends", *Radical Scotland* 31 (1987) 14-15.

149. LITTLE, A *Personal finances in deprived areas.* M.Sc. dissertation, Strathclyde University, 1987.

150. LLOYD, M G & ROWAN-ROBINSON, J "Local authority

responses to economic uncertainty in Scotland", *Scottish Government Yearbook 1988*, 282-300.

151. LOTHIAN R C *Lothian public transport policies*. Edinburgh, 1986, 17pp.

152. LOVE, J & STEPHENS, J "RSD: a comment", *Quarterly Economic Commentary*, 13, 4 (1988) 48-52.

153. McARTHUR, A A "Jobs and incomes", *Regenerating the inner city*, ed. D Donnison & A Middleton, 72-92.

154. MACARTNEY, A "Summary of opinion polls 1986/87", *Scottish Government Yearbook 1988*, 312-317.

155. McCALMAN, J "Going international; the development of export-oriented indigenous electronics firms", *Quarterly Economic Commentary*, 13, 3 (1988) 61-66.

156. McCONNELL, J "Defending local democracy", *Radical Scotland* 32 (1988) 22-23.

157. MacEWEN, M *Housing allocation, race and law*. Edinburgh: Edinburgh College of Art/Heriot Watt University Department of Town and Country Planning, Scottish Ethnic Minorities Research Unit, Research paper 2, 1987.

158. MacEWEN, M "Racial harassment and council housing in Scotland: a discussion of relevant legislation", *Scottish Housing Law News* 3 (1987) 4-11.

159. MacEWEN, M *Racial harassment, council housing and the law*. Edinburgh: Edinburgh College of Art/Heriot Watt University Department of Town and Country Planning, Scottish Ethnic Minorities Research Unit, Research paper 3, 1987.

160. MacEWEN, M "Racial incidents, council housing and the law", *Housing Studies*, 3, 1 (1988) 59-72.

161. McGARRY, J F *The British homogeneity thesis and nationalism in Scotland and Wales*. Ph.D. thesis, University of Western Ontario, 1987.

162. McGREGOR, A et al *An evaluation of community business in Scotland*. Edinburgh: Scottish Central Research Unit, 1988, 82pp.

163. MacGREGOR, B, ROBERTON, D & SHUCKSMITH, M (eds) *Rural housing in Scotland*. Aberdeen: Aberdeen University Press, 1987, 224pp.

164. McILVANNEY, W "Stands Scotland where it did?", *Radical Scotland* 30 (1988) 19-22.

165. MacINNES, J "Recent patterns of change in employment in Scotland", *Quarterly Economic Commentary*, 13, 2 (1987) 68-71.

166. MacINNES, J *Economic restructuring relevant to industrial relations in Scotland*. Glasgow: Glasgow University, Centre for Urban and Regional Research, Discussion paper 26, 1987, 64pp.

167. MacINNES, J & SPROULL, A *Trade union recognition, single union agreements and employment changes in the electronics industry in Scotland*. Glasgow: Glasgow College of Technology, Department of Economics Discussion paper 6, 1988, 44pp.

168. MACKIE, T "The fall and fall of the Scots quoted firm", *Scottish Business Insider*, 4, 9 (1987) 4-5.

169. McLACHLAN, G (Ed) *Improving the commonweal: aspects of Scottish health services 1900-86.* Edinburgh: Edinburgh University Press, 1987.

170. McLEAN, B & SMART, A "Labour in Scotland: what now?", *Left Review* 1 (1987) 3-5.

171. MacLENNAN, D "Rehabilitating older housing", *Regenerating the inner city*, ed. D Donnison & A Middleton, 117-34.

172. MacLENNAN, D, MUNRO, M & LAMONT, D "New and owner-occupied housing", *Regenerating the inner city*, ed. D Donnison & A Middleton, 135-51.

173. McPHERSON,A & RAAB, C *Governing education: a sociology of policy since 1945.* Edinburgh: Edinburgh University Press, 1988, 580pp.

174. McPHERSON, A & RAAB, C "Scottish education: the influence of individual administrators and inspectors", *Contemporary Record*, 2, 2 (1988) 10-11.

175. MADIGAN, R *A new generation of home owners?* Glasgow: Glasgow University Centre for Housing Research Discussion Paper 16, 1988, 56pp.

176. MALLEY, J R *The macroeconomic impacts of foreign direct investment: the Scottish case.* Ph.D. thesis, Glasgow University, 1985, 359pp (BLLD order No. D80146).

177. MARS, T "Glasgow's miles better", *Roof*, Jan/Feb 1988, 21- 25.

178. MARTIN, S "Power politics", *Scottish Government Yearbook 1988*, 200-215.

179. MATHER, A S "The structure of forest ownership in Scotland", *Journal of Rural Studies*, 3, 2 (1987) 175-82.

180. MATHER, A S & MURRAY, A C "Employment and private sector afforestation in Scotland", *Journal of Rural Studies*, 3, 3 (1987) 207-218.

181. MATHER, A S & MURRAY, A C "The dynamics of rural land use change; the case of private sector afforestation in Scotland", *Land Use Policy*, Jan.1988, 103-20.

182. MEEK, B "Waiting in the wings", *Radical Scotland* 31 (1988) 10-12.

183. MIDDLETON, A "Glasgow and its East End", *Regenerating the inner city*, ed. D Donnison & A Middleton, 3-33.

184. MIDWINTER, A "Flawed finance reforms based on belief not evidence", *Local Government Chronicle*, 25.3.1988, 14, 16.

185. MIDWINTER, A, MAIR, C & MOXEN, J *Rural deprivation in Scotland: an investigation into the case for a rural aid fund.* Alexandria: Advise Publishing and Training, 1988, 52pp.

186. MIDWINTER, A et al "A Scottish perspective", *The conduct of local authority business. Research volume 1: The political organisation of local authorities* (London: HMSO, Cmnd 9798, 1987), 157-96.

187. MILNE, K "Holding out", *New Society*, 4,3,1988, 8-9.
188. MITCHISON, A "Playing politics with Scotland", *New Society*, 25.9.1987, 17-19.
189. MOORE, C & BOOTH, S "Hunting the QUARC: an institution without a role?", *Public Administration*, 65, 4 (1987) 455-66.
190. MORENO, L "Scotland and Catalonia: the path to home rule", *Scottish Government Yearbook 1988*, 166-82.
191. MOTHERWELL D C *Annual economic review 1986*. Motherwell, 1986, 67pp.
192. MOTHERWELL D C *Annual economic review 1987*. Motherwell, 1988.
193. MUIR, D "Housing plans and housing needs", *Rural housing in Scotland*, ed. B D MacGregor et al, 59-65.
194. MUNRO, D *Housing and labour market interaction – a review*. Glasgow: Glasgow University, Centre for Urban and Regional Research, Discussion paper 12, 1986, 12pp.
195. NATIONAL AUDIT OFFICE *IDS review of Scottish New Towns*. London: HMSO, 1988, 31pp.
196. NATIONAL AUDIT OFFICE *SDA: involvement with the private sector*. London: House of Commons Paper 478, 1988, 21pp.
197. NICHOLSON, I, SIM, D & WEBSTER, D *Community ownership in Glasgow*. Glasgow: Glasgow D C, 1985.
198. O'BRIEN, R et al *Faith in the Scottish city: the Scottish relevance of the report of the Archbishop's Commission on Urban Priority Areas*. Edinburgh; Edinburgh University Centre for Theology and Public Issues, Occasional paper 8, 1986, 30pp.
199a O'FARRELL, P & HITCHENS, D M *The relative competitiveness and performance of small manufacturing firms in Scotland and the Mid West of Ireland: an analysis of matched pairs*. Edinburgh: College of Art/Heriot Watt University Dept. of Town and Country Planning, 1988, 71pp.
199b O'FARRELL, P & HITCHINS, D M *The relative competitiveness and performance of small manufacturing firms in Scotland and the South of England: an analysis of matched pairs*. Edinburgh: College of Art/Heriot/Watt University Dept. of Town and Country Planning, 1988, 70pp.
200. PAYNE, G & FORD G *Occupational mobility and educational process in Scotland*. Dublin: ISA Research Conference on Social Mobility, 1977.
201. PAYNE, G et al *Education and social mobility*. Edinburgh: SIP Occasional paper 8, 1979.
202. PAYNE, G et al *Employment and mobility in peripheral regions*. Cardiff: BSA Conference, 1983.
203. PEARCE, J & BROOKS, C "Local economic development examined", *Initiatives*, Dec. 1987, 18-20 (Glasgow).

204. PEPINSTER, C & SPRING, M "Glasgow takes the initiative", *Building*, 10.7.87, 31-37.

205. PERMAN, R "A difficult mix of oil and money", *Scottish Business Insider*, 5, 1 (1988) 2-5.

206. P.I.E.D.A *How many owners? A case study of Scottish tenure choice and tenure shift*. Edinburgh, 1987, 37pp (West Lothian).

207. PLANNING EXCHANGE/COSLA *A review of responses to the consultation paper "Scottish Homes"*. Glasgow, 1987, 63pp.

208. PRATTIS, J I "Organisational change and adaptation: community cooperatives and capital control in the Western Isles", *American Anthropologist*, 89, 3 (1987) 567-80.

209. RADICAL SCOTLAND "Grasping the thistle", *Radical Scotland* 31 (1987) 6-9.

210. RADICAL SCOTLAND "Turning the corner at Perth?" *Radical Scotland* 32 (1988) 6-9.

211. REEDS, J "Four square up to the challenge of new deal for Govan", *Surveyor*, 6.6.87, 11-14 (Govan Initiative).

212. REID, J "But(s) he does not understand", *New Statesman*, 19.6.87, 6-7.

213. ROBERTSON, D S & MACGREGOR, B D "Rural housing in Scotland; an assessment of the issues", *Rural housing in Scotland*, ed. B D MacGregor et al, 9-16.

214. ROBERTSON, I M L "Access to the health services", *Regenerating the inner city*, ed. D Donnison & A Middleton, 167-85.

215. ROSENBURG, L & MIDDLETON, A *SSHA house sales research 1987*. Edinburgh: College of Art/HeriotWatt University Dept. of Town and Country Planning, 1987, 61pp.

216. ROSS, D *An unlikely anger: Scottish teachers in action*. Edinburgh: Mainstream, 1986, 158pp.

217. ROSS J "Grasping the doomsday nettle – methodically", *Radical Scotland* 30 (1988) 6-7 (and see 8-9).

218. ROSS, V R *Sofa, so good: a discussion paper on furnished accommodation provided by public sector housing agencies in Scotland*. Edinburgh: Scottish Council for the Single Homeless, 1987, 25pp.

219. ROWAN-ROBINSON, J & LLOYD, M G *Local authority economic development activity in Scotland*. Glasgow: Planning Exchange occasional paper 32, 1987.

220. ROY, S A *Future directions in planning in Scotland*. Ph D thesis, Glasgow University, 1985, 382pp (BLLD number: DX 75429/87).

221. RUSSELL J *Race and planning practice in Scotland 1987*. Edinburgh: Royal Town Planning Institute (Scottish Branch), 1987, 9pp.

222. SALMON, A, CAMPBELL, M, & GALLOWAY, G "Addressing doomsday", *Radical Scotland* 28 (1987) 7-9.

223. SCOTTISH ASSOCIATION FOR PUBLIC TRANSPORT *Making Glasgow miles better: public transport and the city*.

Glasgow, 1987, 29pp.
224. SCOTTISH COMMUNITY EDUCATION COUNCIL *Unemployment: a series of publications with the facts and figures about young Scots today*. Edinburgh, 1987, 42pp.
225. SCOTTISH COUNCIL (DEVELOPMENT AND INDUSTRY) *Towards 2000: a review of trends in the Scottish labour market*. Edinburgh, 1988, 20pp.
226. SCOTTISH COUNCIL FOR CIVIL LIBERTIES *The Scottish prisons crisis in the 1980s*. Glasgow, 1987.
227. SCOTTISH COUNCIL FOR THE SINGLE HOMELESS *Scottish Homes: submission to the Scottish Office*. Edinburgh, 1987.
228. SCOTTISH CROFTERS UNION *A better crofting future*. Broadford (Skye), 1987, 17pp.
229. SCOTTISH DEVELOPMENT AGENCY *Annual report 1987*. Glasgow, 1987, 116pp.
230. SCOTTISH DEVELOPMENT AGENCY *Electronics and support companies in Scotland*. Glasgow, 1988, 51pp.
231. SCOTTISH DEVELOPMENT AGENCY *The engineering industry in Scotland: securing the future*. Glasgow, 1988, 3pp.
232. SCOTTISH DEVELOPMENT AGENCY *North American companies manufacturing in Scotland – Winter 1987*. Glasgow, 1987, 58pp.
233. SCOTTISH DEVELOPMENT DEPARTMENT *Annual estimates of households in Scotland 1981-86*. Edinburgh, HSIU Statistical Bulletin 35, 1988, 4pp.
234. SCOTTISH DEVELOPMENT DEPARTMENT *Housing information paper: tenants' choice*. Edinburgh, 1987, 6pp.
235. SCOTTISH DEVELOPMENT DEPARTMENT *Housing: the government's proposals for Scotland*. London; HMSO (Cmnd 242), 1987, 25pp.
236. SCOTTISH DEVELOPMENT DEPARTMENT *Papers on housing: private rented sector*. Edinburgh, 1987.
237. SCOTTISH DEVELOPMENT DEPARTMENT *Policy review of the Local Government Boundary Commission for Scotland*. Edinburgh, 1988, 6pp.
238. SCOTTISH DEVELOPMENT DEPARTMENT *Private housing renewal: the Government's proposals for Scotland*. Edinburgh, 1988, 15pp.
239. SCOTTISH DEVELOPMENT DEPARTMENT *Public sector rents in Scotland 1986-87*. Edinburgh, HSIU Statistical Bulletin 29, 1987, 12pp.
240. SCOTTISH DEVELOPMENT DEPARTMENT *Scottish Homes: a new agency for housing in Scotland*. Edinburgh, 1987, 24pp.
241. SCOTTISH DEVELOPMENT DEPARTMENT *Tenants' choice: a right for public sector tenants to choose new landlords. The government's proposals for legislation in Scotland*. Edinburgh, 1987, 6pp.

242. SCOTTISH HEALTH SERVICES PLANNING COUNCIL *Report for 1986.* Edinburgh, HMSO, 1987, 21pp.

243. SCOTTISH HEALTH SERVICES PLANNING COUNCIL *Scottish health authorities' review of priorities for the 80's and 90's.* Edinburgh, 1987.

244. SCOTTISH HOME AND HEALTH DEPARTMENT *Health in Scotland 1986.* Edinburgh: HMSO, 1987, 101pp.

245. SCOTTISH INFORMATION OFFICE *Economy of Scotland.* Edinburgh: SIO Factsheet 10, 1987, 27pp.

246. SCOTTISH INFORMATION OFFICE *Ethnic minorities in Scotland.* Edinburgh: SIO Factsheet 30, 1987, 7pp.

247. SCOTTISH INFORMATION OFFICE *Scottish Office.* Edinburgh: SIO Factsheet 20, 1987, 15pp.

248. SCOTTISH LOCAL GOVERNMENT INFORMATION UNIT *A guide to the Housing (Scotland) Bill.* Glasgow, 1988, 4pp.

249. SCOTTISH LOCAL GOVERNMENT INFORMATION UNIT *Rates reform and the poll tax: a guide to the issues.* Glasgow, 1988, 5pp.

250. SCOTTISH LOCAL GOVERNMENT INFORMATION UNIT *A Scottish guide to the Local Government Act 1988*, Glasgow, 5pp.

251. SCOTTISH LOCAL GOVERNMENT INFORMATION UNIT *Scottish homes and jobs: conference report.* Glasgow, 1987, 56pp.

252. SCOTTISH OFFICE *Land use change in Scotland 1986.* Edinburgh: SO Central Research Unit Statistical Bulletin No.3(E)/1987, 1987, 8pp.

253. SCOTTISH OFFICE *Public Expenditure to 1990-91: a commentary on the Scotland programme.* EDINBURGH, 1988, 184PP.

254. SCOTTISH OFFICE *Scottish local government financial statistics 1984-85.* Edinburgh, 1987, 30pp.

255. SCOTTISH SPECIAL HOUSING ASSOCIATION *Scottish Homes consultation paper: a report by the SSHA.* Edinburgh, 1987, 16pp.

256. SCOTTISH TRADES UNION CONGRESS *90th annual report.* Glasgow, 1987, 350pp.

257. SCOULLER, J "The BP bid for Britoil: should Scotland take it lying down?", *Quarterly Economic Commentary*, 13, 3 (1988) 52-60.

258. SECRETARY OF STATE FOR SCOTLAND *Local government finance (Scotland): rate reduction (City of Edinburgh District) 1987-88: report.* Edinburgh: HMSO, 1987, 31pp.

259. SECRETARY OF STATE FOR SCOTLAND *Local government finance (Scotland): rate reduction (Lothian Region) 1987-88: Report.* Edinburgh: HMSO, 1987, 42pp.

260. SECRETARY OF STATE FOR SCOTLAND *Rate support grant (Scotland) order 1987: report.* Edinburgh: HMSO, 1987, 27pp.

261. SHELTER *Response to 'Scottish Homes'.* Edinburgh, 1987, 10pp.

262. SHUCKSMITH, M *Public intervention in rural housing markets.* Ph.D thesis, Newcastle University, 1987, 486pp (BLLD No. DX

80603).
263. SHUCKSMITH, M "Public housing in Scotland: the policy context", *Rural housing in Scotland*, ed. B D MacGregor et al, 17-27.
264. SMITH, P & BURNS, M "The Scottish economy: decline and response", *Scottish Government Yearbook 1988*, 259-81.
265. SPROULL, A & MacINNES, J "Union recognition in Scottish electronics", *Quarterly Economic Commentary*, 13, 1 (1987) 57-63.
266. SPROULL, A & MacINNES, J *Union recognition in the electronics industry in Scotland*. Glasgow: Glasgow University, Centre for Research in Industrial Democracy and Participation Research Paper, 1987.
267. STANDING COMMISSION ON THE SCOTTISH ECONOMY, *Interim report*. Glasgow, 1988, 179pp.
268. STEWART, A "Local government reform", *Radical Scotland* 27 (1987) 11-13.
269. STRATHCLYDE HOUSING LIAISON GROUP *Council housing – still not enough investment*. Glasgow, 1987, 4pp.
270. STRATHCLYDE R C "1984 census of employment results for Strathclyde", *Strathclyde economic trends*, Dec. 1987.
271. STRATHCLYDE R C *The 1984 production results for Strathclyde: source documents*. Glasgow, 1987, 9pp.
272. STRATHCLYDE R C *Government regional assistance to Strathclyde in 1986*. Glasgow, 1987, 17pp.
273. STRATHCLYDE R C *Population, household and housing projections 1985 base. Main report and technical notes*. Glasgow, 1987, 2 vols.
274. STRATHCLYDE R C *The region's economy: the Regional Council's platform for growth*. Glasgow, 1987.
275. STRATHCLYDE R C SHIPBUILDING WORKING GROUP *Strathclyde-built in the 1990's*. Glasgow, 1987, 31pp.
276. STRATHKELVIN D C *Economic development strategy and action plan*. Kirkintilloch, 1987, 16pp.
277. STRATHKELVIN D C *Economic development strategy and action plan: working document*. Kirkintilloch, 1987, 70pp.
278. STUDLAR, D T & McALLISTER, I "Nationalism in Scotland and Wales: a post-industrial phenomenon?", *Ethnic and Racial Studies*, 11, 1 (1988) 48-62.
279. STUDLAR, D T & WELCH, S "Understanding the iron law of andrarchy: effects of candidate gender on voting in Scotland", *Comparative Political Studies*, 20, 2 (1987) 174-91.
280. TAYLOR, B "Going local to survive", *Scottish Government Yearbook 1988*, 62-81.
281. TAYLOR, P *The urban programme in Scotland*, Glasgow: Glasgow College of Technology, Policy Analysis Research Unait Discussion paper 17, 1988, 27pp.
282. TAYSIDE R C *Review of multiple deprivation strategy*. Dundee, 1987, 37pp.

283. TEGHTSOONIAN, K A *Institutional structure and government policy: responding to regional nationalism in Quebec, Scotland and Wales.* Ph.D. thesis, Stanford University, 1987, 549pp (University Microfilms No. DA 8801049).

284. THOMPSON, R J "The SNP: its bases of support 1949-78", *Historicus* 1 (1978), 44-83.

285. TUROK, I "Continuity, change and contradiction in urban policy", *Regenerating the inner city*, ed. D Donnison & A Middleton, 34-58.

286. WAINWRIGHT, H "Scotland", pp 144-52 of *Labour: a tale of two parties* (London: Hogarth Press, 1987, 338pp).

287. WALFORD, G "How important is the independent sector in Scotland?", *Scottish Education Review*, 19, 2 (1987), 108-21.

288. WALSH, D "Racial harassment in Glasgow: research findings", *Annual Report* (Scottish Council for Racial Equality), 1985/86.

289. WALSH, D *Racial harassment in Glasgow.* Edinburgh: Edinburgh College of Art/Heriot Watt University, Department of Town and Country Planning, Scottish Ethnic Minorities Research Unit research paper 4, 1987.

290. WANNOP, U & LECLERC, R "The management of GEAR", *Regenerating the inner city*, ed. D Donnison & A Middleton, 218-34.

291. WANNOP, U & LECLERC, R "Urban renewal and the origins of GEAR", *Regenerating the inner city*, ed. D Donnison & A Middleton, 34-60.

292. WATKINS, L "Improvement policy: the practice of rural authorities", *Rural housing in Scotland*, ed. B D MacGregor et al, 113-118.

293. WHITEFIELD, L *Housing cooperatives in Glasgow: the community ownership programme.* M Phil dissertation, Glasgow University, 1985.

294. WILLIAMS, N J "Recent developments in Scottish housing policy", *Scottish Geographical Magazine*, 104, 1 (1988) 33-35.

295. WILLIAMS, N J, SEWEL, J B & TWINE, F E "Council house sales: ...factors associated with purchase and implications for the future of public sector housing", *Tijdschift voor economische en sociale geographie*, 79, 1 (1988) 39-49.

296. WILLIAMS, N J & SEWEL, J B "Council house sales in the rural environment", *Rural housing in Scotland*, ed. B D MacGregor et al, 66-85.

297. YANETTA, A "Scottish Homes", *Radical Scotland* 32 (1988) 10-11.

298. YOUNG, F "A wind of change blows in from the South", *Scottish Business Insider*, 3, 7 (1986), 42-43.

299. YOUNG, R K "Housing associations: their role in the rural context", *Rural housing in Scotland*, ed BD MacGregor et al, 86-94.

300. YOUNG, S, HOOD, N & HAMILL, J *Foreign multinationals and the British economy.* London: Croom Helm, 1988. See cha p.4.

INDEX TO BIBLIOGRAPHY

THE SCOTTISH GOVERNMENT YEARBOOK 1976-7
Ed. by M.G. Clarke and H.M. Drucker
CONTENTS

1. Our Changing Scotland – M.G. Clarke and H.M. Drucker
2. The New Local Authorities – R.E.G. Peggie
3. The Reorganised Health Service: A Scottish Perspective – Drummond Hunter
4. Unemployment and the Scottish Economy – John Firn
5. Political Reactions to 'Our Changing Democracy' – James G. Kellas
6. Accountability, Professionalism and the Scottish Judiciary – The Rt. Hon. Lord Wheatley and Professor D.N. MacCormick
7. Devolving the Universities: Problems and Prospects – The Very Rev. Professor John McIntyre
8. The Economics of Independence – C.R. Smallwood and Professor D.I. MacKay.

THE SCOTTISH GOVERNMENT YEARBOOK 1978
Ed. by H.M. Drucker and M.G. Clarke
CONTENTS

1. Approaching the Archangelic?: The Secretary for State for Scotland – The Rt. Hon. W. Ross, MP
2. The Scottish Development Agency – Dr L. Robertson
3. The Shetland Experience: A local authority arms itself for the oil invasion – J.M. Fenwick
4. Opposition in Local Government – L.M. Turpie
5. Glasgow's Housing Politics – S.F. Hamilton
6. Health and Health Care in West-Central Scotland – D.Hamilton
7. Consultation or Confrontation?: The Campaign to save the Scottish Colleges of Education – Dr Edith Cope
8. Parliament and the Scots Conscience: Reforming the law on Divorce, Licensing and Homosexual offences – R.F. Cook, MP
9. The Failure of the Scotland and Wales Bill: No will, no way – J. Kerr
10. Devolution: The Commercial Community's Fears – D.J. Risk
11. The District Council Elections of May 1977 – J. Bochel and D. Denver

THE SCOTTISH GOVERNMENT YEARBOOK 1979
Ed. by N. Drucker and H.M. Drucker
CONTENTS

1. Introduction: Towards a Scottish Politics
2. John Mackintosh: An Appreciation – Bernard Crick
   Geoff Shaw: An Appreciation – Bruce Millan
3. The Scotland Bill in the House of Commons – James Naughtie
4. How Scotland Got the Housing (Homeless Persons) Act –Peter Gibson
5. The Crofter, The Laird and the Agrarian Socialist: The Highland Land Question in the 1970s – James Hunter
6. Ten Years After: The Revolutionary Left in Scotland – Neil Williamson
7. Local Health Councils: The Consumers' Voice – Dorothy Bochel and Morag MacLaran
8. Scottish Criminal Policy: The Case for Reform – John Waterhouse
9. Appointed and *Ad Hoc* Agencies in the field of the Scottish Office – Sir Douglas Haddow
10. Public Support for the Arts in Scotland: The Role of the Scottish Arts Council – Michael Flinn
11. The Regional Council Elections of May 1978 – J.M. Bochel and D.T. Denver

THE SCOTTISH GOVERNMENT YEARBOOK 1980
Ed. by H.M. Drucker and N. Drucker
CONTENTS

1. Scotland: Back into the Closet?
2. The Study of Scottish Politics: A Bibliographical Sermon – C.H. Allen
3. The Year at Westminster: The Scotland Act brings down a government; The Criminal Justice (Scotland) Bill – James Naughtie
4. The Devolution Referendum Campaign of 1979 – Ray Permand
5. The Scottish Morning Press and the Devolution Referendum of 1979 – Michael Brown
6. Time to Lay Down Referendum Rules – Chris Baur
7. The 1979 General Election Campaign in Scotland – Peter Hetherington
8. The Scottish Office 1954-79 – Mary Macdonald and Adam Redpath
9. Policy Making in the Scottish Health Services at National Level –

Colin Wiseman

THE SCOTTISH GOVERNMENT YEARBOOK 1981
Ed. by H.M. Drucker and N. Drucker
CONTENTS

THE SCOTTISH GOVERNMENT YEARBOOK 1982
Ed. by H.M. Drucker and N. Drucker
CONTENTS

SCOTTISH GOVERNMENT YEARBOOK 1983
Ed. David McCrone
CONTENTS

SCOTTISH GOVERNMENT YEARBOOK 1984
Ed. David McCrone
CONTENTS

SCOTTISH GOVERNMENT YEARBOOK 1985
Ed. David McCrone
CONTENTS

SCOTTISH GOVERNMENT YEARBOOK 1986
Ed. by David McCrone
CONTENTS

SCOTTISH GOVERNMENT YEARBOOK 1987
Ed. David McCrone
CONTENTS

SCOTTISH GOVERNMENT YEARBOOK 1988
Edited by David McCrone & Alice Brown
CONTENTS